CITY OF BEGINNINGS

translation/TRANSNATION

SERIES EDITOR **EMILY APTER**

A list of titles in the series appears at the back of the book.

City of Beginnings

POETIC MODERNISM IN BEIRUT

Robyn Creswell

PRINCETON UNIVERSITY PRESS
PRINCETON & OXFORD

Copyright © 2019 by Princeton University Press

Princeton University Press is committed to the protection of copyright and the intellectual property our authors entrust to us. Copyright promotes the progress and integrity of knowledge. Thank you for supporting free speech and the global exchange of ideas by purchasing an authorized edition of this book. If you wish to reproduce or distribute any part of it in any form, please obtain permission.

Published by Princeton University Press
41 William Street, Princeton, New Jersey 08540
99 Banbury Road, Oxford OX2 6JX

press.princeton.edu

All Rights Reserved

First paperback printing, 2025
Paper ISBN 978-0-691-26476-9
Cloth ISBN 978-0-691-18218-6
ISBN (e-book) 978-0-691-18514-9

Library of Congress Control Number: 2018936569

British Library Cataloging-in-Publication Data is available

"The New Noah" by Adonis, collected in *Shiʿr*. Copyright © 1958 Ali Ahmad Said Esber, used by permission of The Wylie Agency LLC.

"Al-ʿAhd al-Jadid" [The New Covenant]; "Watan" [Homeland]; "Taʾih al-Wajh" [Face Astray]; "Elegy" [Marthiya]; "Qad Tasir Biladi" [She Might Become My Country]; "Elegy for ʿUmar ibn al-Khattab"; and "Elegy for Bashshar ibn Burd" by Adonis, collected in *Aghani Mihyar al-Dimashqi*. Copyright © 1961 Ali Ahmad Said Esber, used by permission of The Wylie Agency LLC.

"A Mirror for Abi al-ʿAlaʾ" by Adonis, collected in *Al-Masrah wa-l-maraya*. Copyright © 1969 Ali Ahmad Said Esber, used by permission of The Wylie Agency LLC.

Editorial: Anne Savarese and Thalia Leaf
Production Editorial: Ellen Foos
Jacket/Cover Design: Layla MacRory
Jacket/Cover art: Saloua Raouda Choucair, "Experiment with Calligraphy," 1947–1950
  © Saloua Raouda Choucair Foundation
Production: Erin Suydam
Copyeditor: Daniel Simon

This book has been composed in Miller

To Pamela, Saylor, and Nico

CONTENTS

Acknowledgments · ix

INTRODUCTION	Modernism in Translation	1
CHAPTER 1	Lebanon and Late Modernism	21
CHAPTER 2	The Genealogy of Arabic Modernism	52
CHAPTER 3	Figuration and Disfiguration in *The Songs of Mihyar the Damascene*	94
CHAPTER 4	The Origins of the Arabic Prose Poem	121
CHAPTER 5	The Countercanon: Adonis's *Anthology of Arabic Poetry*	147
CHAPTER 6	"He Sang New Sorrow": Adonis and the Modernist Elegy	169
EPILOGUE	Tehran 1979–Damascus 2011	189

Notes · 203
Selected Bibliography · 241
Index · 251

ACKNOWLEDGMENTS

I AM LUCKY to have so many people to thank for their help and encouragement while I was writing this book. It began as a dissertation at New York University, where Xudong Zhang, Philip Kennedy, and Richard Sieburth were my primary mentors. I thank Richard especially for his uncanny ability to make connections between far-flung and historically distant poetries. His spirit of curiosity and friendly criticism made this book a pleasure to write and improved its argument in more ways than I can count. I hope I have done justice to the insightful comments of Sinan Antoon and Peter Nicholls, who read the earliest draft of this work.

Years before I began writing in earnest, while living and studying in Cairo, I received a tutorial in modern Arabic poetry from Mona Tolba. My gratitude to her and Anwar Mughith for their generosity, guidance, humor, and hospitality is unbounded.

I would also like to thank the following friends and scholars for their conversation, advice, and interest in my work over the years: Emily Apter, Negar Azimi, Susan Bernstein, Christine Bustany, Lori Cole, Elliott Colla, Beshara Doumani, Hugh Eakin, Khaled Fahmy, Yousra Fazili, Nicholas Frayn, Forrest Gander, Lara Harb, Bernard Haykel, Seamus Khan, Elias Khoury, Rafil Kroll-Zaidi, Margaret Litvin, Maureen N. McLane, Jeannie Miller, Rowan Ricardo Phillips, Jim Quilty, Kamran Rastegar, Danya Reda, Frederick Seidel, Adam Shatz, Gemma Sieff, Lorin Stein, Jean Strouse, Michael Vazquez, Max Weiss, Kaelen Wilson-Goldie, and Jeffrey Yang.

My special thanks go to Christopher Stone, Arabic teacher, squash partner, and friend. Elizabeth Holt gave me the benefit of her expertise in the International Association for Cultural Freedom (IACF) archives and provided several references when my own went missing. I thank all my colleagues at Brown and Yale Universities, but especially Elias Muhanna for his good counsel and camaraderie. At Yale, I am particularly indebted to Peter Cole and David Quint, who gave my manuscript close readings in its final stages, and for much else.

This book has also benefited from a number of institutional supporters. I'm hugely grateful to the Center for Arabic Study Abroad, which made possible my language studies in Cairo, and the American Council of Learned Studies, which funded a year of dissertation writing. My Morse Year sabbatical from Yale permitted me to finish this book in the convivial environment of the American Academy in Berlin. I thank the staff of the academy for making my stay in Germany so memorable. I also thank the library staffs at the American University of Beirut (in particular Albert Haddad, for the front-page image from *al-Safir*) and the Special Collections Research Center at the University of Chicago, for its help navigating the IACF archive. At Princeton University Press, I thank my editor, Anne Savarese, for her steady hand and consistent support of this book. I also thank Ellen Foos and Thalia Leaf. Yale University's Frederick W. Hillis Publication Fund provided generous support for the production costs.

The jacket of this book features a gorgeous painting by the Lebanese artist Saloua Raouda Choucair. Choucair, who trained in Paris but spent her entire artistic career in Beirut, was a contemporary of the modernist poets I study in this book. Although she never collaborated with the *Shi'r* group, I find that her paintings and sculptures are uncanny visual equivalents of their poetry. I thank Hala Choucair and the Choucair Foundation for permission to use this work.

An earlier version of chapter 5 was published in *Modernism/Modernity*; parts of chapters 3 and 6 were published in an essay written for *Arabic Thought against the Authoritarian Age* (ed. Max Weiss and Jens Hanssen). I thank Johns Hopkins University Press and Cambridge University Press for their permission to reprint.

My greatest thanks go to my family: my mother, my brother, and especially my wife, Pamela. Our two children were born during the writing of this book, and I dedicate it to her and them.

INTRODUCTION

Modernism in Translation

ARABIC MODERNISM was a literary movement of exiles and émigrés who planted their flag in West Beirut during the mid-1950s, when the Lebanese capital became a meeting ground for intellectuals from across the region. West Beirut, a neighborhood known as Hamra, was "the closest the Arab world could ever get to having its own Greenwich Village." For a brief twenty-year period, until the outbreak of civil war in 1975, Hamra was a contact zone for artists and militants from the far left to the far right, nationalists and internationalists, experimentalists and traditionalists. In this highly politicized bohème, journals of ideas flourished and each coterie had its own café. Local banks were flush with deposits from the newly oil-rich states of the Gulf, helping to finance a construction boom that quadrupled the built area of the city in the decade following World War II. This intellectual and economic ferment turned Beirut into a magnet for disaffected thinkers from within Lebanon as well as from neighboring countries. It was a place with all the characteristics of what Roger Shattuck, in his study of the early Parisian avant-garde, has called "cosmopolitan provincialism": an eclectic community of outsiders living on the margins and snitching tips on taste, style, and ideas from elsewhere.[1]

The Arab modernists, like many artistic groups of the early and mid-twentieth century, gathered around a magazine that acted as the nerve center of their movement. *Shiʿr* [Poetry], a quarterly dedicated to poetry and poetry criticism, was founded in 1957 by Yusuf al-Khal, a Greek Orthodox Lebanese with shrewd editorial instincts, who lived in America from 1948 to 1955 and took the moniker for his new journal from Harriet Monroe's famous "little magazine" of the same name. *Shiʿr* published forty-four issues over eleven years (1957–64; 1967–70), including manifestos, poems, criticism, and letters from abroad. Under al-Khal's editorship, *Shiʿr* was an energetically internationalist organ; its openness to foreign literature was one of the ways it defined its "modernity." The magazine had correspondents in Cairo, Baghdad, Berlin,

FIGURE 1A. *Shiʿr* magazine, no. 3 (Summer 1958). The minimalist cover was consistent throughout the life of the magazine.

شِعر   صيف ١٩٥٧

أدونيس	البعث والرماد	٣
بدر شاكر السياب	المسيح بعد الصلب	٢١
يوسف الخال	السفر	٢٥
جورج شحاده	منلق بسبب الافلاس	٢٩
نازك الملائكة	نداء الى السعادة	٣٤
جورج غانم	طفولة	٤٠
بلند الحيدري	شيخوخة	٤٣
فدوى طوقان	هل كان صدفة	٤٥
نذير العظمه	اللحم والسنابل	٤٧
فؤاد رفقه	يوميات مقاتل	٥١
ابراهيم شكر الله	موقف الخوف	٥٥
جبرا ابراهيم جبرا	من مونولوغ لسيدة كسول	٥٩
غولوي كينبل	دار المدرسة	٦٣
إيدث ستويل	قصيدتان	٦٩
الدكتور هنري القيم	رينه شار	٧٣
الدكتور ماجد فخري	مادة الشعر	٨٦
خزامى صبري	قرارة الموجة لنازك الملائكة	٩١
أسعد رزوق	الناس في بلادي لصلاح عبد الصبور	٩٧
منير بشور	رمال عطشى لسليمان العيسى	١٠١
أنسي الحاج	غيوم ظامئة لوديع ديب	١٠٢
	الطين والأظافر لمحيي الدين فارس	١٠٤
	أغاني افريقيا لمفتاح الفيتوري	١٠٥
	عبير الارض لفوزي العنتيل	١٠٧
	اخبار وقضايا	١١١
	المساهمون في هذا العدد	١١٧

FIGURE 1B. Table of contents, Summer 1958. The issue included poems by Adonis ("Resurrection and Ashes") and Yusuf al-Khal ("The Voyage"), as well as works of criticism by Khalida Saʿid and Unsi al-Hajj.

Paris, London, and New York, and it published a range of verse in translation. The physical magazine was also a stylish object, printed in book-sized format with single columns of type and wide margins. The cover was minimalist, featuring only the title in austere and angular calligraphy. Particularly during the early years of *Shiʿr*, its design was remarkably consistent, elegant, and understated. In addition to the magazine, al-Khal established a publishing house, Dar Majallat Shiʿr, which printed criticism, original poetry, and anthologies of foreign verse. He and his wife, Helen, also founded a gallery for contemporary art, Gallery One, where the modernists often convened a literary salon, the so-called *jeudis de* Shiʿr, which hosted Stephen Spender and Yves Bonnefoy among other European luminaries.

In some respects, *Shiʿr* was a typical product of its time and place. Beirut's modernist moment (ca. 1955–1975) coincided with the rise of the Lebanese capital as the center of Arabic intellectual life, usurping the place hitherto held by Cairo. Lebanon's liberal censorship laws attracted writers and editors from across the region. Many of these immigrants were Palestinians fleeing north in the wake of the 1948 *Nakba*; subsequent waves were composed of Egyptians or Syrians escaping the increasingly monolithic regimes of Gamal Abdel Nasser and the Baʿth. As Franck Mermier writes in his study of Lebanon's print culture, "At the end of the 1950s, Lebanese publishing had managed to transform itself into the crossroads of Arabic intellectual production. Unlike its competitors elsewhere in the Arab world, Lebanese publishing enjoyed a striking degree of autonomy from the State and was held almost entirely in private hands." In Fuad Ajami's more skeptical view, "The city's large number of newspapers reflected the worldviews of their patrons, the rival embassies and foreign governments that paid and sustained them. But the press still played with ideas, pointed fingers, debated the issues of the region, and now and then appalled the conservative custodians of proper and improper things." In many histories, Lebanon in these two decades before the civil war was an oasis in the midst of an authoritarian wasteland, "a laboratory of numerous and conflicting tendencies," in the words of Adonis, a Syrian-Lebanese poet who was among West Beirut's immigrants and the preeminent figure of the modernist movement.[2]

This book is a study of that movement, the most significant literary grouping in the Arab world since World War II. It produced a body of work remarkable for its aesthetic ambition and rhetorical coherence. The *Shiʿr* poets' conceptualization of "modernity" or "modernism"—the Arabic word, *al-hadatha*, can be used for both English terms—was immensely influential. As the Syrian critic Muhammad Jamal Barut has written, *Shiʿr* magazine "imposed a specific understanding of the problematic of modernity, one that most closely approaches our own understanding of the word today."[3] Many other literary movements in the region called their own work "modern" (*hadith*). They did this to signal a break with the conventions of classical or "traditional" verse, a willingness to borrow Western forms, or the inclusion of some obviously contemporary aspect of modern life (new technologies, for instance, or radical politics). But these features can be found in virtually any significant poetry written in Arabic during the period.[4] For the *Shiʿr* poets, however, *al-hadatha* was not merely an index of newness or contemporaneity but a tool to redefine poetry as such.[5] "I wonder if they [i.e., the modernists] are ignorant of the limits of poetry?" Nazik al-Malaʾika, a rival Iraqi poet, worried in 1962.[6] One reason for the modernists' success in transforming the concept of poetry is their active supposition that there are no natural limits to this concept—that no one knows in any final sense what poetry is or what its sources of authority could be. "What we did with *Shiʿr* magazine has not been given, even now, its necessary critical reading," Adonis has justifiably argued.

> It had been studied, for the most part, antagonistically; or else it has been studied for what we did with form: the escape from meter, rhyme, inherited standards, etc. But these are surface readings. Our experience at the magazine, as an experience of poetic creativity, was essentially cultural and civilizational—one that transformed the concept of poetry itself as well as the way it is written.[7]

This book begins by tracing the historical and intellectual emergence of the modernist poetry movement. I emphasize the importance of Beirut in conditioning this emergence, not only because of the city's suddenly central and yet anomalous place in the intellectual life of the Arab world, but also for its nodal position in the global history of modernism during the early Cold War. Lebanon's long tradition of diasporic thinkers, along with its characteristic intellectual institutions (the American University of Beirut, the Cénacle libanais, and numerous organs of opinion), deeply affected the version of modernism espoused by the poets of *Shiʿr*. The poets' shared political background in the Syrian Social Nationalist Party, discussed in chapter 2, was equally important in determining their peculiar understanding of modernism. And yet the *Shiʿr* poets' conception of *al-hadatha* was in many ways typical of postwar modernism as an international phenomenon—a coincidence that also requires explanation. After setting out the intellectual and historical parameters of the movement, I analyze the two most aesthetically ambitious poetry collections it published, Adonis's *Songs of Mihyar the Damascene* (1961) and Unsi al-Hajj's *Lan* (1960). In both cases, I show how the intellectual and political history analyzed in the previous chapters affects the formal logic of the poems. The final two chapters focus on the work of Adonis, the signal poet and critic of the *Shiʿr* group, as well as the thinker who most creatively adapted the tenets of Arabic modernism to different historical circumstances. Although Adonis severed ties with *Shiʿr* in 1963, the principles that animated the movement remained crucial to his later writings, even as they addressed new subjects and took on novel forms. My book begins with the history of a literary collective and ends with the work of its most representative and controversial figure.

FIGURE 2. The Phoenicia Intercontinental Hotel, designed by Edward Durell Stone, opened 1961. Popperfoto, Getty Images.

For all its importance to poets writing in Arabic, the *Shiʿr* movement is essentially unknown to English-language readers, including scholars of modernist poetry. Beirut does not figure, for fathomable reasons, among the cities of modernism in Malcolm Bradbury and James McFarlane's seminal collection of studies, *Modernism, 1890–1930*. Paris, London, Berlin, Vienna, St. Petersburg, and New York stake out the geography of the field as envisaged by these essays. Marshall Berman's groundbreaking work, *All That Is Solid Melts into Air*, surveys a similar terrain. Even after the recent "transnational turn," which has added Rio de Janeiro, Shanghai, and Buenos Aires to the purview of scholars, Beirut is still terra incognita.[8] For this reason, the bulk of my book is addressed to the Beiruti movement itself. I hope it may serve in part as an introduction to the work of these poets although it is not intended as a comprehensive survey.[9] Indeed, my deeper ambition for this book is to suggest how much remains to be studied. While *City of Beginnings* is punctuated by close readings of literary and critical texts, it is guided throughout by an argument about Arabic modernism's place in a wider intellectual landscape. Anyone who reads the criticism produced by the *Shiʿr* group, or who examines the list of poets they translated, must be struck by their confident sense of what modernism is and who its major poets are. Sixty years on, with the spatial and temporal boundaries of modernism in constant flux, it is hard to share this confidence.[10] But precisely that feeling of difference is useful in suggesting that the Beiruti movement belongs to a distinct historical period—distinct from our own as well as from earlier eras—which I will call the period of late modernism.

Filling out this period concept is something I attempt in chapters 1 and 2. Here, I will simply suggest that late modernism is the historical moment—roughly, the quarter century following World War II, the earliest and most intense period of the Cold War—in which artistic modernism was formalized and made global. It is the moment when, as Gregory Barnhisel has written, "This formerly radical movement had become the preferred style of cultural elites and, increasingly, the business world in Europe, Latin America, and North America"—and, one might add, Lebanon.[11] A convenient local symbol for this story of formalization and global expansion is the opening in 1961 of Beirut's Phoenicia InterContinental Hotel, the chain's first hotel outside the Western Hemisphere, designed by Edward Durrell Stone, principal architect of New York's Museum of Modern Art. Stone's building, which coincided with his turn toward modernist regionalism, helped create the stereotype of Beirut as "the Paris of the Middle East": a modern, cosmopolitan playground for European and Arab tourists as well as corporate elites. As Lebanese journalist and historian Samir Kassir writes of Stone's modernist icon:

> The building itself was splendid to look at, for its white, delicately perforated façade, its unprecedented scale and height (twelve floors), and its oval swimming pool. But it was the sunken bar that perhaps most vividly captured the spirit of the place: incorporating a large glass wall that allowed guests to relax with a cocktail while contemplating the bikini-clad naiads gliding beneath the surface of the pool. . . . At long last Beirut had its own internationally recognizable building, henceforth a centerpiece of postcard views of the city.[12]

But late modernism as I intend it here is not primarily a period style (nor a lifestyle). It is instead a movement of artistic canonization and revision at a time when, as George Steiner writes, "The apparent iconoclasts have turned out to be more or less anguished custodians racing through the museum of civilization, seeking order and sanctuary for its treasures, before closing time."[13] One noteworthy feature of Arabic modernism is precisely its work of selective preservation, as we shall see in the final two chapters on Adonis's anthologies and elegies. This curatorial sensibility is typical of the period of late modernism, when literary texts and art objects from the first half of the twentieth century were organized into a firm if flexible canon and provided with an ideological rationale, which is that of aesthetic autonomy or purity of medium. Rather than avant-gardist iconoclasm, with its irreverent attitude toward institutionalized art, the ethos of late modernism was one of professionalism or specialized competency. The most powerful account of this ethos remains that of Clement Greenberg, who championed modernist abstract painting for its "use of characteristic methods of a discipline to criticize the discipline itself, not in order to subvert it but in order to entrench it more firmly in its area of competence."[14] By rooting each art's "competence" in its particular medium—whether poetry, painting, or sculpture—late modernism reformulated art history into canons whose internal dynamics were safeguarded from extra-artistic interference. As Theodor Adorno, the most discerning but also ambivalent critic of late modernism, writes, this is the moment of "culture's becoming self-consciously cultural."[15]

The effort to wrest cultural objects free of their historical occasions results in a characteristically late modernist rhetoric of autonomy. This rhetoric is at the heart of the Arab modernists' project. As Yusuf al-Khal writes, to cite one example among many by the *Shiʿr* poets: "The poem as a work of art looks no further than itself, it is an independent creation, sufficient unto itself [*muktafiya bi-dhatiha*]."[16] The implicit sense of al-Khal's name for his magazine is "*Poetry*—and only poetry." In Lebanon, however, the autonomy of literature was not something that had already been "conquered," to borrow Pierre Bourdieu's useful formulation, but rather a rallying cry aimed at securing a margin of independence from the state—a goal that was more plausible in Lebanon than in surrounding countries, where cultural bureaucracies were largely successful in asserting their control over artistic production.[17] The modernists' project was strongly resisted by the region's Marxist and nationalist intellectuals, for whom the separation of literature and politics was anathema. Indeed, the issue of literary autonomy was among the deepest fault lines in the cultural Cold War. Leftist thinkers, in the Arab world as elsewhere, formulated their own poetics and erected their own artistic canons, which emphasized the intrinsically political nature of literary activity. This helps explain why the tone of the Beiruti modernists is so often embattled and even shrill. As opposed to their late modernist peers in Europe and America, the Arab poets could rarely afford the postures of polished certitude. Their anguish arose from the feeling that they had not only to preserve their museum of civilization but also to build one in the face of determined antagonists.

Another characteristic feature of late modernism is that whereas early twentieth-century movements—from Italian futurism and Anglo-American vorticism to French simultaneism and Latin American avant-gardism—were national or regional styles with international circulations, late modernism is the first truly global instance of aesthetic modernism. This difference has too often been ignored, rendering attempts to periodize the phenomenon more and more uncertain. As Franco Moretti has noted, "Until now we have been searching for a non-existent unity—'modernism'—instead of accepting the idea that in early twentieth century literature *there exists no common denominator*."[18] But *late* modernism does have a common denominator, which is a shared ideology of literary autonomy propagated by a global network of institutions and individuals who served as its spokespeople and translators. The Arab poets at the heart of my study quickly grasped what the emerging canon and ideological strictures of late modernism were and injected themselves into its circulatory system (while encountering strong antibodies). They understood how an ostensibly apolitical internationalism combined with strategies of formal abstraction might give them leverage in local debates. The claim of poetic autonomy would help them radically alter the definition of Arabic poetry, in part by subjecting it to the standards of what the *Shiʿr* poets called "world literature." Late modernism is thus a moment of contraction, in which modernism is narrowed by virtue of its formal and ideological specificity, but also of vertiginous expansion in geographical terms.

Most studies of late modernist culture during the Cold War focus on its institutional underpinnings.[19] They are typically uninterested in formal or aesthetic questions—discussions of poetry are conspicuous by their absence—and their critical posture is one of exposure: once the curtain is drawn back on the artists' political bias or institutional support—by the CIA, for example, or the US State Department—the argument is over. Less frequently, scholars have shown how some postwar art—American jazz, for instance, which was enthusiastically exported by the State Department—escaped the rationale of its backers, pursuing agendas that contradicted those of its institutional supporters. In this case, there is no explanatory relation, unless it is an ironic one, between the text or performance and its material conditions: the artists simply outwit their handlers.[20] Another limitation of such studies is that they have concentrated, for understandable reasons, almost exclusively on European and American artists and intellectuals. The North Atlantic was the main theater of Cold War culture, and much of its drama played out in that context. But the dynamics of intellectual exchange were significantly different in Afro-Asian countries, where the existence of national liberation movements (including pan-Arabism) complicated the relatively black-and-white picture that obtained inside Europe.[21]

In contrast with such analyses, this study tries to show how the strictures of late modernism were, in a non-European context, aesthetically productive rather than simply constraining. For the *Shiʿr* poets, the early Cold War is a moment when professionalization—the certification of oneself as a poet according to new global standards—is undertaken *as an adventure*, to use one of Adonis's favorite phrases. It is also the moment when a peculiar brand of political liberalism—militantly anti-Communist, aggressively internationalist, spiritually engaged, and chiefly concerned with negative freedoms—sought to establish itself as a worldwide consensus among non-Soviet-aligned intellectuals.

It was a consensus that presented itself, as liberal politics often has, as "apolitical," motivated chiefly by spiritual concerns or sheer economic rationality. The works of Arab modernism are heavily marked by this midcentury liberal imagination. In their poems and critical writings, abstract individualism is heroized, figures of collectivity are eschewed, local landscapes are sublimated or ignored, and the state is figured as a source of permanent threat. As is often the case with liberal art, the ideological content of Arabic modernist poems is most present where it is most strongly denied. In her analysis of liberal aesthetics during the Cold War, Amanda Anderson notes that critiques of liberalism as covertly ideological (or bloodlessly neutral) have "foreclosed recognition of the formal and conceptual dimensions of active literary engagements with liberal thought." Critiques of liberalism as pragmatically complacent have made it especially difficult to discern liberalism's links to modernist styles of thinking. In most scholarly literature, artistic experimentalism is typically or even exclusively associated with left-wing or right-wing radicalism.[22] The difficulty in linking modernist experimentalism to political liberalism is particularly evident when, as in the case of the Beiruti modernists, the liberalism in question arises in a non-European context whose literary codes and conceptual dimensions are relatively unfamiliar. In Lebanon, a seemingly staid midcentury ideology gave rise to a modernist movement that challenged the principal conventions of Arabic literary culture. Its corpus is one in which spontaneity battles with scholasticism and postures of rebellion are yoked to an abstract poetics. One task of my book is to untangle the contradictions of this radical liberalism.

To insist on the literary dimension of late modernism is not to ignore the ironies of its history. The claim of literary autonomy, along with the accompanying slogans of cultural and intellectual freedom, is compromised if not entirely vitiated when the claimants can be shown to have identifiable political aims or covert institutional support. This study includes a detailed history—the first to be based on archival sources—of the Arab modernists' extensive transactions with the Congress for Cultural Freedom (CCF), the CIA front organization that supported anti-Communist intellectuals throughout the world during the two decades following World War II.[23] *Shi'r* magazine was not funded by the CCF, but its editorial principles echoed without completely endorsing the commonplaces of late modernist culture fostered by the Congress and its liberal allies across the globe. The *Shi'r* group also situated their project carefully within the force field of Lebanese political and intellectual life, even as they pretended to stand above or to the side of it. My analysis of the institutional and historical conditions that made Arab modernism possible are intended in part as a critique of the group's idea of itself as a "nonpartisan," purely (or professionally) poetical movement. It is an attempt, in the words of Giles Scott-Smith, to reveal the (liberal) politics of "apolitical culture." But if the *Shi'r* movement had not done the poetic and critical work that it did, this revelation would hardly be worth the effort. Any critique of the modernist project must take the full measure of its literary successes. The bulk of this study, chapters 3–6, is therefore addressed to that still understudied corpus.

City of Beginnings is situated at the crossroads of poetry criticism and intellectual history. Along with many Arab poets of the period, the Beiruti modernists addressed themselves, albeit at times obliquely, to the signal debates of their day: the relations between cultural power and political power; rivalries between nationalism, secularism, and Marxism; and the transmission of literary authority. To do justice to these debates requires some code-switching between the specialized language of literary criticism and the broader discourses of intellectual, political, and economic history. In that spirit, the rest of this introduction will analyze a lyric poem by Adonis, an important early text that weaves together several strands of Arabic modernist thought and experience. By examining its patterns of allusion, themes, and rhetoric, I hope to suggest the argument of this book as a whole.

"Nuh al-Jadid" [The New Noah] was first published as the opening poem in the Spring 1958 issue of *Shiʿr:*

We sailed on the Ark through rain and mud
with oars promised by God.
We lived while all humankind died,
sailing over the waves while the emptiness
became a chain of corpses we fastened
to our very lives. A window for supplication
opened for us in the sky:

"Lord, why have you saved only us
of all people and created things?
Where will you cast us? Upon another land of yours,
upon our first homeland,
upon the dead leaves and the vibrant air?
Lord, we fear the sun
in our veins. We despair of the light,
we despair of the coming day
and a life lived again from the beginning."

We sailed on the Ark in the rain
with oars promised by God
while the mud covered mankind's eyes.
They perished in the clay but we were saved
from the flood and death, becoming seeds
on a globe that turned while staying still.

"If only we had not become a seed
for creation, for the earth and its generations.
If only we were still clay
or embers, or something in between,
never to see the world again,
never to see its hell or its Lord.
Lord, murder us with all the others.
We yearn for the end, we yearn to be dust,
we do not yearn for life!"

If time returned to the beginning
and waters covered the face of creation
and the earth shook and God said,
"O Noah, save the living for us,"
I would not listen to God's word.
I would go to my Ark with a poet
and a rebel for freedom
and we would set out together
paying no heed to God's word.
We would open ourselves to the flood
and dive into the mud. We would brush away
stones and clay from the eyes of the drowned
and whisper into their veins
that we had returned from the desert,
that we had escaped the cave,
that we had changed the sky of years
and were sailing forth, unbowed by terror
and deaf to God's word.
Our appointment is with death. Our shores
trace a familiar despair we once accepted.
Now we cross an ocean as cold as iron,
sailing beyond the horizon
and paying no mind to that God.
We yearn for a new Lord, a different deity.[24]

Adonis's poem retells a myth of transmission, or translation. In the Old Testament and Qur'anic versions, Noah conveys his cargo safely from the dying world into the new. It is a myth of destruction but also continuity, whose seal is the covenant given by God to Noah and his descendants. In Sura Hud, one of the Qur'anic passages that relate the flood legend, God addresses his prophet after the waters have receded and the unbelievers are drowned: "Noah, get thee down [from the Ark] in peace from Us, and blessings upon thee and on the nations of those with thee" (11:48). Similarly, in Sura al-Mu'minun, God twice promises to raise "another generation" following the destruction he visits upon those who deny the possibility of resurrection (23:31; 23:42). Adonis reverses this myth by rewriting it. While the familiar Noah is a figure of redemption, binding time past to time future through the medium of creed and community, Adonis's Noah is a figure of refusal. He does not want to be the seed for another generation but to remain in the earthly condition of "something in between" [*bayna bayna*]. In this sense, Adonis's Noah bears a family resemblance to all those "childless couples, orphaned children, aborted childbirths, and unregenerately celibate men and women" who, as Edward Said writes, "populate the world of high modernism with remarkable insistence."[25] From the Qur'anic point of view, of course, this wish to remain unregenerate is a heresy that mirrors the unbelievers' denial of an afterlife.

In the long final stanza, Noah imagines a return to the purity of "the beginning," but this time with a difference. The "new" Noah ignores God's command to save the living. Instead of bringing his living charges to harbor, Adonis's prophet dives into the mud, where he uncovers the bodies of the unbelievers. This katabasis is the imaginative heart of the poem, and the figure of an interior descent is one we will encounter several times in this study. Down amid the human clay, Noah opens the eyes of the dead and whispers a new covenant (or revolutionary doctrine) into their veins. The new covenant is in fact an anticovenant, a refusal of the divine promise. "*Waʿd*" [promise], a word that Adonis uses in the second line of stanzas 1 and 3, is often linked in the Qur'an to the Day of Judgment, when the believers' resurrection and the unbelievers' punishment are both assured. In the final stanza, "*mawʿid*" [appointment] is derived from the same root, though here the connotations are not redemptive but defiantly mundane: the only thing promised is an earthly death. Noah's denial of God's promise leads to a yearning for some new telos to his journey, represented not as a shore but a voyage without end—another heretical reversal. The unbelievers, who were drowned after refusing to give credence to the afterlife, are resurrected with a whisper. So the skeptical villains of the Qur'anic myth become the heroes, or at least the most precious cargo, of Adonis's revisionary lyric.

This study is focused on such acts of cultural and literary translation, which were essential to the Arab modernists' achievement. "The New Noah" provides a nice point of embarkation, since it is not only a lyric about an instance of translation—Noah's conveyance of "two of every kind" out of the old world and into the new—but also performs that act by retelling and revising the Qur'anic myth. In a sense, Adonis's revision is a radical one. The villains of the older version are valorized and the divine covenant is suspended, a Nietzschean reversal characteristic of Adonis's early poetry. But despite this overturning, the religious myth subsists as a kind of cultural ballast: the poem's commitment to the new is weighed down by its equally urgent commitment to an ancient model. This divided commitment is reflected in the intricate time structure of the poem, which begins in a crisis-ridden present, segues into a speculative past ("if time returned to the beginning"), and ends by calling for an alternative future ("a new Lord"). In his later critical work, which I discuss in chapter 5, Adonis identifies this temporal structure with the hermeneutical operation of *ta'wil* or allegoresis: a revisionary return to authoritative texts motivated by present concerns (which might also serve as a definition of *translation* as such). The poem's ambiguous commitment to both the new and the old is a commonplace of modernist poetry, whose texts are like gestalt figures, radically experimental or echt traditional depending on how one looks at them. The Mexican poet Octavio Paz, another late modernist, neatly formulates this paradox by calling modernism "*una tradición hecha de interrupciones*," a tradition made of ruptures.[26] In Adonis's poem, the Qur'anic legend is refused and transmitted in the same gesture. And so the ark serves as a figure for Arabic modernism as I attempt to read it here: a vessel or vortex that guarantees the survival of its cargo at the same time it exposes that consignment to unpredictable transformations.

Although I shall argue that translation—in Arabic, "*naql*" or "*tarjama*"— was the characteristic activity of the *Shi'r* group, the modernists described their ambitions very differently. Their own writings stress the importance of literary novelty and tend to relegate translation to a secondary position. The editor in chief of *Shi'r*, Yusuf al-Khal, puts the matter succinctly: "Translation [*al-naql*] is one thing and creation [*al-khalq*] is another."[27] Al-Khal's opposition is a conventional one. It casts literary creation as a heroic activity and translation as a passive technique. My own readings presume a different notion of *naql*. A standard English-Arabic dictionary provides the following equivalents: "*naql* carrying, carriage; conveyance, transportation, transport; removal; translocation, relocation, transplantation; transfer (also, e.g., of an official); change of residence, move, remove; transmission (also by radio); translation; transcription, transcript, copy; tradition; report, account; entry, posting (in an account book); conveyance, transfer, assignment, cession."[28] In this study, translation is not understood as a process of passive reception or linguistic transfer but rather as a historical act of preservation, displacement, and transformation. The modes of *naql* that I examine include anthologization, elegiac inheritance, and genre appropriation as well as translations in the everyday sense of the word in English. Arab modernist poets used these modes to transmit and thereby transform a certain kind of literary cargo, whether foreign or ancient, or foreign because ancient. In their revisionary stance toward the past and their eagerness to translate texts from abroad, the *Shi'r* movement was a continuation of certain strands within the nineteenth-century Arabic *Nahda*, a historical precursor the Beiruti poets were well aware of and often disavowed.[29]

The modernists' rivals frequently accused them of despoiling the cultural heritage [*al-turath*], but the *Shi'r* poets' real achievement, as Adonis's lyric suggests, was considerably more complex. Huda Fakhreddine rightly notes that one of the modernists' signal achievements was to "[hold] a mirror up to the established canon of Arabic culture."[30] While many of their writings adopt an adversarial stance toward the literary tradition, the result of the modernists' many projects, whether critical, poetic, or anthological, was to ensure the survival of that corpus in an altered or translated form. This "internal translation" of the tradition, as Pascal Casanova has termed it, was systematic and consequential.[31] To assert that the *Shi'r* movement is characterized by *naql* is not to denigrate it by comparison with some putatively more original instance of modernism (it is always worth remembering that Pound's great slogan, "Make it new," is a translation from the classical Chinese). My emphasis on the modernists' abilities as translators is meant instead to suggest that their own rhetoric of creativity is a kind of reaction formation, leading us away from the movement's historical origins and actual achievements.

The internal translation of the *turath* was crucial to the modernists' program, but equally important was their translation of European and American poetry. As Yusuf al-Khal writes in the introduction to his *Diwan al-shi'r al-amriki* [Anthology of American Poetry], "One of the guiding principles of *Shi'r* is that a creative engagement with the poetic heritage of the world is necessary for the renaissance of Arabic poetry."[32] Although the French and Anglo-American poetic traditions were the most significant resources for the *Shi'r* poets, they cast their nets widely. During the ten years of its existence (1957–64; 1967–70), *Shi'r* published translations from English (Whitman, Pound, Eliot), French (Valéry, Michaux, Bonnefoy, Perse), Spanish (Lorca, Jiménez, Paz), Italian (Quasimodo), and German (Rilke)—a very partial list. Toward the end of the quarterly's life, there were special issues on contemporary Armenian, Iranian, and Turkish poetry as well as dossiers of Beat poetry and poetry from "the Third World." The magazine's book publishing arm, Dar Majallat Shi'r, published Yusuf al-Khal's American anthology, another of Robert Frost, and a book of selected poems by Eliot, including al-Khal and Adonis's version of *The Waste Land*.[33] As I discuss in chapters 3 and 4, the modernists' translation of the French *poème en prose*—in Arabic, *qasidat al-nathr*—generated fierce polemics about the basic nature of poetry in Arabic. In his earliest manifesto for the *qasidat al-nathr*, Adonis calls it "our ark and our flood."[34] In all these cases of translation, the *Shi'r* poets' criteria of selection and methods of execution were carefully thought out, lending the movement a remarkable theoretical and practical consistency.

The modernists' translations of American and European poetry were part of their effort to restructure the Arabic literary field along internationalist lines. At a moment when national cultures in Egypt, Iraq, and Syria were being formed and their boundaries policed by newly independent states, Beiruti modernists sought to expand the literary field and to remove it from the purview of the nation-state altogether. In the first chapter of this book, I argue that this internationalist strategy must be understood within the context of Beirut's unique role in the intellectual geography of the Arab world as well as the wider background of Cold War cultural politics. Internationalism was a key fact of late modernist culture, inseparable from its central ideological plank of artistic autonomy. For the Arab modernists, radical internationalism allowed them to pivot from an earlier adherence to the politics of Greater Syrian Nationalism, a movement I examine in chapter 2, toward the midcentury liberal ideal of apolitical culture. Arguing that poetry should be released from its moorings in the nation, the *Shi'r* group sought to secure a place on what Yusuf al-Khal called "the map of world literature."[35] Among the many reasons for studying Arab modernism is the light it throws on the recent history of this concept, now at the heart of debates concerning the future of comparative literature as a discipline.

A worry that animates many recent critiques of world literature as a political and pedagogical project is the looming possibility of an intellectual monoculture, or what Erich Auerbach in his 1952 essay, "The Philology of World Literature," calls "a homogenization of human life the world over."[36] One historical corollary of this worry, however, is the demand that non-European literatures exhibit symptoms of national or regional difference—in other words, local color—according to what Aamir Mufti terms "the logic of indigenization." For Mufti, this logic is set in motion during the colonial context of the long nineteenth century, when Orientalist institutions helped provoke the emergence of distinct national literary traditions, particularly in the subcontinent. The dynamics of this colonial logic, which Mufti calls "the dialectic of Orientalism," powerfully foreshadows the encounter between Western scholars and officials and the intellectuals of Afro-Asian nations during the early Cold War.[37] The midcentury moment was also a time when emergent literatures were encouraged, by subtle and not-so-subtle means, to develop and display their regional or national colors. The obvious contradiction at the heart of this indigenizing logic is that non-European literatures were only able to join the ranks of world literature by fully embracing their particularism. The *Shi'r* poets, along with several non-European modernist groupings of the period, explicitly rejected the logic of indigenization. Their poetry displays a palpable aversion to local color and political nationalism even while the poets remained committed to the project of world literature. This commitment involved the Arabic movement in interesting contradictions of its own, as we shall see.

The Beiruti modernists' internationalism suggests another dimension to "The New Noah." For while Adonis's poem is a *naql* of Qur'anic myth, it is also translates, more or less explicitly, a number of maritime tropes from French Romantic, symbolist, and postsymbolist poetry. This lyric tradition, beginning with Lamartine's "Le Lac" ("driven ever onward to new shores"), passing through Baudelaire's various *voyages*, Rimbaud's "Le bateau ivre," and the seafaring epics of Saint-John Perse, was well known to the modernists. In Adonis's poem, Noah's initial ennui and impatience with familiar shorelines gives way at the poem's close to an exhilaration that echoes the famous *envoi* of Baudelaire's "Le Voyage": *"Enfer ou Ciel, qu'importe? / Au fond de l'Inconnu pour trouver du nouveau!"* Viewed through this modernist lens, Noah's rupture with authoritative precedent, his determination to find a new lord to replace the old monotheistic one, could not be more "traditional."[38]

The use of maritime tropes is so common in *Shiʿr*, whether in the original poetry or translations, that it suggests the sea-poem as a full-fledged genre. The Arabic genre, whose ideological significance is discussed in chapter 2, had precedents in earlier modernist movements. "BLESS ALL SEAFARERS," Wyndham Lewis thundered in his manifesto for the first issue of *BLAST* (thinking perhaps of Pound's translation of the Anglo-Saxon poem "The Seafarer"). "BLESS the vast planetary abstraction of the OCEAN." Lewis's encomiums for the sea were balanced against his "blasts" of all the symptoms of British parochialism, from its love of sport to its local climate, hated for its mildness ("the flabby sky that can manufacture no snow"). The Beiruti poets were equally enthusiastic on the subject of the sea. "O boats!" apostrophizes Yusuf al-Khal in his poem "The Voyage" [*al-Safar*]. "O rising ladder, / linking us with those we are not, / bringing us precious things / and taking sweet things from us."[39] The Arab modernists' geography has fixed points of compass, which reflect their appropriation of Orientalist tropes. For them, "the interior" is the desertified origin of a mythical, autochthonous Arab-Islamic civilization: the birthplace of its oldest poetry and revealed religion. In the terms provided by Adonis's poem, the interior is a wasteland of repetition and despair. The sea, on the contrary, is a *domaine de franchise*, as Saint-John Perse calls it, a forum for adventure and exchange. Its heroes are Phoenician entrepreneurs or Levantine dragomen, at home in a Mediterranean world of cultural and commercial give-and-take. The new Noah, driven onward by his obsessive search for the new and the foreign, is a characteristic member of this company.[40]

The Arab modernists' love affair with the sea contrasts with their relative disinterest in the city—another trait that distinguishes them from earlier European and American modernists, for whom the city is the chronotope of contemporary life. It is remarkable how few references there are to the Lebanese capital in the work of the *Shiʿr* poets; it is not so much an unreal city as an unseen city. "I pass through Beirut and do not see it, / I live in Beirut and do not see it," writes Adonis in "The Crow's Feather," a poem from his landmark collection, *The Songs of Mihyar the Damascene* (1961). Arab modernists evince none of the futurist passion for fast cars and new machines (Marinetti and Mayakovsky are conspicuous for their absence from *Shiʿr*'s roll call); they do not swoon over the latest feats in civic engineering (it is not any part of Hart Crane's "The Bridge" that al-Khal selected for his *Anthology of American Poetry* but rather the six "Voyages," which begin, "Above the fresh ruffles of the surf"); the Arab modernists' texts are full of ennui and alienation, but these afflictions have little to do with urban spleen; finally, the poets rarely mention and never plunge into the crowd, despite the fact that between 1930 and 1975 the population of Beirut increased nearly tenfold.[41] But this avoidance of the city is typical of late modernist poetry. As Marshall Berman has noted of postwar movements, "The most exciting work of this era is marked by radical distance from any shared environment. The environment is not attacked: it is simply not there."[42]

In the Arabic sea-poems, the vast planetary abstraction of the ocean is not only a topos that links local culture to Mediterranean and even global streams of literary capital. It is also, as al-Khal writes in his "voyage" poem, "The way of return" [sirat al-ruju']. While the sea facilitates the importation of goods from abroad, it also makes possible the discovery and rebirth of a native heritage. This heritage, as Adonis's poem attests, is often a buried or repressed one. Noah's dive into the clay of creation and his resurrection of the unbelievers—a katabasis we might compare to those of Ulysses and Aeneas, or Pound's first canto, translated by al-Khal in the first issue of *Shi'r*—is a typical instance of Arabic modernism's effort to unearth the heterodox layers of their own literary heritage. "In terms of aesthetic values," Adonis declared in an interview in 1960, "the most astonishing things in Arabic poetry are still buried, unknown to both the common reader as well as the specialist." It is precisely this repressed, resurrected, and revised culture that the modernists sought to transmit to the future.[43]

A final theme of Adonis's poem that helps link Beiruti modernism with wider intellectual currents of the postwar period is the specter of human extinction. "The New Noah" is a dramatic monologue staged at a moment of species-death. Noah and his companions sail the seas while all around them "mankind" perishes in the flood. Arab modernist poets, like many Cold War intellectuals, assigned a great deal of importance to the figure of "man" [*al-insan*]—alternately, "the person" [*al-shakhs*] or "the individual" [*al-fard*]. American readers who come across the Arab poets' repeated, even obsessive references to "the person" might be led to expect a version of confessional poetry or something with a Frank O'Hara–like intimacy, but this is not at all the case. The *Shi'r* poets adopted the figure of "the person" in large part from philosophers of personalism, a Catholic-humanist school of thought, now mostly forgotten, that played a significant role in postwar intellectual life in Europe and elsewhere. For Arab modernists, "the person" is a conceptual abstraction rather than a trope of intimacy. In Lebanon, it was the philosopher and diplomat Charles Malik, a mentor of Yusuf al-Khal at the American University of Beirut, who brought the doctrines of personalism back from his training in the United States and Germany, where he studied with Martin Heidegger (the subject of Malik's doctoral dissertation). Personalists argued for the spiritual dignity of the human person, threatened by the rival materialisms of capitalism and communism. For Arab modernists too, the person is a hero of negative liberty, a lyrical "I" that floats free from the claims of all ideological collectives.

"The person [al-shakhs] is more important than the party, more important than ideology," the Shiʿr poets wrote in an important editorial, early in 1962. "For us, the person and his freedom come first, before anything else."[44] This hyperbolic valorization of the individual, untrammeled by historical circumstance or political commitments, would have important consequences for the Shiʿr group's poetics. Indeed, the modernists' personalist rhetoric, centered on notions of interiority, self-sufficiency, and autonomy, acted in many ways as their theory of lyric poetry.

Outside Lebanon, the figure of man was mobilized by personalists and their allies to effect what historian Samuel Moyn has called the "reinvention under pressure of a self-styled European humanism."[45] For these thinkers, the figure served to anchor and provide conceptual continuity for Western civilization, one that was threatened by the seeming ruptures of Hiroshima and the concentration camps. Personalists repaired that humanistic tradition by tracing it forward from the Christological figure of "the son of man," through Renaissance humanism and Enlightenment notions of "the rights of man," up to the postwar present. "Man" was thus a trope for the viability of cultural transmission and a powerful stay against the forces of disruption. It inhabits the same historical field as a number of homonymous rivals, from Frantz Fanon's "new man" (a collectivist figure of anticolonial struggle), to Albert Camus's *"homme révolté"* (the solitary rebel with a troubled conscience), as well as the anthropological universalism of MOMA's 1955 *Family of Man* exhibit.[46] The postwar reinvention of humanism facilitated the enshrinement of human rights discourse in the UN Declaration of Human Rights, for which Charles Malik was among the principal architects. Seen in this light, "The New Noah" can be read as a parable about the survival of humanism in the wake of a mythical genocide. In Adonis's revision of the monotheistic narrative, Noah represents a heroically secular, dynamic, and individualized notion of the human—a kind of Cold War *Übermensch*.[47]

The Arab modernists' investment in the discourse of man is one example of their eagerness to join a global intellectual culture. One hope for this study is to place Arabic poetry in a dialogue of contemporaries with other postwar currents of thought: humanists, posthumanists, liberals, Marxists, and others. As a movement centered on acts of translation, the Shiʿr group's history illuminates the afterlife of European and American poetry of the early twentieth century. It shows how that corpus was received, transformed, and put to use in a literary milieu—at once foreign as well as uncannily familiar—that was also transformed by the encounter. The history of the Shiʿr group also shows how a version of Cold War liberalism was translated into an alien and in many ways antagonistic terrain, with consequences that are still with us. Focusing on the act of translation has the additional benefit of avoiding sterile disputes about imitation and authenticity. Beiruti modernism can be understood neither as the copy of a European prototype nor as a betrayal of the Arabic poetic tradition. I hope that a concretely historical study of how *al-hadatha* was translated into Arabic intellectual life at a particular time and place—in this case, Beirut during its so-called golden age—might serve as an example of how to study the transmission and circulation of other putative universals, including human rights, liberal democracy, and secularism, all of which remain contentious topics of debate in the Arab world and elsewhere.

CHAPTER ONE

Lebanon and Late Modernism

Beginning in Beirut

It is a scene out of Balzac: a young man from the provinces arrives in the city, hoping to make his fame as a writer. The Syrian poet Adonis arrived in Beirut in October 1956, at the age of twenty-six. "At the time," he writes, "I was haunted by the feeling that I was little more than a ruin: I was broken, disappointed, close to despair." The young Adonis was not fleeing bourgeois mores nor romantic failure, however, but political trauma. He had spent the previous year in prison for his militancy on behalf of the Syrian Social Nationalist Party (SSNP), which he joined as a university student in Damascus. Syria in the mid-1950s was roiled by a succession of coups d'état, most of them originating in the armed forces, where various nationalist groups vied for supremacy. Adonis's misadventure had left him with a feeling of horror for what he calls "the nationalist wasteland." The flight to Lebanon was an escape from these political intrigues and their painful consequences. Adonis's memoir of his early years in Beirut, *Ha anta ayyuha al-waqt* [There You Are, O Time] (1993), is especially valuable for the way it characterizes, in hindsight, the modernists' relation to the city and its intellectual life. The memoir also serves as a retrospective defense of the movement, highlighting its distinctive patterns of thought. Adonis writes of his immigration to Lebanon as a voyage of rebirth, an emergence from the closed world of Damascus—a city attached to dead monuments of culture and riven by violent power struggles—into the new world of Beirut, with its intellectual adventurousness and tolerant social codes. This itinerary, from east to west, from old to new, is one that Adonis traces many times over the course of his long career as poet and critic:

> Beirut. As soon as my feet touched its soil and I began wandering its streets, I felt I was in a different city: not a city of *endings*, as was the case with Damascus, but a city of *beginnings*; not a city of *certainty*,

but a city of *searching*. I felt the city wasn't a completed structure, one you could only enter into as it stood and live in as it was, but rather an open and unfinished project.... The difference between Beirut and Damascus was evident in the streets, in people's behavior, in their relations to one another, in the cultural activity—the newspapers, journals, and clubs—in the cafés, and in the dynamism of everyday life. This difference with Damascus suggested two things: first, an openness to modern gadgets and ideas of all sorts; and second, a kind of neutralism toward past values and the heritage [*al-turath*] in general.... Beirut, looked at from within, was a world escaping from the history that had raised it or given birth to it, a world setting out in the direction of another history, not the one written for it, but one that it would write for itself.[1]

Many retrospective accounts portray pre–civil war Beirut as a place of miraculous *convivencia*, where competing political and intellectual factions lived together peaceably if not always harmoniously. Khalida Saʿid, wife of Adonis and one of *Shiʿr*'s most accomplished critics, begins her own look back at Beirut's *trente glorieuses* with an evocation of the city as a vanished utopia: "Between Independence and the Civil War, a number of cultural and artistic institutions emerged in Lebanon whose peculiar aspirations must seem to us today like idealistic dreams. Their inquiries and explorations created a master plan for what we might call *the lettered city* [*al-madina al-muthaqqafa*]—a city that would nurture thought, the rule of law, knowledge, and the creative life."[2] The neighborhood of West Beirut was the common site for such reveries. Hamra, in the words of sociologist Samir Khalaf, was "the only genuinely 'open' community in the entire Arab world," a place where there was "room for everyone: the devout and the heathen, pious puritans and graceless hedonists, left-wing radicals and ardent conservatives."[3] For Khalaf and others, Beirut's role as refuge and resort for intellectuals from around the region suggests the idea of "Lebanon as a playground," a country characterized by "carefree and uncommitted activity."[4] In such historical accounts, Beirut holds an anomalous yet crucial place in the region's literary geography. It is an intellectual entrepôt where dreams of autonomy—from the state, party politics, and history itself—could briefly flourish. Adonis's memoir is very much in this vein. He argues that Beirutis' "neutralism" toward the past and their eagerness to escape the constraints of history led to a uniquely open civic culture. The city's avidity for modern things and ideas made it an intellectual estuary, "into which flowed rivers of goods of every sort from all over the earth."

Why did this idyll have to end? In his memoir, Adonis suggests that Lebanon's slide into civil war, beginning in 1975, was caused by a dangerous instrumentalization of identities, including sectarian identities. Each group "manufactured a private myth, not within the myth of Beirut, with its variety and differences, but against that myth as well as the myths of other groups." Adonis characterizes this mobilization of identity as "the hegemony of the political":

> The hegemony of the political did not merely destroy the idea of difference, but difference itself; it obliterated not only the idea of culture as dialogue, but also as creativity. In other words it killed off, on the one hand, the rationality of cultural dialogue, a framework in which all kinds of ideas can be entertained . . . and, on the other hand, it deformed all those cultural elements that seem characteristic of Lebanese identity: religion, language, and poetry.[5]

Adonis's narrative is in many ways a compelling account of Beirut's belle époque and subsequent civil conflict. According to this version, the pre-war era is characterized by a species of tolerant disregard between different communities, Sunni, Shia, Maronite, and other. Their common fascination with modern fashions, including things and ideas from abroad, make them less susceptible to the lures of older, more parochial ways of being. Beirut, as a laboratory of culture, is a refuge for the liberal virtues of openness, plurality, and experimentation. It is a city where conflict can be assuaged by rational dialogue. By contrast, the political is the sphere of irrational combat in which each community, whether national or religious, seeks to impose its own interpretation of history on others. The idea that politics, in Arabic *al-siyasa*, is essentially an activity of oppression (rather than liberation, solidarity, or negotiation) is consistent throughout Adonis's oeuvre; in his writing, the Arabic word is usually translatable as "ideology" or even "fanaticism." Where culture is characterized by plurality, *al-siyasa* for Adonis is a struggle for domination; where culture faces toward the future, politics is imprisoned by the past; while culture permits the individual to explore and transform communal attachments, politics fixes identity and makes it into a weapon. In other words, Adonis's argument is not a narrative but a series of antinomies. There is no historical explanation for the hardening of sectarian positions that led to Lebanon's civil war; there is only a claim that the typically modern virtues Adonis associates with Beirut were at some point and for some reason overwhelmed by illiberal "political" agendas. Beirut's golden age is, in this account, a kind of mirage that floats free of its material conditions. Its conflicting ideologies and varied cultural products have no common measure. They belong to two different histories or moments of history.

The presumption of a stark divide between culture and politics is, as we will see, a defining trait of Arabic modernism. In another revealing episode from Adonis's memoir, which he has related more than once, he recalls his time as a student in Syria in the 1940s, when anti-French feeling was strong and nativist sentiments had taken hold among his classmates.

> I remember, for example, that during some demonstrations students would make a pile of foreign books in the courtyard and set fire to them.

What is astonishing to me now is that I never participated, personally, in the burning of a single book, although I did join the demonstrations and was even one of the leaders of the student movements in Tartus (at the school of the *Mission laïque française*) and Latakia (at the preparatory school) between 1944 and 1949. Did I make a distinction, unconsciously, between one's political position toward the foreigner and one's literary position toward him?[6]

Adonis's early verse of the forties and fifties is dominated by the myth of the phoenix, which served as an allegory for the rebirth of the Syrian nation. The same myth lurks behind this anecdote from his school days, but here it is not an ancient nation that rises from the vestiges of a vanquished imperialism. Instead, it is literature that is saved from the fires and passions of nationalism. The modernists often conceived of their task in just these terms.

This chapter and the next urge a different approach to history than that of Adonis and like-minded memorialists of Beirut. Rather than supposing an unproblematic split between politics and culture, I examine the history of how this supposed separation became an ideological position in its own right. This is the Cold War moment of late modernism's emergence, when the vessel of modernist culture was cut loose from its moorings in the nation. Telling the story in this way requires a different set of terms than those employed by Adonis. Or else, it requires a historical analysis of those terms—*openness, creativity, culture, world*—rather than their uncritical adoption. Instead of celebrating antebellum Beirut as a moment of ideological truce, I focus on the antagonistic nature of intellectual exchanges during the period, particularly as seen in literary magazines and journals of opinion. If, as Robert Scholes and others have argued for the European case, "modernism begins in the magazines," the same is profoundly true of the Arabic movement.[7] Intellectual life in Beirut was not so much a playground as a battleground, and this war of position extended beyond the borders of Lebanon. The debates between local intellectuals—nationalist, Marxist, and liberal—reflect the global agon between the main ideological camps of the early Cold War. While the Arab modernists' dreams of artistic freedom were grounded in the peculiar national situation of Lebanon, they were also importantly conditioned by the international play of forces.

The Lebanese Conjuncture

During the three decades following World War II and preceding the outbreak of civil conflict in 1975, Lebanon established a unique role for itself in the region, becoming at once an intellectual center and political outlier. The country received independence from France in 1943 in a separate agreement from Syria, to which it had been joined under an interwar mandate. Christian and Muslim elites shook hands over the National Pact, in which the Maronites relinquished their demands for continued Western military presence in exchange for Sunni acquiescence to separation from Syria (unification had been a primary demand of the Muslim community throughout the Mandate period). A new constitution formalized the Maronites' dominance, establishing advantageous ratios for political positions and reserving the presidency for Christians. The executive was made into a pole of commercial interests, with the result that a small and powerful group of mainly Christian families soon began dismantling wartime economic controls. Under the presidency of Camille Chamoun (1952–58), and with the guidance of Foreign Minister Charles Malik (a significant mentor for the *Shiʿr* poets, as we shall see), Lebanon aligned its foreign policy with Western powers against the nonaligned pan-Arabism of Egypt's Gamal Abdel Nasser. Chamoun's government eventually adopted a militantly anti-Communist rhetoric in line with the Eisenhower Doctrine of 1957, which pledged "to secure and protect the territorial integrity and political independence of such nations, requesting such aid against overt armed aggression from any nation controlled by international communism." Lebanon's pro-trade, pro-Western policies, which were unique in regional terms—and opposed by local Marxist and nationalist movements—would persist with minor alterations for the next thirty years. This period is customarily known as that of the Merchant Republic, which is roughly coextensive with the period of Arabic modernism itself.[8]

Outside Lebanon, the characteristic development in the Arab world during this era was the rapid extension of state power, typically under the auspices of socialist, or quasisocialist, single-party regimes. As historian Hanna Batatu writes in an essay on the Egyptian, Syrian, and Iraqi revolutions: "One of the most significant effects of the revolutions in all three countries was the enormous growth in the role of the government in the life of the people. The impact of the state upon the social structure or at least its capacity to determine the direction of social change was enhanced by its planning powers and its greater influence over the distribution of the national income."[9] This expansion of the state into more and more areas of social life was concurrent with its assertion of hegemony over the field of culture. Here, the Egyptian experience supplies a useful model. Although an extreme version, leading to what Anouar Abdel-Malek has termed "a State monopoly on culture," the Nasserist program was influential at a moment when pan-Arabist politics were spreading across the region.[10] Egyptian officials encouraged centralization in Syria during the three years of union (1958–61) and also in Iraq between 1963 and 1964, when the two countries contemplated unification in the wake of a coup by sympathetic officers in the Iraqi army. Richard Jacquemond gives a précis of how the Egyptian state established its control over the realm of culture and intellectual life in general:

It was only after 1956 that the Nasser regime, reinforced by the Suez Crisis, went on to set up the system of institutions through which it intended to control and mobilize the intellectuals, a system which in its essentials still exists today. This system included the establishment of institutions such as the Higher Council for Arts and Letters (1956) and the Ministry of Culture (1958), as well as the expansion of those state institutions that already existed in the field of theater or radio.... New organizations were created, such as state television in 1960, while others were nationalized, such as the whole of the press in 1960, the film industry in 1961, and an important part of the publishing industry in 1961 and 1965.... On the whole, the state created by the Free Officers continued an ancient tradition of protecting and controlling artists and intellectuals, only acting, in the final analysis, to make this tradition more systematic.[11]

The specter of state culture and its standardized aesthetics haunt the imagination of the Beiruti modernists. It is a recurrent theme in the letters of *Shiʿr*'s foreign correspondents from Egypt, Morocco, and as far away as East Germany. Writing from that divided capital, Asʿad Razzuq, author of an early study of modernist mythography, noted that "The poet in the socialist state receives a very high salary, but he is obliged to commit himself [*yaltazim*] to the causes of the workers and peasants when the State demands it."[12] This concern echoed those of older modernist poets such as Eliot, who worried during the closing moments of World War II over "the dangers which may come from official encouragement and patronage of the arts; the dangers to which men of letters would be exposed, if they became, in their professional capacity, servants of the State."[13]

In Lebanon, by contrast with its neighbors, the state never assumed such powers. Traditions of clientism, encouraged by underfunded French colonial policies; an economy dominated by the trade and service sectors rather than industry; and communal disagreements over the historical identity of the country, all conspired to limit the growth of the central government. This trend was somewhat mitigated during the presidency of Fuad Shihab (1958–64), a former general who sought to build up the state, particularly its security apparatus, and to increase public sector employment in line with regional norms. Shihabist policies met strong opposition, however, most powerfully articulated by the editorialists of *al-Nahar*, a Beiruti daily that was a forum for economic liberalism and anti-Nasserist politics as well as a consistent ally of the *Shiʿr* movement (both Yusuf al-Khal and Unsi al-Hajj served as editors of the cultural page beginning in the mid-1950s). Such countercurrents helped to maintain the relative weakness of the state and to ensure that intellectuals had room to maneuver. A chief reason Beirut became a refuge for thinkers and artists from across the region was the margin of independence it allowed to cultural life. The modernists were aware of the eccentric position occupied by Lebanon and recognized that their own movement was conditioned by its peculiarities. "Our success in poetry," writes Adonis in his memoir, "was essentially due—here is the great irony—to our marginality. Was it not 'the Lebanese margin' [*al-hamish al-lubnani*] that spread the contagion of the modern poetry revolution into the Arab center? Is not Beirut itself proof that the sources of real transformation in the second half of the century came from the margin and not from the center?"[14]

Lebanon's role as a refuge in the postwar period was also the result of a distinct history of relations between intellectuals and the state. Here again the contrasting norm is supplied by Egypt. Beginning with the reign of Muhammad Ali in the first half of the nineteenth century, Egyptian intellectuals did much of their work within the orbit of government institutions, whether as ministry bureaucrats, editors of official newspapers, or teachers at state schools. The Egyptian *wali* sent thinkers such as Rifaʿa al-Tahtawi to Europe for long stays, then brought them home to translate military, scientific, and legal texts into Arabic. A state-centered approach to culture persisted through the colonial period and reached its apogee under Nasser, as Jacquemond notes. This history was the object of bittersweet satire by Egyptian writers such as Naguib Mahfouz, whose cultural eminence was shadowed by his long career as a government clerk. In Mahfouz's novel, *Respected Sir*, an ambitious state employee reflects, "The ideal citizen of other nations might be a warrior, a politician, a merchant, a craftsman or a sailor, but in Egypt it was the government official. . . . Even the Pharaohs themselves, he thought, were but officials appointed by the gods."[15] In the Levant, by contrast, intellectual networks were historically more decentered and geographically far-flung. For *Shiʿr* poets, the relevant precursor was the movement of the *mahjar*—Arabic for "the place of emigration"—a community of freelance critics and poets with branches in North and South America, whose members included Khalil Gibran and Ameen Rihani. The Beiruti modernists often cast themselves as inheritors of the *mahjar* group, whom they viewed as the true trailblazers of twentieth-century Arabic literature.

In postwar Lebanon, a weak state went hand in hand with an open economy. At a time when dirigisme was standard in formerly colonized and Soviet-friendly countries, Lebanon was one of the few states outside Europe to adopt *laissez-faire* economic policies, although as Nadim Shehadeh has noted, *laissez-faire* was really *laissez-aller*: the ideal was not so much production as deregulation. This species of economic liberalism was justified by its supposedly natural fit with Lebanon's mercantile history. Speaking in 1948 at the Cénacle libanais, a forum for elite opinion where Yusuf al-Khal and Adonis would also give important lectures, Gabriel Ménassa, author of the first comprehensive plan for the national economy, argued against the pro-industrial, protective policies favored by Syria, to which Lebanon was then bound by a

Customs Union. Ménassa was a *maître à penser* for Christian liberals known as the New Phoenicians, and in his lecture he recalled Lebanon's "traditional role as a country of transit and distribution . . . [a role] that is given to her and which she has carried out since ancient times." He finished the speech with a characteristically internationalist plea: "May absolute freedom of trade be established between all Arab states, and may all obstacles to the free circulation of persons, goods, and capital between these states be thrown down."[16]

Ménassa's demand for free circulation went largely unheeded by other states in the region, but it found a receptive audience among Lebanon's financial and mercantile elite, which was virtually indistinguishable from its political elite. Beginning in 1948, the government liberalized the exchange market, permitting the free movement of Lebanese capital all over the world; wartime restrictions on currency and financial transactions were gradually lifted; in 1950 the Customs Union with Syria was dissolved, in line with Ménassa's recommendations; and 1956 saw the enactment of the Swiss-style Banking Secrecy Law.[17] The result of these policies was a flood of immigrants, oil money, and imported goods into Lebanon. As early as 1948, nearly a third of the world's gold shipments passed through the country on its way to the Gulf monarchs, and the reflux was equally rich: according to one estimate, two-thirds of the Gulf oil surplus sluiced in and out of Lebanese banks between 1956 and 1966. Meanwhile in Beirut, rather than a state monopoly on culture, a thousand flowers bloomed: the new cinemas in Hamra showed films from Paris, Cairo, Cinecittà, and Hollywood (with subtitles in French and Arabic), the kiosks displayed a similarly cosmopolitan array of journals, and arguably for the first time in the region a consumer society—replete with window-shopping, fashion magazines, and the culture of advertising—arose among Beirut's monied middle class.[18]

Lebanon's experience of modernity was therefore a significant anomaly in regional and even global terms. Unlike other countries in the Middle East, Latin America, and Africa, the connotations of *al-hadatha* in Lebanon were not industrialization, monoculture, and the forced rationalization of economic life. Nor did modernity suggest a strategy of what Samir Amin calls "delinking": economic self-sufficiency driven by import substitution. Instead, with an economy centered on the finance and service sectors—the number of tourists nearly quintupled between 1952 and 1955—in Lebanon the ideology of *al-hadatha* was a fantasy of free exchange and connection with the wider world. Rather than suggesting the iron cage of bureaucratic administration, modernity in Lebanon signaled the enchantments of internationalism—the "open and unfinished project" that so struck Adonis when he arrived in Beirut for the first time in 1956.[19]

The *Shiʿr* poets shared this quintessentially Lebanese vision of modernity. While they consistently cast themselves as members of an adversary culture, the modernists' style of thought, particularly on the question of *al-hadatha*, was in line with a powerful segment of local opinion—precisely that financial and mercantile elite, predominantly though not exclusively Christian, that propounded its ideas at the lectern of the Cénacle libanais.[20] In the social-scientific terms popular at the time, the modernists were more like *integrated* than *alienated* intellectuals; though not employed by the state, and often hailing from minoritarian backgrounds, they shared many of the ideas and the outlook of its planners. Both modernist poets and the mercantile elite—or at least its most articulate representatives—were liberal internationalists of a Cold War type, albeit with Lebanese peculiarities: suspicious of state intervention in cultural and economic spheres, professionalist in ethos, and convinced of Lebanon's special calling in the region, which was not to take sides in political disputes but rather to play the "traditional" role of middleman. The Lebanese planners' preference for open borders and a limited state meant they were deeply skeptical of Soviet intentions in the region, but they were careful to frame their pro-Western orientation as an apolitical commitment to openness and the free circulation of things and ideas. Depending on the occasion, this neutralism could be framed, in Ménassa's terms, as a matter of economic rationality or else as a characteristically spiritual disposition. As Charles Malik wrote in 1952, when he served as Lebanese ambassador to the United States as well as the United Nations, "Lebanon could not be true to East and West alike unless she stood for existential freedom. In the end this is alone her justification. This means freedom of thought, freedom of choice, freedom of being, freedom of becoming. . . . Her basic idea is not political; on the contrary, her political existence is derivative. If she succumbs to the political temptation, to the manifestation of power, she will move from one defeat to another."[21]

The rhetoric of liberal internationalism framed as political neutralism is echoed in the modernist poetics of the *Shiʿr* group. Just as Ménassa argued for Lebanon's postwar integration into global economic markets, so the modernists worked to internationalize the local cultural field. Their magazine expanded the horizons of literary production in a dizzying fashion. Its editorial policy, which emphasized the journal's global reach in the form of letters from abroad as well as reports on the export of its own texts into European languages, helped redraw the map of Arabic poetry with startling swiftness. This redefinition is evident in the poems themselves from the presence of new formal elements, including lexical innovations (transliterated phrases, mythological beings, philosophical terms), prosodic imports (the prose poem), and the transformation of classical genres (the elegy)—all topics addressed elsewhere in this book. It is also marked in the modernists' selection of poems for translation into Arabic. The foreign poets who appeared in *Shiʿr* were not an international hodgepodge. They were carefully chosen as writers whose work had slipped the bonds of national culture and now floated free in an abstract space of transnational exchange. As Adonis writes in a short essay introducing his translation of Saint-John Perse, the chief characteristic of the Frenchman's poetry is "its ability to live on its own, independently," which is why Perse's work "appears, in translation, more worldly [*'alami*] than any other."[22] "Worldliness," understood as an index of abstraction from local circumstances, was a key marker of modernist literature for the Beiruti poets. Many of *Shi'r*'s foreign correspondents reported back to Beirut about the festivals, award ceremonies, and conferences that underpin what we now call "world poetry," and the modernists were the first Arab poets to figure prominently on this stage.

The modernists' rivals in Beirut held markedly different notions of internationalism. The most consistent and clamorous rivals were the pan-Arabist intellectuals associated with the monthly *al-Adab* [Literatures] as well as the Communist thinkers of *al-Thaqafa al-Wataniyya* [National Culture] and its successor *al-Tariq* [The Path].[23] Neither nationalists nor Communists were parochial in any obvious sense. Their magazines were also filled with names of foreign poets and thinkers, though perhaps not as conspicuously as *Shi'r*. The Marxist journals regularly published selections from the emerging canon of Second World literature, from Lu Xun and Berthold Brecht to Nazim Hikmet and Yevgeny Yevtushenko. Suhayl Idris, the editor in chief of *al-Adab*, was a Sorbonne graduate, and his own version of internationalism bore a distinctly Parisian stamp. Jean-Paul Sartre was the journal's tutelary spirit, but it also published works by luminaries of the European antifascist left, from the poems of Lorca to the fiction of Alberto Moravia to the essays of André Malraux. These battling canons of world literature embodied distinct understandings of the relation between nationalism and internationalism. Whereas the *Shi'r* poets valorized "worldliness" against the allegedly parochial space of the nation or the *watan*, both Marxist and pan-Arab writers privileged the latter without presuming any incompatibility between the two commitments. Indeed, what they objected to was precisely the claim that an allegiance to universal values required a rejection of nationalist ideals and sentiments. This was, in their eyes, merely a debased version of internationalism—a version that Marxists, in the Arab world as elsewhere, often referred to slightingly as "cosmopolitanism." The dean of Arab Marxist critics, Husayn Muruwwa, makes this point in a monitory essay on "humanism" directed in part at the poets of *Shi'r*:

> Despite the awakened state of Arab society today, there are still a few among us—perhaps more numerous in Lebanon than elsewhere in the Arab world—who zealously insist on being very "humanist" [*insaniyya jiddan*], *very* humanist in the sense that these gentlemen would like for their "humanism" to transcend their patriotism [*wataniyya*].... They suppose they are able to "uproot" themselves from the ground in which they grew, and they fool themselves—or try to fool others—that patriotism is an impenetrable wall blocking out the horizon and depriving them of light.... But this is a silly and obvious hoax, for

patriotism in this divisive sense is not patriotism at all, but only inane factionalism [al-'asabiyya al-hamqa'].[24]

The Shi'r poets' extreme, antinationalist version of internationalism was at the core of their vision of modernist culture, although, as we shall see, this internationalism was also—ironically—an impediment to certain kinds of collaboration with their counterparts abroad. In the Shi'r poets' view, it was Arabic literature's insufficient worldliness that was holding it back. This is the argument made by editor in chief Yusuf al-Khal at a conference on Arabic literature held in Rome in the fall of 1961, a conference that would become a touchstone for debates about the modernist project in the years to come. Al-Khal's lecture, entitled "The Arab Man of Letters in the Modern World," attempted to identify the causes of what he termed the Arab world's "loss of modernity" [fiqdan al-hadatha].[25] This concern was common to a number of lectures at the Rome Conference, whose participants took for granted that Arab culture was in a state of crisis. In his opening remarks, the Italian novelist Ignazio Silone spoke of the "critical stage" that "Arab civilization" was undergoing in its transition from a traditional to a modern phase.[26] Al-Khal was typically uncompromising, even hyperbolic, in his characterization of this crisis. He claimed that there was "a contradiction between our formal existence in the modern world and our essential existence outside it," and argued that the primary task of Arab intellectuals was therefore to discover "how we can build a modern society in a modern world." Al-Khal identified three major causes of backwardness: Arabs' deference to the literary rather than the spoken language (a concern of al-Khal throughout his career); a long history of political fragmentation; and, most importantly, intellectual parochialism. For al-Khal, the history of Arab intellectual life since the loss of Andalusia in the fifteenth century, "when philosophy died in the East and lived on in the West," is characterized by a spirit of self-segregation. This turn away from the wider world had led to cultural benightedness. To become modern meant once again to enter into "the give and take" of civilizational exchange. But this would also require a ruthless revision of the native intellectual heritage. The Arabic turath needed to be evaluated through the lens of present emergency. "The civilization of man is unified and cannot be broken into pieces," al-Khal declared. "Separating ourselves from it, closing ourselves to it, is death. If we would live, we must connect, we must open up. Anything in our heritage that prevents this is worthless."

Adonis's contribution to the Rome conference, "Arabic Poetry and the Problem of Renewal," frames the dilemma of traditionalism in slightly different terms, though the solutions it offers are similar.[27] Adonis locates the sources of backwardness in what he calls a culture of "pastism," one that does not recognize a rupture between past and present, in which education is centered on memorization and literature is essentially pedagogical. In such a culture, Adonis avers, "Man is understood as an inheritor" rather than as an active subject. A culture that consecrates tradition for its own sake leads to the sort of inward turn described by al-Khal. Modern poets would have to turn outward once again. There is no value to the Arabic heritage, Adonis continued, "except to the extent that it harmonizes with that wider human civilization." He concluded his lecture with a figure of Arabic poetry "knocking on the door of a larger and richer world"—a reprise of al-Khal's typically Levantine admonition to his peers to "open up" and connect with those abroad.

Both Adonis and Yusuf al-Khal agreed that for Arab poets to become modern they needed to end their self-imposed parochialism. To write verse that was "coeval with the civilizational moment in which they live," Arab poets would have to rethink their relation to the inherited tradition and hook up with a larger, indeed universal "human" tradition. This link between modernism and internationalism (and canonical revision) is a constant in the writings of the *Shiʿr* group. But what was on the other side of that door that Arabic poetry was now knocking on? What did Adonis and al-Khal mean by "human" civilization or "the civilization of man"? Did they simply mean "the West"? The corpus of Arabic modernism is full of vague and seemingly vacuous tropes such as "man," "freedom," and "dynamism." An important achievement of the *Shiʿr* group was to marshal these nebulous abstractions into an intelligible poetics. As keywords in the rhetoric of modernism, they also helped distinguish the movement sharply from its rivals. The Rome conference of 1961 was just such a moment of collective self-definition, an opportunity for the Beiruti poets to defend the aims of their movement in front of an international audience. The meeting was a significant crossroads in Arab intellectual life during the Cold War, one in which the arguments and ironies of late modernist culture were articulated with special clarity.

Keywords and Networks

The Rome conference, which took place at the Hermitage Hotel in the embassy neighborhood of Parioli, was sponsored by the Congress for Cultural Freedom (CCF), a global network of artists and intellectuals crucial to the cultural history of the early Cold War. The CCF was founded in Berlin in 1950, in response to efforts by the Cominform—the Soviet-aligned umbrella organization of European Communist parties—to mobilize intellectuals against the US-funded Marshall Plan. The essential task of the CCF was to woo European intellectuals away from communism and toward what the American historian Arthur Schlesinger famously called "the vital center": a redefined, militant liberalism that championed individual freedom and capitalist dynamism against the threat of Soviet totalitarianism. At its peak, writes Frances Stonor Saunders, a historian of the Congress, the Paris-based CCF "had offices in thirty-five countries, employed dozens of personnel, published over twenty prestigious magazines, held art exhibitions, owned a news and features service, organized high-profile international conferences, and rewarded musicians and artists with prizes and public performances."[28] Frank Kermode, who briefly edited one of these magazines, explains that "The congress so lavishly endowed conferences in pleasant places that it became a well-known gravy train, and some who later admitted or boasted that they had always known of its covert connections took full advantage of the Congress's open hand."[29] In 1966 the *New York Times* and *Ramparts* magazine confirmed what had been widely rumored for some time, namely that the CCF was a front for the US Central Intelligence Agency. In the wake of these revelations, the Congress and many of its satellite institutions closed down.

Along with lavishly endowed conferences, magazines played a pivotal role in the activities of the CCF (as they did for the Cominform). If World War II coincided with the demise of the heroic "little magazine," dedicated to fiction, poetry, and the visual arts—Cyril Connolly's *Horizons* already viewed itself as the last of this type—the chain of periodicals funded by the CCF helped establish a new norm for the small journal, centered on political and cultural criticism in the manner of the *Partisan Review*. The first CCF-funded journal was the French *Preuves*, intended to serve as a rival to Jean-Paul Sartre's *Les Temps modernes* and to lure writers from his stable of Soviet-aligned intellectuals. The CCF's flagship publication by virtue of its readership, with a circulation of about forty thousand in the early 1960s, was the British magazine *Encounter*, co-edited in London by Stephen Spender and Irving Kristol (and later Kermode). Other important journals included *Cuadernos*, published in Paris for distribution in Latin America (superseded by the more successful *Mundo Nuevo*), and the socialist *Tempo Presente*, edited in Rome by Ignazio Silone and Nicola Chiaromonte. The CCF also published a number of notable magazines outside the Euro-American sphere of influence, including *Transition* in Uganda and *Quest* in India.[30] These magazines shared their content, so that any contribution might be published more or less simultaneously, in different languages, in Kampala, Mexico City, and Rome. The magazines' tables of contents modeled a similar kind of international egalitarianism. Arab, European, American, and African authors shared the same textual space, as if the hierarchies of politics and power had been temporarily suspended. These juxtapositions had special appeal for writers from outside Europe, whose works enjoyed a refracted glory—as well as an expanded audience—by virtue of their proximity with the names of T. S. Eliot, Thomas Mann, and Benedetto Croce. As Andrew Rubin has noted, "This group of journals not only retained its identity as a corpus and gave a density to the separation between aesthetics and politics but at the same time structured the domain of transnational culture so that certain writers more than others would become recognizable as 'world' literary figures."[31]

For many intellectuals associated with the CCF as well as for late modernist thinkers more generally, the goals of separating aesthetics from politics and internationalizing culture were inextricably linked. By freeing intellectual work from political interference, they sought to construct an ideal realm for collaboration and exchange across national borders. This was the mirror image of intellectual life under the Cominform, where culture was dictated by the state and thinkers were, according to the CCF's way of thinking, essentially propagandists. "Intellectual liberty" became the rallying cry for Congress-affiliated intellectuals on both sides of the Atlantic. In the words of the Freedom Manifesto, a founding charter for the CCF drafted by Arthur Koestler in 1950, neutrality in the face of totalitarianism "amounts to a betrayal of mankind and to the abdication of the free mind."[32] Giles Scott-Smith has usefully described the CCF as an instrument for consolidating the hegemony of the transatlantic non-Communist intelligentsia, in other words, "as the cultural-intellectual equivalent of the political economy of the Marshall Plan."[33] In line with its hegemonic aspirations, the CCF tended to present itself not as a political organization but, on the contrary, as a defender of universal values such as "the free mind" and "human dignity." The Congress's goal of establishing a liberal consensus was remarkably successful in the European theater (and to a lesser extent in Latin America), where the non-Communist left had deep roots and intellectual networks the CCF could reactivate in the postwar period. But when the Congress turned its attention outside Europe, as it increasingly did in the late 1950s, it encountered a very different terrain. In the decolonizing countries of Africa, Asia, and the Middle East, liberalism had relatively shallow roots, and powerful nationalist movements often regarded the United States as an imperial antagonist in the offing. All this made the CCF's task of identifying local allies especially delicate.[34]

The CCF opened its Beirut office in 1954, and the Lebanese capital would henceforth serve as the hub for Congress activities in the Middle East, where, as one CCF consultant opined, "The intelligentsia is politically the most important sector of the population."[35] The choice of Beirut is not surprising given the city's highly developed publishing industry, abundance of polyglot intermediaries, and openness to foreign ideas and institutions. As one American spy wrote in fond retrospect, Beirut "had more banks than New York City and more newspapers than London. By the middle of 1958 it had more confidential newsletters than New York, London and Paris put together."[36] All CCF-affiliated intellectuals who traveled or gave lectures in the region made a stop in Beirut. This ease of access gave pause to some friends of the Congress. One consultant worried that Lebanon was "already the base for numerous international interests," and so "the Congress consequently might acquire an excessively Western flavor."[37] Others warned that the city's openness would inevitably be exploited by ideological enemies. "Beirut is the only possible site that might serve as a base for almost-free culture," Silone conceded after his own tour of the region. But he went on to worry that "in the near future, Beirut will become more and more a hub of intellectual activity thanks to the publication of a communist-inspired review."[38] Despite its many advantages, the CCF office in Beirut was poorly run for the first seven years of its existence—the representative, a former UN official named Beshara Ghorayeb, had few contacts with local intellectuals and a penchant for self-promotion—and it was temporarily closed in the spring of 1960. The Paris office used this opportunity to rethink its mission in the region, including the possibility of establishing a locally published magazine.

The CCF office in Paris was at this time directed by a CIA officer named John Hunt, a graduate of Harvard and the Iowa Writers' Workshop (his first novel, *Generations of Men*, was a finalist for the National Book Award in 1957).[39] Hunt was keen to have a CCF-funded magazine in Arabic. As he wrote to Silone, a trusted adviser to the Paris office, "I'm sure that a prop of this sort in the domain of publications is the best way of supporting our friends in the region and maintaining our presence."[40] Hunt eventually identified Yusuf al-Khal as a possible publisher for the journal, which was to be called *Adab* [Literature]. Al-Khal's credentials as a fellow traveler of Cold War liberals was secured by his long association with the philosopher and diplomat Charles Malik, as we shall see in the next chapter. In the spring of 1960, al-Khal wrote a letter of introduction for Adonis to the Paris office of the CCF—Adonis lived in Paris on a fellowship between 1960 and 1961—boasting that *Shi'r* was "the only magazine for poetry in the Arab world," and adding, "We are now in a midst [*sic*] of a revolution in Arabic poetry worth being expounded and brought to the attention of the outside world."[41] Throughout the spring and summer of 1961, the editor in chief of *Shi'r* was requested to look after CCF friends—Stephen Spender and Jeanne-Léonie Dumont (wife of Gaston Gallimard), among others—on their visits to the region. In August, Hunt expressed the wish that al-Khal might become "our correspondent in Lebanon" and asked him to arrive in Rome a few days prior to the conference so that they might "discuss the publication of an Arabic quarterly."[42] Organizers and attendees alike understood the Rome conference as an audition for al-Khal and the *Shi'r* group, which would determine whether the Arab intellectuals' vision of modernist literature was compatible with that of the CCF and its allies.

The two European luminaries at the Rome conference were Spender and Silone, co-editors of *Encounter* and *Tempo Presente*, respectively. Eleven years previously, they collaborated on a work that helped define the rhetorical parameters of early Cold War culture. *The God That Failed* (1950) was a collection of six autobiographical essays by former Communists and fellow travelers who recounted their initial attraction to the movement and subsequent disillusionment. Several contributors soon migrated into the institutions of the CCF: Silone and Spender became editors for Congress-funded magazines; Arthur Koestler served on its executive committee; and Richard Wright contributed articles for *Encounter*, including his report on the Bandung conference in 1955.[43] Not surprisingly, certain idioms adopted in the book reappear regularly in the magazines. Paeans to artistic heroism, the human condition, and political freedom are the common currency of this milieu. Spender's own conversion narrative ends with a typical peroration. After condemning the Soviet state's co-optation of its intellectual class, Spender writes: "Literature and art are therefore a *témoignage*, a witnessing of the human condition within the particular circumstances of time and place. To make individual experience submit to the generalization of official information and observation, is to cut humanity off from a main means of becoming conscious of itself as a community of individuals."[44] The form of the book itself, a sequence of six short memoirs, emphasized the importance of personal "witnessing" against the abstract collectivism supposedly characteristic of Communist art. As Spender put it more schematically in another essay, "The poet is writing as one person for the reader reading as one person."[45]

Spender was well known to the *Shiʿr* poets. He visited Beirut in April 1961 on a lecture tour of the Middle East, financed by the British Council.[46] He stayed at the British ambassador's residence and gave a talk at the American University of Beirut on the art of autobiography. He was also a guest at one of the "*jeudis de* Shiʿr," the regular salon organized by the magazine, possibly modeled on the "*Mardis de* Preuves," which often included foreign visitors. According to the write-up in the spring issue of *Shiʿr*, Spender talked to the Beiruti poets about the differences between British and French verse culture, remarked on the continuing influence of Eliot on young poets, speculated on the reasons why the prose poem had never caught on in England, and argued that German poetry since Rilke was dead (Spender had collaborated on the first English versions of *The Duino Elegies*).[47] Gloomy surveys of the contemporary scene were a specialty of the English poet, whose articles in *Encounter* vacillate between encomiums for interwar modernists and laments for the present state of literature. This was the period in which Spender was composing and reworking the essays collected in *The Struggle for the Modern* (1963), a book that champions the cosmopolitan modernism of Joyce, Eliot, Lawrence, and Pound against various foreign and domestic rivals. Spender found the older continental avant-gardes, such as Marinetti's futurism, too enthusiastic in their embrace of the newfangled present. But he also disapproved of contemporary poets and critics associated with "the Movement"—Kingsley Amis and Philip Larkin chief among them—whom he found parochial in their anti-experimentalism and adherence to a specifically British literary past. It was only the early Anglo-American modernists who managed to combine a mastery of the classics with a feel for the now. This was a stance Spender called "revolutionary traditionalism," which permitted artists "to view the whole significant past of art at all times and in all places as an available tradition out of which modern forms and style might derive."[48]

For the *Shiʿr* poets, the importance of Spender's visit had less to do with the news he brought, which is rather hastily paraphrased by the magazine's editors, than with the evidence it provided of the Beiruti movement's presence in the circuits of international poetry. The meeting in Rome was further confirmation. In Silone's opening address to the conference, delivered in French (though only the Arabic translation has been published), he evoked Goethe and his idea of *Weltliteratur:*

> I want first of all to stress that interest in Arabic literature has now begun to spread beyond the circle of specialists. No doubt we are still far from that generous opening outward, on a global scale, toward what Goethe called world literature [*al-adab al-'alami*]... yet we feel that neither political and economic facts, nor even a reading of classical texts, can give us the knowledge we seek, which only literature—good or bad—can provide: knowledge of the true life of man, the sentiments, dreams, and agonies that form the Arab man [*al-insan al-'arabi*] at this difficult moment.[49]

This ceremonial rhetoric of community and crisis echoes Silone's letter of invitation to conference participants, in which he wrote, "The colloquium will be consecrated to one of the most pressing questions now facing contemporary Arabic letters: its awakening to modern life and aspiration to communion, alongside other literatures, in a quest for and expression of the human."[50] Silone's hope that the conference would contribute to the wider recognition of Arabic literature was seconded by the lectures of al-Khal and Adonis, who blamed the supposed backwardness of their poetic tradition on its withdrawal from the wider world. Silone and the Arab guests had a more specific notion of "world literature" than is suggested by the Goethean allusion, however. It is not only the mutual enrichment of national literatures these intellectuals envisage, but the creation of a literary space safe from the impingements of politics. For the late modernists, world literature and "apolitical" culture form a Möbius strip. Silone describes the conference itself as a figure for this world-literature-to-come: "The great distinction of this conference is that it is held in a place apart from the relations between states and their political enmities. It is a meeting of men of literature, without distinction among them, whose goal is the discussion of specifically literary issues."[51]

Silone's contrast between political enmity and literary exchange is a commonplace of late modernism, in which a withdrawal from political commitment is the sine qua non of artistic creation. But of course Silone's disavowal of political interest was itself a way of taking sides in the Cold War *Kulturkampf.* To invoke "a place apart," where literary issues could be discussed without fear of censure, was to remind his audience of the Soviet state's enforcement of the party line on aesthetic matters, resulting in that drama of coercion and consent analyzed in Koestler's *The Darkness at Noon* (1940) and later, with more subtlety, in Czesław Miłosz's *The Captive Mind* (1953). In Silone's contribution to *The God That Failed,* he recalls a discussion with the director

FIGURE 3. Ignazio Silone delivering his opening remarks to the Rome Conference. Special Collections Research Center, University of Chicago Library.

of a state publishing house in Moscow in the 1920s: "'Liberty'—I had to give examples—'is the possibility of doubting, the possibility of making a mistake, the possibility of searching and experimenting, the possibility of saying 'no' to any authority—literary, artistic, philosophic, religious, social, and even political.' 'But that,' murmured this eminent functionary of Soviet culture in horror, 'that is counter-revolution.'"[52]

The Congress also pressed its arguments for cultural freedom, meaning freedom from state coercion—"the possibility of saying 'no'"—against European foes. A special target was Jean-Paul Sartre's notion of the *engagé* writer as elaborated in essays written for *Les temps modernes* and collected in his book, *Qu'est-ce que la littérature?*[53] Sartre's polemic against what he called "the temptation of irresponsibility," and his call for "a literature of praxis," had an especially brilliant career in the Arab world.[54] The ideal of *engagement* (in Arabic, *al-iltizam*) became the dominant model among nationalist and Marxist writers for understanding the relationship between intellectuals and politics. Arab writers emphasized the voluntarist and populist elements of Sartre's polemic (and they were baffled by his restriction of *engagement* to prose writers, since for them political commitment was the poet's default posture). In 1953, in the first issue of the pan-Arabist monthly *al-Adab*, Editor in Chief Suhayl Idris wrote, "For literature to be truthful it must not be isolated from the society in which it exists." He called for a "literature of commitment,

FIGURE 4. From right: Tawfiq Sayigh, Yusuf al-Khal, Jabra Ibrahim Jabra, and Adonis at the Rome Conference. Special Collections Research Center, University of Chicago Library.

which issues from Arab society and pours back into it." Idris acquired his doctorate from the Sorbonne in 1952, arguably at the height of Sartre's fame, and his magazine became the principal venue for translating existentialism into Arabic, merging the rhetoric of authenticity, freedom, and anxiety with Arab nationalist politics.[55] Two years after Idris coined the term, a pair of Egyptian critics, Mahmud Amin al-ʿAlim and ʿAbd al-ʿAzim Anis, effectively appropriated it for Marxist intellectuals. In their short work, *Fi-l-thaqafa al-misriyya* [On Egyptian Culture], published in Beirut with an introduction by Husayn Muruwwa, Amin al-ʿAlim and Anis insisted that truly committed literature—their model was the socialist-realist novel—stemmed from solidarity with the working class and not from existential anguish, which they denounced as individualist posturing. For the next decade, debates on the Arab left assumed the necessity of *iltizam* as a condition for meaningful intellectual work.[56]

The unique position occupied by *Shiʿr* magazine in the force field of postwar Arabic literature, explained more fully in the next chapter, is that it resisted the discourse of *iltizam* in the name of poetic autonomy. The modernists countered the demand for socially conscious literature with a lyric poetics. The final lecture of the Rome conference was delivered by the Iraqi poet Badr Shakir al-Sayyab under the title "Commitment and Non-Commitment in Modern Arabic Literature."[57] Al-Sayyab was among the most revered poets of his generation. His "Hymn to Rain," first published in *al-Adab* in 1954, is a landmark of modern Arabic poetry, mixing lyricism, local mythology, and political critique in a work that readers have often compared with *The Waste Land*. Al-Sayyab's Rome talk was an attack on the notion of commitment as defined by Arab Communists. He argued that Communist *engagement* should be translated as *ilzam* ("coercion") rather than *iltizam* ("commitment"). The Marxists' appropriation of Sartre's idea had reduced Arab intellectual life to sloganeering. The warring camps only differed in the terminology of their propaganda: "While the Communist poet repeats the words *peace, peasant,* and *the red flag,* the non-Communist poet says *Arab unity, jihad,* and *mujahidin.*" By contrast, al-Sayyab praised the poetry of Adonis and al-Khal, not as poets who lacked commitment but as poets who had resuscitated an older, less partisan version of the ideal. Al-Sayyab argued that Arab poets of the pre-Islamic and ʿAbbasid periods were also *engagé*—they were spokesmen for the tribe and forcefully represented collective sentiments—and yet, "The degree of humanism and universalism [*al-insaniyya wa-l-shumul*] in the old poets' commitment was far greater than that of committed poets today." To historicize *iltizam* in this way left open the possibility that a less coercive mode of commitment could be found again in the present, and indeed al-Sayyab claimed at the close of his talk that the *Shiʿr* poets were also committed: "But they differ from Communist poets, all of whom are committed as a matter of course, in that Communist commitment is imposed on the poet from outside whereas the commitment of these poets springs from within."

In condemning Communist poets as propagandists, al-Sayyab was performing an act of self-criticism, and it was not his first. Al-Sayyab's political itinerary was an especially tortured one. Born in 1927 in southern Iraq, he became a member of the Iraqi Communist Party after the war, then among the largest leftist parties in the region. In 1953–54 he left the Communists and began supporting the Arab nationalists, whose resistance to British colonialism in Iraq was more resolute than that of the ICP (orthodoxy led the party to downplay the importance of national liberation, which the Soviets still viewed with suspicion). In the summer of 1959, in the wake of bloody clashes between Communists and nationalists in Mosul and Kirkuk, al-Sayyab wrote his own version of an anti-Communist conversion narrative. *Kuntu shuyuʿiyyan* [I Was a Communist], a serial memoir published in Baghdad by the Baathist newspaper *al-Hurriya*, was accompanied by excerpts from *The God That Failed*, which al-Sayyab's biographer speculates that the poet himself may have translated. (In 1955 al-Sayyab published a personal collection of translations, *Anthology of Modern World Poetry*, which included poems by Eliot, Pound, Tagore, and Spender but also Hikmet and Neruda.)[58]

By the late 1950s al-Sayyab had drifted into the orbit of the *Shiʿr* group, whose rhetoric of intellectual liberty—a commitment that springs from within rather than being imposed from without—al-Sayyab supported even as he remained a nationalist in politics. In the spring of 1957 the modernists invited al-Sayyab to Beirut, where he was a guest at one of the first *jeudis de* Shiʿr. In 1960, just prior to the Rome conference, he was awarded the magazine's yearly prize—accompanied by an award of one thousand Lebanese pounds—for his collection *Unshudat al-matar* [Hymn to Rain], released by the magazine's publishing arm Dar Majallat Shiʿr. Adonis edited an anthology of the Iraqi poet's work and would later call him "the real beginning of modernity."[59] In a letter to his friend, the publisher Riad El-Rayyes, Yusuf al-Khal described al-Sayyab's visit to Beirut with gladiatorial relish: "Our movement is on the move: the attacks against us have intensified with the visit of al-Sayyab—from the 'Arab nationalists,' of course, as well as the Communists-disguised-as-nationalists. We responded in kind. Our defense, in brief: We're the true heirs of the Arabic heritage, while you are the false heirs. We represent progress and stem from the best of that tradition, whereas you represent reaction and stem from the worst of that tradition, etc."[60]

Al-Sayyab was never fully converted to the modernists' cause, however. His attempt to rehabilitate the rhetoric of *iltizam*, rather than rejecting it outright as the *Shiʿr* poets tended to do, suggests some of his wariness toward the Beiruti group's project. At the end of his Rome talk al-Sayyab even worried that the "universalist" commitment he ascribed to Adonis and al-Khal was being superseded by a merely "subjectivist"—and to that extent "uncommitted"—poetry of self-absorption. Al-Sayyab's guardedness toward the modernists' radicalism, and his willingness to speak the lingua franca of his Arab peers, ultimately made him a more attractive recruit to the Congress representatives than the *Shiʿr* poets. As we shall see, the Americans became increasingly concerned about the modernists' intellectual intransigence and isolation from their peers in neighboring countries. Following the Rome conference, al-Sayyab was welcomed into CCF networks much more deeply than the Beiruti poets ever were, becoming in effect a financially dependent ward of the Congress, even as he drifted away from *Shiʿr* and back into the nationalist circles of *al-Adab*. Before his death in 1964 of Lou Gehrig's disease, al-Sayyab received a fellowship from the CCF to study at the University of Durham. He also translated several works into Arabic for the Franklin Books Program, a State Department–funded venture for disseminating American books abroad.[61]

In his response to al-Sayyab's lecture, Ignazio Silone (still speaking in French) underlined the Iraqi poet's distinction between political and personal commitment, which he glossed as the difference between a vocation freely chosen by and for the self and one imposed from outside. "The committed writer with a personal mission affiliates himself with society, not the State," Silone stipulated. "He must never accept any commitment that comes from political power, Zhdanov, or a monarch. The sincere, committed writer with a personal mission is true to himself in giving his service to man and his fellow human beings."[62] Silone's invocation of the figure of man, which echoes

FIGURE 5. From right: John Hunt, Badr Shakir al-Sayyab, unknown, and Morroe Berger at the Rome Conference. Special Collections Research Center, University of Chicago Library.

al-Sayyab's remark about "humanist" commitment, is characteristic of him and the CCF more generally. The same figure appears at the end of Silone's essay for *The God That Failed*, which details his revulsion at Stalinist armtwisting during the split with Trotsky in 1927. In the concluding passage, Silone affirms his continuing "faith" in socialism, above and beyond his regretted infatuation with Bolshevist politics. The pious terminology is typical of his post-Communist turn toward Catholicism:

My faith in Socialism (to which I think I can say my entire life bears testimony) has remained more alive in me than ever. In its essence it has gone back to what it was when I first revolted against the old social order; a refusal to admit the existence of destiny, and extension of the ethical impulse from the restricted individual and family sphere to the whole domain of human activity, a need for effective brotherhood, an affirmation of the superiority of the human person over all the economic and social mechanisms which oppress him. As the years have gone by, there has been added to this an intuition of man's dignity and a feeling of reverence for that which in man is always trying to outdistance itself, and lies at the root of his eternal disquiet.[63]

The figure of "man," or "the human person," gathers together all the keywords of late modernist rhetoric. In his heroic solitude and abstraction, "man" is the meeting point for the universalizing discourse of world literature, the ideological insistence on artistic autonomy, and the idealization of creativity ("the eternal disquiet"). The spiritual element suggested by the invocation of "man's dignity"—counterpoised to the degraded realm of the merely material—is also characteristic. Unlike hard-line anti-Communists such as Koestler, an early rival within the CCF, Silone believed that leftist intellectuals should be wooed through appeals to spiritual values and "ethical impulses" rather than polemical confrontation. These ideals of cultural exchange and ecumenical humanism—"commitments" that transcended political allegiances—appeared to offer thinkers such as the Beiruti modernists a way out of their particularism and into that "larger and richer world" on whose door Adonis imagined Arab poets to be knocking.

Late Modernist Ironies

The texts of the Rome conference, along with the network of institutions and individuals it brought together, do not provide an exhaustive context for the *Shiʿr* movement. The Beiruti poets shared or seemed to share a certain vocabulary with their Western interlocutors, but this does not mean they were American agents. There is of course a powerful irony in the fact that CCF-affiliated intellectuals, whose self-conception was premised on their rejection of state-sponsored culture, were echoing official American propaganda and taking American money. Their habits of speech often suggest liberal groupthink rather than an ethos of "searching and experimenting." This doublespeak lies at the heart of late modernist culture. The project of aesthetic autonomy and cultural apoliticism was made possible by the emergence of an international institution—late modernism itself—that promised an escape from the taint of partisan politics. In the event, this promised escape proved to be another, often unwitting form of political commitment. Advanced art became the house style of the vital center. As Serge Guilbaut has argued, "The avant-garde artist who categorically refused to participate in political discourse and tried to isolate himself by accentuating his individuality was co-opted by liberalism, which viewed the artist's individualism as an excellent weapon with which to combat Soviet authoritarianism."[64]

But the ideology of autonomy could also be a stimulant, especially when translated into contexts where liberal politics and literary autonomy were unfinished projects. If as Fredric Jameson has argued, late modernist culture in the US and Europe "transforms the older modernist experimentation into an arsenal of tried and true techniques, no longer striving after aesthetic totality or the systemic and Utopian metamorphosis of forms," the same is not true in Lebanon (nor in Africa, nor Latin America).[65] The difference has its basis in an experience of historical unevenness or noncontemporaneity: the Beiruti poets were translating aesthetic modernism and political liberalism at the same moment their contemporaries in Europe and American were putting these doctrines in a museum. For the *Shi'r* group, in other words, modernism was still an adventure—a *"mughamara,"* to cite Adonis once more—with urgent stakes. Silone's notion of a world literature based on literary exchanges freed from political constraints may seem like a bland reformulation of the Goethean vision, but it seems otherwise when the autonomy of literature is not secured.

The more interesting though less evident ironies of the Rome conference are therefore the ones that divide the participants themselves, revealing the real contradictions at work in the universalist rhetoric shared by organizers and guests. For all their common vocabulary, the Arab poets and their hosts did not agree on the rules of world literature, an incongruity that points more generally to the difference translation makes. One might suppose that the speeches of Adonis and Yusuf al-Khal, with their indictment of provincialism and their eagerness to connect with "the civilization of man," would have been welcomed by their European interlocutors, but this was not exactly the case. The chief respondent to Yusuf al-Khal's talk was Lebanese ethnomusicologist Simon Jargy, who later served as a liaison between the CCF's Paris office and its branch in Beirut. Faced with al-Khal's argument that the task of Arab intellectuals was to strip themselves of the outmoded past in order to recover their "lost modernity," Jargy demurred. The real task facing Arab intellectuals, he argued, was not how to join the modern world, but how to "conserve the distinctiveness of Arabic literature" in the face of "an unstoppable developmentalism." Stephen Spender, in his response to Adonis's talk, expressed similar reservations. He worried that Adonis's "revolt against the traditionalist mentality" was taking things too far. He reminded the audience that T. S. Eliot, for whom Spender fashioned himself as the official interpreter, was both a modernist and a traditionalist. Spender ended his remarks, according to the Arabic transcription, by reproaching Adonis for his "complete disregard for

FIGURE 6. From right: Yusuf al-Khal, Adonis, Ignazio Silone, unknown, and Stephen Spender. Special Collections Research Center, University of Chicago Library.

the ancient heritage of Arabic poetry" and called his conference paper "extremist [*mutatarrifa*] in its demolition of poetic traditions."[66]

It is somewhat breathtaking to read an English poet who knew little to nothing about Arabic literature rebuking Adonis, a *poeta doctus* if there ever was one, for breaking with his own heritage. Jargy's comment makes the same gesture, albeit with more politesse. For the intellectuals of the CCF, the Arab poets and the literary heritage they represent were welcome in the circuits of world literature so long as they faithfully represented their local literary tradition. This is indeed ironic when set against Spender's criticism of the "provincial puritanism" of Leavis and the Movement writers in Britain, whom Spender regarded with cosmopolitan hauteur: "I confess that the idea of limiting the tradition to a few dozen books analyzed by critics who are also teachers of English literature, and who know almost nothing of foreign literature, nothing of the other arts, gives me a sense of choking claustrophobia."[67] Yet Spender and Jargy's responses also express a commonplace of the era, in which dreams of world literature were shadowed by fears of standardization.

This is the concern evoked by Erich Auerbach in his canonical 1952 essay, "The Philology of World Literature." Auerbach begins his philological *rappel à l'ordre* by worrying whether *Weltliteratur* in Goethe's sense of the word is still a viable project. Goethe could take the profusion of national cultures for granted, whereas "Today we are witnessing a homogenization of human life the world over." In Europe, "the leveling process is advancing more rapidly than before," while "everywhere else, standardization is spreading, regardless of whether it follows the Euro-American or the Soviet-Bolshevist pattern." The spread of standardization, which Auerbach links elsewhere in the essay to "a concept of education that has no sense of the past," gives rise to a baleful prediction: "We will have to accustom ourselves to the thought that only a single literary culture may survive in this homogenized world. It may even happen that, within a comparatively short period of time, only a limited number of literary languages will continue to exist, soon perhaps only one. If this were to come to pass, the idea of world literature would simultaneously be realized and destroyed."[68]

Jargy and Spender worry over the same apocalypse of sameness. Writing in *Encounter* two years after Auerbach's essay, Spender laments that "Larger and larger areas of life are today becoming paralyzed by conformity."[69] The logic of the argument against al-Khal and Adonis is therefore easy to deduce. To safeguard the possibility of world literature, one must enforce cultural diversity, which means that Arab poets must write verse that conserves the distinctiveness of their literature and respects rather than revolts against its traditions. Otherwise, world literature will amount to nothing more than what Auerbach calls "The Internationale of Triviality and Esperanto culture."[70] This suggests two subtly different translations of Goethe. For Adonis and al-Khal, the requirements for writing *al-adab al-ʿalami* are "apoliticism" and deprovincialization: Arabic poetry must free itself from regional roots to join its peers around the world. The European hosts of the Rome conference agree on the importance of artistic autonomy, but they also demand that literature—*or at least literature coming from outside Europe*—be "traditional" in the sense of being rooted in the local heritage. To put things somewhat baldly, the Arab poets wanted to write in the international style while the CCF wanted them to write something authentic.[71]

These distinct interpretations of "world literature" were not simply a matter of personal taste. The responses of Jargy and Spender are symptomatic of the CCF's general posture toward the Arab world and its intellectuals. The clearest evidence of a split between the Beiruti poets and their European hosts is that the Arab modernists were ultimately not chosen to publish a CCF-affiliated magazine. Their audition was in this sense unsuccessful, though local opponents continued to argue that *Shiʿr* was funded from abroad.[72] The CCF archives, which have only begun to be studied by scholars of Arabic literature, reveal that in the wake of the Rome conference, Yusuf al-Khal and John Hunt did pursue the idea of collaborating on *Adab*, a journal that would be separate from *Shiʿr* but published by al-Khal and funded by the CCF. Their negotiations came close to succeeding. Shortly after his return to

Paris, Hunt wrote to al-Khal, "Following our talks in Rome last week, I have decided to give Congress support to ADAB. Let me review my understanding of what the arrangement will be: 1) The magazine will be a quarterly, and each issue will contain about 160 pages; 2) You will be the publisher of the magazine and Jargy and Tawfiq Sayegh [sic] will be co-editors." Hunt confirmed that the Congress was willing to pay "something in the neighborhood of $10,000 a year for the magazine."[73] Jargy was already an employee of the Congress, working on Middle Eastern affairs from the office in Paris. Tawfiq Sayigh, who also attended the Rome conference, was a Palestinian graduate of AUB, a lector of Arabic at Cambridge, and a frequent contributor to *Shiʿr*. Sayigh also translated a number of works for the Franklin Books Foundation, including an anthology of contemporary American poetry.[74] In his response to Hunt's note, al-Khal resisted the idea of having co-editors, primarily because Jargy was "not yet known in the Arabic literary field," but finished on a hopeful note: "I am happy about our final agreement to work together, and I am looking forward to successful results for all concerned."[75] This plan never came to fruition, in large part because of Hunt's insistence that the new magazine be representative of Arab intellectual life, or at least his interpretation of it, in a way al-Khal could not accept. Here again, the heart of the disagreement had to with questions of cultural legitimacy and authenticity.

To see why legitimacy mattered so much, it helps to have some sense of official American thinking about the political culture of the Middle East at the time. For the CCF, as for the US foreign policy establishment more generally, Arab nationalism was the most significant and troublesome tendency in the region following the partition of Israel and Palestine in 1948. It required a regional strategy of containment. In the words of US secretary of state John Foster Dulles, Arab nationalism was "an overflowing stream—you cannot stand in front of it and oppose it frontally, but you must try to keep it in bounds."[76] Policymakers were especially worried at the seemingly unstoppable rise of Nasser, who emerged from Bandung and the Suez crisis as a charismatic spokesman for what Americans believed to be a radical version of pan-Arabism. Despite Nasser's professions of neutrality and his leadership of the Non-Aligned Movement, Americans viewed Egypt as straying too close to the Soviet camp. President Eisenhower privately called the Egyptian president "a puppet [of the Soviets] even though he probably doesn't think so." The Eisenhower Doctrine of 1957, ostensibly aimed at protecting the Middle East from Soviet encroachment, was more likely intended to counteract Nasserism, chiefly by supporting conservative neighbors such as Saudi Arabia. When this strategy failed—a year after it was announced, Egypt merged with Syria in the United Arab Republic and seemed to be on the verge of doing the same with Iraq—American experts scrambled to articulate a less confrontational approach. In NSC 5820/1, a document that set US goals in the region during the late 1950s and early 1960s, policymakers distinguished between "Arab nationalism" and "radical pan-Arab nationalism as symbolized by Nasser." They urged the establishment of "an effective working relationship" with the former, in part to choke off the activities of the radicals.[77] In practical terms, this new approach meant that in the Middle East the CCF hoped to lure Arab nationalists away from Nasserism, just as in Europe it hoped to lure leftists away from communism.[78] Wherever it acted, the Congress exploited existing divisions within the political left, attempting to ally itself with intellectuals who had strong local roots and cultural legitimacy but who were nevertheless willing to collaborate with Western institutions. This was a relatively straightforward task in Europe, where a cosmopolitan, non-Communist left was well established, but more difficult in the rest of the world, where rising nationalist currents were strongly opposed to American interventions.

Hunt worried that the CCF's nuanced, not to say quixotic strategy could not be pursued through a magazine edited by a Christian (al-Khal) and an Alawite (Adonis), in a small country already compromised by its government's pro-Western orientation.[79] The modernists were willing to collaborate with foreigners in the name of cultural openness—an example of what Edward Said has called "the natural predilection of minorities to have outside powers sponsor their efforts"—but the Congress was not ultimately convinced that the *Shiʿr* group had enough local legitimacy to be a useful proxy (the CCF was more interested in thinkers like al-Sayyab, whose nationalist credentials made him an especially appealing target for the Americans).[80] In a related vein, Hunt also worried that the modernists' political background in the Syrian Social Nationalist Party, discussed more fully in the next chapter, ensured their isolation from peers in the region: *Shiʿr* magazine was banned in Iraq and had also been banned in Nasser's UAR. In the midst of his back-and-forth with al-Khal following the Rome conference, Hunt wrote a letter to Silone fretting over the hoped-for collaboration.

> My negotiations with Yussuf Al Khal about the quarterly we've planned have run into difficulties. I do believe that such a journal, so long as it is associated with the Congress, should be broadly open to the diverse tendencies and currents of thought one sees in the region, and I have the impression that Yussuf would be likely to run the review in such a way that it would only resonate within a rather small circle.... I have a great deal of sympathy for him as a person and I admire his courageous political stand, but I worry about the degree to which he has isolated himself from other intellectual and political tendencies in Lebanon.[81]

Hunt seems blind to the irony here, but one doubts it escaped al-Khal's notice. The Arab modernists' determination to free themselves from what they thought of as the parochialism of their own heritage—in part by affiliating themselves with the institutions of world literature—meant that the CCF did not recognize them as worthwhile collaborators.

The cultural diplomacy of the Congress called for making fine distinctions between moderate and radical nationalists, useful allies and powerless friends, representative and partisan intellectuals. But its agents were not always able to manage these subtleties. One month after the Rome conference, Hunt wrote his most heavy-handed letter—one that gives the lie to the common argument that the CIA did not interfere in their magazines' editorial decisions—informing al-Khal that he would only publish and distribute the new magazine while the real work would fall to others: "The editor in chief of the magazine will be Tawfiq Sayegh. I insist on this and am not prepared to take an alternative." Furthermore, Hunt went on to write, "As responsible editor, I wish to have a Moslem."[82] Having read the concerns Hunt expressed elsewhere, one assumes that he wanted a Muslim as the legally responsible editor because he believed this would put a more authentic face on the enterprise. Hunt also demanded that the new magazine's association with the Congress be made explicit on the title page—"The Rome seminar has improved our position immeasurably," he assures al-Khal—and that the magazine be housed at CCF offices, with a business manager appointed by Hunt. (As Spender wrote mordantly to Hunt following a visit to the region, "Since everyone in these countries thinks of the Congress as a conspiracy, it is far better to have an open conspiracy than a secret one.")[83] Al-Khal's response to Hunt's letter made no mention of the CIA officer's foray into confessional matters, but he bristled at the demand that he hand over editorial control of the new journal to Sayigh and Jargy. "The magazine, ADAB, was originally projected as a DAR MAJALLAT SHIʿR publication," he reminded Hunt, "and your new plan turns this magazine into a Congress publication, leaving to DAR MAJALLAT SHIʿR a share of the moral responsibility with no fair and aquitable [sic] compensation of any kind."[84] Hunt's letter effectively scuttled the negotiations between the Congress and al-Khal, though the CCF did pay for the first and only year of the quarterly *Adab*, the first issue of which was published in January 1962. After protracted consultations, Sayigh became editor in chief of the CCF-funded *Hiwar* [Dialogue] in the fall of that year. The first issue included an expanded version of Silone's Rome remarks on *engagement* and a new poem by Badr Shakir al-Sayyab, who would become the magazine's correspondent from Iraq. Yusuf al-Khal and Adonis never wrote anything for *Hiwar*, although other members of the *Shiʿr* group, including Unsi al-Hajj, Muhammad al-Maghout, and Jabra Ibrahim Jabra, were frequent contributors. The disagreement between al-Khal and the CCF resulted in lingering resentments. An internal memo of the Congress reported that early in 1962 al-Khal and Adonis gave an interview in a local paper in which they denied any institutional relations between their group and the CCF, asserting that whatever relations did exist were purely "personal." In a letter to the secretary of the Beirut office, Simon Jargy expressed no surprise at the editors' disavowal, but noted that "if they want to talk about incriminating evidence, they shouldn't forget that we have the goods to prove them wrong"—seemingly a reference to the CCF's funding of *Adab*.[85] *Hiwar* lasted for five years, despite intense opposition from local intellectuals, until the *Times* revelations forced it to close in 1967.[86]

The CCF intellectuals and the *Shiʿr* poets seem to speak the same language, or at least to share the same vocabulary of *freedom, creativity, world literature,* and *man*. But this is not quite true, even in literal terms. The Rome conference participants, including the Italian hosts, spoke in English, French, and Arabic, and they met under the aegis of a German. Goethe's *Weltliteratur* does not, however, name the same project as Silone's *la littérature mondiale*, nor al-Khal's *al-adab al-ʿalami*. It is the slippage between these terms that generates the multiple ironies of the conference proceedings and thwarts Silone's hope that European and Arab intellectuals might meet "in a place apart" from political considerations. For the ironies of the Rome conference are ultimately neither formal nor semantic but precisely political. The participants' conflicting interpretations, and their opposing views of what collaboration might involve, result from their unequal positions within the field of late modernism. It was the *Shiʿr* poets' antagonism toward their own literary heritage, their haughty isolation from local (nationalist) interlocutors, and their uncompromising internationalism—their "desire for the world" as Mariano Siskind, in a related context, has usefully termed it—that helped to disqualify the Beiruti movement in the eyes of Hunt and his advisers.[87]

The *Shiʿr* poets translated the keywords of late modernism into their own idiom. From the standpoint of European and American intellectuals, these Arabic versions were unfaithful and even "extreme." Not so extreme as to make conversation impossible, but enough to generate misunderstanding and even to preclude certain kinds of cooperation. There truly is something outlandish about the Arab modernists' project. As we will see in the coming chapters, their rhetoric can be wearyingly insistent, their ambitions impossibly encyclopedic, and their techniques hermetic to the point of incomprehensibility (or untranslatability). All this distinguishes them from the smooth and gentlemanly postures of their European contemporaries. Here we might recall Marshall Berman's evocation of "the modernism of underdevelopment" for its aptness to the Lebanese situation: "In order to be true to the life from which it springs, it is forced to be shrill, uncouth and inchoate. . . . But the bizarre reality from which this modernism grows, and the unbearable pressures under which it moves and lives—social and political pressures as well as spiritual ones—infuse it with a desperate incandescence that Western modernism, so much more at home in its world, can rarely hope to match."[88] Beiruti modernism does indeed spring from a bizarre reality: not only from the historical anomaly of Lebanon itself but also from a specific experience of political militancy and disillusionment that had lasting consequences for the movement. It was because of his membership in the Syrian Social Nationalist Party that Adonis was imprisoned in 1955 and afterward fled to Lebanon, an experience that left the poet "close to despair" but also ready to begin a new life in Beirut. All the central figures of the *Shiʿr* group were at one time active members of this party. But what was the SSNP—a party that is little known outside the region—and how did the Beiruti modernists translate political militancy into cultural "apoliticism"? Having identified the keywords of the *Shiʿr* movement, we now need to trace their historical etymology.

CHAPTER TWO

The Genealogy of Arabic Modernism

Arguments about Autonomy

In late 1961, just months after the CCF conference in Rome, dissident officers in the Lebanese army attempted a coup d'état against the government of Fuad Shihab.[1] The plotters were Syrian Social Nationalists, a party that had enjoyed close relations with the previous regime of Camille Chamoun, to whom they gave armed support during the 1958 crisis that led to a brief American intervention and the installation of Shihab as president. The party resented Shihab's détente with Nasser as well as his reluctance to dismantle the structures of Lebanese confessionalism, the system of quotas intended to temper sectarian rivalries but which also gave them legal status. The rebel officers convinced party leaders to lend their backing to the coup, but the insurrection barely got off the ground. The putschists failed to mobilize support within the ranks, and the civilians promised by the party never materialized. Just hours after the revolt began, on the morning of December 31, government forces arrested hundreds of SSNP members along with most of the leadership. By the end of January, the state had rounded up over three thousand suspects. "At the start of the year," wrote the editorialists at the Arab nationalist *al-Adab*, on the front page of its February 1962 issue, "Lebanon was saved from the terrifying disaster a group of Western imperialist agents plotted for her." Calling it the most dangerous challenge the country had faced since independence, the nationalists claimed that the conspirators had support outside the party membership and that the *Shi'r* poets—not named, but clearly implied—were de facto collaborators:

> Here we must point out that this conspiracy was operative in a number of fields. We at this magazine have tried more than once to expose it in

the field of culture, where the conspiracy was nourished at the hands of a group whose chief aim is the destruction of the Arab heritage, the propagation of anarchy, and the spread of "rejectionism." It has made extremism and madness its law while claiming to truly represent new tendencies in Arabic literature. In that sense, it was an accomplice in this criminal conspiracy that nearly overwhelmed the country.[2]

This charge of criminal collaboration was the final sally of a long campaign waged against the modernists by their Arabist and Marxist adversaries. The critics at *al-Adab* consistently portrayed the *Shiʿr* group as rival nationalists whose poetic program was disguised propaganda. The political goal of the SSNP, as described by the pan-Arabists, was to deliver Lebanon into Western hands. The *Shiʿr* poets' trip to Rome simply confirmed their coziness with the worst elements of neo-imperialism. Ironically, the coup attempt and its aftermath confirmed John Hunt's own sense that the CCF had been right in backing out of negotiations with al-Khal. As Hunt wrote to Albert Hourani two weeks after the failed putsch, he had grown increasingly worried about the *Shiʿr* poets' affiliation with the SSNP (Hunt uses the French acronym PPS for the Parti Populaire Syrien):

> The more I learned about the *Shiʿr* group, the more I felt they were tied in some close way to the P.P.S. This would mean that the Congress would be allying himself [*sic*] with a magazine with a definite parti-pris in terms of local Arab politics. This, of course, is not in line with our overall policy. Therefore, in December, I invited Yussuf to Paris and informed him of my decision.... Given the recent events in Lebanon, I feel more than ever that I made the right decision.[3]

The nationalists at *al-Adab* also accused the modernists of trying to fracture the unity of Arab history, what nationalist writers called "*al-ʿuruba*" [Arabness], and reproached the *Shiʿr* poets for ignoring the native literary tradition—an ironic echo of Spender's remarks to Adonis—in favor of translated texts from abroad. Marxist critics publishing in *al-Thaqafa al-Wataniyya* [*National Culture*] and *al-Tariq* [*The Path*] often echoed these attacks. Writing for the latter, Husayn Muruwwa claimed that the modernist project had two essential goals: "First, to tear up the spiritual and intellectual roots between Lebanese and their Arabic history ... And second, by way of this uprooting, to facilitate the spread of unpatriotic (cosmopolitan) ideas and concepts among Lebanese youth."[4]

In their response to these attacks, the modernists did not dispute their past ties to the SSNP, nor did they defend the party's recent adventurism. Instead, they argued that it was unfair to judge their literary work by their political pasts. *Shiʿr* was devoted to poetry, not to politics, and its pages welcomed contributors of all persuasions: "If our accusers have political criticisms to make against this magazine's poets, such criticisms should be discussed in another context and on a different level—in a place apart from [fi ma'zil'an] the issues of modern poetry and poetic renewal, instead of confusing a political tendency with a poetic tendency, or judging one by the standards of the other."[5] Arabic modernism is defined in large part by its adherence to the principle of literary autonomy, which provided a conceptual anchor for the array of keywords and idioms explored in the last chapter. For the nationalists, however, there was no space between the political activities of the SSNP and the poetic texts of *Shi'r*. They were two elements of one conspiracy against "our Lebanon." The stakes of the debate were not the quality of modernist poetry but the definition of poetry as such: what counts and what does not.

As Pierre Bourdieu and others have shown, the existence of an autonomous literary field is not a natural state of affairs, although that is what Arab modernists and many others have pretended. Instead, it is the result of a historical struggle whose terms and actors vary by case. The chief aim of this chapter is to trace that struggle in the Lebanese instance, with a narrative made up of competing concepts, individuals, and institutions. The exchange between *Shi'r* and *al-Adab* in the year before the Rome conference establishes the terms for that narrative. The debate is also a window onto the world of Beiruti magazines at a particularly charged moment. It shows how the *Shi'r* group's rhetoric, the lingua franca of late modernism, was wielded against local opponents, who marshaled their own repertoire of keywords and concepts.

The first salvo in this war of position was an editorial published by *al-Adab* in February 1961, under the title "*al-Shi'r ... wa-l-hadara al-'arabiyya!*" [Poetry ... and Arab Civilization!]."[6] The article addressed the relationship between the artistic heritage and contemporary practice, between the classical past and the crisis-ridden present. The editorialists argued, as they often did, that modern Arabic literature should identify the "living elements" of tradition and extend those elements in a way that did not compromise literary "authenticity" [*asala*]. Against this vision, they raised the specter of another group, never named, which posited a different account of Arabic literature's past and present. Alluding to the doctrines of the SSNP leader Antun Sa'ada, they wrote:

> This position goes back to a wretched evangelism [*da'wa*] that emerged briefly during the Mandate era and was then quickly extinguished. Its underlying idea was that Lebanon is a Mediterranean country whose civilization was a part of that civilization. As for Arab civilization, it was discounted. The partisans of this program often refused to even recognize the existence of Arab civilization, considering "Arabism" to be a synonym for ignorance, the desert, and the Bedouin way of life.

If the partisans of this position had been sincere in their search for roots, the editorial contended, they would have discovered that the Arabs themselves were the seed bearers of Mediterranean civilization, which was the site of their "authentic self-creation" [*al-ibda' al-dhati al-asil*]. The article concluded with a long citation from an interview with the poet Khalil Hawi in the Beiruti newspaper *Lisan al-Hal*. Hawi, like Yusuf al-Khal, was born into a Greek Orthodox family and had been a member of the SSNP as a young man. He published several poems in the early numbers of *Shi'r* but soon left the group to espouse a version of pan-Arabism.[7] Asked his opinion of postwar Lebanese poetry, Hawi was dismissive. Despite these poets' talk of renewal, he said, they knew little about their own literature and even less about that of the West: "They don't realize that renewal without self-authenticity [*asala dhatiyya*] is blind mimicry."

The next editorial, "*Ula'ika al-muzayyafun*" [Those Hypocrites], was published the following month and dispensed with euphemisms.[8] The editorialists directly accused the *Shi'r* poets of masking their ignorance of tradition by using obscure language and borrowed forms (the specific target was Unsi al-Hajj, whose baffling collection of prose poems, *Lan*, was published the previous year). They also criticized the most recent issue of the magazine, devoted to the war in Algeria. "They write on an issue that they feel coerced to address," the nationalists said about the modernists. "But that issue is foreign to them. They aren't pained by its tragedy in the way that every sincere Arab [*kull 'arabi mukhlis*] is pained by it." Then the editorialists called Adonis out by name. Why hadn't he published any poems in this special issue? Was it because he had received a grant from the French government to spend a year in Paris and was afraid to criticize his patrons? And was this silence not especially shameful in view of the example set by so many French intellectuals—Sartre first among them—who had courageously spoken out against their country's colonialism?

Adonis's response to these innuendos, printed in the spring issue of *Shi'r*, came in the form of a letter from Paris to Yusuf al-Khal.[9] The form is itself a calculated affront, as if Adonis were responding to the nationalists with his back to them. (This gesture, a version of what rhetoricians call "*iltifat*"—literally, a "turning away" or "apostrophe"—is typical of how Adonis conducts political arguments.) The letter began with praise for al-Khal's recently published collection, *Qasa'id fi-l-arba'in* [Poems at Forty], which Adonis describes as "the next step in your poetic experiment: you've leapt over inherited boundaries, going beyond pastism and back to the climate of the sea, linking yourself to its surge and its depths, to its shells and its undulations, its shores and its distances." The fairly baroque terms of this praise make a pointed contrast with Adonis's critique of *al-Adab*. Whereas al-Khal's poems are characterized by their maritime, border-crossing energies, Adonis describes pan-Arabists as trapped in a narrow version of the heritage. Throughout his letter, Adonis eschews *al-Adab*'s rhetoric of "authenticity" [*al-asala*] and "sincerity" [*al-ikhlas*]—along with their etymological connotations of roots [*al-usul*] and purity [*al-khulus*]—and elaborates a typically modernist vocabulary of openness, vitality, and transformation. Nor does Adonis ever mention the nationalists' insinuations about the modernists' membership in the SSNP, treating such arguments with sovereign contempt: "We are beyond all categorization," he writes. "Our attributes are those of the sea surge: movement and creation in an eternal dynamism."

In a revealing passage of his letter, Adonis claims the nationalists' are so mired in the past that he does not even consider them historical coevals—another reason, perhaps, why he does not address them directly. "We have our own proper age," he writes to al-Khal. "We are not their contemporaries except by accident." And just as the present is riven by multiple temporalities, so there are many pasts in the past: "We have our own Arab past," Adonis writes, one that that has nothing to do with the orthodoxy of "al-Ghazali or Ahmed Shawqi."[10] The modernists' past evoked by Adonis is, on the contrary, a heterodox heritage of poets, philosophers, and mystics whose antinomianism makes them the forerunners of modernism. Here, Adonis mentions the names of Imru' al-Qays, Abu Nuwas, Abu Tammam, al-Mutanabbi, Abu al-ʿAlaʾ al-Maʿarri, al-Hallaj, al-Razi, and Ibn al-Rawandi. This countercanon of *illuminés*, rebels, and heretics appears again and again in Adonis's oeuvre. The names and emphases differ depending on the occasion, but the heroic attributes are consistent. Each protomodernist is, as Adonis writes at the end of his letter from Paris, "A man of refusal [*insan al-rafd*] . . . a man of novelty . . . a man of beginning and the eternal sea-surge [*insan al-bidaya wa-l-tamawwuj abadan*]: this is what we look forward to, this is the good news we bring."

Adonis's epistle is one skirmish in a wider war for the Arabic *turath*, or literary heritage, examined more fully in chapter 5. The modernists' revision of the classical past was systematic and influential, but it was also vigorously contested. In *al-Adab*'s response to Adonis's Paris letter, an editorial published in July 1961 entitled *"Al-Wujuh al-mustaʿara!"* [Borrowed Faces], the nationalists ridiculed Adonis's claims to a private *turath* and went so far as to accuse him of *shuʿubiyya* [chauvinism], a mode of anti-Arab invective popular among Persianate writers of the classical period. "When have Adonis and his friends ever called themselves Arabs?" the editorialists of *al-Adab* wonder. "When has the party they belong to ever stopped proclaiming the bankruptcy of Arabism?" How could Adonis square his talk of "rejection" with his commitment to the SSNP party line? The editorialists promised this would be their last word on the subject, but history intervened in dramatic fashion.[11]

The failed coup of December 1961 put the modernists once again on the defensive. They now stood accused not merely of cultural betrayal and political cowardice but of being accomplices in a conspiracy directed from abroad. The fact that several of them had just returned from a CCF conference in Rome did not help matters. The *Shiʿr* poets' editorial in the spring issue of 1962, a ten-page apologia that ran at the front of the issue and bore a collective signature, is one of the most significant texts in the magazine's history—not so much for what it says as what it explicitly does not say.[12] The modernists declined to renounce their youthful activism. "Yusuf al-Khal and Adonis did not and will not trade away their party past," the editorial declared. "For a person's past, his lived experience, is not like a shirt he puts on and takes off every day." Instead, they would continue to meditate on the meanings of that experience, but in the form of "a silent, internal dialogue" rather than in a public forum. At the same time, the editorialists argued, "Man cannot be judged according to his past":

> The past is no more than a shadow fleeing before the great sun latent in the depths of the human person. The person is in this sense greater than the past, greater than what he was, or presently is. The person is a pure future. In the same way, *Shi'r* magazine embodies nonfactionalism in its richest sense: we mean nonpartisanship, we mean an absolute and universal openness that grants the person a space of freedom for his experimentation and dynamism. For us, the person is more important than the party, more important than ideology; for us, the person and his freedom come first, before anything else.

The modernists' refusal to grapple explicitly with their political past sets a crucial task for criticism, one that builds on the analyses of contemporaries and tries to correct their inevitable shortcomings. I believe the nationalist and Marxist critics were right to insist on the importance of the *Shi'r* poets' affiliation with the SSNP, but they mistook the reasons for this importance. The editorialists at *al-Adab* regarded the *Shi'r* poets as a competing nationalist group, albeit one that refused to acknowledge itself as such (hence their rhetoric of hypocrisy and mask-wearing). But as the modernists pointed out in their defense, Yusuf al-Khal had publicly resigned from the SSNP fifteen years previously, while Adonis "has grown out of his party affiliation, moved beyond its concepts and doctrinal principles, and renounced all party activity as of four years ago." Indeed, there are few traces of Sa'ada's Greater Syrian ideology in the pages of *Shi'r*, and those that remain are not disguised so much as transformed. Though the modernists were not pan-Arabists, they had no interest in destroying the Arabic *turath*. Adonis's interest in that heritage—a revisionary interest, to be sure—was evident by the early 1960s and would deepen in the years to come.

Al-Adab's writers misrecognized their opponents largely because the modernists' real ideology was a historical novelty rather than a dissimulated nationalism. To understand the importance of the *Shi'r* group's political past requires a narrative of how they turned away from the SSNP and toward that "larger and richer world" of international modernism and midcentury liberalism. It is a distinguishing fact about the Beiruti poets that their modernism emerges from an experience of political defeat and subsequently comes to serve as a substitute for that failure. The stages of this emergence will take some time to tease out. What does it mean, in historical terms, to grow out of politics? What were the landmarks of the modernists' march toward "nonpartisanship"? And what traces did their party experience leave in their poetry?

What follows is an attempt to re-create the "internal dialogue" about their pasts as militants that the *Shi'r* poets chose not to make public. This narrative is centered on the career of Yusuf al-Khal, who as editor in chief played a leading role in determining the principles of the *Shi'r* movement. But the real protagonists of the story are institutions: the political party, the university, the Cénacle, and the little magazine. These settings constitute the backstory to al-Khal's engagement with the institutions of late modernism itself—the global network of actors and discourses examined in the last chapter. This focus on institutional history is intended, in part, as a corrective to the *Shi'r* poets' insistence that modernist literature is the work of heroic, deracinated individuals. At each step of the way, the Beiruti modernist project was affected by its institutional affiliations as well as the various audiences these institutions addressed, or imagined themselves to address. The figure of *al-insan* [the human being] or *al-shakhs* [the person] plays a pivotal role in this story. It allowed the *Shi'r* poets to turn away from political militancy toward a heroized notion of cultural struggle, a shift with consequences that have lasted into the present. The modernists' march toward nonpartisanship was always a hesitant one, hedged by scruples about a past the poets never simply repudiated but found more useful to reinterpret, repurpose, and sometimes repress.

Syrian Literature and World Literature

Antun Sa'ada, founder and charismatic leader of the Syrian Social Nationalist Party, was born in 1904 in the village of Shweir, in present-day Lebanon (then under Ottoman suzerainty). His father, Khalil Sa'ada, a Greek Orthodox physician, active Mason, and anti-Turkish pamphleteer, soon left the village for Egypt and then Brazil, where he settled among São Paulo's large émigré population. Brazil and Argentina were centers of the southern *mahjar*, a lively intellectual community that sprang up during the last two decades of the nineteenth century in South America. Levantine identity, the role of literature in civic life, and calls for Syrian or Lebanese independence were the common topics of debate in this milieu, which was closely in touch with intellectual currents in the homeland.[13] For Khalil Sa'ada and his son, as for so many diasporic thinkers, exile was the nursery of nationalism. The elder Sa'ada founded a newspaper, *al-Jarida* [The Register], as well as the monthly *al-Majalla* [The Journal], which served as mouthpieces for his party, the Democratic Patriotic Party, whose antisectarian, anti-French platform would deeply influence his son's political outlook.

Antun Saʿada joined his father in South America following the First World War. He helped edit *al-Jarida*, joined the same Masonic lodge, learned German, and read widely if also haphazardly in European scholarship on the rise of nations, classical antiquity, and world history. Returning to Lebanon in 1930, he found work as a German tutor for students at the American University in Beirut and soon began recruiting university students for his new party, which he founded in November 1932 as the Syrian National Party. "The whole movement was an odd mixture of modernism, of scientism, with something extremely old, even archaeological." This is how Michel ʿAflaq, founder of the rival Baʿath party, described the SSNP.[14] The party began as a secret society in Beirut, but its membership grew rapidly and it soon established cells as far north as Tripoli, where Yusuf al-Khal joined in 1934. Mandate authorities discovered the existence of the party in late 1935, and much of the leadership was swiftly arrested. Saʿada himself was sentenced to six months in jail, and it was during this period that he wrote *Nushuʾ al-umam* [The Emergence of Nations], a key text in the history of the SSNP. The work is not a manifesto, nor an exposition of the party platform; instead, it is an autodidactic blend of anthropological speculation and *Weltgeschichte* that sought to establish an intellectual framework for Syrian nationalism.[15]

For Saʿada, the glue of national life is not language, ethnicity, or religion but geography. It is the peculiar configuration of mountains, rivers, and shorelines that gives rise to a nation's distinctive attributes: "The nation finds its base, before anything else, in a specific territorial unity with which a group of people interact and inside which they mix and become unified."[16] This idea is not original to Saʿada but a commonplace among Levantine Christians of the period (and comparable to the ideas of the Canaanite movement in Mandate Palestine). Georges Samné, a Greek Catholic from Damascus, had argued for the existence of a separate Syrian nation, including Lebanon, in *La Syrie*, a book published in 1920. Samné was secretary of the Paris-based Comité Central Syrien, and his work advocated for the autonomy of Syria, whose populace was not, in his view, Arab at all. The Jesuit intellectual Henri Lammens, a professor at Beirut's Saint-Joseph University, argued in his own *La Syrie* (1921) that Syria was a country with natural frontiers: the Taurus mountains in the north divided it from Turkish Anatolia; the desert to the east and south divided it from Iraq and the Arabian peninsula; and the sea bordered it to the west. These boundaries were more or less the same as those proposed by Saʿada in *The Emergence of Nations* (though after World War II he expanded them to include Iraq, parts of Iran, and also Cyprus).[17]

Unlike the narrowly ethnic nationalisms of eastern and central Europe or the religious nationalism of Zionists and Lebanese Maronites, Saʿada's territorial nationalism assumes a blend of subnational groups: "The limited environment is a crucible that fuses the life of these groups and mixes them vigorously together," he writes, "so that they acquire a particular personality [*shakhsiyya khassa*], like the one acquired by bronze via the mixing of copper, tin, and lead." Syria, with its long history of settlement stretching back to the Stone Age and including subsequent alloys of Canaanites, Hittites, Arameans, and Arabs, provides the best example of a melting pot that had fused its demographic strata into "one temperament and one personality [*shakhsiyya wahida*]."[18] Saʿada's secularism is a corollary of this inclusive historical vision. The separation of religion and state—a practice whose origins Saʿada traces to the Umayyad caliphate, the capital of which was Damascus, thereby qualifying it as a "Syrian" dynasty—was a key element of the SSNP's political platform.

Saʿada's downplaying of ethnic and religious elements in Syrian nationalism made his party especially attractive to the region's minority communities, for whom neither a narrowly Lebanese nationalism nor a broader pan-Arabism held much appeal, since the one was essentially a Maronite ideology while the latter was often suspected of having a disguised Sunni agenda. As the historian Labib Zuwiyya Yamak writes, "The Maronites opposed [the SSNP] because it negated the existence of a Lebanese nation, and the Muslims rejected it because of its avowed anti-Arab and anti-Muslim orientation. Consequently it was forced to seek its adherents among those dissatisfied groups and militant minorities that did not share the national aspirations of the majority."[19] Many of the poets and thinkers who would later write for *Shiʿr* came from just such dissatisfied and marginalized groups: Yusuf al-Khal and Khalil Hawi were both born into Greek Orthodox families; Adonis's background is Alawite; and the Syrian poet Muhammad al-Maghout came from Ismaili stock. Al-Khal was the oldest of these poets and the first to join the party. In the mid-1930s, he wrote a number of articles for party organs that focused on questions of sectarianism and secularism. In the modernists' later insistence on "nonfactionalism," there is a distinct echo of Saʿada's emphasis on religious pluralism.

In 1938, having spent much of the previous three years in jail, Saʿada left Lebanon for a recruitment tour among the émigré communities of Brazil and Argentina, where he had lived in his youth. In October 1939, following the outbreak of hostilities in Europe, French authorities declared martial law in Mandate territories and banned the SSNP, effectively marooning Saʿada in South America, where he remained until 1947. It was during this period that he composed his short work, *al-Siraʿ al-fikri fi-l-adab al-suri* [The Intellectual Struggle in Syrian Literature], a strange and remarkable document of nationalist poetics that Adonis later acknowledged as "the first, most important work that formed my ideas and poetic outlook" and an essential element in "our understanding of the true meaning of poetic modernity in Arabic."[20] Despite its importance to the modernists, Saʿada's tract has rarely been read as a coherent theoretical statement (nor has it ever been translated).

The Intellectual Struggle collects several articles written by Saʿada for the party organ, *al-Zawbaʿa* [The Storm], in the latter part of 1942. These pieces were then published in book form in 1943, in Buenos Aires. Upon his return to Lebanon in 1947, Saʿada oversaw the publication of a second edition, noting that only a few copies of the original version had arrived in the homeland.[21] This peripatetic history is mirrored in Saʿada's account of the book's genesis, an intricate mise-en-scène that foreshadows the book's themes and arguments:

> In May of this year [Saʿada is writing in December 1942], there fell into my hands a copy of the second number of the first year of *al-ʿUsba* magazine, published in São Paolo, Brazil—the February issue, 1935. The copy had a dirty cover and several pages were torn away; the remaining pages were loose and falling to pieces. Despite this, I resolved to examine these pages and give them my full attention. I found they contained an exchange between three Syrian men of letters [*udabaʾ suriyyin*]: Ameen Rihani, Yusuf Nuʿman Maʿluf, and Shafiq Maʿluf. The exchange was in the form of three letters containing opinions and theories on poetry and poets. Now, poetry and poets belong to the subject of literature, which had attracted my attention because of the muddle and mess one finds there. (5)

Al-ʿUsba was the literary journal of al-ʿUsba al-Andalusiyya [the Andalusian League], a group of Levantine intellectuals based in São Paolo who formed an important part of the southern *mahjar*. Of the three poets named by Saʿada, only Shafiq Maʿluf (1905–76) was a member of the league. Born in Zahle, a mountain village east of Beirut, Maʿluf moved to São Paulo in 1926, where he became a textile manufacturer and poet. Before leaving home, Maʿluf published a long work called "*al-Ahlam*" [Dreams], the poem that is the subject of the three epistles discussed by Saʿada. The first letter was by Ameen Rihani, a well-known novelist, poet, and essayist, born in Freike, just outside Beirut, and largely educated in New York; the author of the second was Yusuf Nuʿman Maʿluf, Shafiq's uncle, who edited the Arabic-language newspaper *al-Ayyam* [The Days], also in New York. The letters by Rihani and the elder Maʿluf, along with an initial response from the poet, were written in 1926, from Freike, New York, and Zahle, respectively. Before the series of epistles was published in *al-ʿUsba* in 1935, Shafiq appended a short retrospective note, written in São Paulo. To summarize: Saʿada's book is composed and published in Buenos Aires, where he has come across a tatty, seven-year-old literary magazine from São Paulo, in which an Arabic poem written in 1926 in the Lebanese town of Zahle gives rise to an exchange between writers living in the United States, Lebanon, and Brazil.[22]

I have lingered over Saʿada's exordium for two reasons. The first is to suggest the extraordinarily fluid and far-flung geography of Levantine literature. Reading the texts of this imaginary community, whose members were more likely to meet in print than face-to-face, requires constant shifting between local and transnational contexts. The fluctuating borders of the *mahjar* group sketch out in advance the geography of Arabic modernism. Both movements were diasporic intellectual communities made possible by the circulation of little magazines, though the *Shiʿr* movement did not confine itself to the nodes of émigré life, seeking additional outposts in the capitals of Europe, America, and the Arab world. The modernists often paid homage to the earlier émigrés. *Shiʿr*'s second issue included Shafiq Maʿluf's poem "A Dancer" (sent from São Paulo), and he later hosted one of their *jeudis de* Shiʿr. Khalil Hawi wrote a critical study of Kahlil Gibran, and Yusuf al-Khal translated *The Prophet* into Arabic.[23] Saʿada is in this sense a vanishing mediator—what in Arabic is called a *hamzat al-wasl*—between the *mahjar* and modernism: he links the two movements by articulating terms for the former's eclipse. The second reason for entering into such detail is to emphasize the pointedness of Saʿada's qualification of all three writers as "Syrian men of letters." It is doubtful that the Maʿlufs or Ameen Rihani would have claimed this identity except in a loose and provisional fashion. The letters themselves, large parts of which are cited by Saʿada, are more concerned with the questions of "Eastern" or "oriental" poetry rather than "Syrian" poetry, and this is arguably true of *mahjar* literature more generally. But Saʿada's characterization is carefully considered. Indeed, the putatively accidental origin of his tract—the hoary trope of a book that "fell into my hands," which Saʿada uses more than once in his pamphlet—conceals a systematic intent. The thrust of his argument is that to write Syrian poetry, in the special sense Saʿada understands it, is not at all a parochial activity. On the contrary, it is only by writing a specifically national poetry, by availing oneself of its peculiar traditions and resources, that one joins the ranks of what Saʿada repeatedly calls "world literature" [*al-adab al-ʿalami*].

The overcoming of parochialism is what motivates the comments of the elder Maʿluf and Rihani on the poem "Dreams." Both letters, which Saʿada quotes at length, note what Rihani calls "a tone of melancholy and sadness" that pervades the poem, a tone he finds in too much poetry from the East: "For what good is the poet who weeps and cries just like the rest of mankind?" (14). Similarly, Yusuf Maʿluf counsels his nephew to be "imitated" rather than "imitative," and to cease writing "laments over empty encampments and wasted ruins, which is what most Eastern writers do, and especially the poets among them" (15). The abandoned campsite, *al-atlal*, is undoubtedly the oldest topos of Arabic poetry, and the idea that poetic innovation demands a turn away from it is almost as old. Both Maʿluf and Rihani urge the author of "Dreams" to move beyond such old-fashioned and provincial verse. To be a true poet means to rise above this tradition of lamentation. "Read Isaiah rather than submerging yourself in the tears of Jeremiah," suggests Rihani. "If you must go back, go back to Shakespeare and Goethe" (14).

For Saʿada, however, a true literary renaissance will not be achieved by returning to Eastern traditions of lamentation, nor to the classics of the West. "Going back to Shakespeare and Goethe will not, of itself, be of much benefit,"

Saʿada writes in response to Rihani, "unless there already exists an intelligent and self-aware culture that follows the principles of the Syrian soul. Of what benefit to Arabic literature was Egyptian poet Ahmed Shawqi's return to Shakespeare, other than producing a copy, a distortion, and an imitation that added less than a mustard seed to the wealth of world literature?" (Saʿada's reference is to Shawqi's 1927 play, *The Fall of Cleopatra*). Here is the dialectical logic constantly at work in Saʿada's writings as well as those of many twentieth-century nationalists: national literature comes into being *as* world literature, just as nationalism is itself a universalist project. As Saʿada writes in *The Emergence of Nations*, "When we speak of Syrian culture we mean the role played by Syrians in advancing universal culture, a role that combined sowing, planting, seafaring, trading, and invention of the alphabet and the city-state." Al-Khal frequently borrows the same logic, as for example in an editorial published in the SSNP organ *al-Makshuf:* "We want to participate in human literature [*al-adab al-insani*] on the basis of our national literature."[24] In this sense, all literature is first and foremost national literature, hence Saʿada's penchant for labeling even medieval poets such as Abu al-ʿAlaʾ al-Maʿarri or Abu Nuwas as "Syrian." It is worth noting the difference between this notion of world literature and the one articulated by Silone and other late modernists. Rather than a corpus of autonomous texts circulating in an abstract, unified, and cosmopolitan space, Saʿada imagines world literature as an uneven, heterodox site where the various national traditions vie for status. The *struggle* in the title of his work refers not only to the struggle to renew Syrian literature but also to the struggle of that literature to achieve recognition.

Saʿada's model for a successful national culture is the mythico-philosophical tradition of German Romanticism and Wagner, which is not surprising given the anti-French platform of his party. What distinguishes the products of German culture, in Saʿada's view, is that they are at once universal and particular, or universal by virtue of their particularism. It is through his treatment of Germanic myths in the *Ring Cycle* that Wagner becomes a "philosopher," which is to say, a creative artist of universal significance (53–54). Similarly, it is Schiller's treatment of the Thirty Years' War, "a quintessentially German topic," that secures for his work "world status" (67–68). (Saʿada seems to have in mind Schiller's *Wallenstein* trilogy as well as his *History of the Thirty Years' War*.) When Saʿada turns his attention to the works of a nascent Syrian literature, it is this universal dimension he finds missing. Part of Saʿada's aim in composing *The Intellectual Struggle* was to recruit young poets to the party and to provide them with an intellectual basis for their art. This recruitment effort is most evident in the third chapter of Saʿada's book, "From Darkness into the Light," in which he discusses the works of two poets, Shafiq Maʿluf, author of "Dreams," and Saʿid ʿAql, one of Lebanon's leading poets.

Saʿada's interest in the work of ʿAql and Maʿluf stems from these poets' own investment in local myth and the recovery of ancient literature. Saʿada describes a meeting with ʿAql in the summer of 1935 in Lebanon after reading his verse play *Bint Yaftah* [The Daughter of Jephthah]. Saʿada writes that he had found the poem a promising debut, though ultimately too "bookish." He encouraged the young poet to seek his subject matter not in the Old Testament but rather in the rich history of ancient Syria. ʿAql did just that in his 1944 play *Qadmus*, which takes up the Greek-Canaanite myth of Cadmus and Europa. News of this work, which reached Saʿada in South America, raised his hopes for an inaugural work of Syrian renewal. But in an aside included in the second edition of his book, published in Beirut in 1947, he announced his disappointment with the play. "The author has colored historical facts and traditional myths with a narrow localism" (64), he wrote, frowning at ʿAql's drift into an exclusively Lebanese-Christian Phoenicianism. (Later in his life, ʿAql became notorious for advocating the replacement of Arabic script by Latin characters and the use of Lebanese dialect in printed texts.)

Saʿada's disappointment with Shafiq Maʿluf has a similar basis. He concentrates his remarks on Maʿluf's long narrative poem "*Abqar*," first published in 1936 in São Paolo.[25] The title is a toponym for the legendary home of the jinn, the muses of Bedouin poetry. The poem recounts a Dantesque journey into a fantastical landscape where the narrator meets many creatures and personages of pre-Islamic myth, whose sources are detailed in Maʿluf's scholarly introduction. "ʿAbqar" is in this sense a dive into the pagan sources of Arab poetic inspiration. But for Saʿada this material is too limited. Maʿluf's jinn and hybrid monsters are not the universal "legends" [*asatir*] employed by Wagner but only local "superstitions" [*khurafat*]. He finds the boneless seers and make-believe birds of "ʿAbqar" too peculiar, irrational, and grotesque: "This kind of superstition has no point," he complains, "except to suggest the condition of the peoples who hold to it, so different from those majestic legends with their philosophical coloring that deal with the material and spiritual issues of life." Saʿada's critique of ʿAql and Maʿluf lines up neatly with his party program. Both his politics and his poetics refuse the tenets of narrow Lebanese nationalism and nostalgic Arabism alike. But if both of these mythical sources were too provincial, where should Syria's writers look for inspiration?

Here, as is often the case with modernist poetry and nationalist politics, archaeology came to the rescue. "Secrets from Syrian Hills" was published in the *National Geographic* magazine in July (Tammuz) 1933.[26] The article's author, Claude Schaeffer, was the lead archaeologist at Raʾs Shamra in northern Syria, site of the ancient trading city of Ugarit, where excavations had begun in 1929. Among the more spectacular finds of these digs were several libraries containing clay tablets inscribed with a heretofore unknown cuneiform script, later identified as Ugaritic, "The world's earliest known alphabet," according to the article's subtitle. This Semitic abjad was eventually deciphered by experts in Paris and Jerusalem, and several of the cuneiform texts turned out to be "epics of old Phoenicia," dating back to the fourteenth century BCE. "Long before Homer's immortal 'Iliad,' Phoenician authors in Ugarit wrote epics about the strange adventures of a legendary hero called Taphon," Shaeffer told his readers. He then summarized a number of other Phoenician myths, including the death and resurrection of Aleyan-Baal (a version of the Tammuz myth), Baal's slaying of a seven-headed serpent (a precursor of Isaiah's mention of the Leviathan [27:1]), and the tale of Adon, "Adonis of the classical Phoenicians."

How Saʿada came across this issue of *National Geographic* he does not say. Perhaps, like the fortuitous discovery of *al-ʿUsba* with which he begins his book, it was a lucky find of his South American exile. In *The Intellectual Struggle*, Saʿada cites Shaeffer's article extensively in his own translation. It is easy to make out the reasons for his enthusiasm. At the moment Saʿada was composing his tract, nationalist elites across the region were wresting control over ancient patrimonies—Hittite, Semitic, pharaonic, Phoenician, and Archaemenidian—away from European archaeologists and using the past uncovered in the dig pits as the basis for national histories. In his study of interwar archaeology in Turkey, Egypt, Iran, and Iraq, James Goode writes, "Buried within the national domain lay the remains of the ancestors, and it became the responsibility of archaeology to establish links between the past and the present, to provide the evidence to support the national narrative."[27] Saʿada argued that poets too should play a fundamental role in establishing this narrative. It was clear to him that Raʾs Shamra gave the Syrian avant-garde—a group that did not yet exist, or that had not yet come to self-consciousness—all the material it needed for a literary renaissance. Schaeffer's digs had uncovered the Ur-literature of the West. The Ugaritic legends pre-dated the Homeric epics and Old Testament stories, and Saʿada was quick to claim them as the ultimate source for these more canonized origins: "Among the discoveries made at Raʾs Shamra, near Latakia, is astonishing evidence of the greatness of Syrian imagination and Syrian thought about life and great issues. These findings announce nothing less than the following fact: the most important Greek myths and the most important stories of the Jews in the Old Testament are taken from Syrian sources." And then again, with undertones of resentment: "How often historians and scholars have praised the Greeks for the greatness of their myths, most of which—or the most important of which—go back to Syria," Saʿada writes. "The world is indebted to us for great philosophies, yet they say that all of us are exclusively indebted to the Greeks" (86). The epics of Ugarit gave Saʿada what he was searching for: an indisputably ancient literature, one that pre-dated both Arab and Western traditions, whose mythic substructure could bolster a project of national renewal. What Siegfried and Brünnhilde were for Wagner, Baal and ʿAthtart could be for the Syrians—a gateway to world literature. After the discoveries at Raʾs Shamra, all that remained was for the rising generation of poets to transmit or translate these myths to a wider audience. As Sa'ada writes at the close of his work:

> True literature must be a perfect transmission [*naqil*] of new thought and new feeling arising from a new weltanschauung [*al-nazra al-jadida*] to the sensibility and consciousness of the wider collective, to the hearing and sight of the world. In this way, it becomes a national and a global literature: it raises the national community up to the level of this new weltanschauung and illuminates the community's path toward the world.... Our literature cannot be reborn, nor will we possess a world literature—one that demands the world's attention and claims a lasting, world-class value—except by this route. (91)

The use of myth by the Arab modernist poets, particularly before the founding of *Shi'r* and during the first few years of its publication, has been extensively analyzed.[28] The epithet "Tammuzi," often used to qualify the early work of Adonis, Yusuf al-Khal, and Khalil Hawi among others, was coined by Jabra Ibrahim Jabra in a review published in *Shi'r* in 1958, and it was Jabra who first translated Sir James Frazer's "Adonis, Attis, Osiris," the first part of the fourth book of *The Golden Bough*, into Arabic.[29] The common denominator of these poems, essentially national allegories for a nation-to-come, is their obsession with the theme of death and rebirth. This narrative is typically refracted through the life cycles of legendary beasts such as the phoenix and salamander or through the adventures of mythico-historical figures such as Christ, Orpheus, and Tammuz/Adonis. Early criticism, much of it produced by the modernists themselves, tended to ascribe the poets' obsession with this theme to the influence of Eliot and in particular to the mythical method of *The Waste Land*.[30] But the *Shi'r* poets' familiarity with Eliot came relatively late, and any claim of association with his work should be viewed as a first step toward the repression of Sa'ada's earlier and more profound intervention.

The most consequential aspect of Sa'ada's nationalist poetics was not his discovery of a theme. It is true that the resurrection myth provides Tammuzi poetry, of which Adonis's "The Earth Spoke" and "Resurrection and Ashes" are the preeminent examples, with a narrative template.[31] But the stories of Adon and Tammuz have little importance as such; *The Intellectual Struggle* provides the barest summary of these matters. Instead, for Sa'ada, it is the de-provincializing of Syrian poetry that provides the ultimate rationale for the transmission of indigenous myth. It is this ambition, the determination to put Arabic poetry "on the map of world literature," that became fundamental to the modernist project and marked the poets' own way of talking about their aims. It is an aspiration that survives long after the poets' party memberships and their fascination with the mythic method were renounced for good.

The Turn to Personalism

For Saʿada, the project of literary revival, like the project of national revival, was a collective one. The only "personality" that occurs in his text is that of the national group, whose "particular personality" [*shakhsiyya khassa*] is the result its unique environment and historical development. Reading the remarks of Yusuf Maʿluf on "Ahlam," Saʿada condemns the suggestion that a poet should seek first of all to be "imitated" rather than "imitative." For Saʿada, such counsel reveals an unfortunate desire for personal fame. "This is an utterly individualistic principle," Saʿada shakes his head, "which might be explained by the fact that the speaker is the addressee's uncle and therefore solicitous of his personal well-being." Saʿada's dismissal of individualism stems from his conviction that a literary revival will not be accomplished by isolated artists. Literature is an epiphenomenon of national life, the true engines of which lie elsewhere: "Literature cannot cause renewal on its own, spontaneously," he declares in the second chapter of *The Intellectual Struggle*. "Renewal in literature is an effect rather than a cause. It is the result of . . . a spiritual, material, social, and political revolution that transforms the life of an entire people."[32] The quasi-epistolary form of Saʿada's own tract, so careful to situate itself in a shared intellectual endeavor, however imaginary or far-flung, is a symptom of this commitment to collectivity.

The modernists often repeated Saʿada's claim that a literary revolution required more than technical innovation, that it required a transformation at the level of the weltanschauung, which is how I will translate their Saʿadist slogan, "*al-nazra al-jadida*" (literally, "the new way of looking"). This notion is often cashed out, particularly in Adonis's writings, by figuring the poet as a seer or possessor of visions, rather than a mere craftsman.[33] But here already we see a strategic relinquishing of Saʿada's belief that cultural renewal would supervene a "material, social, and political revolution." The *Shiʿr* poets' idea of modernity consistently gave emphasis to the cultural struggle and individual heroism, while gradually giving up on the idea of political commitment. How is it that the modernists came to rewrite *shakhsiyya* as a personal rather than a collective term? How did the individual, and not the nation, come to be the protagonist of their adventure?

This revision was chiefly the work of Yusuf al-Khal, and it marks the first step on his path toward becoming editor in chief of *Shiʿr*. Al-Khal was the first of the modernists to join the SSNP, when it was still a secret society. He joined the Tripoli cell in 1934, after graduating from the local secondary school. Al-Khal spent the next several years writing for party organs on subjects such as the liberation of women, Arab versus Western music, and the genius of Antun Saʿada. Following the leader's departure for South America in 1938, the journals were closed and French authorities outlawed the party soon afterward (in part because they suspected that Saʿada had ties with Fascist and Nazi parties in Europe). The persecution of the SSNP that began after Saʿada's departure may have encouraged al-Khal to go back to school. He studied political science and economics at the American College in Aleppo, then spent two more years teaching Arabic in the Lebanese city of Sidon. In 1942, at the age of twenty-five, he matriculated to the American University in Beirut, where he began working toward a degree in philosophy.

The shift from clandestine militancy in Tripoli to life as a student in Beirut was crucial to al-Khal's development. It signaled a turn away from political activity and toward the professional sphere, a gradual but decisive transition that would leave its imprint on the magazine al-Khal went on to establish. The university neighborhood of Hamra was the most varied and lively space in Lebanese and arguably Arab intellectual life. This was due in large part to the presence of AUB itself, founded by American missionaries in 1866 as the Syrian Protestant College (it was secularized in 1920). Originally a mixed suburb of Greek Orthodox, Sunni, and Druze families, Hamra became home to a community of Protestant converts around the turn of the century and eventually served as a magnet for émigrés from all over the Arab world. When al-Khal arrived, AUB was one of the premier training schools for regional elites. Its graduates were "eagerly sought by the new governments bent on new programs of reform and modernization." It was also during the interwar years that the first generation of Arab scholars trained in Europe and America came to AUB to establish a culture of expertise. "There is no question," writes Samir Kassir, "that AUB was the premier center of cultural and ideological extraterritoriality in Beirut in the twentieth century."[34] Prominent thinkers such as Constantine Zurayk, Charles Issawi, and Anis Frayha taught at the university during this period and founded some of its most important journals and research centers, a trend that was helped by the simultaneous rise of a well-connected and technically skilled publishing industry. The interwar years are in this sense at the origins of the professionalization and globalization of Lebanese intellectual life, a legacy that *Shiʿr* extended into the realm of literature. The modernists' commitment to poetry—to poetry and nothing else—reflected a deeper historical transition. The rise of a professional intellectual class slowly led to the replacement of the older ideal of the *adib* or *muthaqqaf*—both words near equivalents to the French *homme de lettres*—best exemplified by Egyptian thinkers such as Taha Husayn and Tawfik al-Hakim. Compared to the cultural authority enjoyed by these generalists, the subsequent generation of intellectuals had a narrower remit yet one with more solid institutional support in the form of academic departments and specialized fields of study.

Samuel Weber has analyzed the process of professionalization by noting "the tendency of the professional to present himself as relatively autonomous in his field," since the services he or she renders "are not merely specialized (as are those of the auto mechanic), they are, in a crucial sense, *incommensurable*, and upon this incommensurability the distinctive autonomy and authority of

FIGURE 7. Charles Malik delivering his address, "Asia and Africa Ask Searching Questions," to the World Council of Churches, 1954. Photo: John Dominis, The LIFE Picture Collection, Getty Images.

the professional is founded." Weber describes the origins of such authority in a way that recalls the Arab modernists' own historical conjunction: "The emergence of professionalism may be understood as . . . an effort to establish a measure of self-control, not, to be sure, on the part of isolated individuals, but on that of a group, seeking to define and to maintain a certain identity in the face of an extremely dynamic, unsettling, and powerful reorganization and transformation of society." The *Shiʿr* poets were not academics, although some earned higher degrees and taught at university from time to time. But it is the professionalist ethos of their movement, their insistence on the authority granted by autonomy, that makes their movement so expressive of its historical moment. What distinguished the *Shiʿr* poets from their *engagé* contemporaries was their gamble that professionalization and its corollary, independence, would not lead to isolation or the ivory tower but would instead give the poets access to the new global institution of late modernism. As Franco Moretti has written in a related context, "Specialism, for this happy generation, is freedom."[35]

For al-Khal, the key figure at AUB was the philosopher and diplomat Charles Malik, another charismatic thinker whose influence upon a whole generation of Arab thinkers has been mostly ignored by intellectual historians. Edward Said, a nephew of Malik's by marriage, has written a lively personal recollection of the summers he spent in the mountains of the Lebanese

Chouf, debating the merits of Nasserism with his uncle. Said felt the philosopher's influence, "not only in the perspectives and ideas he introduced me to but in the dignity of the kind of moral-philosophical inquiry he had engaged in, which was so lacking either in my formal education or my environment." And yet Said also calls the older man "the great negative intellectual lesson of my life, an example which for the last three decades I have found myself grappling with, living through, analyzing, over and over and over with regret, mystification, and bottomless disappointment."[36] Malik's sway over the Beiruti modernists and Yusuf al-Khal in particular was if anything more powerful. Ten years older than al-Khal, Malik also came from a Greek Orthodox family in northern Lebanon (he eventually converted to Roman Catholicism). He was educated at a Presbyterian missionary school in Tripoli and then at AUB, where he received a degree in physics and mathematics. In 1932 he began his graduate work in philosophy at Harvard under Alfred North Whitehead, and after a year in Freiburg, where he studied with Heidegger, Malik returned to Cambridge to write his dissertation, "The metaphysics of time in the philosophies of A. N. Whitehead and M. Heidegger."[37] Malik returned to Lebanon in 1938 and founded the philosophy department at AUB. He also gathered around him a cohort of handpicked students, *al-Rabita al-falsafiyya al-'arabiyya* [The Arab philosophy union], who received special instruction. Al-Khal was one of this cohort.[38] In a review of Malik's autobiography, written many years later, al-Khal called his former teacher "the highest 'peak' of our intellectual heritage since Averroes," and qualified Malik as "a true revolutionary," the sort of teacher-prophet "who leads you, sooner or later, to renew your life by changing your mind. You become a person who has discarded the old person and dressed as a new one—a second birth, from on high."[39]

Al-Khal's encounter with Malik was indeed a turning point in the poet's intellectual life. The philosopher facilitated his pivot away from the SSNP toward the ideal of apolitical literature, from militant nationalism toward militant liberalism, a development that typifies the *Shi'r* group as a whole. Yet significant elements of Sa'ada's program were carried over into the modernist venture, most importantly his aim to establish Arabic poetry among the ranks of world literature. Both Sa'ada and Malik were adamantly anti-Arab-nationalist in their political orientation, which must have facilitated al-Khal's conversion. The nationalist leader and the philosophy professor, soon to become a politician himself, met at least once during the winter of 1937, which gave rise to a brief correspondence between them. The subject of their exchange was the nature and function of philosophy, particularly in what Malik called, with the Western perspective he invariably adopted, "the Near East." It is this perspective that Sa'ada specifically objects to in his letter. After Malik had sent Sa'ada the text of a lecture he delivered to the women's college at AUB in the spring of 1938, Sa'ada wrote back in appreciation but also to note two points of disagreement. While Malik asserted, in a phrase quoted by Saʿada, "I hardly think I am mistaken when I say that we do seem to have a very strong antiphilosophical streak in our very being," Saʿada reminds him that "in the past, before our great setbacks" (presumably a reference to Ottoman and French rule), idealist philosophy was no stranger to Syria. And in response to Malik's encomiums for Greek and European thinkers, from Socrates to Nietzsche, Saʿada encourages Malik to seek the buried streams of his native intellectual tradition, "So that you may discover yourself—your authentic self, with all its beauty and power—thereby becoming a philosopher and not a translator of philosophy [*naql al-falsafa*]." Not surprisingly, Saʿada wanted to mobilize philosophy (like poetry) within his project of national awakening, a more concrete route to universality in his view than the abstractions of metaphysics.[40]

What did al-Khal learn from his philosophy teacher? What practical lexicon or new weltanschauung did he take with him from the seminars at AUB? There are few sources that give us a picture of Malik as a thinker during this period, when he does not appear to have published any articles. From personal letters and memoranda, we know that Malik envisaged the university not merely as a training ground for "young men who can function as reliable employees of the I.P.C. [Iraqi Petroleum Company]," but rather as an incubator for "great heroes of intellectual freedom in the modern world." Malik's teaching syllabus was what he called "the Greco-Roman-Christian humane synthesis."[41] Hisham Sharabi, a Palestinian intellectual historian who studied philosophy at AUB during the early 1940s, remembers Malik's "religious idealism," his domineering style in the classroom, and mentions reading the works of Kierkegaard, Jacques Maritain, and the spiritualist philosopher Nikolai Berdyaev.[42] Malik's philosophy reader, which surveys a tradition from Thales to Whitehead, is centered on the study of "great masters." In his introduction to the seminar, he writes, "Nothing can help to realize our human, spiritual potentials more effectively than the sustained, reverent wrestling with great minds."[43] But it is not until Malik began his career as a diplomat in 1945 that he began to publish his work for a general audience. Between 1945 and 1955 Malik held a number of official posts: minister plenipotentiary in Washington, DC; Lebanese representative to the Commission on Human Rights (becoming chair in 1951 after Eleanor Roosevelt's retirement); Lebanese ambassador to the United States and the United Nations; and president of the UN General Assembly. In 1956 Lebanese president Chamoun appointed Malik as minister of foreign affairs, a post he held for two years before returning to his professorship at AUB. There is no indication that the work he wrote as a diplomat represents a significant change in Malik's style or preoccupations as a thinker. On the contrary, his writings are evidence of the attempt to bring a philosopher's professional terminology to bear on questions of world affairs.

In the broadest terms, Malik's oeuvre is a peculiarly Cold War combination of Christian theology, international relations, and humanist philosophy—roughly the same mixture one finds in his American contemporary, Reinhold Niebuhr. In his English writings, which preponderate, Malik adopts the role of an analyst and interpreter of the East who addresses himself to a Western, chiefly American audience.[44] Although there are passages of dispassionate analysis, Malik's primary genre is that of the anti-Communist polemic. He seeks to outline a strategy for Western policy in the Near East, which is for him the most important theater of the Cold War. In that region, according to Malik, the war is being lost because the West has abandoned its faith in itself. The countries of the Near East, like others in the Third World, are underdeveloped and therefore dependent on aid from abroad. This dependency makes them vulnerable to Soviet blandishments. Malik rates the intellectual attractions of Marxism very low—he finds dialectical materialism "nauseatingly superficial and false"—but argues that the Communists are winning because the West is fighting the war on their terms, the "materialist" terms of "economic and social justice."[45] This is not the West's natural terrain and does not allow for the deployment of its most important and still "unbroken" traditions: the Hellenic tradition of reason and philosophy, and the Christian tradition of charity and love. "The ultimate crisis," Malik writes, "is entirely spiritual."[46] It is on this battlefield that the Cold War must be fought: "The East thirsts for nothing more than this message, a message not of money and machines, but of spirit and truth."[47]

To win the battle for hearts and minds, Malik calls for the West to turn back to the sources of its own authentic traditions. His most striking evocation of this process is his demand for a "Western revolution," which is to say, "a return of the West to itself":

> The West owes it to itself, independently of any external challenge, to rise to the highest it already is and knows. This rise is simply a repentant homecoming, an authentic return to itself. For I repeat what I have said before: In a great revolutionary age, when everything is on the move, when everyone everywhere is awakening, when no level of existence is without its ferment—in such an age, for the West to exist-as-usual and *not* to develop its own distinctive revolution—this is the tragedy of the day.[48]

The passage is typical of Malik's writings. It yokes the jargon of authenticity to a specifically Christian call for repentance, and it employs the trope of revolution while advocating an essentially conservative reconstruction of the West.[49]

Two elements of Malik's liberal imagination need emphasizing. The first is the special role he allots to Lebanon. Malik's call for a Western revolution is in fact a call for the West to rediscover itself in the East as the historical fountainhead of Christianity. Malik consistently describes this redemptive return to the East as a movement of "love," or suffering through identification: "Those who approach the East not knowing themselves what they are after, obviously cannot suffer for the East. Only those who identify themselves with the East, because they love it, not indeed for what it is, but for what it might and ought to be under God, shall eventually redeem it."[50] In order for this spiritual or humanist rapprochement to take place there must be a mediating term, and for Malik this is the role that Lebanon is uniquely suited to play. On one hand, this is the result of what he characterizes as Lebanon's history of autonomy, a tradition of relative independence that dates back to the late Ottoman period. More profoundly, it stems from Lebanon's belonging to both the Christian West and the Muslim East. "Lebanon has a positive vocation in the international field," Malik writes in a *Foreign Affairs* article of 1952. "It is not political. It is spiritual and intellectual. It consists in being true to the best and truest in the West and East alike. This burden of mediation and understanding she is uniquely called to bear."[51] While much of Malik's anti-Nasserist and anti-Soviet writings on the Near East are explicitly interventionist, this way of thinking does not apply to Lebanon. Instead, the singular position of Malik's native country means that it must be safeguarded as a spiritual resource, protected from what he calls "the political temptation":

> Lebanon should remain open to the East and the West so that both worlds could feel at home in it. The wonderful intellectual and spiritual liberties of Lebanon should not be sacrificed no matter in what name and for what cause. . . . Eastern and Western statesmen can combine to work out adequate guarantees for Lebanon as an authentic home of freedom—freedom of enterprise, freedom of thought, freedom of conscience, freedom of being and freedom of becoming.[52]

Lebanon's potential as a mediator can thus be fulfilled only if its traditional autonomy and freedom is respected. Realpolitik must make an exception. "The principle of international politics is power," Malik writes in an especially grandiloquent passage, "but Lebanon's power is reason, truth, love, suffering, being."[53]

These tropes of Lebanon as an interpreter or translator between East and West, as the home of freedom, and as a spiritual refuge are conspicuous in the poetry Yusuf al-Khal wrote in the early 1940s, while he was Malik's student at AUB. Much of this verse was published in al-Khal's first collection of poems, *al-Hurriyya* [Freedom] (1945). In *"Hadhihi al-ard liyya"* [This Earth Belongs to Me], a celebratory poem for the newly independent state, al-Khal writes, "There is no salvation for the East without the intercession [*shafaʿa*] of Lebanon / Nor any sacrificial soldier for the West." ("*Shafaʿa*" is a conspicuously ecumenical choice of word, since both Jesus and Muhammad are figured in their respective traditions as intercessors for mankind on the Day of Judgment.) Similarly, in *"Lubnan"* [Lebanon], he apostrophizes, "O singular, inconceivable country / the first to Arabize its face / and Westernize its character." In *"Biladi"* [My Country], he evokes the trope of Lebanon as refuge:

"The poor man takes shelter with us / so that he might sing, and also he who seeks aid, / and he who has been made to roam." The title poem, the longest in the book, is a teleological history of freedom, beginning with an evocation of Egypt's pyramids, built by slaves, and ending with a paean to Lebanon as the inheritor of Greece and "the eternal standard-bearer of liberty."

These baldly patriotic poems were all written several years before al-Khal's public resignation from the SSNP, but their emphasis on Lebanon as the historical home of freedom already indicate a turn away from the ideology of Greater Syria. The poems are not evidence al-Khal's conversion to a narrow or exclusivist nationalism; rather, they suggest his pivoting away from a poetics of indigenous, mythical renewal and toward a poetics of intercession between East and West, Islam and Christianity. These tropes persist in al-Khal's political writings of the early 1950s. In 1954, as Chamoun brokered talks between the Baathists of Iraq and Syria, al-Khal wrote approvingly of the Lebanese president's willingness to play "the role of middleman" [*dawr al-wasata*]. Al-Khal's political writings are squarely within the tradition of midcentury liberalism that sought to present itself as apolitical—because motivated primarily by spiritual concerns—despite its evident anticommunism. Like Malik, al-Khal ascribed Lebanon's importance in foreign policy terms to its political autonomy, or autonomy from politics, as well as to its civilizational inheritance: "Lebanon is free and there is nothing that can force it to fall in line with any of the Arabs' tribal, familial, or authoritarian pacts. More than that, Lebanon is a pure lover, who hates no one and betrays no cause. . . . It is the homeland where two heritages meet: the Christian and the Islamic."[54]

The second element of Malik's thought that needs emphasizing is its insistence on "the infinite worth and dignity of the human person."[55] This Christian humanism was a fundamental tenet of midcentury personalism, a neo-Thomist movement that argued for a spiritualist "third way" between individualist liberalism and totalitarian communism. Personalism's most prominent international advocate was the Catholic philosopher Jacques Maritain, who supplied much of the intellectual framework for the postwar discourse of human rights.[56] Malik also played a crucial role in introducing this philosophy into policy circles. Samuel Moyn has noted "the striking prominence of Christian social thought among the framers [of the Universal Declaration of Human Rights]," whose preamble affirms the signatories' faith in "the dignity and worth of the human person," and he suggests that "Malik was perhaps the key figure in the negotiations."[57] For Malik, the dignity of the person was rooted in the divine and provided a through line for two and a half millennia of Western history. "The unity of the Western tradition," he wrote in 1953, "can be shown to go back, in a continuous manner, to people who lived some twenty-five or thirty centuries ago in Greece and Palestine. The essence of this view is, one the one hand, the subordination of Man to God, and, on the other, the recognition of the ultimacy of the individual human person."[58] The spiritual dignity of the person was thus a bulwark against both the "radical immanentism" of Marxist thought, which reduced humanity to its economic and social conditions, as well as the atomistic tendencies inherent in liberal capitalism. Against these rival materialisms, Malik speaks in Heideggerian accents of ontic unfathomability: "Man is very deep," he assured one audience in 1962. "He is a veritable abyss."[59]

Maritain took care to distinguish bourgeois individualism, which in his view led to moral selfishness and statolatry (i.e., fascism), from Christian personalism, which acknowledged "that personality tends by nature to communion." But Malik's zealous anticommunism led him to downplay the person's communal affiliations, and the Arab modernists would arguably go even further in this direction.[60] Malik describes the person as a figure of radical autonomy and limitless potential, an abstraction that stands above any collective:

> If one believes that the individual human person, with his inner joy and freedom, and with his infinite spiritual possibilities, is the most precious thing in the world, so much so that when we think of God we cannot think of anything higher than to speak of Him as a person—then one cannot be indifferent to a doctrine and way of life that subordinates the human person to the Party or the Collective or the State.[61]

This is from an article written for *World Affairs* in the winter of 1961; the long editorial that ran in *Shi'r* a few months later is a close paraphrase: "For us, the person is more important than the party, more important than ideology; for us, the person and his freedom come first, before anything else." Given his emphasis on the person, it is no surprise that when Malik called for "a Western revolution," he began by imagining its heroes. "A revolution means first of all revolutionaries," he writes more than once in *Man in the Struggle for Peace* (1962). The present, Malik claims, is an eschatological moment, "perfectly cut for the highest heroism of the spirit":

> The heroes called for will outgrow by a million degrees all mediocrity and shallowness.... Every word they utter will weigh a world. They live and move and have their being in directness and silence, in certainty and truth, in death, rapture, and triumph, and in utter simplicity. In the solitude of their being, they are always transfigured and transformed in the presence of the ground of all being.[62]

Al-Khal's political writings from this period hew closely to Malik's spiritual-humanist anticommunism. In an editorial written in 1955, al-Khal argued that "The disagreement between us and Communism is not a matter of economic theories nor methods of governance, it is a disagreement over the true nature of man."[63] But it is in the field of literature that al-Khal made his most original contribution, extending his teacher's philosophy into a subject that Malik himself rarely discussed. Al-Khal made the figure of the person into the lynchpin for a distinctively late modernist poetics.

The most significant early text on this figure is al-Khal's lecture "*Fi Falsafat al-shiʿr*" [On the Philosophy of Poetry], delivered at AUB in late 1945.[64] The lecture is in large part a gloss on Maritain's *Art and Scholasticism* (1920), a work that Malik may well have introduced to al-Khal in his philosophy seminars; al-Khal would later translate, via intermediary English versions, a selection of Maritain's prose.[65] *Art and Scholasticism* sought to re-inject Thomistic categories and a Latinate lexicon into debates about contemporary art. For Maritain as for Eliot, who translated the French thinker's essays for *The Criterion*, the modern world was heir to an "immense intellectual disorder inherited from the nineteenth century." This chaos required contemporary intellectuals to tread carefully, making neat distinctions between speculative and practical orders, "Doing" and "Making," *ad bonum operantis* and *ad bonum operas*. An admirer of Baudelaire and Picasso, Maritain claimed to find a classical rigor in the best modern works: "I know nothing in contemporary production more sincerely *classical* than the music of Satie." The necessary condition for producing such works of "integrity," "proportion," and "clarity" is a separation of the artist from his work. The artwork, according to Maritain, is autonomous. It stands "outside the human sphere; it has an end, rules, values, which are not those of man, but those of the work to be produced." The production of art requires that the artist give himself over to these rules entirely in a movement of spiritual surrender:

> Hence the tyrannical and absorbing power of Art, and also its astonishing power of soothing; it delivers one from the human; it establishes the *artifex*—artist or artisan—in a world apart, closed, limited, absolute, in which he puts the energy and intelligence of his manhood at the service of a thing which he makes.[66]

The separation of the maker from his object means that "The Artist is subject, in the sphere of his art, to a kind of asceticism, which may require heroic sacrifices." The artisan's devotion to his craft must be total; he must even keep his work pure of any Christian intention to edify or propagate the faith. The production of art is, for Maritain as for many modernists, a strictly "disinterested activity."[67]

Maritain's portrait of the artist as a sacrificial hero was very much to al-Khal's taste. In "*al-Shaʿir*" [The Poet], a short poem written in 1941, he figures the poet as a Christ-like outcast, "a symbol of truth in a world that has strayed, / crucifying his soul to ransom others."[68] In his commentary on Maritain's text, in which "the artist" is quickly replaced by "the poet," al-Khal explains his notion of self-sacrifice by suggesting a nicely scholastic distinction between "the personality of the poet as a man" and "the personality of the poet as a creator":

This struggle [between the two personalities] determines the poet's greatness and heroism, for the artist must preserve, with respect to the work he creates, his personality as a creator and overcome his personality as a man; in other words, he must create in a place apart from the influence of everyday duties, social rules, and moral obligations. If we see in his creation the influence of these duties, rules, and obligations, then it is only by accident.[69]

Al-Khal's distinction echoes Maritain's ideal of a "deliverance from the human" as well as Eliot's description of the artistic process in "Tradition and the Individual Talent" as "a continual self-sacrifice, a continual extinction of personality." But whereas for Maritain and Eliot this is primarily a movement of ascesis, for al-Khal it is a movement of self-overcoming. The poet achieves greatness not by extinguishing his personality but by identifying it solely with the activity of literary creation, an activity he undertakes in "a place apart" from all other activities. This personalist conception of *al-shakhsiyya* as an undetermined, solitary figure stands in defiant opposition to Saʿada's collectivist notion, according to which a people's "personality" is the symptom of their historical environment, with its particular boundaries and demographic mixture. In this way, through his encounter with Malik and Maritain, al-Khal began to replace political struggle with poetic heroism.

The *Shiʿr* poets would go on to situate the trope of "the person" or "man" at the heart of their thinking about genre, prosody, and literary inheritance. It is a conceptual crux of the movement, and its historical emergence links the Arabic modernist project to a specific global conjuncture constituted by the onset of the Cold War, a reinvention and defense of "the Western tradition," and the honeymoon of Lebanese independence. For the Beiruti poets, it also emerges in tandem with a turn away from political nationalism. In a statement published in *al-Nahar* in late 1947, al-Khal along with several other party militants made public their break with the SSNP. Entitled "The Issue of Freedom of Thought in the Nationalist Party," the signatories declared that "freedom of thought, not the party apparatus, was the first condition for cultural and intellectual work," and they criticized Saʿada for imposing "dictatorial" control over the party following his return to Lebanon earlier that year.[70] In this way, the terms of Malik's anticommunism were effectively turned on the nationalist leader, who was executed by Lebanese authorities a year and a half later, in July 1949. Yusuf al-Khal's encounter with Malik provided him with the resources to make a personalist revolution very much like those European and American intellectuals, many affiliated with the CCF, who at precisely the same historical moment repented of their "totalitarian" pasts and embraced a militant form of liberalism. The philosopher-theologian supplied the keywords and concepts not only for the turn away from Saʿada's politics but also for the salvaging of his global ambitions for Arabic literature.[71] In 1948, when he was appointed head of the Lebanese delegation to the newly constituted United Nations, Malik took al-Khal along with him to America. During the debates that swirled around Article 18 of the Universal Declaration of Human Rights, the article on religious freedom, Malik was especially resolute—and ultimately effective—in arguing for the inclusion of the right to conversion within the scope of the article.[72]

The Sea-Poem and the Cénacle

The seven years al-Khal spent in the United States were his apprenticeship as a publisher and translator. With Malik's assistance, al-Khal found work as an editor for the UN Bulletin before being assigned as an interpreter for a mission to Libya, then in the process of formalizing its independence. After leaving the UN in 1952, al-Khal remained in New York City as a freelancer. He established a private news service and then became the editor in chief of *al-Huda* [The Right Way], a small daily with a largely Maronite readership.[73] Al-Khal wrote frequent editorials on subjects ranging from Eisenhower's policies in the Middle East, to the literature of the *mahjar*, to American literature. It was during this period that al-Khal came to know the work of those poets he later translated in his *Anthology of American Poetry*, an unacknowledged abridgement of F. O. Matthiessen's *Oxford Book of American Verse* (1950), which included selections from Anne Bradstreet ("A Letter to Her Husband") through Robert Lowell ("The Dead in Europe"). Al-Khal returned to Beirut in 1955. "The homeland has claims upon me," he wrote in his last editorial for *al-Huda*, "and I have a mission in life that I have found it is better to pursue there."[74] In speaking of this mission, perhaps al-Khal was already thinking of founding a magazine, one where his familiarity with American poetry, along with his skills as editor, entrepreneur, and translator, could be put to use.

Al-Khal's lecture at the Cénacle libanais in early 1957, "*Mustaqbal al-shiʿr fi lubnan*" [The Future of Poetry in Lebanon], was a foundational moment in the history of *Shiʿr*.[75] The venue was particularly auspicious. Established in 1946, the Cénacle served as a Lebanese public square presided over by the intellectual, financial, and political elite of the country. In the words of its founder, the Maronite intellectual Michel Asmar, it was a place where one might go "to pursue one's cultural education, in an atmosphere of true science and the pure desire for learning at the hands of experts and leading opinion makers of the country." During the first decade of its existence, the Cénacle's lectern was dominated by Christian thinkers, though Muslim and Druze leaders also received a polite hearing. Visitors from abroad included Léopold Senghor, Louis Massignon, and Alfred Toynbee (whose ideas about the world-historical importance of creative minorities was tailor-made for his Lebanese audience). The Cénacle was also an ally of the CCF.[76] Several friends of the Congress, such as Silone and the Swiss personalist Denis de Rougemont, gave lectures at the Cénacle during their tours of the region, and John Hunt admired its clubby ecumenicalism. The invited speakers often addressed subjects related to the political economy, seeking to define a realistic path for a small, newly independent state with long-standing commercial and intellectual ties to Europe as well as the Arab hinterland. They also spoke about the fraught question of national identity. The founders of the Cénacle insisted on the unique role Lebanon had to play in the Middle East, convinced that, in the high-minded words of Asmar, "The intellectual radiance of Lebanon has not dimmed ... and its message to the East still carries in its folds the most nourishing seeds."[77]

Al-Khal's lecture was designed to flatter these notions of Lebanon's distinctive place in the region and its mission of enlightenment. Although his talk is typically cited for its concluding ten principles, often taken as a manifesto of the modernist movement in Arabic poetry, the body of the lecture contains arguments and strategies that are equally foundational. Al-Khal's speech at the Cénacle was a declaration of his newly acquired expertise in American poetry. It serves notice of his determination to establish himself as a translator or "intercessor" between international modernism and his local audience—one that was primed to welcome such a message.

Al-Khal begins his talk by suggesting that Lebanese poetry is a young tradition, dating back only to the "court poets" of emir Bashir Shihab II in the early nineteenth century. Yet this origin is already a moment of decline. Al-Khal characterizes the poetry of Butrus Karami, Nasif al-Yaziji, and Niqula al-Turk as a literature of rhetorical mannerism. He cites al-Yaziji on the death of poetry: "My soul was saddened at the humiliation of poetry, and when sure of its death I dressed in black. / Its circulation is scarce these days: despite its cheapness, the market doesn't move." But al-Yaziji's own verse did not point the way to a new beginning. Nor, according to al-Khal, was the neoclassical and Romantic poetry of the late nineteenth and early twentieth centuries much better, with their sentimental "glorification of the past and adherence to nature." Even the love poetry of Saʿid ʿAql, reputedly the most modern of al-Khal's contemporaries, represents no advance over the seventh-century ghazals of ʿUmar ibn Abi Rabiʿa (an echo of Saʿada's complaint that ʿAql's poetry was merely "the literature of books," rather than "the literature of life").[78] "Contemporary Lebanese poetry is not modern poetry except in a chronological sense," al-Khal claims. "In terms of form and genre, there is no difference between it and the poetry of the ancients. Indeed, the ancients' poetry often contains more novelty than that of the greatest moderns." The modern world, in al-Khal's description, is continuously moving forward—an unsteady, anxiety-inducing, but finally exhilarating advance. Girded with scientific discoveries and technological innovations, "man no longer regards his place in existence with humility and resignation, but rather with a look of mastery, creativity, and self-confidence." Al-Khal reminded his audience of political developments during the previous quarter century: a worldwide depression, the rise of fascism, the Spanish Civil War, the use of the atomic bomb, the founding of the UN, and the Universal Declaration of Human Rights. This was the age of the car, the plane, and modern appliances. And yet, al-Khal complains, Lebanese poets continue to write as if nothing had changed since the days of Bedouin romances—a symptom of the "loss of modernity" that he would diagnose in his Rome lecture four years later. Al-Khal cites a long poem by ʿAql whose refrain is an apostrophe to the night: "Fly away with us, O night, fly away, you wild passion." As a corrective to such sentimentality, he presents a partial translation of the American poet Robinson Jeffers's "Night"—a poem, al-Khal says disarmingly, "which requires no commentary."

The apposition of Jeffers and ʿAql is hardly self-explanatory for us, however. And though he enjoyed far more esteem in the 1950s than now, Jeffers would have been unknown to most if not all of al-Khal's audience at the Cénacle. There is little in the meditative stanzas of "Night" (a poem included in Matthiessen's anthology) that points to an obviously modernist disposition. There are no cars, planes, or washing machines in Jeffers's poem. "The fretfulness / of cities" is evoked with a shudder. The absence of such objects and settings helps point up the distinctiveness of Arabic modernism, whose canon overlaps with the European and American versions while not being fully congruent. Like "Night," the poems that would come to typify *Shiʿr* stand aloof from the built environment around them; their landscapes are un-citified and starkly allegorical. This avoidance of the city is as characteristic of Arabic modernism as the immersion into urban life is to so many of its precursors. It is an evasion that reflects the modernists' particular vision of Lebanon. The audience for al-Khal's lecture would certainly have recognized the solemn Pacific scenery of Jeffers's poem—the "prone ocean" that is the subject of its first stanza and the "dark mountain" that is the subject of the second—as an uncannily Lebanese landscape. In his address to the same Cénacle in 1953, the banker, politician, and essayist Michel Chiha averred, "Phoenicia is, first of all, the sea. Mount Lebanon is, by definition, the mountain. The interpenetration of mountain and sea is what has constituted our republic."[79] More specifically, al-Khal's translation of Jeffers's ode is among the first instances of the modernist genre of the sea-poem, a characteristic import of the *Shiʿr* poets and one that resonated with the Cénacle's founding ideas. Before looking more closely at al-Khal's Arabic version of Jeffers's poem, it will be helpful to know the parameters of this political imaginary.

Phoenicianism was a common denominator to several nationalist groups in mandate-era Lebanon. Taking their cue from the vogue created by Ernest Renan's excavations of the coastal town of Byblos in the 1850s—and quickly followed by the publication of Flaubert's *Salammbô*, set in the Phoenician colony of Carthage—these political and cultural associations claimed the ancient seafarers as their progenitors. For some Maronite thinkers, such as Charles Corm,

Lebanon's Phoenician past provided historical proof that Lebanon was essentially distinct from its Arab-Muslim neighbors, a Mediterranean country oriented toward Europe, and particularly France, in both culture and politics. The hymnal poems of his most famous literary work, *La Montagne inspirée* (1934), though written in French, were declared by Corm to have been "translated from Lebanese"—not the local dialect of Arabic but rather the ancient Phoenician.[80] Michel Chiha, a prominent member of the Cénacle, did not insist on the historical claims of Phoenicianism but argued that modern Lebanon should model itself on a putatively ancient model of "the merchant republic." For Chiha, it was Lebanon's unique geography, its specific combination of mountains and coast that determined its inhabitants' historical role as traders and travelers. Michelle Hartman and Alessandro Olsaretti have shown how Chiha's ascription of a Phoenician-Mediterranean past for Lebanon helped buttress his argument for "a financial-mercantile oligarchy" and "a laissez-faire economic regime advocating both low taxation and no restrictions on the movement of capital and goods."[81] Chiha's call was echoed by many of those who addressed the Cénacle. Gabriel Ménassa, whose lecture was evoked earlier, based his plea for free trade and the abolishment of the Customs Union with Syria on Lebanon's "traditional role as a country of transit and distribution ... [a role] that is given to her and which she has carried out since ancient times."

Phoenicianism was not confined to Maronite ideologies. Antun Saʿada also claimed the Phoenician past for his own brand of radically secular nationalism. For Saʿada, the Phoenicians, whom he often calls Canaanites, were not only the inventors of the alphabet. They were also founders of the first city-state, a political model they exported to Greece, and rulers of the world's first maritime empire. As Saʿada writes in *The Emergence of Nations*, while other historical peoples viewed the sea as a limit to territorial expansion, Phoenician thalassocrats made the Mediterranean into a space for exploration and conquest:

> When Phoenician ships began navigating this sea and came into contact with other islands and shores suitable for colonization, they directed all their efforts to these new possibilities, which for other peoples had been an obstacle. They cast off the burdens of land and turned toward the burdens of the sea. ... In this land "abundant in milk and honey," the Canaanites did not cleave to the principle of deep-rooted conservatism that so often characterizes the peasant attached to the soil, but rather awoke to new possibilities. We might say that the Syrian people as a whole were not profoundly conservative in this way, because of the trade that linked them continuously to the outside world by way of war, exchange, and colonization.[82]

The Phoenician political and mercantile innovations that Maronite thinkers reserved for Lebanon Saʿada simply claimed for the wider Syrian nation, which was for him the cradle of Western civilization and the birthplace of its distinctive political institutions, literary techniques, and systems of myth. The sea that serves as a setting for so many Arabic modernist poems is thus a medium of translation in which foreign goods are traded for local manufacture. It is a site of entrepreneurial adventure and civilizational exchange.[83]

Al-Khal's translation of Jeffers's poem skillfully brings out these resonances. Here is the first stanza of "Night" in the original:

> The ebb slips from the rock, the sunken
> Tide-rocks lift streaming shoulders
> Out of the slack, the slow west
> Sombering its torch; a ship's light
> Shows faintly, far out,
> Over the weight of the prone ocean
> On the low cloud.

Al-Khal's translation rearranges the syntax, so that the ship's faint light [*daw' safina khafit*], the one human element in this twilit seascape, comes at the close of the stanza and acquires a more pointed brilliance. The following stanza's solemn apostrophe to the soul, "You like the ocean have grave depths [*aghwar*] where she [i.e., the night] dwells always," would have had peculiarly philosophical undertones for al-Khal's audience. Seven months previously, they had listened to Charles Malik's lecture, "*al-Wujud bi-l-fi'l*" [Active Existence], in which Malik spent several passages analyzing the word "*aghwar*," explaining that "the deep [*al-'umq*] cannot be known except in depth [*fi-l-'umq*]"—a tautology with a nicely Heideggerian ring that recalls the Psalmist's "deep calleth unto deep."[84]

The final stanza of Jeffers's poem carries presentiments of death, which it expresses through a maritime simile: "I and my people, we are willing to love the four-score years / Heartily; but as a sailor loves the sea, when the helm is for harbor." The lines urge an acceptance of contingency; our love of life must be tempered with the knowledge that, like any voyage, it will eventually come to an end. Al-Khal's translation is rather different. In the first place, it suppresses the conjunction "but," which removes any sense of apposition or qualification: we are to love life as heartily as sailors love the sea. This does not suggest an attitude of wisdom so much as a readiness for adventure. This interpretation is also suggested by al-Khal's word choices. Jeffers's "my people" is ambiguous between the intimate sense of "people who share my outlook on life" and the abstract sense of "mortals." Al-Khal's "*sha'bi*," on the other hand, is explicitly political. In the context of al-Khal's lecture, "*sha'b*" names a national community, a folk, as when at the end of the talk he argues as his fourth principle that Lebanese poetry must borrow its language from "the life of the people" [*hayat al-sha'b*].[85] This connotation, which makes Jeffers's sailors into an allegory for the nation, would not have seemed at all strange to an audience accustomed to thinking of the Lebanese as a historically "seafaring people."

Al-Khal's interpretation of the poem's last lines is even more pointed. Jeffers writes, "A few centuries / Gone by, was none dared not to people / The darkness beyond the stars with harps and habitations." This is an indictment of older superstitions about the cosmos, whether religious or secular, as complacently anthropocentric, turning the random scatter of stars into humanly meaningful constellations. True daring would be to resist anthropocentrism and grant that the universe has no particular message for us. This acknowledgment is fundamental to Jeffers's "inhumanism," with its "shifting of emphasis from man to not-man; the rejection of human solipsism and recognition of the transhuman magnificence."[86] Al-Khal either misses the double negative or, more likely, ignores it. His own version reads, "A few centuries gone by / no one dared / to people [or "colonize": *istitan*] the darkness beyond the stars." This is to turn Jeffers's meaning on its head. It suggests that the courage of modern thought is not to bid farewell to yesterday's mythology of harps and habitations, a phrase al-Khal suppresses entirely, but to press on into the unknown, like Saʿada's Phoenician colonists (or NASA). Al-Khal is equally adventuresome in his handling of the last two lines of "Night." Having moved beyond the old superstitions, Jeffers concludes, "But now, dear is the truth. Life is grown sweeter and lonelier, / And death is no evil." This is a stoic acknowledgment of the poet's mortality, his ultimate dissolution into the natural world. Viewed from this "inhuman" perspective, death is no evil, but neither is it good—it is simply the end. Al-Khal's translation inserts a line break after "truth" and suffixes that word with an unstoical exclamation mark. Jeffers's "dear" is rendered "*ma ahabba*" [how lovely], which sheds the English word's connotations of hard-earned experience and becomes a slogan for enlightenment: "How lovely is the truth!" In a similar vein, al-Khal renders "lonelier" as "*awhad*," a word that is ambiguous between "more solitary" and "more unique." So the melancholy of the original ending is brightened and solitude is tinted with heroism. Al-Khal's translation is, in other words, a strikingly unintuitive, personalist interpretation of Jeffers's poem.[87] In a virtuosic misreading, al-Khal converts Jeffers's bleak transhumanism into a parable of humanist fortitude set in a specifically Lebanese seascape. This makes it difficult to read the last line of the Arabic version—"And death is no evil"—as an acceptance of finality or cosmic reintegration. Al-Khal's choices as a translator, and indeed the whole trend of his argument, suggest that death is "no evil" because it heralds a new beginning. The ship's light in the first stanza, we realize in retrospect, was not faint because it was about to vanish, but because it was far away and coming closer: an approaching dawn after the west (or the West) has finally sombered its torch.

Jeffers's "Night" is not an obvious text to demonstrate the workings and attractions of modernist poetry. It is neither contemporary in its themes nor unconventional in its poetic techniques. Jeffers was notoriously anti-internationalist in politics, and his American readers certainly did not recognize his sensibility as modernist. In a famously critical review, Yvor Winters described Jeffers as an essentially "romantic" poet, whose deification of Nature was an unfortunate inheritance from Wordsworth.[88] In this sense, it is only al-Khal's resolutely unfaithful Arabic translation that qualifies as a modernist poem—a poem, moreover, crafted with a particular audience in mind: the intellectual and political elite of the Cénacle libanais. "Some works are created by their public," runs a famous aphorism of Valéry. "Other works create their public." Al-Khal's translation does both. It relies on his audience's recognition of certain tropes and narratives—the seascape, national rebirth, entrepreneurial and existential daring—while teaching his public to read these signs *as modernist*.

At the end of his lecture, al-Khal lists the ten principles he believes should guide the future of Lebanese poetry. These are concise restatements of the arguments of his lecture, written in the bulletin form of a manifesto. Principles six through nine are the most significant. Six affirms the personalist credo that "man" [*al-insan*] must be "the first and last subject" of poetry. Any poetry that does not place man at the heart of its practice—by substituting God, or nature, or a collective—is "shallow and artificial." The next principle advocated an awareness of the "spiritual-rational Arabic heritage," a remembrance, perhaps, of al-Khal's apprenticeship in Malik's AUB seminars. The eighth called for "a plunge into the spiritual-rational European heritage," a figure that looks forward to Noah's descent into the mud of creation, along with many other modernist katabases. Finally, al-Khal's ninth principle urged Lebanese poets "to benefit from the poetic experiences of literary writers of the world. For the modern Lebanese poet must not fall prey to the danger of isolationism, as the ancient Arab poets did with respect to Greek literature" (a reference to the lack of classical Arabic versions of Greek poetry, even as the works of Aristotle and Galen were endlessly translated and commented on).[89] These four principles of al-Khal's Cénacle lecture transform the mixed lexicon he inherited from Saʿada and Malik into an editorial policy for his modernist magazine. To place "man" at the vortex of foreign and domestic (inter- and intralinguistic) translation, with the aim of joining the ranks of world literature: such is the program of *Shiʿr*.

Translation as Origin

In his front-page editorial to the March 1956 issue of *al-Adab*, Editor in Chief Suhayl Idris noted that translation had become an issue for Arab intellectuals in a historically novel fashion.[90] Although modern Arab writers were not the first to translate works from abroad, the sheer quantity of foreign texts had become worrisome. Idris noted that translations were now "inundating the literary marketplace, so much so that during the past few years the ratio of original works to translated works is in absolute decline—a decline most striking in the recent Arabic-language production in Lebanon." Idris acknowledged that translations had the potential to enrich Arab readers' sensibilities and contribute to the renewal and development of culture. But he also cautioned that the objective conditions for this transmission did not yet exist. "There is no doubt that the tools of translation we now possess are not such as to make them consistently useful and fruitful. For we have very few translators with the proper skills and equipment: a technical proficiency in the foreign language, and an expertise in its linguistic and rhetorical depths to match their proficiency in the mother tongue." Idris recalled the proverbially free adaptations of the nineteenth century, characterized by their "excessive liberty" [*al-tasarruf*], and concluded by reminding his readers of the old chestnut, "*traduction-trahison*," whose political connotations were in this context particularly clear.

The *Shiʿr* poets displayed none of Idris's hesitancy toward translation, nor did they doubt their professional credentials. "Translation is part of *Shiʿr*'s mission," the editors wrote in the spring issue of 1962. "Through its translations, this magazine attempts to introduce the important works of world poetry to the Arabic reader. One of the magazine's priorities is to transmit this work in its original dynamism—the dynamism of content as well as form—with a view to the influence this type of translation may have in provoking a renaissance of Arabic poetry."[91] For the *Shiʿr* poets, importing foreign texts was one way to establish one's claim to be a modernist. Their advocacy of free trade in literary matters—al-Khal's principle of "anti-isolationism," with its roots in Malik's philosophical syllabus—did indeed expose the local field to an enormous "inundation" of foreign texts. And it was by way of these translations that they aimed to establish new sources of avowedly nonpolitical, cultural authority, along with new formal protocols and techniques.

The *Shiʿr* poets' insistent linkage of modernist poetry to acts of translation is their most Poundian inheritance. Jacques Amateis, al-Khal's biographer, suggests that Ezra Pound was "the most significant cultural influence on Yusuf al-Khal's literary and artistic character."[92] In some cases, this influence was direct and explicit. The second principle of al-Khal's Cénacle lecture, "the use of a lively image [*al-sura al-hayya*], whether objective or subjective, where the ancient poet used a simile or metaphor," is a restatement of Pound and F. S. Flint's first principle of imagism, viz., "Direct treatment of the 'thing,' whether objective or subjective." In other instances, Pound's inspiration was more diffuse. The American poet's intuition that the best way of making it new was to make it foreign, that literary innovation might result from an estrangement through ancient or "exotic" codes and structures, was consistently instructive for the Beiruti poets. This lesson is strongly felt in the inaugural issue of *Shiʿr* in 1957, which features two significant translations from the English: a short text by the American poet Archibald MacLeish and Yusuf al-Khal's version of Pound's first canto.[93] Canto I is, of course, already a translation, being an English (or neo-Anglo-Saxon) version of Andreas Divus's Latin translation of *The Odyssey*'s *Nekuia*, a narrative of Odysseus's trip to the underworld that Pound believed to be older than the rest of the poem. The translation of a translation of a translation, al-Khal's Arabic text asks to be a read as a charter statement for his modernist magazine. His version of Pound-Divus-Homer suggests that modernism is itself a movement in translation, which establishes its peculiar authority through feats of importation and exchange.

Al-Khal sets his course as a translator by the standard of fidelity. In the commentary he appends to his translation, al-Khal describes his version as being "without any *tasarruf*"—that is, without excessive liberties or alterations. This was a consistent principle of al-Khal's professionalist approach to *naql*. In his introduction to the anthology of poems by T. S. Eliot, translated by multiple hands, he writes, "Our one concern is a commitment to reliability and precision."[94] Fidelity and precision are relative virtues, of course, as evidenced by al-Khal's version of Jeffers's "Night." By comparison with previous generations of Arab translators, however, who habitually embellished and transformed their source texts, al-Khal's translation tracks the English version quite closely, though he does not attempt to reproduce Pound's archaicisms ("ell-square pitkin," "dreory arms," and "bloody bever" are all rendered into a contemporary idiom), nor does he follow the original's exaggerated enjambments or dangled phrases ("since toils urged other" has no Arabic equivalent at all).[95] Perhaps the most striking feature of al-Khal's lack of *tasarruf* is his decision to transliterate, rather than translate, the series of Latin phrases that end Pound's poem. "Venerandam," "Cypri monumenta sortita est," and "orichalchi," phrases that Pound takes from a Middle Latin translation of the Second Hymn to Aphrodite, are all rendered into homophones in Arabic script. This kind of metaphrasis points to Beiruti modernism's characteristic combination of fidelity to the foreign original with an estrangement from contemporary norms in Arabic.[96]

Al-Khal's fidelity to Pound went beyond translation in the technical sense of the word. From his critical and poetic writings, it is clear he also took Pound as a kind of life model. In the note to his translation of Canto I, al-Khal mentions Pound's "renunciation" of his homeland, his life abroad, his anti-Romanticism, his "musical" rather than merely formal championing of *vers libre*, and his ambition, in the *Cantos*, to tell "the truth of history" rather than repeat the officially sanctioned version. The autobiographical tenor of all this is striking. Al-Khal also mentions, not incidentally, Pound's "encouragement of the American poet Harriet Monroe to establish *Poetry*," the magazine from which *Shi'r* took its name.[97] And al-Khal's loyalty to Pound went deeper than this. In an editorial he wrote for the daily *al-Nahar* in January 1956, Al-Khal called for Pound's release from St. Elizabeths Hospital, a controversy that Lebanese readers were unlikely to have followed very closely. Finally, in "To Ezra Pound," the opening poem of his 1958 collection, *al-Bi'r al-mahjura* [The Abandoned Well], al-Khal figures Pound as a suffering Christ to whom the speaker promises new life (another example of al-Khal's conflation of poet and martyr). The closing lines of al-Khal's dedicatory poem go so far as to imitate Pound's anti-Semitism, though in a traditionally Christian register, while also suggesting translation as an act of redemptive transmission: "If the Jews crucified you there / then you shall be resurrected here." Typically, al-Khal's fidelity to a prior model of modernism is framed as a return to more ancient sources: his imitation of Pound translates the American poet as an *imitatio Christi*.[98]

Al-Khal's translation of Pound also left its mark on the poetry he wrote and published in the early issues of *Shiʿr*. This is worth noting, if only to provide a first instance of how the modernists' translations re-echoed in their "originals," rendering that conventional distinction problematic. Al-Khal was a more imaginative editor than he was a poet. His verse tends to exemplify his critical and ideological beliefs, often crudely. But the poems are nevertheless valuable for just these programmatic qualities. In the note that follows his Arabic version, al-Khal argues that Pound's first canto establishes "the axis on which the *Cantos*' themes will pivot" and identifies these themes as "the sea voyage, the conversation with the dead, and the three ages: the classical, the Renaissance [*al-nahda*], and the present." Al-Khal's best-known sea-poem hews very closely to the patterns he identifies in Pound.

"*Nida' al-bahr*" [The Call of the Sea] is a trilogy consisting of "*al-Duʿa'*" [The Call], "*al-Safar*" [The Voyage], and "*al-ʿAwda*" [The Return]. The second and third sections of this poem were published in *Shiʿr* in the summer and fall issues of 1957—that is, immediately following the translation of Pound—and the trilogy is the final sequence of *The Abandoned Well*. The opening poem is written in the first-person plural and evokes an anonymous collective stranded in a desert landscape of ruins, dust, and sun. The poem sketches a movement of reorientation, away from exile in the land of the dead and toward the sea, a topos of salvation and origins. The poems opens, "And we turned our faces: the sun was / dust on the boats, and the horizon / a broken sail." The initial conjunction (*wa*) is significant in several ways. To begin the narrative in medias res signals not only the movement of reorientation to follow but markedly follows the opening line of Canto I, "And then went down to the ship." In fact, each poem of al-Khal's trilogy begins with "*wa*"—a provocative *incipit* for a poem in Arabic—and the second poem, "The Voyage," opens with a line whose echoes are explicit: "*Wa fi-l-nahar nahbut al-marafiʾ al-amana*" [And by day we go down to the ports of safety]. (*Habata*, "to go down," is the verb al-Khal uses to translate Pound's first line: "*Wa idhdhaka habatna ila-l-safina*.") Al-Khal's trilogy is in this sense a re-sounding of the Poundian katabasis. The dead it carries up into the light are the spirits of modernism.[99]

"The Voyage" is the central poem of the trilogy and worth quoting at some length:

> And by day we go down to the ports of safety,
> to the boats with sails unfurled for travel.
> We call out, O our beloved sea, O
> near one, as near as our lids to our eyes,
> we come alone.
> Our companions behind those mountains chose
> to remain sleeping while we chose to travel.
> Here, the shepherds told us
> of distant islands yearning for danger,
> despising rest or caution,
> of islands that battle fate
> and sow teeth to make cities in the waste:
> letters of light that write the tale
> and fill the eyes with light,
> by whose dazzling color
> old men dream of youth.
>
> So we board the ships carrying
> glass and pine wood, carrying silk
> and wine from our country, carrying fruit.
> We shout, O boats!
> O rising ladder
> linking us with those we are not,
> bringing us precious things
> and taking sweet things from us.

As in "The Call," the first poem of the trilogy, the Syrian interior beyond the mountains is a place of stagnation, slumber, and ingrown fatalism: in other words, an Orientalist stereotype of the East. The sea, on the contrary, is a free-trade zone for adventure and encounter with others. It is also a space of origins, a cradle of cities, alphabets, and civilization itself. This idea of the Levant as the birthplace of ancient learning and mythology occurs again in the final stanza of the "The Voyage" when, before the raising of anchors, sheep are slaughtered on the shore, as they are prior to Ulysses' colloquy with the dead in Homer's *Nekuia*: "One for Ashtarut, one for Adonis, / one for Ba'al." The third, concluding portion of the poem, "The Return," is a monologue spoken by the Ashtarut herself—the goddess of war and fertility first named in the Ugaritic texts whose major centers of worship were the Lebanese port cities of Sidon, Tyre, and Byblos. She looks forward to the return of her lover Adonis/Tammuz, "His sail like a white cloud at evening," bearing foreign gold, ivory and jewels. Al-Khal's trilogy is, in other words, a Phoenician fantasy that recalls the nostalgic fictions indulged at the Cénacle. At a time when Lebanon's economy was becoming more and more dependent on the international banking and service sectors, primarily to handle oil profits made in the Gulf countries, his sailors still trade the silk, glass, wood, and wine of an older economic era—older even than the *Odyssey*.

All newness needs sanction. Just as Saʿada discovered a Syrian nationalist pantheon in Raʾs Shamra that predated all Western mythologies, so al-Khal's sea-poem plunges past its modernist and classical intertexts to identify with an even more ancient (but neglected) local tradition. Al-Khal's version of Pound's version of Homer in the first issue of *Shiʿr* is not only a translation of American modernism and the ur-text of the Western canon. It is also a translation, like his version of Jeffers's "Night," that anchors foreign texts within a local imaginary—the cultural Phoenicianism that explains and conditions the genre of the sea-poem. In this way, the act of translation imports new and foreign sources of literary authority while investing them with the prestige of an indigenous antiquity. For al-Khal and the other Beiruti modernists, the translator's voyage out is also "the way back."[100]

The second translation in the inaugural issue of *Shiʿr* proposes a distinct though ultimately complementary notion of what *naql* does. The opening pages feature a short, untitled text in Arabic attributed to the American poet Archibald MacLeish.[101] The placement of the text before the issue's title page, as well as its declaratory tone, suggest its purpose as a manifesto for the new magazine. This is in itself an extraordinary choice, signaling the paramount role that translation would play in the *Shiʿr* group's self-conception and suggesting that its mission as a magazine was in some sense authorized by acts of importation. Indeed, the formal fact of its being a translated text written by Archibald MacLeish is in many ways more striking than what it says.

The text begins with a stock figure in the modernist discourse of crisis, "an anxious and troubled generation" for whom poetry holds little interest. The real problem is not generational, however, but rather economic and existential. "The enduring core" of the crisis, writes MacLeish, is the result of "standardization," a midcentury trope for Weberian rationalization, along with its corollary, the emptying out of "the singular and urgent experience of life." MacLeish goes on to argue, like Spender and any number of late modernists, that poetry is precisely what grants the individual access to unstandardized, personal experience. Poetry is a method of self-knowledge more immediate than sociological statistics or the generalizations of philosophy. Individual experience is, in this account, both the source of literary authority and its proper subject. The antagonist of this mild-mannered polemic is a familiar one: the standardized aesthetic of Second World countries where anonymous collectives and tyrannical states coerce artists into making propaganda instead of poetry. This Cold War commonplace, which al-Khal shared with the artists of the CCF and many other late modernists, is laid out in the text's final paragraph, which contains the clearest statement of what would become the principle of *Shiʿr*'s editorial policy, one that distinguished the magazine from its contemporary rivals in the region: "It is not necessary for those who practice the art of poetry in a time such as ours to write political poetry, or to attempt to solve the problems of the age with their poems; they must rather practice their art for its own ends and according to its own requirements."

If MacLeish's text is an undistinguished specimen of late modernist argument, al-Khal's decision to place it on the front page of his new magazine is a significant choice. The most obvious question is, why MacLeish? Like Robinson Jeffers, MacLeish would have been unknown to Arab readers. There were no translations of him into Arabic before al-Khal included two poems in his *Anthology of American Poetry*, published by Dar Majallat Shiʿr in 1958. But MacLeish was hardly an obscure figure. On the contrary, he was a writer of tremendous institutional authority—a type of that midcentury species Evan Kindley has called "poet-administrators"—and certainly the most decorated American poet of his time (and perhaps any other).[102] Since MacLeish is not much read now, outside his much-anthologized poem "Ars Poetica," it is worth recalling the imposing particulars of his curriculum vitae: a friend of Hemingway, Dos Passos, and Fitzgerald in Paris in the 1920s, he was appointed librarian of Congress in 1939 by Roosevelt, went on to become assistant secretary of state, president of the American Academy of Arts and Letters, Boylston Professor of Rhetoric and Oratory at Harvard, a speechwriter for Adlai Stevenson, winner of three Pulitzer Prizes (two for his poetry) and a National Book Award, the Bollingen Prize, a Tony Award (for his Broadway play, *J. B.*), an Academy Award (for his screenplay of *The Eleanor Roosevelt Story*), and a Presidential Medal of Freedom. In his prose essays after the war, MacLeish worked to canonize the modernism of Pound, Eliot, and Yeats in part by rejecting political readings of their work. In his dialogue, *Poetry and Opinion*, MacLeish intervened in the debate over the 1949 Bollingen Prize by arguing on Pound's behalf, in typically late modernist fashion, for the separation of politics and poetry (though MacLeish had made a name for himself in the late 1930s precisely for advocating a public-spirited, not to say *engagé* poetics). But it was his institutional credentials that made MacLeish especially effective in securing Pound's release from St. Elizabeths in 1958, in part by drafting a letter of support signed by Frost, Eliot, and Hemingway and delivered to the US attorney general by Guy Davenport.[103]

MacLeish's institutional authority also explains some of his appeal to Yusuf al-Khal, whose literary career shows a talent for affiliating himself with powerful political figures, from Malik and the Cénacle to MacLeish and the CCF. "It often seemed to me," Adonis writes cuttingly but accurately of al-Khal in his memoir of the period, "that his primary passion was to make institutions [*yuʾassis*], and that his interest in establishing institutional strictures was greater than his interest in writing poems."[104] It is, of course, precisely al-Khal's talent for establishing institutions—magazines, galleries, and publishing houses—that made him an especially attractive interlocutor for John Hunt and his allies. Under al-Khal's editorship, *Shiʿr* never showed much interest in MacLeish's American contemporaries in the Black Mountain or New York schools, though the former were the most explicitly Poundian of all the midcentury groupings, and it was not until the late 1960s that the Beiruti magazine published a selection of the Beats. In this light, MacLeish's status as a tutelary spirit for *Shiʿr* becomes a vivid index of the movement's professionalist ambitions: the Arab modernists did not seek, in the way of historical avant-gardes, to break down the wall between art and life, nor to sublimate one into the other.[105] Instead, they sought to establish an institution. MacLeish, like his British counterpart Stephen Spender, represented a powerful link to the heroic modernism of the early twentieth century, whose energies he helped codify. Al-Khal was also alert to the ways in which MacLeish's own poetry rhymed with late modernist themes, particularly the trope of man. "Brave New World," one of the two poems by MacLeish that al-Khal translated for his *Anthology of American Poetry* (the other is "The End of the World"), is an apostrophe to Thomas Jefferson that echoes the discourse of Malik and other militant liberals while yoking it to a conventional rhetoric of novelty: "There was a time when tyrants feared / The new world of the free. / Now freedom is afraid and shrieks / At tyranny.... What's changed is freedom in this age. / What great men dared to choose / Small men now dare neither win / Nor lose."

Perhaps more striking than its author is the fact that the inaugural text of *Shiʿr* is a *naql:* a manifesto in and for translation. It is a choice that testifies to al-Khal's shrewd assessment of the local literary landscape and the opportunities it offered for establishing a new review. With its first issue, *Shiʿr* entered a literary field that was highly differentiated in ideological terms. Pan-Arabist, Marxist, and Lebanese nationalist magazines already filled the kiosks of Ra's Beirut. *Sawt al-Ajyal* [The Voice of Generations], a monthly edited by the father of Unsi al-Hajj, represented the SSNP. *Shiʿr* distinguished itself by devoting its pages exclusively to poetry—to professional poetry one might say—and by refusing to be identified with any party or sect. MacLeish's assertion that it is simply "not necessary" to write political poetry put into question the principles of the field itself. In this sense, Suhayl Idris's worry about the effect an "inundation" of translations would have on contemporary Arabic literature was justified: translations changed the rules of engagement. Here again, Arabic modernism's openness to world literature and its doctrine of literary autonomy function, somewhat paradoxically, as two sides of the same program: poetic self-sufficiency is secured by the *naql* of new authorities.

MacLeish's manifesto in *Shiʿr* is not accompanied by any commentary or contributor note. Nor is there any indication of a source for the text—or even a translator, though it is safe to suppose that it was al-Khal himself. It is as though MacLeish himself wrote the text in Arabic or as if, in elaborating his thoughts on the person as a "solitary being," he was ventriloquizing the philosophy of Charles Malik. MacLeish's cultural authority goes unremarked in the pages of *Shiʿr*. Instead, the American poet, translated here for the first time into Arabic, is simply presented as a porte-parole for the universal ideology of modernism, a movement of individuals floating free of past affiliations, whether political, sectarian, or otherwise. Al-Khal's selection and translation of MacLeish's manifesto is in this sense very similar to his use of Jeffers's "Night." Manifesto and poem are abstracted from their place in the authors' oeuvre and presented as purely modernist texts or, more complexly, as texts that will exemplify for Arab readers what "modernism" means. For al-Khal, translation is this act of abstraction, alteration, and re-authorization. With the publication of his magazine's first issue, the modernist program was complete, though the arguments were just beginning.

Appendix #1: Archibald MacLeish's text for Shiʿr *(Winter 1957)*

There clearly exists a widespread opinion that poetry, whatever it was in the past, is not today a principal object of interest to a troubled and anxious generation. But the truth, as far as I am concerned, is just the opposite.

The relation of poetry to life is the one described by Aristotle and repeated by Wordsworth, even if somewhat differently. That is, poetry is a means to knowledge of a certain kind. For Aristotle, it is a means to reveal the harmony of life. For Wordsworth, it is a method of sensual perception, able to transmit the truth, "truth, not individual and local, but general, and operative . . . carried alive into the heart by passion." Until the psychologists prove their claims, poetry remains the only method by which man—as an individual [*ka-fard*], as a person [*ka-shakhs*], as a solitary being who must rely on himself in all that confronts him—is able to understand his experience and know himself. Religion, for those who have religion, may reveal the causes behind the causes; ethics and philosophy may impose their generalizations; but poetry alone allows the individual, as a man, to enter directly into the singular and urgent experience of life.

The enduring core of our ever-changing crisis is the problem of the individual human being in a world that grows increasingly standardized. In a time such as this, the importance of poetry is necessarily greater. It is greater, at least, for those who believe and hope to establish a society based on the individual life [*al-haya al-fardiyya*]—in other words, on this life, for it is the only one there is. There is nothing more essential to the establishment of such a society than to make real the truth of this direct, personal relation to life and to experience—the life of man and the experience of man, each peculiar to him. This is the relation true individualism is based upon. So long as man's notions are not peculiar to himself and connected to his own experience of life, then there is no life for him except by way of others. And in that case, he does not possess himself, for he has no self.

It is not necessary for those who practice the art of poetry in a time such as ours to write political poetry, or to attempt to solve the problems of the age with their poems; they must rather practice their art for its own ends and according to its own requirements, knowing that by way of their art they have touched on the life of some here and now and in the past, and may do so again in the future.

CHAPTER THREE

Figuration and Disfiguration in *The Songs of Mihyar the Damascene*

Against Inwardness

Of all the figures produced by the Arab modernists, it is Mihyar, the gloomy, many-sided hero of Adonis's *Aghani Mihyar al-Dimashqi* [*The Songs of Mihyar the Damascene*], who most powerfully represents the *Shi'r* poets' conception of man. *The Songs of Mihyar*, published in 1961, has always been recognized as crucial to Adonis's poetic itinerary—"the initial, definitive disruption," in the words of his English translators—as well as the *Shi'r* movement more generally.[1] In many accounts, this book is the turning point between Adonis's apprenticeship in the mythic methods of the Tammuzi school and his own mature poetry, between a dependence on models of Near Eastern legend and his own mythology of *al-insan* (the human being). This reading was programmed early on in the critical reception of Adonis. As the young Syrian philosopher Adel Daher put it, writing in the pages of *Shi'r* soon after the collection's publication, "I do not hesitate to say that *The Songs of Mihyar the Damascene* is a new experiment in the manufacture of man" [*tajriba jadida fi san' al-insan*].[2]

"Man" would seem to be a theme for rhetoricians and philosophers rather than poets. Only a stereotypical versifier of the age of Eisenhower—the pipe-smoking, professorial master of ceremonies—would attempt to make lyrics out of such ponderous abstractions. "What great men dared to choose / Small men now dare neither win / Nor lose." It is precisely because of such sententiousness that "the poetry of the fifties" has become a catchphrase for official culture of the most wearisome sort. But Beiruti modernism is, in its origins, a poetry of the fifties. The movement's interest stems from its untimeliness, and its situation on the edge of the modernist heartlands. In the Arab poets' work, the figure of man becomes surprisingly fruitful (just as liberalism becomes surprisingly radical). The *Shiʿr* group insisted on its contemporaneity with poetry movements in Europe and the Americas, but it emerged at a moment when modernist verse in those places was being put into museums and university syllabuses, when its disruptive energies were being integrated into the *longue durée* of humanistic culture as a phase of "revolutionary traditionalism," in Spender's memorable oxymoron. The Arab poets took advantage of the local opportunities that modernist novelties offered, even as those opportunities were steadily closing off elsewhere. They made lyrics out of conceptual universals and translated the politics of Cold War liberalism into a transformational poetics; they refused to write poems full of local color and wrested themselves away from the particularism of the nationalist imaginary. As a result, the Beiruti poets' characteristic works are unnervingly abstract. They seem to obey a taboo on particulars of any sort, turning each poem into a stained-glass landscape of allegorical signifiers.

It is not surprising therefore that one of the poets' most enduring tropes, *man* or *the person*, is originally a philosophical figure. "To say that man is a *person* is to acknowledge his status as a subject, a center of perspective, and not an object among other objects," explains the French-speaking philosopher René Habachi, a consistent ally of the *Shiʿr* movement, in his address to the Cénacle libanais in 1960. Habachi's philosophy sought to reconcile Marxism and existentialism by insisting on the notion of freedom-through-labor, what Habachi called "transcendence": "This transcendence is that of a new world, that of human interiority—the inside [*ce dedans*] that constitutes our inviolable intimacy ... an inalienable inside that opens out of itself toward the truth, refusing any violent imposition from the outside [*dehors*]."[3] This personalist rhetoric of novelty, subjectivity, transcendence, and interiority provides the *Shiʿr* poets, and Adonis in particular, with the basic elements of a lyric poetics. Habachi's formulations are close to those of Charles Malik and many other spiritualist philosophers of the midcentury, who sought to secure a refuge for human agency in a world they perceived as growing ever more unfree (including in the capitalist West). The Arab modernists actively conflated poetic and philosophical vocabularies, a habit traceable to Antun Saʿada, for whom Germanic legends belong to world literature rather than local folklore precisely because of their "philosophical coloring." But what does a poetry of man sound like? How does it reconcile a liberal commitment to philosophical universals with lyric poetry's pull toward the particular?

The theme of man is announced at the outset of *The Songs of Mihyar*. The collection's epigraph translates a line from a late fragment of Hölderlin, "Warum, o schöne Sonne, genügst du mir?" [Why do you not suffice me, beautiful sun?], and then swerves dramatically away from the German original: *"Wa fajʾatan yaʾti, yasqut alayna al-muqiz / al-gharib / al-sawt al-ladhi yakhluq al-nas"* [And suddenly he comes, falling upon us, the strange awakener, the voice that creates mankind]. This is the first evocation we have of Mihyar the Damascene: a substitute for the sun, a mixture of the translated and the transcendent, of citation and invention, at once *homo faber* and *faber hominis*. The opening section of the book, "The Knight of Strange Words," fills in this sketch. As with the other six sections of the book except for the last, it begins with a prose text that Adonis calls a *mazmur* or "psalm." The first "Psalm" is a solemn evocation of Mihyar, still unnamed, but conjured up through a series of dynamic verbs: he *approaches*, *names*, *knows*, and *transforms*; he is said to "peel man like an onion" and to "create his genus, beginning with himself." The characteristic features of this genus, of which Mihyar is the original and perhaps solitary species, are enumerated in another poem of the collection's opening section, "*al-'Ahd al-jadid*" [The New Covenant], a ritualistic eulogy of the hero:

> He does not know how to speak this speech.
> He does not know the voice of deserts.
> For he is a seer, stony-slumbered.
> For he is freighted with far-off tongues.
>
> There he is, advancing under the ruins
> in a climate of new letters,
> offering his poetry to the melancholy winds,
> rough and enchanting like brass.
>
> For he is a tongue roiling among the masts.
> For he is the knight of strange words.[4]

Like many modernist poems, the geography of "The New Covenant" is split between sand and sea, between "the deserts" [*al-barari*] of the present and "the masts" [*al-sawari*] that beckon. As many critics have noted, Adonis's hero shares his name with Mihyar al-Daylami, an eleventh-century Zoroastrian convert to Shiism best known for his elegies to 'Ali, Husayn, and his mentor, the great Shia poet al-Sharif al-Radi. Perhaps the most memorable anecdote about al-Daylami is the quip of Sunni enemies that his conversion only guaranteed that he would be moved from one corner of hell to another. Adonis's poetry is a dense tissue of allusions, and so it is tempting to read "Mihyar" as a persona or mask (in Arabic, *qina'*) that figures an estrangement from one's native place and traditions.[5] Indeed, Adonis consistently presents Mihyar as a poet whose marginality is an index of his originality. Mihyar's ignorance of "this speech"—that is, "the voice of the deserts"—is a sign of his vocation; aphasia is a symptom of true poethood. In "*al-Sadafa*" [The Seashell], Mihyar declares, "I do not fear the way of muteness for I am a hot wind, / I am the seashell."

Mihyar is also a figure of extreme solitude. Unlike many poetic questers, he has no companions, nor is he tempted by any spirit of *eros* (it is not often noted how essentially innocent these songs are). Throughout *The Songs of Mihyar*, the hero's solitude is coupled with tropes of inwardness, such as the seashell. "He hides himself in the waves, among seashells," is one of the first images we have of Mihyar. Another figure of involution is the snail: "We live in the folds of the city, / like snails behind their shell." The running tropes of despair [*al-ya's*] and melancholy [*al-ka'aba*], which I will come back to later in the chapter, also seem to be symptoms of inwardness. Certainly the "melancholy winds" to which Mihyar bequeaths his poetry in "The New Covenant" are a kind of microclimate, fencing him off from others as definitively as his inability to speak their tongue. At other moments in the text, Mihyar is more declarative. "I erase the traces and stains of my inside" [*dakhili*], he says in the second "Psalm," prefiguring many disfigurations to come. "I wash my inside, keeping it empty and clean. In this way, underneath myself, I live." Or again, in a resonant phrase that returns us to our original subject: "I dwell in the seashells of dream, I announce the interior man" [*al-insan al-dakhil*].[6] In other words, Mihyar is less the persona of some historical figure such as Mihyar al-Daylami than he is a persona of the person, a mask of Man.

Adonis's yoking together of the figure of man with a rhetoric of interiority determined much of his collection's critical reception, which dutifully repeats the tropes of the poems. An early response in the pages of *Shi'r* by Halim Barakat, who went on to become a well-known novelist, casts Adonis as a successor to the *mahjar* school.[7] But while the older generation of émigré poets supposed that "heroism consisted in calling for a voyage across the earth's surfaces," Adonis sets his contemporaries a "deeper and more difficult task": namely, "voyages into the interior" [*al-sufur fi-l-dakhil*]. In the next issue, Adel Daher, a doctoral student in philosophy at New York University, gave Adonis's collection a self-consciously philosophical reading. Daher argues that the "adventure" of Mihyar dramatizes "a return to the self," which he links to Husserl's dictum, "*zurück zu den Sachen selbst*," a return to the things themselves, interpreted as a call to return to "the private and the concrete." Daher figures this return to the self as "an act of folding inward," a liberation from both the chains of the past and the "tyranny of the collective." The liberated subject is likened to the Leibnizian monad, governed by "laws particular to the self," which Daher opposes to the "mass-man" of Ortega y Gasset. In this way, Mihyar becomes a philosopher among philosophers, a translator for the tenets of personalism:

> From the moment Mihyar recognizes this generalized man, he turns away from him: "He recognized the others / so threw a stone upon them and turned away" ("*al-Akharin*"). Where did he turn toward? He turned toward the self, an introversion, a form of personalist spelunking [*istighwar tashakhusni*]. Indeed, Mihyar ... dives into his interior: he defines his relation to the outer world and understands

his historical condition not according to any ready-made givens, or to any truths except those he discovers inside himself. He does all this in a place apart from generalized man: "Nothing binds us together, and everything divides us," Mihyar tells us ("Psalm").[8]

The early interpretations of Barakat and Daher, which link the figure of *al-insan* to a discourse of inwardness, autonomy, and subjectivity, have influenced later writings on Adonis and the *Shiʿr* movement. Dounia Badini's recent study, *La Revue* Shiʿr / *Poésie et la modernité poétique arabe*, is the most comprehensive examination of the *Shiʿr* poets to date, but one that often takes the modernists' declarations at face value. Badini, like Barakat and Daher, supposes that what is at stake in the figure of man is "subjective experience," expressive of "poetry's orientation toward the *interior space [l'espace du Dedans]*." She returns to this trope, borrowed from Henri Michaux, at the close of her study, in an effort to summarize what she takes to be the key innovation of the *Shiʿr* poets: "If one searches, despite everything, to find a sort of thematic unity that transcends diversity, it would reside in that obsessive quest for the *interior space*, in opposition to an exterior space, in other words a collective space, which has for a long time oppressed the poet and limited his creativity."[9]

Arabic modernism is hardly the first modernist movement to be canonized for its ostensible turn toward the self. Fredric Jameson has argued that "a thematics of subjectivity tend illicitly to contaminate 'theories' of modernity," and that "older ideologies of the modern have been misleading in their insistence on some 'inward turn' of the modern or on its increasing subjectivization of reality." Against this putative orientation toward *l'espace du dedans*, or indeed a discovery of the unconscious, Jameson suggests that modernist texts be read instead as symptoms of "an apocalyptic dissatisfaction with subjectivity" or even a "longing for depersonalization."[10] For Jameson, who draws his references from late-nineteenth and early-twentieth century European and American modernisms, this dissatisfaction is symptomatic of a crisis in bourgeois subjectivity. Rilke's Delphic admonition, "You must change your life," is not to be understood as an ethical directive aimed at the individual subject but as a slogan of utopian transformation, paralleled in Jameson's account by Rimbaud's "*Je est un autre*." Mihyar does not exemplify a crisis in subjectivity so much as he does Beiruti modernism's struggle to achieve, for the first time in Arabic letters, a particular kind of lyric subjectivity. Mihyar is Adonis's most powerful attempt to establish the authority of an autonomous individual called "*al-insan*"—a figure unsanctioned by any collective and which acquires its legitimacy from exclusively literary sources.

The struggle for autonomy is never conclusive, however. Its texts inevitably bear some trace of the effort spent to pry them free of their historical occasions. This chapter tracks the emergence of Mihyar, the persona of personhood, from its origins in political militancy into a liberal poetics of autonomy.

In this sense, the narrative has the same endpoints as the story told in the previous chapter of Yusuf al-Khal, in which a modernist cultural program is salvaged from the shipwreck of nationalist politics. Here the narrative is not an intellectual genealogy but rather follows the logic of literary forms and figures—an approach meant to suggest the potential of an alliance between intellectual history and formalist poetry criticism. I try to explain how collective defeat and the subsequent renunciation of political activity left its mark on a poetics that is avowedly "nonpartisan," abstract, and universal. Following Jameson, I argue that Mihyar's "turn" is not to be conceived of as a turn *inward* but rather as a series of *turns away*—first of all, from the commitment to nationalism. I will even suggest that the figure of apostrophe or the Arabic *iltifat*, both words meaning "a turn away," is the central trope in Adonis's canonical collection. While the turn inward is supposed to establish a new kind of subjectivity or person, Adonis's apostrophes enact a drama of displacement and disfiguration. The first and in some ways most significant turn away is from Damascus itself, Mihyar's native place, the Syrian capital that Adonis in his memoir calls "a city of endings."

The Road from Damascus

The Songs of Mihyar the Damascene was published in 1961, the same year Adonis formally resigned from the SSNP.[11] Adonis's membership in Antun Sa'ada's party began when he was a schoolboy in Tartus, and he was by his own account "a very active member."[12] Adonis's earliest poems, written in the late 1940s and early 1950s, are essentially national allegories, written in response to Sa'ada's demand for a distinctively Syrian literature based on indigenous myths. In *The Intellectual Struggle*, Sa'ada faulted the Maronite poet Sa'id 'Aql for the "narrow localism" of his retellings of biblical and Canaanite stories, advocating a philosophical approach that would launch Syrian poetry into the ranks world literature. Adonis's early poems try to match the mythic ambitions of 'Aql's *Qadmus* while transcending his stubbornly Lebanese, and therefore parochial, frame of reference. In his long poem, "Delilah," published in 1950, Adonis retells the Old Testament story but makes the Philistine Delilah the protagonist of the myth—in his introduction to the poem he calls her "a Syrian nationalist heroine"—while Samson is cast as a Jewish villain who takes violent advantage of his Syrian hosts' hospitality. (The poem is clearly a response to the *Nakba* of 1948: for the SSNP, Palestinians were a "southern Syrian" community.)[13] Four years later, Adonis published another long poem, "The Earth Spoke," which was dedicated to Sa'ada and transforms the party chief, executed in 1949, into a mythical martyr figure in his own right. Written in the persona of the Syrian earth, the poem is an elegiac variant of the national allegory: it does not narrate the emergence of a national community so much as it laments the loss of one and looks forward to its future resurrection. Syria is represented as being in exile from herself, the present wasteland counterpoised against a past abundance: "What is it that I awake to—my meadows without blooms, my hills without flowers? / The guardians of my vineyards do not keep company with the stars, nor do lights play in the eyes. / I am a hidden treasure: where are my sons?"[14] Adonis has never permitted the republication of his early nationalist poetry, or else—as in the case of "The Earth Spoke"—he has republished selected fragments that often transform the original in dramatic fashion. While Saʿada is explicitly the elegiac subject of "The Earth Spoke," the figure of the leader was excised from all later editions of the poem, an excision that is symptomatic of Adonis's attitude toward his political past, which is consistently repressed and just as persistently returns.

In the spring of 1955, a year after receiving an undergraduate degree in philosophy from the Syrian University in Damascus, Adonis was arrested during a roundup of party members following the assassination of Colonel ʿAdnan Malki, a charismatic army officer, by a member of the SSNP. The assassination and its aftermath was a turning point in the history of the party in Syria. In the words of a party historian, "Malki's assassination was seized upon by the leftist elements in the army, as well as by the Baath, as the opportunity *par excellence* to liquidate the SSNP as a political force."[15] The repercussions were also severe for Adonis. "The accused were arrested, persecuted, and removed from their jobs," he later recalled in an interview. "I spent eleven months in prison. A year of torture, a true hell. I believed that a country governed in such a way must be very close to the abyss, and that I had to get out." It was not only his treatment in prison that convinced Adonis to quit Syria. The regime was also asserting its power over the cultural field, making it impossible to be the sort of poet that Adonis aspired to become. "The dictatorship in Syria went beyond the political realm to fasten its grip on all aspects of social and cultural life. I remember those masses of French books that they piled up in the courtyards and then burned as a sign of their refusal of the other," he says in the same interview. Adonis arrived in Beirut in the fall of 1956, finding that "Lebanon offered, in effect, more openness and more liberty."[16]

Adonis has told the story of this migration from Damascus to Beirut many times, in different registers. In his 1993 memoir, *There You Are, O Time*, the journey out of Syria becomes a narrative of rebirth, an emigration from the closed world of primitive politics into the city of modern things and ways of being. In chapter 5 we will see how another version of this topography anchors Adonis's long poem "*al-Saqr*" [The Hawk], whose hero is ʿAbd al-Rahman, the exiled Umayyad prince who fled Damascus in 750 and traveled west to establish the emirate of Cordoba. *The Songs of Mihyar* stakes out this territory for the first time. It establishes a geography of exile, assigning specific yet durable structures of feeling to the various topoi named in the poems. Mapping out this terrain, or at least its borders and central nodes, will allow us to better recognize the routes that run through it.

"Damascus" as a proper noun appears only once, and rather pointedly, in *The Songs of Mihyar*. This hapax occurs in the poem *"Watan"* [Homeland]:

> To faces drying out behind masks of melancholy,
> I bow. To roads where I left tears
> for a father—dead, green as a cloud,
> sail-faced—
> I bow. To a child sold
> so that he might pray, so that he might shine shoes
> (all of us in my country pray, all of us shine shoes),
> and to a stone on which I wrote, with my hunger,
> that it is the rain rolling down, that it is the lightning,
> and to a home [*bayt*] whose soil I carried [*naqaltu*] with me in my ribs,
> I bow. All this is my homeland, not Damascus.

Damascus is named only in the negative. The topos is marked as taboo, as if in obeisance to the Orphic or modernist injunction, "Don't look back." And Mihyar never does. "Where were you?" someone asks in *"Hiwar"* [Dialogue]. "I did not answer her," says Mihyar. "I did not know the word." This suggests that "Mihyar the Damascene" is a kind of misnomer or identity *sous rature*.[17] Mihyar repeatedly refuses his origins and embraces his exile. "He is the wind that doesn't retreat, the water that doesn't return to its source," the first "Psalm" intones. "He has no ancestors, and in his footsteps are his roots." In Adonis's early verse, exile is a historical condition in which the nation is estranged from its own deep past. In "Homeland," however, exile becomes a metaphysical identity as well as a source of poetic creativity. A conventional pun in the penultimate line allows us to read *"bayt"* as both "home" and "line of verse" and suggests that Mihyar's exile from Damascus is an immigration into poetry, a patria he henceforth carries or translates [*naqaltu*] inside himself as a devotee. We should finally note the bitter parenthesis of "all of us in my country pray, all of us shine shoes." By shifting the grammatical person from singular to plural, the poet identifies himself with a collective, but only on the basis of its humiliation. Exile is thus motivated not only by a repulsion from the group but also by a repulsion from the self as a member of the group. The poet's dissatisfaction with subjectivity, to borrow Jameson's phrase, stems from his revulsion at being tied to others.

The key poems of *The Songs of Mihyar* are not national allegories—texts that assume or project an identity between the lyrical subject and a collective one—but allegories of alienation. They rewrite tropes of national rebirth into a poetics of vagrancy, in which the speaking subject turns away, in disgust, melancholy, or anger, from a national community. The emigration out of Damascus persists in all these texts as a kind of buried anecdote or germ of historical narrative that motivates the figural displacements. *"Marthiyat al-ayyam al-hadira"* [Elegy for the Present Days] is an exemplary text in this regard and one of the most important of Adonis's oeuvre. It is his first experiment in the prose poem and a text that narrates the emergence of Mihyar—or at least the figure that will come to be called "Mihyar"—from the cradle of the sea. Adonis rewrote the poem twice in the late 1950s and early 1960s (in the 1980s he did so again), which suggests the importance he attached to it.

The first version, entitled *"Wahduhu al-Ya's"* [Only Despair], was published in *Shiʿr* in the fall of 1958.[18] Earlier that year, Syria had merged with Egypt to become the United Arab Republic, a pan-Arabist political experiment that foundered three years later. The move toward unification was initiated by Syrian Baathists, who feared a coup d'état by local Communists and appealed to the Egyptian president as a savior who would allow the regime to maintain itself in power. The move was fiercely resisted by remnants of the SSNP, of which Adonis was still a member though he no longer lived in Syria. The opening sections of "Only Despair" mark the text as an occasional poem, a bitter lament for what Adonis clearly felt to be a foreign invasion. The initial tableaux evoke a barbarian influx into the poet's country: "Here are men burning water / Coming from a land with no sky / A horde of spillers-of-blood. / Here they are in our poor house / Pissing on the welcome mat / And putting out the lamps." Adonis mocks the Syrians' hope for a foreign savior, one who in fact never showed much enthusiasm for unification and always held his Baathist allies at arm's length: "In my country there is a god / To whom all brows turn / Though he is never seen." The poet compares the Egyptians to Mongols and calls them "men of the sand," hungry for "the fruit of the sea." Their invasion sparks a massive emigration toward the coast, the deep horizon of Syrian culture. "When will I hear your sea-song above the pharaonic ruins?" the poet asks his country in unmistakably Phoenician accents. "When will I see the key of the sea stained with purple, stained with the spirit?"

Adonis included "Only Despair" in his second collection of poems, *Awraq fi-l-rih* [Leaves in the Wind] (1958), with minor modifications. But when he republished the poem in 1961, including it also in *Songs of Mihyar*, Adonis undertook a substantial revision and used his new title, "Elegy for the Present Days."[19] The rewrite removed all direct references to the Egyptian "invasion," which came to an end the same year *The Songs of Mihyar* was published. Instead of a conquest that leads to a reflux of refugees, the collective migration toward the coast becomes curiously unmotivated, as if the sea itself were exerting a natural or gravitational pull. The landscape of the poem is arid and menacing, a version of the wasteland, but the poem's specifically political occasion has been erased. Here is the opening episode of the poem in full:

Exile's trucks
cross the borders
through songs of exile
and sighing flames.

> The wind is against us and the ash of war covers the earth. We see our spirit flash on a razor blade, a helmet's curve. The brackish springs of autumn salt our wounds.
>
> Doom drags at history's face—our history needled with terror, a meadow of wild thorns.
>
> In what salt rivers will we wash this story, stale with the smell of old maids and widows back from the hajj, our history stained with the sweat of dervishes' loins, its springtime a feast for locusts?
>
> Night thickens and a new day crawls forth over dead sparrows. The door rattles but doesn't open. We cry out and dream of weeping and the eyes have no tears.
>
> My country is a woman in heat, a bridge of lusts. Mercenaries cross her, applauded by the massing sands. From distant balconies we see what there is to see: animals slaughtered on the graves of children; smoking censers for holy saints; the black rock of tombstones. The fields are full of bones and vultures. The heroic statues soft cadavers.
>
> So we go, chests bared to the sea. Old laments sleep under our tongues and our words have no heirs.
>
> We reach out for alien islands, scenting a virgin strangeness in the sea's abyss. We hear the sorrowful moan of our ships at port. Sorrow: a new moon rising, evil in its infancy. Rivers issue into the dead sea, where the night births weddings of sea-scum and sand, locusts and sand.
>
> So we go and fear scythes us down, crying out on muddy slopes. The earth bleeds all around us. The sea is a green wall.[20]

The poem shares its initial topography and trajectory with the opening poem of Yusuf al-Khal's trilogy, "The Call of the Sea," which also begins with an anonymous collective making its way through a ruined land toward the Mediterranean basin. Both poems are katabases, narrating a voyage out of the interior and toward the coast. In other ways, however, the poems are quite different. There is nothing in al-Khal's poem to match the density of discrete particulars in Adonis's "Elegy"—the razor blades and helmet curves—which give his poem the vividness of nightmare. More significantly, the modes of the two poems are distinct. Whereas al-Khal's trilogy narrates a triumphal march to the sea as the matrix of Mediterranean civilization, the subject of Adonis's long poem is a funeral procession: "So we go, chests bared to the sea. Old laments sleep under our tongues and our words have no heirs." Rather than dramatizing a community's reconciliation with its ancient origins, Adonis's poem is an exile's lament—albeit one that has been abstracted from its historical occasion, thereby transforming rootlessness into an ontological condition.

The second section of "Elegy" prolongs this melancholy—"the years are lean and still," "the dust of cemeteries grips our eyelashes"—then abruptly shifts into a new register with two apostrophes. The first address is toward the earth: "O earth the color of emigration, the color of wind—will a new wind awaken against the sand?" The second is to the rain, a version of what classical Arabic poetics calls an *istisqa*': "O rain, O rain that washes wastes and ruins, O rain that washes corpses, be gentle, too, and wash my people's history." The imploration to "be gentle" (*taraffaq*) again echoes al-Khal's address to the sea in "The Call" ("*Taraffaq bina, taraffaq, taraffaq!*"). In both poems, the apostrophe dramatizes a turn away from the dead land, locus of the "wounds" of history, toward an open horizon. The possessive suffix of "*shaʿbi*" [my people] is a pointed use of the first-person singular in a poem that has heretofore been narrated by the collective "we." But though the grammar of "*shaʿbi*" makes a claim of unity, the narrative of the poem marks an initial scission between the speaker and the collective. Following the prayer to rain, this split between "I" and "we" is emphasized in eight lines of rhymed and metered verse, in which "my people" is abruptly described in the third person:

> They do not know the wounded rock
> Is a poem suffocating on the lips.
> They believe the braying buffalo
> Is a dove, or a flower, or a god.
> And one day death rattles rise up
> In a country of starving frogs
> And a locust or stray ant
> Brings us bread and prayer.

The lines juxtapose elements of the plaint and the curse, the characteristic ambivalences of exile. The speaker's people live in the land of poetry, but they do not know it, cannot hear it, and perhaps are complicit in its suffocation. They look abroad for salvation and confuse a demagogue's braying (an implicit reference to the populist Nasser) with a promise of divine intervention. Rather than cultivate their native genius, they let their country starve until they will settle for the blandishments of bread and prayer. The poet styles himself as a spurned prophet, a man of the people, who persist in rejecting his good offices. The speaking self, the poetic "I," emerges out of this scene of mutual rejection and disaffiliation.

The following section dramatizes this emergence and forms the crux of the poem. At first, the prayer for rain seems to have been answered. The collective moves on horseback through a suddenly fertile landscape: "We washed the day clean, and now the stones are silken beneath our feet, the backs of our mounts are a horizon, and their hooves are the cardinal winds. Here is our route—we wed the lightning bolt, wash away the earth's decay and fill it with the scream of new things." The migration to the coast becomes a sea voyage in which a strange creature rises up to greet them.

From the headstrong boats crossing the dead sea another wind breaks, shaking the city gates. Tomorrow they will open and immolate the city's harvest of locusts and sand.

We will build above the abyss to endure in the mouth of the future—

This is the threshold [*'ataba*] of the future:

"A dark man, rising from the sea, full of the panther's bliss, he teaches refusal, proffers new names, and beneath his eyelids crouches the eagle of the future.

"A dark man, rising from the sea, untempted by the carnivals of corpses, full of the world, full of winds that sweep away plague. His winds' creative breath compels the stone to love—to dance and to love."

It is a scene of parturition: *ecce homo*. The Zarathustra-like figure who rises up from the waves—his animal familiars recall Nietzsche's "Song of Melancholy": "This is your blessedness / the blessedness of panthers and eagles"— bears many of the qualities that will come to identify Mihyar, the inventor of new names whose creed is "refusal." In the final section of the poem, the *Übermensch* speaks in propria persona, but only to say farewell: "Carrying my books, I go to live in my heart's shade, to weave the poems' silk into a new sky"; "I leave my companions behind me, the iron bars, the prisons." The emigration from Syria, here as elsewhere is Adonis's writing, is an immigration into poetry and language. The speaker's tone is a mixture of despair and defiance, a heroic melancholy that will also typify the figure of Mihyar: "And I go with nothing but my long sorrows and stellar distances. . . . I go and the bee of exile honeys my brow." (Later it is "despair" that is "a star on the brow": two idioms for the stigmata of poetic prophethood.) "We go," the refrain of the poem's first section, here gives way to "I go." The speaker bids farewell to the collective: "Farewell, O age of flies in my country. . . . My homeland is not yet achieved, my spirit is far away, and I am free of all possessions." It is this movement of turning away that constitutes the entire burden of his speech: the birth of lyric from the spirit of elegy.

Maître du navire

"Elegy for the Present Days" is a pivotal poem in the modernist corpus. It narrates a number of transitions, or translations: from allegory to lyric, from partisan to nonpartisan, from occasional poem to metaphysical meditation, from Damascus to the sea. The prosody of the poem enacts another kind of shift, which would be especially momentous for the *Shi'r* movement. "Elegy" features several passages in metered verse—including the opening quatrain and the eight-line jeremiad noted above—but is mostly written in prose. This mixture of verse and prose, of lyrics and "psalms," is one of the most striking formal elements of *The Songs of Mihyar* and can be traced back to "Only

Despair," Adonis's first experiment with the prose poem. As we shall see in the next chapter, the prose poem or *qasidat al-nathr* was a new and controversial form in Arabic poetry in the late 1950s, one that Adonis and Unsi al-Hajj in particular championed in the pages of *Shiʿr*. At stake in these debates was nothing less than the nature of poetry itself: if poetry was not, as the ancient critics had it, rhymed and metered speech, then what was it? And who had the authority to revoke or revise these definitions?

Adonis's apprenticeship in the *qasidat al-nathr* came through his versions of the French poet Saint-John Perse, another late modernist figure like Spender, Silone, or MacLeish, whose poetry and criticism helped define the orthodoxy of the day but whose works have now fallen into a deep historical trough. Any recovery of the midcentury moment, whose characteristic idioms and habits of thought now seem suddenly distant, has to grapple with the work of Perse, whose international eminence was at the time rivaled only by Eliot. (Eliot's one serious work of translation was Perse's *Anabasis* [1924], just as Perse's only published work of translation, intended as an homage, is the first section of Eliot's "The Hollow Men.")[21] Perse was also a figure of great institutional power, the sort of intellectual, like Charles Malik, whom the *Shiʿr* poets often gravitated toward. Perse was a native of Guadeloupe, the scion of a wealthy family of solicitors and planters, who rose through the ranks of the Quai d'Orsay until he became secretary general of the Foreign Ministry in 1933. Exiled and stripped of his citizenship by Vichy, he fled to America in 1940 where he was given a post at the Library of Congress by his close friend, Archibald MacLeish. The four poems of this period, *Exil, Pluies, Neiges,* and *Poème à l'Étrangère*, are all meditations on exile and what Perse calls, in the first of these poems, "the search for a pure place" [*la recherche d'un lieu pur*] in the New World.[22] In 1960 he was awarded the Nobel Prize in Literature, due in part to the advocacy of UN secretary-general Dag Hammarskjöld, who translated Perse's *Chroniques* into Swedish. "What a proud privilege is ours," Perse exclaims in his acceptance speech (translated into English by W. H. Auden). "Faithful to its task, which is nothing less than to fathom the human mystery, modern poetry is pursuing an enterprise which is concerned with man in the plenitude of his being.... Dedicated to its goal and free from ideology, it knows itself to be the equal of life, which needs no self-justification."[23]

In *Shiʿr*'s fall issue of 1957, a year before the publication of his first prose poem, "Only Despair," Adonis translated "*Étroits sont les vaisseaux*" [Narrow are the ships], the ninth and longest section of Perse's longest poem, *Amers* [Seamarks] (1957). Adonis appended several pages of commentary to his translation, noting that the poem "is deemed to be the poet's greatest work."[24] *Amers* begins with an apostrophe to the sea, imploring it to lend the poet its powers of dynamism as well as, implicitly, the genealogical powers of precursor poets such as Homer, Virgil, Pindar, and Paul Claudel. The invocation also promises a poem in praise of the sea—the eulogy or *fête* is the central mode of

Perse's poetry—which will be a kind of literary summa: "The nuptial chant, O Sea, will be for you the chant: 'My last song! My last song! Which will be the song of a man of the sea.'"[25] After the opening invocation, the poem includes nine "strophes" of varying lengths spoken by distinct personas: the Master of stars and navigation, the Tragediennes, the Patrician Women, a poetess, a girl prophet, the daughter of the city. The final strophe, the portion of the poem translated by Adonis, is a dialogue between a pair of lovers: a woman of the seashore and a man, "*maître du navire*," who pilots his ship alongside and away from the land. The strophe is an agon of constraint and liberation, eros and solitude. While the woman declares her desires frankly and laments her lover's absence, the pilot is one of those restless subjects, like Adonis's new Noah or Mihyar, who spurn domestic pleasures for epic (and curiously empty) conquests. The woman often addresses him with a mixture of awe and pity: "O you haunted, like the sea, by things that are great and distant, I have seen you with knit brows seeking beyond woman. Does the night you steer through have no island, no shore? Who is it in you that always alienates and denies himself?" As it develops, Perse's long poem reveals itself as a choral masque: its multiple speakers are all hierophants of the sea, who have come to play their parts and sing their songs of praise on the shoreline. The poem closes with a tableau that suggests the theatrical and erotic nature of what we have been reading: "The lover washes himself of his nights. And the man with the mask of gold removes his gold in honor of the Sea."

Perse's poetics of exile, along with the eloquent undulations of his verse, are especially evident in Adonis's poetry of the late 1950s and early 1960s, and he would go on to translate the French poet's oeuvre in its entirety. Adonis's conception of the prose poem, unlike that of Unsi al-Hajj, examined in the next chapter, is deeply marked by the example of Perse. As opposed to the shorter *poèmes en prose* of Baudelaire, Rimbaud, and Mallarmé, which often take the form of delirious anecdotes set in Paris, Perse's prose poems are typically long, indeterminate in their setting, and grounded in lyric modes such as the ode or eulogy. Adonis's versions also tend to be long and lyrical, and to eschew urban settings. Of all his translations, Adonis's versions of Perse have attracted the most commentary. Critics have accused Adonis of plagiarizing the French poet and of misunderstanding the originals.[26] But Adonis's translations were more significant than these narrowly polemical debates suggest. The encounter with Perse provoked Adonis's most acute thoughts on the act of translation, and it had profound consequences for his own poetry as well. Indeed, the important *turn* or *passage* I have been tracing—from Damascus to Beirut, from nationalist politics to international exile—pivots on this affiliation.

It is arguable whether any other poet of the twentieth century was so handsomely translated as Perse, a fact it is easy to forget now that his star has dimmed. The translations themselves often draw attention to this history. The 1949 revised edition of T. S. Eliot's version of *Anabase* includes a bibliography of translations in a half-dozen European languages. These include the 1926 Russian version, with a preface by Valéry Larbaud; the 1929 German version, translated by Walter Benjamin and Bernard Groethuysen, with a preface by Hugo von Hofmannsthal (Benjamin's involvement in the project was in lieu of Rilke, who had translated Perse's *Images à Crusoé* in 1925); the 1930 English version, translated by Eliot himself; and the 1936 Italian version, translated by Giuseppe Ungaretti.[27] Translating Perse during the interwar years was thus a kind of passport to international modernism. In 1931 Octavio Paz borrowed a line from *Anabase* as the epigraph to his first published poem. And Perse was equally fêted by late modernists of the postwar period, such as MacLeish, Spender, and Giorgos Seferis.[28]

Adonis, another late modernist, was aware of these precursors. In the commentary he wrote for his own version, he mentions Eliot, Ungaretti, MacLeish, and Hofmannsthal as previous translators (in fact, MacLeish and Hofmannsthal never published translations, though they wrote essays of appreciation).[29] And like them, Adonis places special emphasis on the freedom of Perse's poetry from constraints of place and time. Hofmannsthal, for example, in his preface to *Anabase*, credits Perse with "the renewal of lyrical inspiration," declaring that "the action itself dispenses with historical, ideological or social allusions." Eliot, in his own preface, claims that he required only one reading of the poem to grasp that "no map of its migrations could be drawn up." For Adonis, it is precisely this "ability to live on its own, independently," that explains why "[Perse's] poetry appears, in translation, more worldly than any other." Here again, in typical late modernist fashion, autonomy is proffered as the sine qua non of world literature. It is Perse's exile from history and from geographical constraints that allows him to construct what Larbaud calls his "planetary monument of poesy."[30] Throughout his career, Adonis would link Perse to the ideals of worldliness and modernity. As he declares in a short commentary written seventeen years after he published his first translation, "Let me say that I am influenced by everything that goes on in the world. Great poetry is the wind of the world—anyone who takes a breath is influenced—and the poetry of Saint-John Perse is a crucial part of the wind of the modern world."[31]

In a lecture delivered to the Fondation Saint-John Perse in 1993, Adonis recounts an illuminating anecdote of how he discovered *Amers* and what he hoped to accomplish by translating the poem into Arabic.[32] In the summer of 1957, Adonis writes, he and Yusuf al-Khal visited the editor Albert Adib at the Beiruti offices of his magazine, *al-Adib* [The Man of Letters], where both poets had previously published work:

> In front of Adib, on his desk, I saw an issue of the *Nouvelle Revue Française*, which I leafed through out of curiosity. On the first page was "*Étroits sont les vaisseaux*." I left my friends to their conversation and plunged into the poem, part of a long poem, *Amers*, whose author was

Saint-John Perse. It was the first time I had heard the name. I was immediately captivated by the text. I had the impression of reading something that arose from the deepest part of myself.

This story of the fortunate *trouvaille*, a kind of message in a bottle, is immediately reminiscent of those lucky finds that pattern the narrative of Antun Saʿada's *The Intellectual Struggle*. There too, the circulation of little magazines among exiles and émigrés offers a figure for the world-literature-to-come. And in both cases, the seemingly random discovery of a foreign text provokes self-recognition. For Saʿada, letters from his compatriots and news of the discoveries at Raʾs Shamra send him down into the deep strata of indigenous mythology; similarly, Adonis's "plunge" into the sea of *Amers* turns out to be a dive into the depths of the self. Convinced that modern poetry required turning one's back on the sterile traditions of the interior and embracing the maritime energies of exile, Adonis must have experienced an uncanny frisson at reading the first page of Perse's strophe: "À la mer seule, nous dirons / Quels étrangers nous fûmes aux fêtes de la Ville. . . . En vaine la terre proche nous trace sa frontière. Une même vague par le monde" [Only to the sea shall we say what strangers we were at the celebrations of the City. . . . In vain does the surrounding land trace for us its confines. One wave throughout the world].

In his lecture, Adonis explains that his interest in *Amers* was not merely aroused by the discovery of a poetic sensibility so close to his own. He was also struck by the idea that Perse could be used strategically, to establish the legitimacy of the *qasidat al-nathr:* "The idea suddenly came to me that the translation of this poem would, through its lyrical force, through its splendor and density, provide a solid support for the very principle of the prose poem, which was categorically refused by the dominant literary milieu. We wanted to demonstrate, on the contrary, that it was possible for the Arabic language to find in it a new means of poetic expression." All poetic invention requires authoritative precedent. This is a principle modernist poetry consistently acknowledges and just as consistently disavows. In line with the method established by al-Khal in his own essays and translations, Adonis envisages the creation of a modernist genre through the *naql* of new authorities. As I have noted in the previous chapter, the signal achievement of the *Shiʿr* poets was not merely to have translated a large corpus of foreign poetry, but to have customized their editorial and compositional methods for a particular context, suggesting to their local audience—Lebanon's intellectual elite—that by reading certain foreign texts, including some that may have seemed very abstruse and remote, they were plunging into the deepest portions of their own historical identity. The appeal of a text such as Perse's was not only its illustrious provenance but also its strange at-homeness in Beirut. It is not by coincidence that *Amers* is another instance of the sea-poem, that modernist genre peculiar to the *Shiʿr* poets and whose most salient examples—Pound's first canto, Rimbaud's "The Drunken

Boat," the first song of Lautréamont's *Les Chants de Maldoror*, and "Narrow are the vessels"—are translations.[33] In Arabic, *"bahr"* can mean both "sea" and "meter," a coincidence that lends itself to some characteristic modernist punning. In the opening line of the first "Psalm" of *Songs of Mihyar*, the hero is depicted as an Atlas figure: "Yesterday he carried a continent and moved the sea from its place" [*naqala al-bahr min makanihi*] (13). Reading "translated" for "moved" and "meter" for "sea," we get the modernist program for importing the prose poem into Arabic: It translated the meter from its place.[34]

In the same lecture, Adonis offers a description of the challenge he faced in translating *Amers*. It also serves as a statement of his general theory of *naql*, announced in the distinctive rhetoric of the sea-poem:

> *Il faut que le poème dans sa nouvelle patrie trouve un lieu d'ancrage, une demeure, et qu'il apparaisse comme s'il en était l'authentique propriétaire. Combien est malheureux le sort du poème qui se présente dans son expatriation tel un mendiant, un clochard, un désœuvré! Autrement dit, il faut que cet exil s'apparente à une naissance seconde. Et le seul garant qui permette à l'expatriation de devenir domiciliation est d'être intégrée dans un haut langage poétique.*
>
> *J'avoue que lorsque j'ai entrepris la traduction de Saint-John Perse, je n'étais pas certain que l'arabe, émanant du désert, pourrait cerner cette mer lyrique et épique qu'est le texte persien. Mais, au fur et à mesure que j'avançais, la certitude m'est venue que le désert et la mer se rejoignent dans cet océan plus vaste, plus riche, je veux dire l'homme.*

[In its new country, the poem must find a place to drop anchor, a home of which it must seem to be the authentic owner. How unfortunate is the fate of the poem that appears in its expatriation to be a beggar, a vagrant, someone with nothing to do! In other words, exile must become like a second birth. And the only guarantee that allows expatriation to turn into domestication is for it to be integrated into a high poetic language.

I admit that when I undertook to translate Saint-John Perse, I wasn't certain that the Arabic language, born of the desert, could encompass that lyrical and epic sea that is the text of Perse. But as I progressed, I became certain that the desert and the sea come together in that larger and richer ocean which is man.]

The aim of translation is to provide the foreign poem with a suitable harbor. In the case of Perse, this requires the use of a specifically literary register. "I said to myself: Saint-John Perse must become an Arab poet through me," Adonis writes at the end of the lecture, admitting that "I may have led Perse astray in trying to Orientalize him." This is, we might say, an extreme version of "domesticating" translation (it may also be a sly mockery of the Qur'anic warning that only those who have been led astray [*al-ghawun*] will follow the poets: Q 26:224). Adonis's notion of translation is very far from Yusuf al-Khal's professionalist ideal of *naql* "without any liberties." But what the *Shiʿr* poets' versions suggest over and again—here al-Khal and Adonis agree—is that the plunge into the foreign is simultaneously an act of self-legitimation, an assertion of one's citizenship in the republic of man.

This legitimating intention is evident in the many translations of Perse scattered throughout the text of "Elegy for the Present Days." The second section of the poem includes a prayer for rain that I have previously cited: "O rain, O rain that washes wastes and ruins, O rain that washes corpses, be gentle, too, and wash the history of my people." As several critics have pointed out, the passage echoes the implorations in the seventh strophe of Perse's poem *Pluies*, with its refrain of "*Lavez, ô Pluies!*" More specifically, the last phrase of Adonis's text, "*ighsil tarikh shaʿbi*" [wash the history of my people], rewrites Perse's "*Lavez, lavez l'histoire des peuples*," although Adonis has characteristically altered the grammatical person of the speaker from third to first. The act of translation is more complex than this, however. The prayer for rain, or *istisqaʾ*, is a venerable, indeed pre-Islamic poetic genre in Arabic, and one that had been prominently revived Badr Shakir by al-Sayyab's "Hymn to Rain" (published in *al-Adab* in the summer of 1954). The insinuation made by Adonis's echoing chamber is that Perse, the most recherché of modern French poets, is himself the translator, all unknowingly, of an ancient Arabic speech-act. In rendering Perse into Arabic, Adonis was also reactivating the oldest poetry in his own language. In the same way, Adonis's experiment in translating the prose poem begins in exile from its own language and ends by claiming a dual citizenship in "le désert et la mer."[35]

There is one further instance of translation in "Elegy for the Present Days" that has not been previously noted by critics. This is Adonis's use of the word "*ʿataba*," which I have translated as "threshold," and which Adonis uses to translate Perse's "*seuil*." The word occurs ten times in "*Étroits sont les vaisseaux*" and nineteen times in *Amers* as a whole, often as an alternate name for the seashore, the female speaker's domestic space. As she implores her lover, "Do not be a harsh Master to me by silence and by absence. O loving face, far from the threshold [*baʿidan ʿan al-ʿataba*]." Roger Little has shown that "*seuil*" is a keyword in the poetry of Perse.[36] It is used to striking effect as early as *Anabase* ("All glory to the threshold of the tents!") and is especially prominent in *Exil* and *Amers*, two poems of the seashore written in America. In the opening lines of *Exil*, the first poem by Perse after his flight from France and dedicated to Archibald MacLeish, the poet stands on the beach facing the Atlantic swells: "Doors open onto the sands, doors open onto exile, / The keys are with the lighthouse keepers, and the sun is spread-eagled on the stone of the threshold" [*l'astre roué vif sur la pierre du seuil*].[37] In *Amers*, the connotations of the word extend beyond liminal space of exile to name a more abstract, though also erotic site of passage—a kind of birth canal to *l'outre-mer*.

In a section of the poem's "Chorus," which follows the last strophe, the pilot reaches the limits of the Mediterranean and encounters a vision of the watery sublime: "And beyond opens the foreign Sea, at the exit from the straits, which is no longer the sea of labor, but the major threshold of the greatest Orb and the extreme threshold of the greatest Age."

Adonis does not, to my knowledge, use "*'ataba*" in any poems preceding his first translation of Perse, but the word appears several times, quite pointedly, in *The Songs of Mihyar*, where it names a topos of transgression, exile, and resurrection. Here is the entire text of "*Ta'ih al-Wajh*" [Face Astray]: "Face astray—I pray to my dust / and sing my estranged soul, / to a miracle still unfulfilled / I cross a world burned / by my songs and push forward the threshold." The *'ataba* is in this case a frontier between the old world, consumed and purified by flame, and the unnamed new world, whose exploration has just begun. In Mihyar's fourth "Psalm" the word is linked to the sea, and specifically to the cry of Xenophon's ten thousand, itself a convention of the sea-poem. Mihyar addresses his compatriots while also looking for an escape route: "I cannot live with you. I cannot live except with you. You are a sea surge [*tamawwuj*] in my senses. There is no escape for me from you. But scream—the sea, the sea! And hang the pearls of the sun over your thresholds." A third instance comes in one of the final poems of the collection, the four-line "*Marthiya*" [Elegy]: "You, dead on the cross, / O my friend, / the road flowers traced your face / and behind your steps walked the threshold." In these lines, the imagery of which owes a great deal to Yusuf al-Khal, the poet affiliates himself with the crucified addressee, whose resurrection is figured as a passage over the *'ataba*. All these resonances are at play in a phrase from "Elegy for the Present Days" that we have already read, which immediately precedes the birth of Mihyar from the sea: "This is the threshold of the future." At this moment in the poem, the passage over the threshold signals the grammatical turn from a collective to the singular. It is also a passage across the *seuil* of the seashore, from the desert of the opening sections to the open sea of the future. These transitions reflect the deep narrative or rite of passage that structures *The Songs of Mihyar* as a whole: the katabasis away from Damascus, a national space inhabited by an identifiable collective, toward the coast of international exile. The prose poetry of Perse is for Adonis a spirit of this threshold, a *genius loci* of displacement. So it is fitting that we should find one of Perse's keywords precisely here, at the crossroads of so many migrations.

Knight of the Sorrowful Countenance

"Who are you?" "Where were you?" These questions, which begin two poems of the same title, "*Hiwar*" [Dialogue], echo throughout *The Songs of Mihyar*. They also seem to set a task for critics and readers.[38] The hero of the collection offers a number of self-identifications, though the most obvious one, "I am Mihyar the Damascene," is conspicuously missing. For example: "I am a prophet and a skeptic"; "I am proof [*hujja*] against the age"; "I am the enchanter of dust"; "I am the lord of spirits"; "I am the lord of betrayal"; "I am the thunderbolt's stone"; "I am the banner hanging from a fugitive cloud's eyelids"; "I am the coming morning and the map that draws itself"; "I am like the seashell"; "I am, like you, wind and earth." Each of these self-identifications poses riddles of its own. To solve them, we might be tempted to consult Nietzsche or to parse the connotations of "*hujja*," a legal term signifying "testimony" or "evidence," but one that also belongs to the lexicon of Shiite prophetology, where it is a figure of authoritative interpretation, God's "proof" to man. All this suggests that the poems of *The Songs of Mihyar* are designed to provoke exegesis. "Who are you?" is a question that gives critics something to do, like solving a puzzle or lifting up a mask.

No text is entirely innocent of such solicitations, and no criticism can entirely avoid them. The solicitations of *Mihyar* are only especially blatant. This is due in part to Adonis's relentless and wide-ranging allusiveness; reading his poetry, we are always aware of the missing footnotes. Adonis's critical writings are also heavily invested in the defense of obscurity, what he calls "*al-ghumud*." Remarking on the poetry of the famously difficult ʿAbbasid poet Abu Tammam, Adonis writes: "His is not a twilit obscurity, but rather a translucency one might truly describe with the words of Cocteau on Mallarmé: 'Obscure as a diamond' [*ghamid ka-l-mas*]."[39] A similar solicitation is made by the rhetoric of profundity with which he surrounds his hero, a verbal spell that encourages us to believe we are in the presence of a mystery we might hope to solve with sufficient erudition and patience. Many critics proceed under this spell. Daher and Barakat, after suggesting plausible precedents—Odysseus, Zarathustra, Leibniz's monad—identify Mihyar as figure of "man," a philosophical subject or subjectivity to whom they add a congeries of attributes: creativity, interiority, heroism. The afterlife Mihyar enjoys in Adonis's later collections reinforces the suggestion that Mihyar is a figure with definite traits and a stable identity. In this way, Mihyar, "the knight of strange words," "the barbarian priest," "the Adam of life" (more solicitations), survives the collection that bears his name.

What if we approach these solicitations in a different manner? Rather than take "Who are you?" as a riddle to be solved, we might read it as a figure of speech, and specifically as an *iltifat*, often translated as *apostrophe*, since both words mean "a turn away." Figuratively speaking, the poet or speaker turns his back on the reader to address another, an object, scene, person, or perhaps himself. It is a trope of tropism. Grammatically, this turn involves a switch of persons, usually from third to second or second to third (the Arabic term is somewhat broader, however, since it can be used to denote any such change of person).[40] We have already noted some of the apostrophes that structure "Elegy for the Present Days," a poem that enacts Adonis's turn away from a collective *we* toward an exilic *I*. But trope is characteristic of *Songs of Mihyar* as a whole. Read as a figure of speech, "Who are you?" does not solicit an exegesis of the lyric subject. Instead, it provides an example of how subjectivity emerges from the movement of rhetoric. We are not asked to identify a figure but rather to track the process of figuration—in the words of Jonathan Culler, "the animicity enforced by apostrophe."[41]

The poem "Dialogue" nicely dramatizes this process. The poem is one of many in Adonis's collection that heroize the rejection of religious conventions. Here as elsewhere, Mihyar is a figure of defiant impiety. But the rhetoric of the poem is more intricate. Its opening line confirms the suggestion that we understand its question as an apostrophe: "Who are you, whom do you choose, O Mihyar? / Wherever you turn, it is God or the devil's abyss, / an abyss that goes, or an abyss that comes, / and the world is a choice." After this beginning, the poem stages another *iltifat*, shifting from second to first person, as if the anonymous speaker of "O Mihyar" has indeed animated its addressee into speech: "Neither God nor the devil do I choose / for both are walls, / both block my vision, / shall I replace a wall with a wall?" Responding to the invocation of "O" by speaking in his own voice, Mihyar refuses the terms proposed to him. Asked to establish his identity ("Who are you?") by turning one way or the other, he simply turns *away*. The poem is a dance of strophe, antistrophe, and apostrophe. This movement is repeated throughout the collection, in which we watch Mihyar whirl and whirl again. This gesture of continually looking away (but never looking back) is symptomatic of Adonis's own turn away from nationalist politics. It is an evasion that marks this particular collection as well as the modernist movement in general, whose literary project stems from its unacknowledged loss of political agency. But before making that diagnosis, we should note how deeply the trope of apostrophe structures *The Songs of Mihyar*.

The poems of the volume's first section, "Knight of Strange Words," are exclusively descriptive, even hymnal in their repetitions and solemnity. As with "The New Covenant," they evoke Mihyar in the third person, and the voice is typically in the first-person plural, as though it belonged to some unnamed community awaiting or witnessing the advent of a new prophet. Beginning in the second section, "The Enchanter of Dust," Mihyar speaks for himself: "I carry my abyss and I walk. I wipe out the roads that end, I open the roads that are long, like the wind and the earth." This initial change of person is quickly followed by others. The two poems entitled "Dialogue" begin with apostrophic questions and end inconclusively, either with Mihyar refusing the terms of the interrogation or simply refusing to answer. To the question, "Where were you?" he responds, "I did not respond. I did not know the word." In "It Is Enough for You to See," Mihyar is again the subject of an apostrophe and again keeps an enigmatic silence: "It is enough for you, O Mihyar / to guard the secret that God erased." The section takes its name from a poem spoken in the voice of Orpheus: "I am the language of a God to come, / I am the enchanter of dust." Here, thematic echoes between the voices of Orpheus and Mihyar suggest that one persona has adopted or turned into another, a kind of double prosopopoeia, mask upon mask. That suggestion is extended in the final poem of the second section, "Odysseus," in which the wily Greek, apostrophized by king Alkínoös, sounds like both Mihyar and Orpheus: "Here I am in fear and fruitlessness, / not knowing how to stay, how to return." (Just as Adonis's rewrite of the Noah myth imagines a sea journey without end, his Odysseus never returns to Ithaca but remains a figure of exile.) The poems of the third section, "The Dead God," are all spoken by Mihyar in the first person except the last, where Mihyar addresses himself in the second person. All these texts are full of Mihyar's own apostrophes, or turns away from his readers: "O Mother"; "O winds / O childhood / O bridge of tears"; "O my earth"; "O death, my friend"; "O my songs"; "O Odysseus"; "O Orpheus"; "O words of disease"; "O grave, O my end at the beginning of spring."

The penultimate section of the book ends with "The New Noah," a poem of synthesis and summarization. For its inclusion in *The Songs of Mihyar*, Adonis rewrote the text he had originally published in *Shiʿr*, dividing the poem into two sections that make a sharp division between the plural, prayerful voice of the first four stanzas and the singular, heroic voice of the long last stanza. Noah's "I" is animated, quite explicitly, by God's apostrophe ("O Noah, save the living for us"), an imploration from which Noah pointedly turns away: "I would not listen to God's word." The persona of Noah bears a family resemblance to all the other masks of Mihyar. Like Odysseus, he is a seafaring quester in search of the new; like Orpheus, he visits an underworld and whispers with the dead. The poem, with its multiple changes of person—the conclusion returns to the plural voice—and answering apostrophes ("O Lord," "O Noah") is a microcosm of the collection.[42]

This compressed review suggests that *Songs of Mihyar* is not structured, as its title might suggest, as a narrative with a central hero. Although the collection begins with a propulsive surge, "He advances, unarmed as the forest, and like the clouds he does not retreat," it quickly stalls. Instead of a quest, there is a dizzying series of turns and returns. The trope of adventure is constantly invoked, but Mihyar has no actual adventures. Unlike the epic or mythological precursors he summons, Mihyar has no tests, no romances, no battles, no rites of initiation. Although he is given magnificent and portentous words to pronounce, he performs no deeds—the traditional requirement of classical heroes, including the heroes of Arabic prose romances. Rather than a hero, Mihyar is, in the apt words of his English translators, "a hero-shaped space."[43] The landscape Mihyar strides through is mostly unpeopled, and his apostrophes are so many attempts to animate the emptiness—including the empty or abstract space of his own persona. My literal-minded suggestion is that there are no confrontations primarily because Mihyar is always turning away from them. Sometimes this turn is toward himself, the sort of "introversion" that Adel Daher describes, but more often it is toward another element of the landscape or mythical confrere. The collection is in this sense a continuous *iltifat*, a potentially endless chain of prosopopoeia.

Mihyar's multiple personas and lack of adventures suggest that he is a typically *modernist* hero—that is, a hero who performs no deeds but retains the ambition to represent a certain kind of totality. Mihyar's attempt to personify that storehouse of mythical and literary wisdom summed up in the names of Zarathustra, Odysseus, Orpheus, Noah, and others gives the lie to his own emptiness in the same way that ideological encomiums to the figure of man, evoking "his inner joy and freedom" along with "his infinite spiritual possibilities," ultimately signal the figure's vacuity. Yet Mihyar's abstraction is also the condition for his universality. Franco Moretti, in his study of the modern epic, suggests that a certain kind of emptiness is characteristic of modernist attempts to recapture the totalizing ambitions of the classical genre, from Goethe's *Faust* to Joyce's *Ulysses*. Remarking on the strange fact that Faust, for all his infernal powers and grand plans, is essentially an idle spectator of the poem's action, Moretti suggests that "We see in Faust's inertia the only chance for modern epic totality. If Hegel is actually right, and in the modern world 'the vitality of the individual appears as transcended,' then nothing is left but to seek 'the universal individual of mankind' *in passivity*. In this new scenario, the grand world of the epic no longer takes shape in transformative action, but in imagination, in dream, in magic."[44]

The modernist epic takes shape in the imagination—or in rhetoric. As with the examples studied by Moretti, the adventure of *The Songs Mihyar* does not belong to the protagonist but rather to the figurative logic of the poems, to their strenuous efforts of authorization and re-authorization. The adventure of reading is not to decode—to ferret out allusions, to unmask the hero—but rather to register the movement of dissatisfaction, in which identities are continually essayed and set aside. This restlessness is a symptom of modernism's search for forms and personae of authority at a moment when older authorities are no longer available (and new political authorities are refused). Here I will cite Richard Poirier's essay, "Modernism and Its Difficulties," which proposes a similar approach to the difficult-by-design texts of Anglo-American modernism, particularly Eliot, Pound, and Joyce: "The ostentatious learning, the cultural displays, the mechanical structurings would not then be taken as directives to the reader that he or she must look behind these things for heavy significances but as indications instead of extreme procedural hesitancy. They are forms of stamina, persistence, of discipline where there exist no other forms of authority."[45] In the poems of *The Songs of Mihyar*, this hesitancy and stamina is legible in the desperate apostrophes of its hero, who invokes a succession of authorities, literary or legendary, only to discover their writ has expired. As Poirier puts it, "An active authorial presence . . . can be found, if not in any of the styles, then in the transitions, the modes of variation among them. It is to be found not in any place, despite all the formal placements made available, but in the acts of *displacement* by which one form is relinquished for another."[46]

Reading Adonis's poetry for its acts of displacement rather than its ostentatious philosophical learning suggests that "Mihyar" is not so much a figure as a movement of disfiguration. As Mihyar announces in his opening "Psalm," "I erase and await the one who erases me." Tracking this movement of identification and erasure requires us to be sensitive not only to the declarative force of Adonis's language but its substitutions and shifts of person. While criticism has mostly paid attention to the hero's self-affirmations, the collection enacts a dialectic of doing and undoing, address and evasion, facing and defacing. In "You Have No Choice," Mihyar apostrophizes himself: "What then, you destroy the face of the earth? / Then draw another, different face." This movement of disfiguration finds its clearest articulation in the group of elegies, in Arabic "*marathi*," that form the seventh and final section of *The Songs of Mihyar*. We will return to these texts in chapter 5, an examination of the modernist elegy as a genre. Here I will simply note that Adonis's *marathi* to the second Caliph ʿUmar ibn al-Khattab, as well as the ʿAbbasid poets Abu Nuwas, al-Hallaj, and Bashshar ibn Burd, form the collection's most concentrated sequence of apostrophes. They are the culmination of its rhetorical procedures—further confirmation that the adventure of *The Songs of Mihyar* does not belong to its titular hero but rather to its sequencing of tropes.

The elegy is an especially aggravated case of apostrophe. Here, the "animicity" bestowed by invocation wars against the recognition of death. In Culler's account of the elegy, which caps his own analysis of apostrophe, the genre "replaces an irreversible temporal disjunction, the move from life to death, with a dialectical alternation between attitudes of mourning and consolation, evocations of absence and presence."[47] There are two short poems from the final section of *Songs of Mihyar* entitled simply "*Marthiya*" [Elegy].[48] The first of these is the elegy addressed to a crucified figure so common in the poems of Yusuf al-Khal. The anticipation of resurrection in the last two lines, "the road flowers traced [*rasamat*] your face / and behind your steps walked the threshold," employs an ambiguous imagery of inscription and erasure. The blooms that "trace" the face of the addressee also cover it over, in the way of funereal flowers. This ambiguity goes back to the earliest uses of "*rasm*" in pre-Islamic poetry, where it names both the erasure of dwelling places by the rain as well as their visible traces or vestiges, often compared to writing in the sand.[49] (Inversely, the idiom "*rasama sharat al-salib*" [to trace the sign of the cross], which we will encounter in a prose poem by Unsi al-Hajj, denotes a "tracery" that leaves no permanent marks.) The second "Elegy" also lacks a specified addressee, yet its lexicon suggests the apostrophe is directed to Mihyar:

The dust sings you, raises its poems toward you
offering your steps to the abysses,
elegizing these traces [*hadhihi al-baqaya*]
of your songs, your visions.

The dust covers the glass of seasons.
It covers the mirrors [*al-maraya*]
and it covers your hands.

The transitive use of *"yughanni"* [sings] in the opening line suggests *extols* or *glorifies*. The verb is countered by its metagram, *"yughatti"* [covers], in the second stanza. These two verbs, governed by the same noun, suggest the customary task of elegy, to praise and to bury. They also enact the dialectic of figuration and disfiguration, presence and absence, that we followed in the preceding "Elegy." Here too, the movement of the poem pivots on the notion of a trace, relic, or vestige. The rhyme of *baqaya–maraya* [traces–mirrors] is the key pairing of the poem. The mirror is where Mihyar, the elegized subject, turns to see his face, or perhaps the face of one of his mythical *prosopa* (it is not a single mirror but several). As in the iconography of melancholia, the mirror is an emblem of figuration and fleetingness: "the glass of seasons" picks out just these elements of fragility and evanescence. In this sense, the mirror functions much as the elegy does, animating its addressee and claiming some of his power, only to subsequently mark his demise. "Elegy" has a specular form, rhyming its first and last lines by way of the second-person pronominal suffix (*ilayk* [toward you] and *"yadayk"* [your hands]), as though to mark the elegy's provisional existence as an apostrophic address. The poems of dust finally erase all the figures of this text: mirrors, seasons, and hands (a conventional symbol of power). Yet the figures' traces are still legible, like letters in the sand. The deictic *"hadhihi"* [these] points to the text that is dissolving in front of us, or else to the series of "songs" and "visions" that constitute *The Songs of Mihyar* as a whole. In this way, the process of disfiguration leaves its own figures, its *rasamat* or *baqaya*, in the form of elegies.[50]

Because it closes with a series of *marathi*, it is tempting to read *The Songs of Mihyar* as a work of mourning. If so, who or what is the mourned object? Presumably not the stipulated addressees. What would it mean to mourn Mihyar, al-Hallaj, or Abu Nuwas? The disparity and number of elegized figures suggests they are essentially substitutes for one another, like the masks of Odysseus, Orpheus, and Noah in earlier poems of the collection. What these figures finally have in common is no more than the poet's apostrophe, as he turns from one to another. Let me suggest that these elegies are therefore not to be read as works of mourning but rather as the traces of melancholia. This diagnosis is if anything too obvious, since the poems flaunt their symptoms. We have already noted the omnipresence of *"al-ya's"* [despair] and *"al-ka'aba"* [melancholy] in *The Songs of Mihyar* and their role in the poems' rhetoric of inwardness, a reflection of the traditional association between melancholy and contemplation. But sadness is also the sign of a spiritual aristocracy, a valorization of the saturnine temperament observable in other periods of literary history.[51] In "The Barbarian Priest," Mihyar is *"al-khaliq al-shaqiyy"* [the miserable creator], a formulation that links misery to the mania of poetry (hence Adonis's frequent rhyming of *"ka'aba"* [melancholy] with *"kitaba"* [writing]). Other poems intimate that *ya's* is a sign of prophethood. In "The Face of Mihyar," Mihyar is "the one who refuses the imamate / Leaving his despair as a sign / above the face of seasons."

Melancholy is therefore a remarkably productive pathology. It sets the poet apart from others, but this is precisely what his art requires. Granting the poet a vision of monotony and waste, melancholy becomes a working principle of dissatisfaction. Whereas mourning requires the recognition of a lost object or person so that the work of withdrawal and recathexis can begin, the melancholic refuses to acknowledge loss. In Freud's canonical account, the melancholic may know *"whom* he has lost, but not *what* he has lost in him."[52] Julia Kristeva goes beyond Freud's diagnosis to show how this refusal of recognition can be aesthetically productive, how in her words, "beauty emerges as the admirable face of loss." By placing the lost thing under taboo and designating it as henceforth un-representable, the artist generates a search for substitute satisfactions, however temporary and ultimately inadequate (melancholy, like analysis, is interminable). Translated into the terms of this chapter, the melancholic is characterized by his continual acts of displacement. Unable or unwilling to acknowledge the lost thing, he turns away from it, seeking compensatory structures and authorities through a series of imaginary filiations, what Kristeva calls "anaphora of the unique object."[53]

I will suggest that for Adonis and for the Arab modernists more generally the unique lost object is nationalist politics, which they consistently refuse to name or to recognize. Here my reading of the modernists' elegies parts company with readers such as Culler, who resist any historicization of lyric poetry, and who read the apostrophe as the epitome of lyric address. Instead, Adonis's turn to the lyric and its characteristic tropes, as exemplified in the poems of his most canonical collection, must be understood within a historical narrative of his turn away from a particular history of nationalist militancy. In the chapters that follow, we will see further examples of how the death of a collective political project—the *Shiʿr* poets' common experience in the SSNP—motivates their melancholy strategies of evasion, substitution, and exclusion. The road from Damascus is the road from politics to poetry, henceforth understood as irreconcilable sources of authority. The road is therefore a crossroads, a threshold or a turning point, where the poet renounces the tutelary spirits of his political past and begins his search for new, literary substitutes. Many phantoms gather here: Odysseus, Abu Nuwas, Saint-John Perse. The poet apostrophizes each in turn and then turns away for further summons. The exclusion of politics, which is *Shiʿr*'s editorial and ideological raison d'être, is not a strategy of censorship so much as it is a productive prohibition—hence the various tropes of repudiation or denial scattered throughout the corpus of Arabic modernism, from Adonis's *al-rafd* [refusal] to Unsi al-Hajj's more radical *lan* [will not]. By placing old authorities under a succession of taboos, modernism generates the new *via negativa*.[54]

For Arab modernists, the loss of politics is the enabling condition of their poetry, the engine of its various displacements and reauthorizations. This is also why the ideology of autonomy—the absolute separation of poetry from politics—is best understood not as a positive slogan but rather a gesture of repression, made over and again in the *Shiʿr* poets' editorial decisions and strategies of translation. "The essence of repression lies simply in turning something away, and keeping it at a distance, from the consciousness," Freud writes in "Repression." Such repeated exclusions bear witness to the recalcitrance of the material—the threatened return of the repressed—and also to its generative, libidinal energies. In *The Songs of Mihyar*, politics survives through the traces of its repression.

"*Qad Tasir Biladi*" [She Might Become My Country] is another—final—poem of the road from Damascus, Adonis's compulsively retraced itinerary. Here the speaker is figured as a variant of the *angelus novus*, a refugee who can only escape if he never looks back:

> Here I am climbing, rising above the morning of my country,
> above her ruins and her peaks.
> Here I am freeing myself from the weight of death inside her.
> Here I am estranging myself from her
> just to see her,
> so that tomorrow she might become my country.

CHAPTER FOUR

The Origins of the Arabic Prose Poem

The Measure of Man

No modernist genre provoked more controversy than the prose poem or *qasidat al-nathr*. When the *Shiʿr* poets began translating and publishing their own versions in the late 1950s, local critics accused them of traducing the long tradition of Arabic poetry, in which meter (and rhyme) held a paramount place until well into the twentieth century. In her seminal study, *Qadaya al-shiʿr al-muʿasir* [Problems in Contemporary Poetry], published in 1962, the Iraqi poet Nazik al-Malaʾika called the prose poem a "strange and heretical innovation," wondering if its advocates were perhaps "ignorant of the limits of poetry?" A decade or so earlier, al-Malaʾika and her Iraqi peers had pioneered a new verse form of their own, *al-shiʿr al-hurr* [free poetry], which maintained the meters formalized by al-Khalil ibn Ahmad al-Farahidi in the eighth century but varied the number of metrical units per line, doing away with the caesura that marks the majority of Arabic poems written before World War II. Al-Malaʾika, a pan-Arabist in politics, believed that her innovations were sanctioned by the canons of the Arabic *turath*, and even styled herself as a present-day al-Khalil. The antagonism between her and the *Shiʿr* poets was thus a rivalry between innovators. Al-Malaʾika and many other critics argued that by composing a type of poem that did away with meter entirely, the Beiruti modernists were not writing poetry at all. Though she was herself a translator and keen student of English Romantic poetry, al-Malaʾika accused the modernists of looking abroad for poetic models. She called *Shiʿr* a magazine "published in the Arabic language with a European spirit."[1]

What are the limits, or borders, of poetry? Are they coextensive with national or linguistic borders? Is translation always an act of heresy—a letter divorced from the spirit? While scholarly commentary on the Arabic prose poem has centered on questions of prosody, seeking to locate the modernists' innovations within a long history of metrical experimentation, the real stakes of the debate about the new form was the definition of poetry as such, its sources of authority and relation to its readers.[2] The *Shiʿr* poets were aware of these stakes. In the magazine's collective response to al-Malaʾika, published in the spring of 1962, they argued that her criticisms displayed "an ignorance (or pretended ignorance) of the nature of poetry, as well as a lamentable backwardness in viewpoint and understanding." The claim that poetry could be defined by something as external, arbitrary, and antiquated as verse meters only revealed al-Malaʾika's parochialism. In his review of *Problems in Contemporary Poetry*, Yusuf al-Khal accused the Iraqi poet of having "donned a schoolmarm's veil of traditionalism and close-mindedness, ignorant of everything that has happened and is happening as regards the development of poetical and artistic experimentalism in the world." If the prose poem is not really a poem, he asks rhetorically, then what are we to call the texts of "the great world poets"—Baudelaire, Lautréamont, Artaud, and Perse—who wrote in this form?[3] For the Beiruti modernists, literary experiments happening elsewhere, especially in Paris or New York, could serve as authoritative precedents for Arabic poetry. The limits of what could legitimately be called "*shiʿr*" did not coincide with the limits of Arabic but with the limits of translation.

It was chiefly through their activities as translators that the modernists expanded the boundaries of poetry, and the *qasidat al-nathr* was their most radical experiment of this sort, a translated genre or genre in translation whose emergence challenged the protocols of the local literary field. For the Beiruti poets, and for many Arab poets after them, the prose poem is the signal genre of world literature. We have already seen how Adonis's interest in Perse was motivated by his desire to find "a solid support for the very principle of the prose poem," and that one of the signal attractions of Perse's poetry was its translatability. The genealogy of translators—Eliot, Ungaretti, Benjamin—is precisely what made Perse's verse "more worldly" than any other. For the modernists, the metrical strictures of classical verse, still maintained by poets such as al-Malaʾika, were emblematic of Arabic culture's own rigidity. "*Étroit la mesure, étroit la césure*": "Narrow the meter, narrow the caesura," Perse writes in *Amers*, a formula for the Arab modernists' own most passionate convictions.[4]

The modernists claimed that the *qasidat al-nathr* allowed poets to introduce a new form of music into Arabic verse. This new music, they argued, was uniquely in tune with the rhythms of modernity itself.[5] This is one of the chief contentions of Adonis's manifesto, "On the Prose Poem," published in the spring 1960 issue of *Shiʿr*. Adonis's essay, which set the terms for the modernists' defense of the new form, was written at the beginning of a yearlong fellowship in Paris, where he encountered Suzanne Bernard's magisterial study, *Le Poème en prose de Baudelaire jusqu'à nos jours*, published in 1959. Bernard's keywords, "brevity," "intensity," "gratuity," and "interiority"—a concise lexicon of late modernist poetics—were systematically invoked by the modernists in their apologies for the *qasidat al-nathr*. The *Shiʿr* poets also echoed Bernard's description of the form as a quasi-anarchistic gesture of individual rebellion against classical norms. "The prose poem," Bernard writes, "is born of a revolt against all the formal tyrannies that prevent the poet from creating an individual language and force him to pour the soft clay of his phrases into ready-made molds." Bernard argued that the prose poem was exceptionally suited to its times, calling it "a *modern* form, adapted to the present day, to the interior impulses and aspirations of modern man." The form's modernity was proven by its self-sufficiency. At the end of her study, Bernard cites André Malraux's *The Voices of Silence*: "There is a fundamental value of modern art ... which is the very old will to create an autonomous world, *reduced for the first time upon itself.*" For Adonis too, the form's modernity and autonomy are what lend the prose poem its distinctive music: "The prose poem has its music, but it is not a music that submits to the old, canonized rhythms. Instead, it is a music that responds to the experience of dynamism and our new life—a rhythm that renews itself in every instant."[6]

The modernists' concept of music stood in contrast to the ideas of al-Malaʾika, who argued that music was precisely what made poetry and prose incompatible. Al-Malaʾika's definition of poetry is explicitly rhetorical: a poem is only a poem if it provokes the emotions of its listeners (al-Malaʾika, unlike the modernists, consistently imagines the relation between poet and audience as one between a speaker and auditors). Furthermore, a poem's affective power is ultimately a function of its music, which for al-Malaʾika is reducible to its meter [*wazn*]: "Meter is the spirit that electrifies the literary material and makes it poetry, for there is no poetry without the meter, no matter how the poet stuffs his work with images and sentiments. Indeed, images and sentiments do not become poetic, in the true sense of the word, unless touched by the musician's fingers, unless some meter beats in their veins." Al-Malaʾika traces this definition of poetry back to the earliest period of Islam, when it was conceived of as a species of magic or enchantment the poet wielded over his listeners. But prose, according to al-Malaʾika, lacks this ability to sway the feelings its audience: "There is no doubt that prose, because it lacks this affective music, also lacks that special ability of poetry to thrill the emotions and touch the heart. And so prose was mainly used for scientific study and objective researches, so much so that we now call poetry that does not give us a feeling of musical ecstasy [*la yutribuna*] 'prosaic.'"[7]

The idea of *tarab*, or musical ecstasy, is crucial to al-Malaʾika's poetics, and it is the *Shiʿr* poets' emphatic rejection of this mode of experience that defines their own sense of the prose poem's modernist music. For al-Malaʾika, *tarab* is the most basic and widespread poetic affect. Even a listener who cannot distinguish well-metered verse from broken verse—al-Malaʾika supposed that most people fall into this group—can experience the *tarab* that poetry paradigmatically affords and prose does not.[8] "*Tarab*" is a notoriously difficult word to define: "A term denoting poetic and musical emotion, evoking a broad spectrum of sentiments, from the most private to the most violent: pleasure, enjoyment, emotional trauma, exaltation," according to a standard reference. More descriptively, *tarab* is a state of intense vibration or *Stimmung* experienced by both musicians and audience, linked to one another by a loop of "ecstatic-feedback." At the moment that al-Malaʾika was writing, the term also had a marked political resonance. The two decades after World War II were preeminently the era of the Egyptian *mutribin*, Umm Kulthum and ʿAbdel Wahab, whose songs were broadcast on Egyptian radio across the region, giving rise to what Virginia Danielson has termed a pan-Arab "*tarab* culture," an experience of being-together in a musically induced ecstasy. Al-Malaʾika, like most contributors and readers of *al-Adab*, was an enthusiastic supporter of Nasserism, and *tarab* was in this sense a figure for the new political solidarities associated with anti-imperialist pan-Arabism. By putting *tarab* at the heart of her poetics, al-Malaʾika was making clear her political leanings, arguing that aesthetic innovation was compatible with a politics of authenticity. *Tarab* is an experience that is pan-Arab but also uniquely Arab. Hence, like the Spanish "*duende*," to which it is often compared, "*tarab*" is a famously difficult word to translate.[9]

The modernists' defense of the prose poem is premised on their rejection of *tarab* as a mode of musical experience. This rejection is often coupled with a dismissal of al-Khalil's metrics, to which al-Malaʾika remained faithful in her fashion. For the modernists, varying the number of feet per line only produces poetry composed in the sequence of the metronome. On the first page of "On the Prose Poem," Adonis writes, "Khalilian rhythm is a physical peculiarity of Arabic poetry, one intended most of all for *tarab*. And in this sense it offers a delight to the ear rather than an aid to thought." In the same vein, Unsi al-Hajj writes in his introduction to *Lan*, the other foundational document for the modernists' defense of the new form: "It may be that when you read [a prose poem] (Henri Michaux, Antonin Artaud . . .), if you read it aloud, for the purpose of pleasure or of being carried away, you will leap up and deny that this is poetry, since you find no magic in it, no *tarab*." In Khalida Saʿid's supportive review of *Lan*, she discovers precisely this absence: "Unsi al-Hajj does not sing, nor explain, nor write elegantly. He does not compose in stanzas, nor does he avail himself of the phonic elements of words and letters. He has none of the sweetness, the sparkle, the cozy mood of the *mutrib*. All these things are foreign to his own mood." The modernist poet is not a *mutrib*, but this does not mean the prose poem is devoid of music. Instead, it suggests that its model of music—"without rhythm and without rhyme, flexible and fitful enough to adapt itself to the lyrical movements of the soul," in Baudelaire's foundational description—is to be found elsewhere.[10]

The modernists' antipathy toward *tarab* can be traced to the writings of Sa'ada, who is at the origin of so many of their characteristic attitudes. Sa'ada's interest in music is evident as early as his first stay in South America, when he covered concerts at the São Paulo Conservatory for his father's monthly, *al-Majalla*.¹¹ In 1932, having returned to Beirut to recruit members for his new party, he published a didactic novel of ideas, *Faji'at hubb* [A Love Tragedy], which features a long dialogue on the virtues of Eastern versus Western styles of music (the novel is palpably a relic of Sa'ada's time tutoring undergraduates at AUB while also attempting to recruit them to his party). He excerpted this dialogue at length in the second chapter of *The Intellectual Struggle* as a preface to his discussion of Beethoven's symphonies and Wagner's operas, his chief examples of national art forms that qualified as philosophical universals. "Music is not merely the language of emotions," the protagonist of *A Love Tragedy* admonishes his listeners, "it is also the language of thought and understanding." Sa'ada goes on to relate an anecdote or parable from his own life:

> A few years ago, in São Paulo, Brazil, I heard a Syrian journalist who considered himself a great man of letters saying that he had gone to the Municipal Theater of that city to hear one of Beethoven's famous symphonies. He was seated only a short while before he could no longer bear to listen and got up to leave, astonished at the idiocy of those able to sit without boredom, for an hour or more, listening to music in which there was no *tarab*. [. . .] To drive away his distress, he asked the Syrian in whose office he was telling this story to put on a few songs of the sentimental Egyptian *mutriba*, Umm Kulthum! Nor did he stop there, but called out to a friend of his who was passing by, "Come over here, this song is to die for [*li-namut bi-hadha-l-ghina'*]," not realizing that he had spoken the very truth with this phrase, by which he meant something quite different!¹²

For Sa'ada, as for his literary disciples, *tarab* is the mark of provincialism. It is the music of rustic voluptuaries rather than poets, and its raptures are a sign of spiritual death. Sa'ada's censure of Umm Kulthum's sentimentalism, "a delight to the ear rather than an aid to thought," parallels his censure of Shafiq Ma'luf's "*Abqar*," which he faults for its merely sensual conception of love and reliance on local superstitions. Sa'ada's preference for the "philosophical" compositions of Beethoven and Wagner over the emotive dirges of the *mutribin* is echoed by many of the *Shi'r* poets as well as subsequent modernists.¹³ During the period in which he wrote for and edited party publications, Yusuf al-Khal composed several articles on Eastern and Western music, in which he inveighed against the influence of Egyptian music, "devoid of art or taste, filling the soul with waves of lethargy, despair, grief, and degeneration." A number of Unsi al-Hajj's early pieces of journalism for *al-Adib* are reviews of biographies of classical composers, notably Chopin and Beethoven, who became for him prototypes of the *poète maudit*. Even those *Shiʿr* poets who never belonged to the party often echo Saʿada's preferences. In the introduction to his 1959 poetry collection, *Tammuz fi-l-madina* [Tammuz in the City], Jabra Ibrahim Jabra notes that while he refused the use of "monotonous" meters, his own prosody will be recognized "by anyone familiar with orchestral music," since his long poems in particular are "built along the lines of a symphony." And Adonis writes, in an important early essay, that modern poetry is defined by its "symphonic construction, allowing it to embrace all life, all reality."[14]

The modernists distinguished between traditional verse, governed by an external, rule-bound music—the prosody codified by al-Khalil—and the music of the prose poem, which was based on "personal experience" or the dynamic rhythms of the self. In "On the Prose Poem," Adonis writes that "The world of music in the prose poem is a personal, private world, as opposed to the world of music in metered poetry, which is a world of arbitrary congruence, rules, and analogies."[15] These remarks are echoed by al-Hajj in his introduction to *Lan*: "The music of meter and rhyme is an external music, a music that has remained the same while the world is in transformation, because man is in transformation, because of a new sensibility." The "rules" of the new genre, al-Hajj writes—putting the word between quotation marks to suggest his ambivalence toward any notion of rules in poetry—spring "from the soul of the poet himself," from his "interior experience."[16] This conception of music as subjective experience is one with deep roots in philosophical aesthetics, beginning with Hegel and continuing through the German tradition of what Carl Dahlhaus has called "absolute music."[17] The chief figures of this tradition—Beethoven, Wagner, Nietzsche—are precisely the ones we find in the writings of Saʿada and his followers. The prose poem is the culmination of the modernists' project of translating Saʿada's nationalism into a poetics of self-sufficiency and hermetic subjectivity. The *qasidat al-nathr* was a genre with extravagantly "worldly" credentials that the *Shiʿr* poets theorized as a new musical form, an autonomous, symphonic work of art that sprung from the poet's most "private" experiences.

The prose poem, as understood by the Beiruti modernists, seems to arise from an act of auscultation, or attention to interior rhythms. But how do these rhythms synchronize with the dynamism of modernity? How does the private music of the prose poem accord with what Adonis calls "the rhythm of our new life, a rhythm that renews itself in every instant"? The same puzzle arises in the modernists' theorizations of the genre's source of authority. Does the *qasidat al-nathr* originate abroad, or does it well up from the self? We have noted that the *Shiʿr* poets often translated foreign authors such as Robinson Jeffers and Saint-John Perse as though they belonged to a hoary native tradition. But the Arab modernists' most common way of harmonizing these sources is to suppose a subject, namely "man," who serves as a figure of mediation, translating from one side of this caesura to the other. We recall Adonis's description of his own experience of translating the prose poetry of Perse: "I admit that when I undertook to translate Saint-John Perse, I wasn't certain that the Arabic language, born of the desert, could encompass that lyrical and epic sea that is the text of Perse. But as I progressed, I became certain that the desert and the sea come together in that larger and richer ocean which is man." This echoes the rhetoric of Perse's Nobel speech, where he claims that, for the poet, "One law of harmony governs the whole world of things. Nothing can occur there which by its nature is incommensurable with man [*qui par nature excède la mesure de l'homme*]. The worst catastrophes of history are but seasonal rhythms in a vaster cycle of repetitions and renewals."[18] "*La mesure de l'homme*" is a pun on the genitive: the (poetic) measure of man as well as man the (universal) measure. In Perse's figure of man-as-translator, a subject whose private rhythms are in sync with the wider seas of history, we have the *Shiʿr* poets' most powerful version of "world harmony." "*Une même vague par le monde*," Perse writes in *Amers*, "One wave for the world." This is the late modernist sublime, a vision of man's limitlessness. What is especially remarkable about the work of Unsi al-Hajj is its attempt to expose the boundaries of this theorization, to mark the limits of man and of poetry.

Under the Sign of Cancer

Although Adonis published his first prose poems in 1958, it was Unsi al-Hajj's collection *Lan*, published in 1960 by Dar Majallat Shiʿr, that put the *qasidat al-nathr* at the heart of debates about the modernist movement. The prose poems of *Lan* are the most radical and bewildering of all the texts produced by the *Shiʿr* poets. They provoked outrage among critics and impassioned defenses by the movement's supporters. "Unsi is the purest among us," Adonis wrote at the time. "We others are more or less soiled with traditionalism."[19] It is fair to say that al-Hajj courted the controversy. The very title of his book is a provocation: "*lan*" is a particle used to negate the future tense in formal Arabic. It is another trope of refusal, like Adonis's "*al-rafd*," though here the amputated syntax—the closest English equivalent is perhaps "won't"—suggests some terminal taboo or limit of poetic expression. Al-Hajj prefaced the first edition of *Lan* with a long introduction that serves as an *apologia pro libro suo* as well as a defense of the genre. Many of al-Hajj's formulations are borrowed from Adonis's essay, "On the Prose Poem," but al-Hajj's text is better read as a performance piece than a work of sustained argument. He styles the writer of prose poems as a *poète maudit* [*shaʿir malʿun*], "cursed in his body and in his very existence," who pits himself against the forces of "political reaction, stagnation, and religious and ethnic fanaticism." Many of al-Hajj's claims seem designed to justify the harshest suspicions of the modernists' critics, who consistently argued that *Shiʿr* was out to demolish the Arabic literary heritage. Al-Hajj wrote that the modern poet's "first duty is obliteration," and against those who would "accept the inheritance of decline," he announced his own slogan: "Destruction and destruction and destruction [*al-hadm wa-l-hadm wa-l-hadm*]." Al-Hajj argued that the political, cultural, and educational institutions of modern Arab life had produced a populace of "slaves, ignoramuses, and fools." In the face of such entrenched conservatism, he averred that the modern poet had one of two options: "Suffocation or madness."[20]

The pan-Arabists at *al-Adab* were contemptuous of all this attitudinizing. They called al-Hajj, then in his early twenties, "utterly foul-mouthed and lacking in manners." In another editorial, they described him as "a trifling youngster who wants to get famous through vulgarity, insolence, and silly obscenities." The nationalists were especially offended by al-Hajj's aggressively unliterary lexicon. They pointed to his use of *"al-mirhad"* [toilet] as an example of the surrealists' lamentable influence (typically, while al-Hajj complains of being suffocated by parochialism, the nationalist writers worry about foreign contaminations).[21] These accusations of impropriety and name-calling point to a deeper critique. To say that al-Hajj was "lacking in manners," in Arabic *"qillat al-adab,"* was to impugn his literary authority: *"adab"* means "letters" or "literature" as well as "manners," and so a lack of social politesse doubles as illiteracy. For the modernists, however, a certain kind of illiteracy was praiseworthy and even desirable. In a congratulatory letter from Paris, where news had reached him of the publication of *Lan*, Adonis joined arms with al-Hajj against those whom he called "the partisans of heritage" [*al-irthiyyun*]: "The heritage isn't a pivot for us—neither a wellspring, nor a circle that surrounds us. Human existence is our pivot and our wellspring: everything else, the heritage included, circles around that." For the modernists, it was crucial to break with inherited modes of literacy in order to write truly "human" poetry, and this is what the *qasidat al-nathr* allowed them to do. As Adonis wrote to al-Hajj, signing off from Paris: "Through you, our poetry comes nearer to being poetry."[22]

For al-Hajj the prose poem is indeed an illiterate form, so long as literacy is understood as the acquisition of fluency with the cultural past. His own work suggests, by contrast, that the *qasidat al-nathr* emerges from an experience of suffocation, aphasia, and confinement—paradigmatically, a confinement within the body. In al-Hajj's introduction to *Lan*, he calls this experience of fleshly enclosure *"al-saratan"* [cancer], which he takes as a sign of the modern zeitgeist:

> We are in the age of cancer. This is what I say and it makes everyone laugh. We are in the age of cancer: here, and on the inside. Art either keeps pace or dies. It has kept pace—the afflicted are those who have created a new world of poetry: when we say Rimbaud, we point to a family of the sick. The prose poem is the daughter of this family.
>
> We are in the age of cancer: in prose, poetry, everything. The prose poem is the creation [*khaliqa*] of this age, its ally and its destiny.[23]

The symptoms of this disease, as we find them in the prose poems themselves, are verbal outbursts, shouts of protest against the feeling of self-strangulation. Unlike the smooth undulations of Adonis's prose poems, Al-Hajj's versions are exclamatory episodes, more akin to Rimbaud's *Illuminations* than Perse's lyrical sequences. The title of one poem, "A Shriek That Starts and Stops," sums up the collection, which proceeds fitfully through a sequence of stutters, stammerings, and shrieks. "I seek a virgin scream," al-Hajj writes, "but do not find even a hesitant murmuration."[24] These verbal ejaculations, some of them in the form of curses or obscenities, are the symptoms of physical discord. "The body awakes!" the poet exclaims in the explicitly Rimbaldien prose poem "*Fasl fi-l-jild*" [A Season in the Skin]. "The skin lifts like the lid of a coffin. / It gushes! / It flares open like nostrils."[25]

The body is the dominant topos of al-Hajj's early prose poems and translations. It is typically an adolescent or disorganized body, one that refuses to behave and is therefore watched, scolded, made ashamed of itself. (One of al-Hajj's pen names for his regular column at *al-Nahar* was "*murahiq*" [an adolescent].) But it is also a sick body, one that has already begun to decompose. In "Season in the Skin," the Christian trope of bodily resurrection is undermined by putrefaction—swelling and smelling—as well as entombment. Indeed, in al-Hajj's poetry the experience of having a body is often likened to the claustrophobia of being en-coffined. "Where shall I flee when I am the horizon?" the poet asks in "*Huwiyya*" [Identity], a restatement of Rimbaud's parody of the Cartesian cogito, "*Je me crois en enfer, donc j'y suis*" [I believe myself in Hell, so that's where I am]. If Yusuf al-Khal is a poet of crucifixion and rebirth, al-Hajj is a poet of incarnation and the descent into the body. In the words of his French translator, al-Hajj is "a Christian Gnostic."[26]

For all his claims to a Rimbaldien legacy, it is al-Hajj's translation of Antonin Artaud—another gnostic in Susan Sontag's influential reading as well as "one of the last great exemplars of the heroic period of literary modernism"—that established the peculiar lexicon of al-Hajj's early poetics, his working notions of embodiment and articulation, cancer and contagion.[27] Al-Hajj's *naql* of Artaud was the most extensive translation project he published in *Shiʿr*. His Arabic versions appeared in the fall 1960 issue, contemporaneously with the publication of *Lan*, along with a substantial commentary. Other important translations would follow, including a selection of poems by André Breton and a version of the biblical Song of Songs.[28] Al-Hajj's folio of Artaud translations includes seven early poems ("*Cri*," *Poète Noir*," "*Musicien*," "*L'arbre*," "*Nuit*," "*L'amour sans trêve*," and "*Prière*"), the prose poem "*L'enclume des forces*," an excerpt from "*Van Gogh le suicidé de la société*," and two late poems, "*Lettre à Pierre Loëb*" and "*J'étais vivant*." Al-Hajj's title for the selection is "Eleven Poems," and in his commentary he treats Artaud almost exclusively as a poet. The theatrical writings, though mentioned, are unanalyzed.[29]

The selection of early poems adds up to an idealized portrait of the *poète maudit*, a trope one finds everywhere in al-Hajj's early work: "The little celestial poet" of *"Cri,"* who is also "the little lost poet"; the eponymous "dark poet"; and the apostrophized figure of *"Nuit"*: "Poet, that which invests you / has nothing to do with the moon." *"Musicien,"* a pastiche of Baudelaire, may have been included for its fusion of several themes important to al-Hajj: music, the sea, and the artist as a conjuror of demons. These early poems mostly date from the period of Artaud's involvement with the surrealists, and the opening of al-Hajj's supplementary essay is a discussion of Artaud's break with Breton. In recounting this split, al-Hajj takes his cues from Artaud's 1927 text, "In Total Darkness, or the Surrealist Bluff," a response to the surrealists' tract "In the Light of Day," which announced Artaud's expulsion from the group and their commitment to communism.[30] "The whole root, all the exacerbations of our quarrel, turn on the word 'Revolution,'" Artaud writes. "For each man to refuse to consider anything beyond his own deepest sensibility, beyond his inmost self [*le moi intime*], this for me is the point of view of the complete Revolution." Al-Hajj comments:

> Among the deepest causes that distanced [Artaud] from [the surrealists] is that they sought to include only two goals within their revolution, the social and the political, whereas Artaud understood revolution to be a human revolution [*thawra insaniyya*]. The political revolutionary cannot commit himself to his own individual freedom because he cannot commit himself to the individual freedom of his enemy. The political revolutionary is a social oppressor, a collective oppressor. (95)

This is a familiar argument, borrowed from the philosophy of personalism, that salvages the humanist subject by distinguishing it from the fallen, material realm of politics, which is identified with the collective's tyranny over the individual. Many texts by Artaud lend themselves to such spiritualist readings. Al-Hajj cites the series of lectures Artaud delivered in Mexico in 1936, for example, where his anti-Marxist polemics often have recourse to the trope of man as a figure of integrity and interiority (Artaud's *"homme"* is an anthropological figure rather than a philosophical one: he is archaic rather than abstract). As Artaud writes in "Man against Destiny," "A preoccupation with the external functions of Man leads one away from a profound understanding of Man. And there is a whole world in the mind. The Communist revolution ignores the internal world of thought." In "First Contact with the Mexican Revolution," another text from this period in which Artaud had become fascinated with the vitalism of exotic cultures, he writes, "We expect from Mexico a new concept of Revolution, and also a new concept of Man which will serve to nourish, to feed with its magical life this ultimate form of humanism that is being born in France."[31] But al-Hajj's reading of Artaud does not ultimately seek to make him another example of the humanist discourse of man. Instead, he situates Artaud at the limits of this discourse. Where humanism posits the continuity of a certain cultural or even civilizational inheritance, Artaud casts doubt on the possibility of literary or linguistic transmission. While exalting man's "internal world of thought," he also suggests that interiority may ultimately be a trap.

For al-Hajj, the fundamental distinction between the surrealists and Artaud is one between health and illness. In his diagnosis, the contrasting symptoms are chiefly verbal. The surrealists, who declared "the well-known lack of frontiers between nonmadness and madness" (Breton's phrase in *Nadja*), nevertheless remained outside the experience of illness. Al-Hajj writes, "They escaped from their stammerings and muteness to talk about stammering and muteness in a language proper to them, a language that took its distance from the experience itself" (98). Surrealist automatic writing, in al-Hajj's description, was an exercise in eloquence, tracing the grooves already established by convention. Artaud, on the other hand, writes from within illness, which is what makes him so difficult to understand. The illness in question is not madness, however. The trope of *la folie* (or schizophrenia), so common in later studies of Artaud in France, is hardly mentioned by al-Hajj. Instead, the disease he is concerned with is *al-saratan*: "Perhaps his affliction with cancer is the key to his world, to its many obscurities and hallucinations. The rotten blood circulating in his veins was not living blood, but the blood of cancer. In this way, we begin to understand the impossibility for Artaud to live, to be in harmony, to realize himself, to think with clarity and organization [*bi-intizam*]" (96).

Al-Hajj's understanding of cancer as a passionate experience of suffering and incarnation reflects his reading of Georges Charbonnier's early, somewhat florid study, *Antonin Artaud* (1959), which al-Hajj cites extensively in his own essay. Charbonnier writes, "For all the pains he suffered throughout his life, for all the tortures of electroshock, Antonin Artaud did not die of these pains nor these tortures. He died of a cancer in the rectum. He was strangled by the anus. . . . Artaud slowly and ineluctably came to inhabit his body [*incarné son corps*], and when the incarnation was complete, the cancer finally choked the life out of him."[32] Cancer, in al-Hajj's text, is also a disease that strangles the subject from within, but it is essentially a disease of the blood, a species of *mauvais sang* in which the body drowns itself. This claustrophobic vision is most powerfully present in al-Hajj's prose poem *"Afaf Yabas"* [Desiccated Purity], a nightmarish anecdote that combines in typical fashion the themes of sexual anxiety, claustrophobic confinement, artistic creation, and the fear of pollution or impropriety:

> The only thing I recall is that I was in a ditch, gobbling up my own body until it was dead, and then I regretfully stuffed the cadaver so that it might live again. The door was not closed. I was hiding and fantasizing and in that way comforting myself. Then she came in and the blood

spilled like coffee and for the first time I cleaned up. Then she screamed in my face, "I found you!" So I kissed her like a pervert and ran away to the city cemeteries.

The resurrection of the body, whose blood is rotten with cancer, is reimagined here as an act of "stuffing," as with a doll or scarecrow, and the poem ends with the imploration: "Invent for us a purity with no blood!"[33] In a similar vein, the opening poem of *Lan*, "*al-Huwiyya*" [Identity], ends with the iconic phrase "Modern blood" or "New blood" [*dam hadith*], which sounds at once like a prayer and the demand for a new Eucharist.

At other moments of his supplementary essay, al-Hajj writes of cancer as a disease of disorganization: "The cancer hatched in Artaud's anus and spread all over his body, dismembering him." This figuration of the body as a site of dismemberment is made vivid by the second poem translated by al-Hajj, "*J'étais vivant*," taken from the special edition of *84* magazine dedicated to Artaud and published immediately after his death.[34] The poem ends with a series of refusals or surgical amputations: "To open one's mouth is to give oneself up to miasmas. / So, no mouth! / no mouth / no tongue / no teeth / no larynx / no esophagus / no stomach / no belly / no anus // I will reconstruct the man I was." The organs named and negated in this poem are those of speech, or else the body's hollows and orifices. (It is not by chance that al-Hajj's second volume of verse bears the acephalous title, *Ra's maqtu'* [A Cut-off Head].) While the last line of Artaud's poem promises a project of humanist "reconstruction," the figure it gestures toward is radically closed off to the outside: all means of egress have been sealed shut. In this way, an obsession with interiority as a space for creative adventure, or as the last refuge of the spirit, tips over into a vision of absolute immanence, "a metaphysics of the flesh," in Jacques Derrida's phrase, or humanism with no exit. In short, a trap.

The Limits of Translation

Between 1965 and 1969, the late texts of Artaud were the subject of studies by Derrida and Gilles Deleuze that helped establish the themes of posthumanist discourse in France. For both Derrida and Deleuze, Artaud represents a figure of humanism's limits: "The limit—the humanist limit—of the metaphysics of classical theater," in Derrida's case, and the limits of Oedipal subjectivity and sense-making in the work of Deleuze.[35] These essays were written amidst a general turn in the late 1960s toward post- or antihumanism in philosophy and the social sciences, whose landmarks in French thought are well known: the rediscovery of Heidegger's "Letter on Humanism," Derrida's essay "The Ends of Man," Michel Foucault's announcement, at the end of *The Order of Things*, that "man is an invention of recent date," and Louis Althusser's attack on Marxist pieties of the early postwar period: "Our primary theoretical, ideological and political (I say political) duty today is to rid the domain of Marxist philosophy of all the 'Humanist' rubbish that is brazenly being dumped into it."[36]

This antihumanism does not, of course, provide a context for al-Hajj, who published his work on Artaud in 1960. If anything, the relation works the other way around. A number of central themes in the essays of Derrida and Deleuze—translation and articulation, the body and the limit—are prefigured in the writings of al-Hajj, suggesting that skepticism toward the discourse of man occurred outside Europe well in advance of its collapse on the continent. Indeed, it is worth noting the strict contemporaneity of *Lan* with Frantz Fanon's *Wretched of the Earth* (1961), with its ringing conclusion: "Let us leave this Europe where they are never done talking of Man, yet murder men everywhere they find them, at the corner of every one of their own streets, in all the corners of the globe. For centuries they have stifled almost the whole of humanity in the name of a so-called spiritual experience."[37] A reception history of Artaud that juxtaposes al-Hajj's reading and translations with the essays of Derrida and Deleuze makes clear the untimeliness of al-Hajj's work in both local and international terms. In questioning the viability or transmissibility of humanism, al-Hajj was also formulating radical doubts, never really acknowledged by his peers (nor by subsequent scholars), about the modernist project of *Shiʿr*.

In *"La parole soufflée,"* an essay written in 1965, Derrida situates Artaud at an extreme of Western metaphysics, a tradition he simultaneously belonged to and sought to demolish, in the manner of deconstructionist criticism itself: "Artaud keeps himself at the limit," Derrida writes, "and we have attempted to read him at this limit."[38] Derrida construes Artaud's work as a protest against the Western dramaturgical tradition, which subjects the actor's living voice to a preexisting text. In classical theater, the actor never speaks in his own name but always in the words of another, the offstage prompter (in French, *souffleur*) or playwright who robs the speaker of his proper speech and forces him to speak what is, in effect, a foreign language. "Henceforth," writes Derrida, summarizing Artaud, "what is called the speaking subject is no longer the person himself, or the person alone, who speaks. The speaking subject discovers his irreducible secondarity." Derrida goes on to show how Artaud constantly links this loss of what is proper to the loss of propriety, so that the speaking subject's dispossession of his language is equivalent to the body being soiled by its own works or waste ("All writing is pig shit," Artaud famously declared). At the root of Artaud's critique of classical dramaturgy and the body it produces is his resistance to articulation as such—the articulations of language as well as the articulation of the body (its differentiation into organs). As Derrida explains, "Articulation is the structure of my body, and structure is always a structure of expropriation." In place of the classical theater of dispossession, in which the subject is robbed of his body and his word, Artaud imagines—rather sketchily, based on ideas of "Oriental Theater" exemplified by Balinese dance troupes he saw at the Colonial Exposition of 1931—a theater that restores integrity to the flesh, in which the superstition of texts is replaced by a concrete language of "objects, silences, shouts, and rhythms," "a genuine physical language with signs, not words, as its root." For Derrida, however, Artaud's substitution of "the metaphysics of flesh" for the false spiritualism of classical theater is a reversal that remains within the parameters of Western metaphysics. The ideal of a reconstituted but nonarticulated body—it is in this context that Derrida quotes Artaud's poem, "*J'étais vivant*"—is a fantasy of self-presence, a desire for what Derrida terms "One's-proper-body-upright-without-detritus."

The fantasy of a "body without organs" is a central trope in Gilles Deleuze and Félix Guattari's critique of orthodox psychology and political economy, *Anti-Oedipus* (1972). In elaborating this notion, which they insist "is not at all a notion or a concept" but rather "a set of practices" or else "a limit," they too cite "*J'étais vivant*," whose program of amputations they read as a resistance to articulation or organization as such: "The body suffers from being organized in this way, from not having some other sort of organization, or no organization at all. . . . In order to resist using words composed of articulated phonetic units, [the body without organs] utters only gasps and cries that are sheer unarticulated blocks of sounds."[39] Artaud's mistrust of articulation was also, explicitly, a mistrust of translation, which he viewed as yet another mode of dispossession. In *The Theater and Its Double*, he writes that for classical theater, where the written script has the status of sacred writ, the director "is merely an artisan, an adapter, a kind of translator eternally devoted to making a dramatic work pass from one language into another."[40] For Artaud, in other words, classical theater is a mise en scène of translation. It is a structure in which the subject comes into speech through a language that precedes him and is therefore not his own, discovering what Derrida terms the enunciating subject's "irreducible secondarity."

Artaud's critique of articulation and translation is the premise for Deleuze's earliest encounter with the poet, an essay in which Deleuze first identified the body without organs. In the thirteenth chapter of *The Logic of Sense* (1969), a study of Lewis Carroll's Alice books, Deleuze reads Artaud's partial translation of "Jabberwocky." Composed in 1943, Artaud's version of Carroll's nonsense poem was one of several translations he produced at the psychiatric hospital Rodez. Artaud had written almost nothing in the six years prior to his internment, and the exercises, suggested by his supervising doctor, were intended as a type of writing-cure. It was hoped that by submitting to the discipline of translation, the discourse of the other, Artaud would be able to rejoin society and, so to speak, himself. The therapy seems to have been a success—it is after Rodez that Artaud enjoyed his final burst of poetic productivity—if only because it activated Artaud's deep *hostility* toward translation. Artaud's version of "Jabberwocky" is in fact a hyperbolic mistranslation, a defiant refusal of the precursor's authority. "Not *after* Lewis but *against* him," as Artaud writes. Artaud's French version begins by mimicking the syntax of the original: "'Twas brillig, and the slithy toves / Did gyre and gimble in the wabe" becomes "Il était roparant, et les vliqueux tarands / Allaient en gibroyant et en brimbulkdriquant." Beginning with that final word, however, the translation veers abruptly away from Carroll's poem. The third and fourth lines read: "Jusque là lò la rourghe est à rouarghe a ramgmbde / et rangmbde a rouargambde." This is, Deleuze writes, "the language of schizophrenia." Rather than tracking a semantic or syntactical sequence, Artaud's version lets itself be guided by the material flow of guttural and consonantal sounds, as if he were swallowing and noisily digesting the English sonnet. It is not a transmission of sense so much as an attempt to decompose the structures of language, what Deleuze calls "a progressive and creative disorganization." Deleuze juxtaposes Carroll's brand of organized, "logical" nonsense with what he considered to be Artaud's more profound version, centered on "the painful passion of the body." Carroll's clever paradoxes, along with the almost graspable gibberish of "Jabberwocky"—rendered comically sensible by Humpty Dumpty's interpretations—require "a very strict grammar." But Artaud's howls and babblings destroy grammar, syntax, and the sense-making work of interpretation. (It was during his stay at Rodez that Artaud began composing his so-called glossolalic texts: "pesti anti pestantum putra," etc.) These shrieks and shouts emerge from the depths of the schizophrenic body, "An organism without parts which operates entirely by insufflation, respiration, evaporation, and fluid transmission (the superior body, or body without organs of Antonin Artaud)."[41]

Deleuze's reading suggests that the fantasy of a body without organs emerges from a failure of translation and might even be a figure of that failure. In his letter to Henri Parisot, an editor of many surrealist texts and translator of Carroll into French, Artaud wrote, "I haven't done a translation of 'Jabberwocky.' I tried to translate a piece of it, but it bored me. . . . It is permissible to invent one's language and to make the language speak with an extragrammatical meaning, but this meaning must be valid in itself, that is, it must come out of anguish. . . . 'Jabberwocky' is the work of an opportunist who wanted to feed intellectually on someone else's pain." Here again, translation and its necessary failure is linked to the experience of being robbed of what is proper to the self—its own pain or anguish. Whatever its therapeutic effects, Artaud continued to think of translation as a loss of self, which is perhaps why his own versions are so willfully "unfaithful." Artaud comes back to this experience of dispossession at the end of his letter, where he makes a somewhat surprising declaration: "'Jabberwocky' is nothing more than a sugar-coated and lifeless plagiarism of a work written by me, which has been spirited away so successfully that I myself hardly know what is in it."[42] The notion that a predecessor might have plagiarized one's own work is a paradox worthy of Borges, but it also describes the rather ordinary experience of translation, in which the words one writes always already belong to someone else.

In the essays of Derrida and Deleuze, Artaud marks the limit between a humanist ideology of unbroken cultural inheritance and a posthumanist vision of the body as a nexus of creative disorganization. This is already where, several years earlier, al-Hajj explicitly situates his own translations and commentary. To say that Artaud "keeps himself at the limit" is to suggest the ambiguity of his position. For both al-Hajj and Derrida, Artaud's oeuvre remains faithful to the humanist discourse of man, although for al-Hajj this is still a revolutionary discourse while for Derrida it confirms Artaud's fatal complicity with Western metaphysics. The project of humanist restoration promised in *"J'étais vivant"* ("I will reconstruct the man I was") is indistinguishable from its deconstruction: "No mouth / no tongue / no teeth."[43]

Situated at the limit of humanism, Western metaphysics, and sense-making, Artaud is a grand figure of crisis. The violent interruptions of his work cast doubt on the viability of cultural transmission, and so, not surprisingly, an anxiety of inheritance runs through the corpus of commentary on Artaud. What would it mean to declare one's affinity with a writer who refuses to acknowledge any predecessors or heirs? "I, Antonin Artaud, am my son, my father, my mother, and myself," Artaud declares in "Here Lies," a poem often cited by Deleuze: "I don't believe in father / or mother // don't have / papa-mama." In his essay on the theater of cruelty, Derrida asks, "Under what conditions can a theater today legitimately invoke Artaud's name? It is only a fact that so many directors wish to be acknowledged as Artaud's heirs, that is (as has been written), his 'illegitimate sons.'" Derrida looks askance at all such claims of inheritance but goes on to specify what sorts of theater, including that of Brecht and the situationists, must be considered "unfaithful."[44] In Deleuze and Guattari's texts, the same anxiety informs the tension between the "sterility" of the body without organs and its identification with eggs of various types (the Dogon egg, the world egg, the tantric egg: so many alter-egos of Humpty Dumpty). This tension gets resolved with a typically Deleuzian sleight of hand, by which Artaud's actual sterility, or failure, becomes a virtual fertility, or success. "Even if Artaud did not succeed for himself," Deleuze writes, "it is certain that through him something has succeeded for us all."[45]

For al-Hajj, an Arabic translator of Artaud, the dilemmas of inheritance and fidelity are especially acute. All translators are perhaps unfaithful heirs, and their status is made more untenable when the source text is determined to block all possibility of transmission. In al-Hajj's remarks on Artaud's break with the surrealists, he suggests that while Breton's movement settled for conventional codes of eloquence and so became "a reproduction [or biological descendant: *tanasul*] rather than an interruption" (98), Artaud's poetry is defined by its ineloquence, its reluctance to transmit itself to contemporaries or future generations. "I am writing for illiterates" is Artaud's typically paradoxical formulation.[46] For al-Hajj, this ineloquence or illiteracy is a symptom of cancer, conceived as a state of bodily immanence: "This is why is it so difficult for us to speak with Artaud. He blocked the road by refusing all relations and ties, by slipping beyond being, beyond the word, into the void.... In this way poetry reaches, with him, the limit of untransmissibility [*hadd al-imtinaʿ ʿan al-intiqal*]" (99). Artaud experienced this "untransmissibility" as a kind of physical ailment. "There is something that destroys my thought," he writes in one of the famous letters to Jacques Rivière, quoted by al-Hajj, "which is robbing me even of the memory of those idioms with which one expresses oneself and which translate accurately the most inseparable, the most localized, the most living inflections of thought."[47] Articulation is the successful translation of one's thoughts to the mouth or to the page, which is precisely the movement that is blocked by the spread of cancer. "Why is it that he, Antonin Artaud, is unable to translate, into an understandable language, the thoughts that circle through his head?" al-Hajj asks (97). As in the readings of Derrida and Deleuze, al-Hajj suggests that for Artaud articulation and translation are in fact the same problem, the problem of "organization," defined as an articulated language or body threatened by the metastases of *al-saratan*.

Cancer cannot be transmitted, yet it is nevertheless what Artaud communicates to his contemporaries, including his readers. For Artaud does have a determinate sense of audience (in Roger Shattuck's estimation he is "more histrionic finally than gnostic"). "Let all coproloquists listen," Artaud writes in an early essay cited by al-Hajj, "all aphasiacs, and in general all the disinherited of language and of the word [*les discrédités des mots et du verbe*], the Pariahs of Thought. I speak only for them."[48] Coprolalia, a fit of involuntary swearing or obscenity, is a tic that regularly interrupts the poetry of al-Hajj, who certainly counts himself among the "disinherited," those "deprived of authority over phrases and the word," in the Arabic translation. Impotence, an inability to speak or a refusal of the power of the word—including, prototypically, the Word that is Christ—is essential to al-Hajj's poetics of translation, as we shall see.[49] The authority and continuity of speech are what Artaud's texts relentlessly put in doubt. The howls, hesitations, and exclamations that interrupt his late poems are what make Artaud untranslatable. And yet, al-Hajj writes, "Artaud's cancer is what he bequeaths, it is our scorched inheritance" (102).

The inheritance of cancer is al-Hajj's most complex figure for a modernist crisis of transmission. This is also a crisis in the ideology of *al-insan*, that figure of heroic isolation and spiritual persistence, guarantor of what Charles Malik calls "the unity of the Western tradition." For it is precisely the individual's isolation that cancer turns into a source of affliction. In her acute review of *Lan* published in *Shiʿr*, Khalida Saʿid makes this point by contrasting the horror of cancer with the more familiar (even romantic) fear of "death," which she suggests has become a literary cliché—she may be thinking of Nazik al-Mala'ika's fascination with the theme—now subject to modernism's taboo on the out-of-date.

> Death has become a familiar, domesticated beast, no longer terrifying. Some poets sing to death and embrace its phantom, heroes fall in love with it, martyrs chase after it, the despairing call out to it. Death is not cancer. . . . Cancer is a wild, undomesticated kind of death, making its victim suffer, stalking him organ by organ. . . . Death is essentially common, collective, and subject at times to solace. The cancer victim remains alone, for cancer is individual. Here is al-Hajj addressing the original cell of cancer: "You enter us not like the plague, O original nakedness." Not like the plague. This is crucial. The plague is a collective state, it is contagious [*tantaqil*: transmissible]. Cancer remains isolated. It better articulates the solitude of man, the solitude of the poet himself.[50]

Cancer is what does not allow the poet to articulate himself; it is what confirms his solitude. But it is also the condition that best "articulates" or expresses this solitude. Cancer is, in other words, a peculiarly modern affliction, a sign of the times. It poses the question of how and what the poet may communicate when he has no community; how he can authorize his speech when he has no authority; how he can translate the untranslatable. If, as al-Hajj asserts, the prose poem is "the creation of this age," what origin story can the poet tell about his work, and what authorities attend its birth?

Heretical Origins

These questions can helpfully illuminate what is al-Hajj's most memorable and puzzling *qasidat al-nathr*, "The Bubble of Origin, or the Heretical Poem" (see the English translation at the end of this chapter).[51] The poem was initially notorious for its sexual content. "The Bubble" is a masturbator's confession, a "story" [*hikaya*] that revolves around the adolescent speaker's sexual shame. But its narrative moves quickly past this risqué premise into properly surrealist territory: a dramatic confrontation, alternately comic and violent, between the poet and his seed—the "bubble" of the title, the personified object of shame, whose name is Charlotte. Al-Hajj's interest in tabooed forms of sexual experience is a distinguishing feature of his poetry, and the coupling of impotence and sexuality—"A real man has no sex," Artaud writes—sets him apart from his modernist peers, whose poetry is chaste by comparison.[52] Another characteristic of al-Hajj's prose poetry is its reliance on anecdotal narratives, as opposed to the work of Adonis, for example, structured by more conventionally lyrical tropes such as the apostrophe. I suggest that "The Bubble" is ultimately a narrative about the origins of the prose poem itself, a parable or parody of genesis. In her critique of the *qasidat al-nathr*, Nazik al-Mala'ika called the form "a strange and heretical innovation." Al-Hajj welcomes this censure, flaunting it in the title of his poem, and asks us to consider what sort of heresy the text represents as well as what sort of legitimacy it might thereby claim.

To speak of heresy implies a standard of orthodoxy. For al-Hajj's poem, this is the Bible and in particular the books of the evangelists.[53] The most explicit indication of the religious intertext is Charlotte's initial stammering, "Verily verily I say I say unto you unto you," as though the Christly idiom had caught in her throat, or as if she were struggling to remember her lines. The poems of *Lan* feature a number of such citations or mistranslations. "*Al-Ghazw*" [The Conquest], for example, features the speech of a phallus, a "*qutb*" or "pole," who declares, in a parody of the Sermon on the Mount, "Whosoever shall smite my right testicle hits the mark, for I have lost the left. And whosoever shall find me my left testicle let him eat it, for I shall lose my right." This parody is equivocal between Christ's teaching about when to pluck out one's eye and when to turn the other cheek. Probably both are being mocked, as though virtuousness leads to castration. Another target is the sacrament of the host ("let him eat it"), as we are asked to consider what organ or body part is incarnated in the ingested wafer. This is a literalist's question, and many of al-Hajj's parodies are motivated by this mode of skepticism—one with a long history in the dissident Catholic tradition, including the Maronite branch—that interprets sacred texts according to the letter rather than the spirit. In "A Scream That Stops and Starts," the savior's commandment, "That ye love one another," is placed in the mouth of a seducer. In all these cases, al-Hajj's *naql* of Christ's speech leeches away its legitimacy, substituting figures of impotence (or lechery) for the authority of the Word.

The deeper heresy of "The Bubble" lies in its complex parody of the creation story itself, or rather of several origin stories found in the holy text. The idea that the speaker is engaged on "a work of creation" is evoked several times—always with scare quotes, so to speak—as when he boasts of "forever embarking upon creation," or of meditating upon "the enigmas of creation," or, most crucially, in Charlotte's curse, which warns the speaker that he will "not be created again." The poem's opening heresy is a surrealist one. The first long paragraph situates the speaker's work of creation in the context of a wet dream, subsequently the washroom [*al-hammam*], and then, to make the deflation more emphatic, the workaday toilet [*al-mirhad*]. There is a marked contrast between the poet's "work" [*'amal*], where he only ever seems to go to the bathroom—a satire of professionalism?—and the "work" of God in Genesis: "And on the seventh day God ended his work which he had made [*faragha 'an 'amalihi alladhi 'amala*]; and he rested on the seventh day from all his work which he had made [*jami' 'amalihi alladhi 'amala*] (Genesis 2:2). The toilet is thus the scene of origin, a place where the poet is "forever embarking [*atabahhar*]." Coming in the midst of a narrative about rain, seeds, and seeding, this phrase suggests that the myth of Noah is among the many stories of creation and re-creation at work here (which is why I have hazarded the translation of "embarking," though the standard sense of "penetrating" or "delving into" is also relevant). Charlotte's first question for the poet, "Are you he, the boat?" leaps directly from the poem's dream-work. It is an initial interrogation of the myth itself, as if in doubt of its relevance or powers of persistence. We recall that Adonis extoled the prose poem as "at once our ark and our flood," but al-Hajj approaches the legend with characteristic skepticism. Elsewhere in *Lan* he writes, "I saw Noah, that old spinster."[54]

To set a myth of creation in the toilet is one kind of heresy, a gesture of coprolalia typical of al-Hajj. A more sophisticated variety sneaks into the phrase "*abdhul dhati*," literally, "giving away myself" or "sacrificing myself," which the poet uses to describe his acts of self-abuse. The idiom recalls that of John 3:16: "For God so loved the world that he gave his only begotten Son" [*badhala ibnahu al-wahid*], as well as Galatians 1:4, Timothy 2:6, and Titus 2:14, all passages in which Christ is said to "give himself" [*badhala nafsahu*] as a ransom for our sins. Here the heresy is aimed at the literary act itself. It figures masturbation, the unfruitful and unlawful spilling of seed, as the poet's version of creation and sacrifice. In this parable of inspiration, poetry is imagined as a crime of solitude. This is al-Hajj's characteristically mischievous interpretation of Yusuf al-Khal's demand that the modernist poet-as-creator "must create in a place apart from the influence of everyday duties, social rules, and moral obligations." It is also another instance in which al-Hajj's *naql* of the New Testament effectively de-authorizes the Word, as though the act of translation were a denial of potency, or an exposure of false potency, as well as a claim of solidarity with "the disinherited of language and of the word."

Masturbation is paradigmatically a vice of adolescence, a refusal of the passage to adulthood and its duties of procreation. So it is fitting that the fundamental crisis of "The Bubble" is one of transmission. This is evident in the poem's various figures of dissemination. The poet's finger/phallus is said to "seed" [*tansul*] Charlotte from its tip, and Charlotte later warns him, as if in reproach for the excess of his habit, "You will disseminate seed by seed [*sawfa tunsal nasla nasla*]." Her warning suggests that autoeroticism leads to a kind of wasting away, as if the poet were draining himself of his vital juices and stripping himself to the bones. This notion is of a piece with al-Hajj's obsessive imagination of cancer as a disease of mortification or decomposition. Such imaginings are implicit in Charlotte's subsequent curse, which tells the poet that after his bones are thrown to the night he will not be resurrected because of his blood, suggesting that this is the "rotten blood" of *al-saratan*. The popular superstition linking masturbation to cancer may lurk in the background of Charlotte's speech, and we have seen that al-Hajj consistently figures the disease as one whose symptoms are those of blockage, interruption, and the failure of transmission. Here the biblical precedent is again relevant. For it is after the flood that God reiterates the words of creation, now addressed to

Noah and his sons, "be ye fruitful, and multiply," and establishes his covenant, "with you, and with your seed [*naslikum*] after you" (Genesis 9:9). The same word is used elsewhere to figure Christ as the bridge between dispensations, reminding the faithful that he is "of the seed [*min nasl*] of David" (John 7:42; Romans 1:3). In al-Hajj's poem, however, the speaker's *nasl* is a figure of impotence and dispersion rather than fruitfulness. "I have no inheritor," al-Hajj writes elsewhere in *Lan*, "my offspring is barren, it is my end and their end."[55] "The Bubble" thus combines an anxiety about the stymied passage to adulthood with an anxiety about being (already) at the end of a line, a quintessentially modernist worry, whose creations fall into desuetude before they have a chance to mature.

"The Bubble" is a mise-en-abyme of literary creation, a prose poem that is an origin story of the prose poem—a form of literary self-stimulation. So it is no surprise that Charlotte, the poet's heretical seed, bears a French name and is rather difficult to understand. At times this is because she chokes on her words, or the words of a quoted text, while at other times it is because her own diction is obviously "literary." Much of the poem's humor depends on the sudden swings between vulgar and self-consciously elevated speech, between everyday and religious idioms, an alternation characteristic of al-Hajj's prose poetry. But if Charlotte is an allegorical figure—she is, as she says, "a sign" [*'alama*]—it is not entirely clear what she is an allegory for. Charlotte is not merely the poet's seed, a speaking persona for his "work of creation," but also the object of his guilty fantasy (a French girlfriend). In other words, she is both a personification of the poet's work as well as its reification (an alienated thing). Especially in the final scene, Charlotte acquires a violent autonomy, standing over and against the speaker as the hostile product of his own "labor." The speaker's fear of Charlotte, one that is disavowed or displaced throughout the narrative, is the loss of his potency as a speaker or poet. It is this loss of authority that the translated genre of the *qasidat al-nathr* continually promises and threatens.

The ultimate question posed by the "The Bubble" is whether the speaker will let his creation go out into the world or whether he will keep her to himself. The question emerges from the poem's rhetoric of "going in" and "coming out," of "putting away" and "breaking open." These alternations follow the logic of sexual shame: the speaker is always rushing into the toilet and always hesitating to emerge. This dilemma of whether or not to make oneself or one's utterance public, to be "forced into the open," as the final line says, is the dilemma of articulation, which lies at the heart of al-Hajj's poetics (as with Artaud). For it is not only Charlotte who struggles to articulate herself: the speaker maintains a near-silence until the end, and his own words are marked by the same stutters and falterings. In the last long paragraph, a game of word-golf leads from "forest of fear" [*ghaba min al-mawt*] to "end of fear" [*ghaya min al-mawt*] to "sign of fear" [*aya min al-mawt*]. "Say something!" Charlotte pleads, or demands, and the speaker promises to do so—"wait until I go out"—but then breaks his promise as soon as he leaves the bathroom. *"Ughadir"* [I go out] echoes Charlotte's declaration, *"lam naghdur bika!"* [we have not betrayed you!]. The etymological rhyme, stemming from the root verb *"ghadara,"* conjoins ideas of "going out" and "betrayal." It is a conjuncture at the heart of many discourses of translation, inevitably anxious about the borders between domestic and foreign, loyalty and disloyalty, orthodoxy and heresy.

When the speaker does finally speak, his words are equivocal. He qualifies them as "theatricalizing" [*atamasrah*], a neologism that suggests self-consciously histrionic behavior—a kind of false articulation, or fit of prompted speech. This is perhaps the most explicitly Artaudian moment of al-Hajj's poem. Artaud's critique of the theater springs from his objection to its reliance on a preexisting text, and for al-Hajj that text is the Bible. The speaker's next-to-last speech is indeed prompted by a biblical idiom, which he characteristically mistranslates. "Go from my nail unto the wind, and keep going [*istamirri*]," is a parody of Eve's creation from the rib of Adam, as well as a deflation of the injunction to "go forth and multiply." *"Istamirri"* [keep going] has a comically stilted and hapless feel to it, as though the imperative were being mocked in its utterance. What hope is there for seed cast to the wind? This is like asking what hope there is for an Arabic *poème en prose*, or indeed for any translation lacking the articulate authority of a mother tongue. The question is an urgent one for al-Hajj, a poet who consistently confuses the limits of translation with the limits of creation. The speaker's last line, in which he contemplates being forced out into the open, is the fear of articulation in general. It is a fear that his own utterances, once they come out of his mouth, out of hiding, will find no audience no matter what language he or they happen to speak.

In al-Hajj's heretical creation story, the *qasidat al-nathr* springs from an act of autogenesis (or autoeroticism). This narrative lends support to a late modernist conception of the prose poem's self-sufficiency, its formal autonomy and organic unity, slogans that al-Hajj, like the other *Shiʿr* poets, repeats again and again. With more acuity than his colleagues, however, al-Hajj intimates that this same conception leads to sterility, to a genre of poem that has no authority and perhaps no audience, but is rather a dialogue between self and seed. Here again, the autonomy of the *qasidat al-nathr* should not be understood as a positive slogan but rather as a productive censure or act of refusal—in al-Hajj's case, a refusal of articulation or "the authority over phrases and the word." For al-Hajj, translation does not secure its legitimacy by finding eloquent equivalents, as it does for Adonis. Instead, it is an act of de-authorization, a denial of the Word: here again, the modernists sanction their own speech *via negativa*.

It is not only religion that al-Hajj subjects to his corrosive skepticism; like all Beiruti modernists, he also refuses to grant politics any authority over poetry. Indeed, politics is the one limit to poetry the modernists invariably insist on. To conclude, I will note an exacerbated case of this insistence: al-Hajj's *"Nashid al-bilad"* [Country Song] the penultimate prose poem of *Lan*, which conjoins the refusal of politics, authority, and articulation in remarkable fashion.

What is initially striking about the poem, a translation of which is appended to this chapter, is its promise of some explicitly political content. The title is a distortion of *nashid al-watan* [national anthem] as well as the *Nashid al-anashid* [song of songs], and in fact the poem is a kind of antianthem or nonsong. The text is most obviously a parody of the nationalist's love of country. "Syria, my beloved, you've given my dignity back to me, you've given my identity back to me," ran a popular anthem of the period. Al-Hajj's poem begins, "O my country, from the depths I do not call unto you, I have not read your story and I wish you a womb I rip to pieces." The apostrophe, a conventional opening to an anthem, is taken back in the act of invocation. Al-Hajj's *iltifat* reprises Adonis's use of the trope as a movement of turning toward and turning away. Addressing his country, the speaker refuses to address his country, just as while invoking the psalmist's *de profundis*, he also denies that he is doing it, purposefully depriving himself of the authority conferred by those depths. The figure of the shredded womb recalls one of *Lan*'s most powerful images of disinheritance: "I am shot into the air," al-Hajj writes in the opening poem of the collection, "I claw at the air with my tendons and my womb is sewed shut."[56] These images work in implicit contrast to those of the "Song of Songs," whose rhetoric of love and fertility is replaced by one of violation and barrenness. In similar fashion, the commonplaces of nationalist ideology, which idealize political relations as familial ones ("sister Egypt," for example), is mimicked and mocked. The mother-beloved is made into a whore and a breeder of grotesque hybrids. The poet's relation to her is hyperbolically hostile: "I am not a white light, but I'll snuff you out all the same. You're swollen with fury and my nail punctures your pelvis." This last image is ambiguous between a monstrous birth (if the nail emerges from inside) and some form of rape. It suggests the violence intrinsic to any act of inheritance and a rejection of ideologies that cover up this violence with a rhetoric of natural relations. While nationalist thought typically insists on the political community's antiquity and rootedness—"Its glory is the cedar, symbol of eternity," runs the Lebanese national anthem—al-Hajj's poet denies the nation's past and future, and he condemns its present to a ruined sterility: stones breeding stones.

The poem's five stanzas or paragraphs are interrupted by the exclamation "Traitor!" which serves as a choral curse upon the speaker (and also the anathema commonly flung at translators). The final paragraph embraces the accusation:

> It's all right, calm down, you've come to me for empathy. Come closer. Keep coming. Again, again. One step more. Open your ear. Lean over (rest easy on my belly). Open your ear. Lean over

a little more
you can hardly hear—it's so excessively hot—my wind!

This is, of course, an adolescent prank—an exercise in coprolalia. In the same vein, Artaud (mis)translates, *"Car christ en hébreu de la pétaille / veut dire pet d'âne"* [For Christ in vulgar Hebrew / means a donkey's fart].[57] But al-Hajj's prank exhibits a consistent logic. The wind, *"al-rih,"* on which the speaker of "The Bubble" cast his seed, is a figure for the limits of articulation. Here, all the blocked stutterings of al-Hajj's work find expression in "bodily speech," a literalization (or vulgarization) of the claim that poetry is the music of man's "interior experience." It is only in this way—with their backs turned, so to speak—that the modernists consent to address the political collective or, indeed, the lay reader, who cannot help but put herself in the uncomfortable place of this poem's addressee. The taboo on political speech is the limit of poetry, a repression that generates new forms of expression, new forms of verse, which may initially seem like heresies.[58]

Appendix #2: "The Bubble of Origin, or the Heretical Poem," Unsi al-Hajj, Lan (1960)

Charlotte gushed forth from the finger, white, alone, where the coal thickens and sweats, where fruits come to be.

I will tell my story. One day I went to sleep and while I slept the rain was also verifying the earth. I wept until the rain slept and then rose and went to the washroom and observed a strange phenomenon. I was still hidden and would have gone out from the washroom in a natural, everyday fashion had it not been for Charlotte. She was coming out of my finger, effortlessly, gracefully. I tried to assist her, but she was quick to perish and I quickly grasped that she was quick to perish and so I went to work and forgot. At work it was necessary that I go into the toilet, where I am forever embarking upon creation, and as usual I brushed my glance upon my hand while I was giving away my only self. There I noticed Charlotte at ease. I looked at her more intently and found that she was looking back at me. So came I closer to her and came she closer too. I bent over her until my own sight pained me and suddenly

I realized there was something I had neglected to put away. So I put it away and then returned to my object of interest until I broke open the riddle's secret.

I perceived that Charlotte, whom my finger was seeding from its tip just below the nail, had gone ahead of the caravan—an advance scout! On the spot, I resented her. I said to her:

—What do you want?
She craned her neck around and answered:
—Are you he, the boat?

Then she said:

—I have come to say unto you: Verily verily I say I say unto you unto you. Verily the bindings will be loosened. Verily we are abandoning you. Verily are you dispersed, a most wicked dispersion. Please maintain respect for us, for we have not betrayed you!

Then she said:

—Farewell!

Then she said:

—I am a sign. Thy end will come by way of me and by way of other signs than me. The signs will cover you. You will disseminate seed by seed until your naked flesh is exposed and then will your naked flesh fall away revealing your bones and then will your bones be thrown into the night.

Then she said:

—Such are we!

Then she said:

—You will not be created again with that blood, you dog!

Then she said:

—Say something!

So I said:

—Wait until I leave the toilet.

When I did, I pounced upon Charlotte and wiped her out. That night I awoke to meditate, as so often, upon the enigmas of creation. Suddenly I saw Charlotte on my finger. I made the sign of the cross and Charlotte grew larger. Here I became afraid, then I became afraid, then I became afraid, until I was a forest [*ghaba*] of fear. After I had become a forest of fear I went back and became an end [*ghaya*] of fear. After I had become an end of fear I went back and became a sign [*aya*] of fear. And so the morning dawned and the sparrows chirped and I was seized by an overwhelming need for the toilet. I had hardly entered before Charlotte pushed me against the wall, tore off my clothes, and beat me to a pulp.

When she was satisfied, I said to her, panting:

—I will let you grow, I will not wipe you out.

Then I said:

—You asked me to say something?

Then I said:

—So I will speak.

Then I said, twisting my head and theatricalizing:

—Go from my nail unto the wind, and keep going.

Then I said, shivering:

—I know you are the first symptom of all that will force me into the open.

Appendix #3: "Country Song," Unsi al-Hajj, Lan (1960)

O my country, from the depths I do not call unto you. I have not read your story and I wish for you a womb I rip to pieces.

—Traitor!

O my country, I marry you to pollute myself. Your luck with me was very bad. You're going crazy, how can I not see it? Are you really going crazy? We went to the shops and a bullet tempted you, it aroused you, but you didn't shoot. Are you really your country? Your bird is black smoke. The one who chases you is cast down by disappointment; your conqueror perfects his heart, which he hangs, O my country, on your hole.

—Traitor!

Why, O my country? There's no tomorrow coming and the past is invisible. Trust me. You arouse me with accusations. Your prostitution is a low-flying moth. I'm not a white light, but I'll snuff you out all the same. You are swollen with fury and my fingernail punctures your pelvis, you breeder of fox-cats! I do not cast you out, I do not abandon you. The present is cast out and abandoned, you breeder of stones with stones. O death, death, death that senility has covered in moss!

—Traitor!

O my country. If I called out to you in death, he would spare you. I would make him more spacious. I would decorate his braids with my dung. Let my member raise your flag—I give you this fantasy (for I'm a Christian), I fill you with the fantasy that you are my member. Believe me—it will relax your nerves. You are my member! Are you my member?

—Traitor!

O my country, my member is the night. You refuse my mockery, so what shall I give you?

—Traitor!

It's all right, calm down, you've come for empathy. Come closer, I'm still here. Keep coming. Again, again. One step more. Open your ear. Lean over (rest easy on my belly). Open your ear. Lean over

a little more

you can hardly hear—it's so excessively hot—my wind!

CHAPTER FIVE

The Countercanon

ADONIS'S *ANTHOLOGY OF ARABIC POETRY*

Internal Translation

The corpus of European and American poetry that Beiruti modernists translated into Arabic was the local variant of an emergent global canon—the canon of modernist poetry itself, made to serve as a counterweight to the engagé verse of poets affiliated with the Communist world. The strict political divisions of the early Cold War resulted in a literary partisanship nearly as severe. In the Arab world and elsewhere, Pablo Neruda, Nazim Hikmet, and Paul Éluard rarely appeared in the same journals as T. S. Eliot, Octavio Paz, and Saint-John Perse. For all their scruples about translation and the worrying influx of foreign texts, Arab nationalist and Marxist magazines in Beirut regularly published poets of the Second World in Arabic versions. Rather than correspondence from Paris and New York, they published reports on conferences of the Arab Writers' Union in Damascus or the latest contents of *Novy Mir* and *Literaturnaia gazeta*. And while the modernists hosted Spender and Bonnefoy at their *jeudis de* Shiʿr, the leftists fêted their own celebrities. When Hikmet visited Beirut in the spring of 1960, the editors of the Marxist monthly *al-Tariq* arranged for readings and published a folio of translations into Arabic of the man they called "the great Turkish world poet."[1] In this way, the political binaries of the immediate postwar era generated parallel networks of translation and consecration, which in turn produced rival canons of world literature.

They also produced rival canons of Arabic literature, the subject of this and the following chapter. Alongside the work of foreign translation, the modernists and their opponents engaged in a fierce struggle over their own literary heritage or *turath*. Both camps saw their task as a cultural salvage. This is how Husayn Muruwwa, the most erudite Arab Marxist critic, identified the aims of the Beiruti monthly *al-Thaqafa al-Wataniyya* [National Culture]:

> Among our most basic goals since the founding of this journal was to go back to our Arabic cultural inheritance, in all its historical variety, in an attempt to dig up its greatest treasures from beneath the rubble of time and neglect. We know that many of these treasures were buried, at times intentionally and at others out of ignorance. But the element of intention predominated, for the great treasures of Arabic thought, whatever their historical provenance, were the expression of new ideas in intellectual, social, and political life, emerging from the movement of progress [*al-tatawwur*], which struggled against the ideas of an old and dominant conservatism.[2]

This struggle over the terms of cultural inheritance reprised, sometimes self-consciously, interwar debates in Europe between Fascists and their leftist or liberal humanist critics. As György Lukács writes in "Thomas Mann and the Literary Heritage," an essay published in 1936:

> The battle for heritage is one of the most important ideological tasks of anti-fascism in Germany. National Socialism has used its state power and monopoly in order to falsify in the most ruthless manner Germany's entire political and cultural past. From university to primary school, from the fat "learned" tome to the small, popular, crudely demagogic pamphlet this work of falsification has proceeded on a large and systematic scale. The demagogy of mass propaganda has no qualms about turning every great figure of the past into a simple forerunner of National Socialism.[3]

For Muruwwa and other Arab Marxists, the past that needed rescuing from the falsifications of conservatism, as well as the Orientalist scholarship Muruwwa considered its accomplice, was "the culture of the people" [*turath al-shaʿb*], a tradition of resistance to the ruling elites of Arabo-Islamic history. It also meant establishing the "unity" [*wihda*] of this cultural heritage above and beyond its historical variety. In practice, uncovering a tradition of dissent within the medieval corpus meant a revisionary account of its major figures, now reread as allies of the subaltern classes. Throughout the late 1950s and early 1960s, Muruwwa wrote dozens of short essays on writers of the classical period, published in *al-Thaqafa al-wataniyya* and *al-Tariq*. In his article on Ibn al-Muqaffaʿ, an eighth-century courtier and translator of *Kalila wa Dimna* (an Arabic adaptation of the Sanskrit *Panchatantra* by way of a Middle Persian version), Muruwwa argued that *Kalila and Dimna* was not "an interloper in Arabic literature by way of translation, but rather native to the core of our national literature." He showed that the prose style of the fables was consistent with Ibn al-Muqaffaʿ's works on court etiquette and statecraft, suggesting that translation should serve as a mode of literary nationalization. Muruwwa also argued that Ibn al-Muqaffaʿ's Persian bloodline did not prevent him from being an essentially Arab thinker—Muruwwa criticized ideas of racial unity as passionately as he defended those of cultural unity—and that his moralizing against the sway of money made him a "progressive" critic of the caliphate. Muruwwa performed similar salvage operations on the ʿAbbasid poets Abu Nuwas, whom he defended against accusations of anti-Arabism, asserting the poet's "deeply rooted [*asil*] place in our heritage and in our history," and also al-Mutanabbi, who despite his suspect parentage was also "the great poet of Arab unity [*al-ʿuruba*]." By such means, Muruwwa and his colleagues sought to establish a curriculum that would counteract what he called "the reactionary pedagogy followed by most of the schools responsible for the acculturation [*tathqif*] of the youth in our country." This new curriculum would both safeguard the integrity of Arab culture and activate its resources of revolution.[4]

The modernists also sought to establish a curriculum that would provide an oppositional model of "acculturation" or *Bildung*, but one that was distinct from the model proposed by leftists. Adonis was the major figure behind this revision of the *turath*. I have already cited his letter to Yusuf al-Khal, written from Paris in the wake of attacks by the nationalists at *al-Adab*, in which Adonis claimed, "We have our own Arab past." This past-within-the-past is that of modernism itself, a countertradition of misfits and rebels as well as several properly canonical figures whom Adonis sought to reclaim for the present. "A culture advances, spiralwise, via translations of its own canonic past," George Steiner writes.[5] The advance is a spiral because the canon is always in flux, always retranslating its own translations.

Adonis's countercanonical efforts were first published in the pages of *Shiʿr*. Beginning in the summer of 1960, Adonis curated a selection of poetry for each issue under the rubric "*Min turath al-shiʿr al-ʿarabi*" [From the Heritage of Arabic Poetry]. These selections, published without commentary, were excerpts from major and minor poets of the pre-Islamic, *jahili* era. The chosen texts were short, often no more than a couple of lines, with ellipses to mark the use of editorial scissors and nothing to suggest their textual provenance. The result is a version of the *turath* that is decontextualized and broken into pieces: the heritage in fragments. Adonis also curated prose selections from the medieval tradition, publishing them under the oxymoronic title *al-Madi al-muʿasir* [The Contemporary Past] in *Shiʿr*'s short-lived sister magazine, *Adab*. The first selection was a short text by the twelfth-century Persian mystic Suhrawardi, "*al-Gurba al-gharbiyya*" [The Western Exile], an allegory of the soul's imprisonment in matter and its yearning to return home to the east of the spirit. Suhrawardi, who wrote in both Arabic and Persian, was not a canonical philosopher in the Arabic tradition, nor was he ever translated into Latin. It was only during the mid-twentieth century that his works began to be systematically collected, primarily by the French orientalist Henri Corbin, whose 1952 critical edition of Suhrawardi is the source of Adonis's excerpt. In his introductory note, Adonis mentions the difficulty of understanding

Suhrawardi's esoteric philosophy, "based on a sequence of symbols and secret correspondences," but suggests it is precisely this difficulty, as well as Suhrawardi's estrangement from the orthodox canon, that makes his writings "contemporary." At the end of his note, Adonis cautions his readers that the allegory of the soul's reversion to its spiritual home should not be read as "a return to the past, but rather a return to the beginning [*al-bad'*], which is also its destiny."[6] Rather than nostalgia for past glories, Adonis's fragmentary folios sought to locate the futurity that inheres in certain marginalized texts of the tradition.

Adonis's interest in the *turath* deepened over the next decade, affecting his poetry and criticism in important ways. The summa of these archival efforts was *al-Thabit wa-l-mutahawwil* [The Fixed and the Dynamic] (1973), a four-volume study based on his dissertation for the Université Saint-Joseph supervised by Boulus Nwiya, an Iraqi Jesuit scholar of mysticism and student of Louis Massignon. *The Fixed and the Dynamic* is a synoptic study of Arabo-Islamic history, including social movements, literature, and theology from the pre-Islamic period through the early twentieth century. Like his leftist rivals, Adonis critiques the "fixed" heritage—embodied for him in the institution of the caliphate, enforcer of intellectual and spiritual conformism—and attempts to identify, within that heritage, resources of resistance. As he writes in his introduction:

> If change presumes the destruction of the old, traditional structure, this destruction cannot be carried out by means of an instrument from outside the Arabic heritage, but must be carried out instead by means of an instrument from within. The destruction of a principle [*asl*] must be carried out by way of the principle itself. Therefore, this destruction does not imply an allegiance to any non-Arab past, nor to any non-Arab heritage, but implies instead a transcendence of that past and that heritage using tools provided by them.[7]

This idea of cultural authority is notably distinct from the one we find in Adonis's earlier work, where formal innovations in Arabic could be legitimized by the precedent of "world poets" such as Saint-John Perse. The difference is representative of Adonis's steady drift, beginning in the mid-1960s, into a version of cultural Arabism: his resignation from *Shi'r* in 1963 coincides with a resolute turn toward the texts of the Arab-Islamic tradition, whose canon he would spend the next several decades reinterpreting and reshaping. In an interview given at the time, he went so far as to claim that "In political and economic terms, 'the Nasserist event' is the most significant in Arab history for more than a thousand years.... And the crisis of Arabic culture is that it is not yet at the level of this event."[8] Adonis's idea of the Arabic canon is very different from Muruwwa's, however. His tradition-within-the-tradition is largely made up of heterodox figures: marginalized individuals (scientists, mystics, rationalist philosophers), revolutionary social movements (the Zanj Rebellion, the Qarmatians), and dissident intellectual currents (atheism, the Muʿtazila, and especially esoteric Shiism). Adonis's study does not confirm the unity of the classical tradition, which both Marxist and nationalist intellectuals emphasized, but argues instead for a plurality of pasts within the past. Some of these dissident and diverse histories left few traces. As Adonis notes, much of what is known about the Qarmatians, a syncretistic, millenarian movement of the tenth century, comes by way of their antagonists:

> When I insist on revealing and studying what has been suppressed or stifled, I mean to emphasize those aspects of our cultural past that can help illuminate its vivacity, variety, and plurality of vision [taʿaddudiyyat al-nazar]. It can also help erase the picture of it given to us by the dominant regime: a picture of unity, atavism, and monotony. I do not suggest we should return to the past, but that we should reevaluate it, radically and completely . . . to reveal its variety and pluralism [taʿaddud].[9]

Adonis's consistent method for excavating the buried pluralism of the *turath* is the classical hermeneutic operation of *ta'wil*. The Arabic word is derived from the root verb *aala*, meaning to return or revert, and the literal meaning would be something like "a reversion to the origin." Often translated as "allegorical interpretation," *ta'wil* is typically contrasted with *tafsir*, where the latter connotes the literal interpretation or periphrasis of a Qur'anic text as opposed to its figural interpretation provided by the former. Like many scholars, Adonis associates *ta'wil* with the Shiite exegetical tradition, connecting the practice of allegorical interpretation with the "esoteric knowledge" [ʿilm al-batin] of the imams. As a contemporary scholar has written, "The Quran has an outer dimension (zahr), and an inner dimension (batn); its inner dimension has yet another dimension, up to seven inner dimensions."[10] It is easy to see the appeal of this interpretive method for Adonis, whose recourse to the categories of exoteric [zahiri] and esoteric [batini] readings become more and more frequent: if his intellectual touchstones become increasingly Arab during this period, they also become increasingly Shiite. For Adonis, orthodoxy privileges clarity and unity of expression. In the words of the eighth-century polymath al-Jahiz: "The best speech is that whose meaning [maʿna] is on the surface of its expression [zahir lafzihi]." By contrast, the heterodox tradition is characterized by its ambiguity and polysemy. Against al-Jahiz's praise of clarity, Adonis cites a line from one of Abu Nuwas's love poems, which characterizes the beloved's flirtations as "singular in expression [lafz], multiple in meaning [maʿani]." Just as figural speech opens itself to multiple readings, so *ta'wil* unlocks the heritage to a plurality of interpretations. As Adonis writes more than once, "Metaphor is in the realm of poetry what *ta'wil* is in the realm of thought."

In this light, the whole of Adonis's encyclopedia can be read as a massive *ta'wil* of the *turath*—that is, a revisionary fracturing of its unity and an attempt to identify the historical precursors of an as-yet-unrealized Arab modernism. Adonis argues that the mystical tradition of the Sufis first displaces divine law in favor of human experience; that Qarmatian social organization points toward an equitable, nonsectarian distribution of wealth; and that the medical experiments of al-Razi and the alchemical speculations of Jabir bin Hayyan planted the seeds of the scientific method. Adonis's allegorical interpretation of the *turath* recovers its lost or muffled voices and reveals their uncanny contemporaneity. As he writes at the end of his study, in a passage that amounts to a *ta'wil* of *ta'wil*, a modernist interpretation of a classical figure of thought: "The literal, etymological derivation of *ta'wil* signifies 'a return to origins,' but its historical meaning is 'the interpretation of origins according to the needs of what follows.' It means, in other words, the interpretation of the ancient according to the needs of the modern [*al-muhdath*]." To borrow Auerbach's more familiar terminology, all these individuals and trends—rationalists, atheists, and Sufis—are the *figura* of modernity: fully historical phenomena that also point toward a future historical fulfillment.[11]

While Muruwwa and other critics often accused the *Shi'r* group of seeking to uproot or even destroy the Arabic literary past, the modernists' project was largely one of reconstruction and reconfiguration rather than demolition. Both modernists and leftists were engaged in the practice of *ta'wil*, understood as a revision of the native heritage according to the needs of the present. It was their clashing interpretations of those contemporary needs that determined which legacies they strove to transmit. The act of intralinguistic inheritance is what Pascal Casanova has helpfully termed "internal translation":

> The task of what might be called internal translation, which is to say bringing the national language forward from an ancient to a modern state, as in the case of translations from ancient to modern Greek, is one way of annexing, and thereby nationalizing, texts that all the great countries of Europe had long before declared to be universal, by claiming them as evidence of an underlying linguistic and cultural continuity.[12]

This describes very well the salvage operation of Muruwwa, who reclaims the ancient past from European orientalists and their local collaborators. ("Even the dead will not be safe," as Benjamin writes in his own meditation on the need to salvage the past from a victorious conformism.)[13] Muruwwa's *naql* of ancient texts is in this sense like Ibn al-Muqaffa'"s "nationalizing" translation of *Kalila wa Dimna*, which appropriates a Sanskrit-Persian text for the Arabic canon. Adonis's internal translations also make a claim of underlying cultural continuity—or renewed continuity after a centuries-long interruption—but his gesture of annexation is the very opposite of "nationalization." Instead, his transmissions of classical texts aim to uncover a native modernism that escapes and undermines national strictures: a local tradition, like the Syrian myths discovered by Antun Saʿada, still waiting for the recognition of its universality.

The rest of this chapter focuses on an especially rich case of internal translation, Adonis's *Diwan al-shiʿr al-ʿarabi* [Anthology of Arabic Poetry], a three-volume florilegium published between 1964 and 1968 whose origins are in the dossiers of pre-Islamic poetry first published in *Shiʿr*. The *Diwan* was the most consequential revision of the classical heritage undertaken by Adonis, a work fully as synoptic as his later encyclopedia, including verse from the *jahili* period through the late nineteenth century. It is a massive critical project that hews strictly to the original impetus of *Shiʿr*, a movement based on the paired goals of literary autonomy and deprovincialization. How do these goals affect Adonis's decisions as an editor of the corpus of classical poetry? As a collection of citations from the *turath*, the *Anthology* is a work of internal translation in which source and target texts are exactly the same, though provided with a new context. "Repetition is the purest concentrate of translation," Steiner writes. "To repeat identically is to translate along the axis of time."[14] This displacement in time makes all the difference, however. While Adonis's counter-canon seeks to restore those voices silenced by orthodoxy, his own choices, tailored to the needs of the present, impose their own exclusions and repressions.

Modernist Museums

"*Al-shiʿr diwan al-ʿarab*," runs an ancient maxim: "Poetry is the archive of the Arabs"—that is to say, a record of their historical experience and the epitome of their literature. It is poetry that records the earliest tribal battles, the so-called *ayyam al-ʿarab* of the pre-Islamic period, and which serves as an ongoing repository of aesthetic and ethical values. Even in the contemporary period, many Arab poets, including Adonis, have styled themselves as the custodians of patrimony. This stance would seem at odds with modernism's own commitment to newness and its often aggressive rhetoric against the literary past. In the same way, there is something paradoxical about the very idea of a modernist anthology of classical poetry. How does one canonize, or institutionalize, a practice of rupture? In his introduction to the first volume of the *Diwan*, Adonis explains his motives for compiling the anthology by pointing to a contemporary crisis of pedagogy, what Muruwwa calls "acculturation." The historical dilemma, for both Adonis and Muruwwa, is that the archive of poetry has been continually shaped by history's victors, who have handed it down in an ever more falsified form:

> This poetic museum [*al-mathaf al-shiʿri*] aids in the reconsideration of poetry as the original creative force in Arab life. For poetry's role in the present has begun to recede from the level of its authentic mission [*risalatihi al-asliyya*] in Arab life. This phenomenon is a crisis and

we must face up to it. Whether the causes of this crisis are political or religious, or traceable to the nature of our historical stage, none of this allows us to turn our attention or our studies away from it.[15]

The crisis is one of cultural translation. It involves the difficulty of handing down a certain heritage or "mission" (*risala*: message, epistle)—in this case, the heritage of Arabic poetry—from generation to generation. Later on in his introduction, Adonis laments the fact that the rising generations are no longer interested in Arabic poetry, "Because the mentalities and methods that transmitted it [*naqalathu*] to them could not see in poetry farther than the syntax, meter and topoi that were mutually agreed upon, and the norms that had been generally sanctioned" (I 12). The pedagogical crisis would thus seem to spring from a fatal institutionalization of poetry, which now finds itself caught, as Adonis says elsewhere, "between the ignorance of the youth and the dogmatism of old men."[16] What had once been an authentic part of Arab life has degenerated into a scholastic exercise. But the problem of institutionalization seems rather different from the crisis of transmission. In fact, it seems less a corollary of this crisis than a possible solution, since the survival of poetry is guaranteed rather than threatened by its inclusion in a curriculum. The tensions in Adonis's argument come into focus around the figure of the "museum" [*mathaf*], a word he uses several times as a metaphor for the *Anthology* itself. It is an odd figure to have chosen, for if the crisis confronting poetry is its loss of mission, then it is not easy to see how placing it in a museum counts as a solution, since a museum is precisely where we put the art of the past to rest. As Adorno notes, "Museums are like the family sepulchers of works of art. They testify to the neutralization of culture."[17] (Or as Filippo Marinetti abbreviates the idea in his futurist manifesto: "Museums: cemeteries!") But in fact Adonis has in mind an institution that does not testify to the neutralization—or nationalization—of culture so much as to its renewal or resurrection. "This anthology," Adonis writes, "is the bringing-back-to-life [*ihya'*] of Arabic poetry" (I 11). Or again, in an overtly Nietzschean idiom: "This heritage museum strengthens our faith, we who believe in the necessity of transformation and the generation of new values, against those who cling to culture literally, repeatedly, and coercively" (I 10). The establishment of an imaginary museum, in other words, is not an act of clinging to heritage but rather an attempt to set it free from itself.[18]

The history of twentieth-century modernism provides several points of comparison for understanding the rhetorical and formal features of Adonis's *Diwan*. Scholars of modernism have mostly ignored the anthology as a genre, focusing their attention on its more clamorous cousin, the manifesto, whose history extends from the futurists to the situationists, passing by way of Pound, Lewis, and Breton. But the corpus of modernist anthologies is at least as extensive, and in fact both stem from the same author. Marinetti published *I poeti futuristi* in 1912, three years after his better-known *Manifesto*. The anthology is reported to have sold thirty-five thousand copies in Italy, and the form's popularity during what Chris Baldick has termed "the great age of anthologies" is due in large part to this inaugural effort.[19] The anthologies edited by Pound are legion, from the early coterie collections, *Des Imagistes* (1914) and *Catholic Anthology* (1915), up through the *Active Anthology* (1933) and including Chinese translations such as *The Classic Anthology Defined by Confucius* (1954). (The *Cantos*, which Louis Zukofsky once called "a living museum of facts," is itself a kind of poem-anthology or bric-a-brac of citations.) America's "anthology wars" of the 1960s were in some ways a repetition of the battles first waged by Pound and his contemporaries, though now Pound's own poetry figured among the spoils. In Spain, the importance of Gerardo Diego's *Antología poética en honor de Góngora* (1927), a collection that reintroduced Góngora to modern poets, is well known. (The later prose anthologies of Borges—his *Antología de la literatura fantástica* (1940) as well as his later self-anthologizations, *Antología personal* (1961) and *Nueva antología personal* (1968), not to speak of his various *bibliotecas*—amount to a defiantly personal version of the canon of world literature.) Contemporaneously with Adonis's *Anthology*, Gerald Moore and Ulli Beier's *Modern Poetry from Africa* (1963) eschewed the poetry of *négritude* and introduced Ibadan modernists such as Wole Soyinka and Christopher Okigbo to readers in the metropole.[20]

One reason for the popularity of anthologies among these movements is that it accomplishes a necessary task of all modernisms—and does so more efficiently than the manifesto—which is the rewriting of literary history. In the anthology, the textual past is reformulated as a collage, effecting what Jameson has called modernism's "powerful displacement of previous narrative paradigms."[21] This revisionary operation is particularly evident in collections that take a long historical purview. Consider Diego's *Antología poética*, published in Madrid on the three hundredth anniversary of Góngora's death. The volume gathers together poems that evince a common "magnetic attraction" toward the baroque master. Arranged in chronological order, the poems are either dedicated to Góngora or written in imitation of his style. "It is a sort of inside-out anthology [*una antología al revés*]," Diego explains, "one that does not seek an author's personal style in all its autonomous plenitude, but rather its filiation and genealogy, traced to a precursor whose attraction deforms in some sense that style's most characteristic qualities." Elsewhere, he describes the collection as a "core sample from the geography of our poetry during the three centuries of its evolution."[22] This depersonalized, genealogical narrative allows Diego to suggest that *el Gongorismo* is a persistent modernist element whose unearthing in the present has the power to transform the landscape of Spanish poetry. It is hardly by chance that the last two poems of the anthology are Don José Iglesias de la Casa's "*Letrilla*," published in 1793, and then Rubén Darío's Parnassian "*Trébol*," published in 1905. In this way, the blandly curatorial collecting and arrangement of poems becomes a polemic against the nineteenth century, though it does so negatively, by way of a displacement or repression. The anthology succeeds in rewriting, via citation, the history of Spanish poetry as one with a modernist telos, here represented by the figure of Darío.

Adonis's *Anthology* presents a more complex version of this narrative strategy, marked by its own repressions and reshufflings. The three volumes of the *Anthology* are arranged in chronological order, according to a well-established scheme of Arabic literary history: the first volume consists of excerpts from pre-Islamic poets as well as those contemporaneous with Muhammad's revelation; the second includes poets from the eighth to tenth century, the golden era of ʿAbbasid rule; the last volume is dedicated to the nine-hundred-year-long decline, approximately coterminous with the Mamluk and Ottoman periods, characterized by a baroque poetry of "craft and artifice." The last period ends with the poetry of Khalil Gibran, whose work signals the beginning of the modern era.

Adonis wrote a lengthy introduction for each volume of his *Anthology*. In the first essay, which describes the ethos of pre-Islamic poetry, Adonis takes a famous phrase from the seventh-century poet Tamim Ibn Muqbil as his guide: "Were that man was a stone." Here is the clear-eyed heroism Adonis discerns at the heart of *jahili* sensibility: the poet's knowledge of life's brevity and his obsessive desire to overcome it, even at the price of petrification.[23] The world of these early poets, as evoked by Adonis, is absolutely profane. No gods or spirits populate the wadis, and the poet "possesses nothing but the earth." But the earth, which is nothing but desert, has no lessons to teach, no comfort to offer, no hidden meanings to reveal. Confronted by an impassive nature or the mute ruins of an abandoned campsite, the *jahili* poet's response is a reckless fatalism. It is this spirit we find careening through the poetry itself. For Adonis, the pre-Islamic *qasida* is a quest romance in which the hero "goes outside of his self in order to find himself":

> [Ibn Muqbil's phrase] reveals ... a yearning for mastery over frailty and death. Discovering himself, the Arabic poet also discovers the absurdity of the world upon which his destiny nevertheless depends. So his self develops into a split oneness: there is no link between the self and what it contemplates; the more it contemplates, the greater its realization of the abyss that separates it from the world. When man's separation from the things that surround him becomes clear, his essential lack is also clarified, leading to a thirst for a completion that is not achieved except in the outside. (I 16)

In Adonis's telling, the pre-Islamic poet-hero discovers over and again that nature is nothing more than a trap for his imagination. It is this extravagant will-to-timelessness that connects all modes of *jahili* poetry. Just as the lyric poet of the *qasida* wants to become a stone in order to master time, so the ʿ*udhri* love poet wants his night with the beloved to last forever.

Adonis's introductory essay to the second volume of his *Anthology* marks a historical shift, turning from the nomadic life of the desert to the settled life of towns, from the *badiya* to the *hadar* in the traditional apposition. In the *fourmillante cité* of 'Abbasid Baghdad, the poet is confronted not by an indifferent nature but by an undifferentiated crowd. Instead of embarking on an outwardly directed quest, the poet retreats into himself. He spiritualizes the world outside, making it a reflection of his inner vision. Baghdad is where the poet discovers alienation [*al-ghurba*]. "Feelings of alienation and disconnection from others—of being 'an echo of life,' as Abu Tammam expresses it—this is the sap that courses through the experience of Abu Nuwas, Abu Tammam, al-Mutanabbi and Abu al-'Ala'.... These feelings of alienation and disconnection are the context and motive for irony [*al-sukhriyya*]" (II, *mim*). Irony is, for Adonis, the master trope of 'Abbasid poetry, expressive of the poet's turn away from the city crowds and his new penchant for obscurity and hermeticism. Adonis cites an anecdote from Abu Bakr bin Yahya al-Suli's tenth-century *Akhbar Abi Tammam* [Anecdotes of Abu Tammam], in which the poet is asked by one of the uncomprehending masses, "Why do you not say that which is understood?" To which the poet responds, "Why do you not understand that which is said?" (II 3). 'Abbasid poetry is the result of this dialectic of interiorization and alienation. Radically set off from his environment, the poet discovers the self as the origin of the world: "He will choose alienation," Adonis writes of al-Mutanabbi, "believing there is no greatness except in himself" (II 21).

This summary suggests how Adonis rewrites a conventional narrative of pre-Islamic and 'Abbasid poets in a manner that reproduces the categories of Romantic and modernist (in this case, *symboliste*) poetry. In the first period, the *jahili*-Romantic era, the heroic imagination pits itself against an exteriorized nature in a sequence of quest adventures. In the second, the 'Abbasid-modernist era, the poet of Baghdad-Paris retreats into an interior world of analogies and symbols, whose incomprehensibility is a symptom of his estrangement from the crowd. Adonis's rewriting is a narrative *trompe l'oeil*, making it seem as though Arabic modernism preceded by eleven centuries the French version on which it is modeled. To make this feat more plausible, Adonis takes advantage of some lexical coincidences stemming from the verb *hadutha* ("to be new"), from which *al-hadatha* ("modernism") is derived. In the critical debates of the classical era, poets were schematically divided into the ancients (*al-qudama'*) and the innovators (*al-muhdathun*). The latter term had sacrilegious connotations: in legal texts, a *muhdath* is one who invents a saying or *hadith* and attributes it to the prophet, so that innovation and invention become synonyms of unlawfulness. Adonis takes the fact that *al-hadatha* (modernism) shares its root verb with *al-muhdathun* (aesthetic innovators, or inventors of illicit sayings) as etymological sanction for the argument that Arabic modernism occurred in the eighth century. It also lends to that movement an implication of heresy, which is fully in line with the *Shiʿr* poets' idea of themselves.

In a comparison that has become notorious, Adonis asserts that Abu Tammam, the most difficult and recherché of all classical poets, was the "Mallarmé of the Arabs," and that Abu Nuwas, a libertine famous for his wine poetry, was the "Baudelaire of the Arabs." Joseph Massad, among others, argues that Adonis's comparison "anachronistically render[s] Europe, not Arab-Islamic civilization, the reference."[24] But it is probably more correct to say that the reference is not so much Europe or the West as it is "modernism," and that the trope in play is not anachronism but *taʾwil*—the allegorical interpretation of the past according to the needs of the present. (In fact, this species of temporal reversal is a modernist commonplace: for Pound, Omahitsu was "the real modern—even Parisian—of VIII cent. China.")[25] By inserting the French model of modernism into the Arabic tradition itself, Adonis's *Anthology* promises the pleasure of something new that was always already there. This pleasure points to the belatedness of Arabic modernism as a historical experience, one that Adonis's figure of a *mathaf* captures perfectly, suggesting the movement's determination to make its belatedness a strength and to make the museum a site of resurrection.

Differentiation and Autonomy

Classical tradition links the first anthology of Arabic poetry to reasons of state. According to one version, it was the first Umayyad caliph, Muʿawiya [d. 680], who ordered the transmitters of verse, the court *ruwa*, to select twelve exemplary poems, the so-called "Suspended Odes" [*muʿallaqat*], for his son to study in written form (a similar anecdote is told of a subsequent Umayyad caliph, ʿAbd al-Malik [d. 705]). This educational rite seems to have been transmitted across the change of dynasties. According to a later medieval tradition, it was the ʿAbbasid caliph al-Mansur who commanded the Kufan philologist al-Mufaddal al-Dabbi [d. 780] to collect poems by lesser-known poets and teach them to his son, the future caliph al-Mahdi. Al-Dabbi's collection, *al-Mufaddaliyyat*, was the most celebrated of all early Arabic anthologies. In addition to providing a myth of royal *Bildung*, or *adab*, this anecdotal tradition also narrates the transition from orality to literacy, from a poetic culture based on the memorization of poems to one in which they are archived in written form. András Hámori notes that the commissioning of poetry anthologies for the education of princes "may have been a royal habit, or a topos of literary history."[26] This transition or crisis recalls the Platonic mythology of the *pharmakon* and obeys a familiar supplementary logic: to ensure dynastic continuity and the transmission of culture across generations, the caliph avails himself of the technology of writing; but this new art of memory, while preserving the traces of oral culture, also signifies the end of that culture and its own special techniques of preservation. There is a nice etymological wit to these narratives, since one common derivation of *"diwan"* is from the Arabic *"dawwana"* (to collect, write down, or register), while another is traced back to the Persian *"deve"* (mad, devil), used to describe secretaries or court functionaries.[27] The *diwan* or record of poetry is thus figured as an archive of the state.

Medieval traditions about the *diwan* give us some coordinates for understanding Adonis's very different conception of the anthology, which is deeply aware of these older stories and their implications. Rather than ensuring dynastic continuity through a new cultural technology, Adonis's anthology attempts to delink the literary heritage from the state and thereby secure the autonomy of poetry and of poets. As he writes at the beginning of his introduction, Adonis's goals for the *Anthology* are explicitly pedagogical, aiming to combat an entrenched tradition that distorts the Arab reader's relation to poetry:

> This is the tradition of politics, the state [*al-dawla*], power struggles, and everything that accompanies them—a tradition that persists in one form or another and has influenced, to a great degree, a large portion of the rising generations. The *Anthology of Arabic Poetry* attempts an immediate appeal to the heritage itself, to disseminate beauty and poetry as these things were understood by the Arab poet, far from caliph or tribe, proving that it is wrong to define poetic work according to its political or creedal content. Nor it is possible to judge the work by political standards. This anthology consists of poetry that serves no school, creed, state, or person. (I 10–11)

Adonis's notion of poetic autonomy means *autonomy from the state*. For him, the contemporary *dawla* is essentially unchanged since the Umayyad caliphate of the seventh century, where for the first time "culture and state became one."[28] Like all Arab modernists, Adonis watched in alarm as bureaucrats in Cairo, Damascus, and Syria, casting themselves as the agents of popular, anti-imperialist revolutions, gradually established control over intellectual life, including the power to establish literary canons and hierarchies of taste. Adonis's *Anthology* argues that a true, modernist revolution would interrupt this long tradition of statist "acculturation." By differentiating culture from the state, Adonis establishes the poet as a figure of splendid isolation, "far from caliph or tribe"—a phrase that once again recalls Yusuf al-Khal's stipulation that the poet "must create in a place apart." It is his apartness from political institutions that provides the poet with a direct relation to "the heritage itself." In this way, Adonis's modernist museum—his anthology—is figured as an institution of pure mediality, facilitating a link between reader and poetry or reader and poet. This is the properly ideological moment of Adonis's argument. For to conceive of the *Anthology* in this way is to pretend that the whole editorial apparatus—its methods of selection and rearrangement as well as the prefatory material of the introductions themselves—has no mediating role, and to represent a mediate relation as though it were an immediate one is the very definition of ideology.

This late modernist logic of differentiation, or autonomization, does not stop with the separation of poetry from the state but goes on to differentiate modernist poetry—"pure" poetry—from its literary rivals as well. For Adonis, these rivals are the poets and intellectuals of the *Nahda* ("revival," "awakening," "renaissance"), a broad historical term referring to various nineteenth-century movements of reform that arose in response to the Napoleonic invasion of Egypt. The shock of this encounter with the enlightened West is typically supposed to have roused the Arab world from its dogmatic slumbers and thrust it violently into modernity.[29] The problem posed by the *Nahda* to Arab modernists is thus similar to the problem posed by Romanticism to European modernists. In both cases, a movement fueled by innovation is confronted by a precursor whose claims to novelty appear equally urgent. In the case of Arabic modernism, a specifically Lebanese phenomenon, this agon was aggravated by the fact that the historical center of the *Nahda* was Egypt. Egyptian intellectuals were the first to undertake translations of European technical and artistic works—from François Fénelon's *Télémaque* to Jean Cruveilhier's *Anatomie pathologique du corps humain*—in a manner that struck Beiruti modernists as uncomfortably similar to their own project.

Modernism's typical response to the difficulty posed by its precursors is to undertake a process of internal differentiation, a movement of self-division that allows modernism to assert its continuity with the rewritten past while distinguishing itself from its contemporary rivals.[30] In Adonis's account, as we have seen, it is the corpus of ʿAbbasid poetry that is recoded in a modernist idiom of irony and estrangement, and then claimed as a precedent. Modernist poetry's chief rival, the movement from which it has to differentiate itself, is that of the Egyptian *Nahda*. Adonis claims that the *Nahda* poets were unable to wrest poetry free of its mobilization by the state, the sine qua non of his own brand of modernism:

> Unsurprisingly, the formalist perspective, which dominated what we call the era of the *Nahda*, was unable to be creative, to truly understand the particularity of the poetic heritage and the meaning of its rebirth [*ihya'*]. Nor did it understand what is worth reviving and what deserves neglect. For the *Nahda* did not offer, from our literary and poetic heritage, anything except works that vacillate between two tendencies: commonplaces and didactic parables on one hand, and on the other, politics and whatever goes with it in the way of poems of praise and blame [*madh wa hija'*]. It did not give us anything except works in which the person of the poet [*shakhsiyyat al-shaʿir*], his views and experiences, is not foregrounded. Instead, what gets foregrounded is the character of the society: its habits, traditions and established

conventions. Works, in other words, that cannot possibly benefit a true poetic *Nahda*. (I 12)

Adonis's critique of the étatist intellectuals of the nineteenth-century *Nahda* is an analogue of his campaign against contemporary opponents, the nationalist poets (many of them Nasserists and in that sense "Egyptian") whose committed verse he excludes from the realm of poetry.[31] In this way, all possible positions, whether Romantic, modernist, or *engagé*, are included in Adonis's narrative, which weans the poet away from the tribe, the caliphate, and finally his historical peers. The "individual" is in this sense whatever is left over from the dynamic of differentiation. He is a figure of *difference* in the mathematical sense of the word: the result of a process of subtraction. In his review of the *Anthology*, Husayn Muruwwa criticized Adonis on just these grounds. While Adonis claims to have no editorial method but to rely instead on his "personal" [*shakhsi*] taste, Muruwwa notes that personal taste is itself a method, one that "abstracts [*tajrid*] poetry from its conditions of time and place." He accuses Adonis of "exaggerating the individual isolation of Arab poets, making each one of them a world unto himself," and complains of Adonis's practice of taking lines of poetry out of context: "Can one make this fragmentation [*tajzi'*] the basis for a generalized judgment, one that allows the critic to judge Arabic poetry on purely individualistic grounds?"[32] Where Adonis saw alienated nomads, Muruwwa saw *engagé* intellectuals; where Adonis saw a tradition in fragments, Muruwwa saw a unified corpus.

True to his credo that the destruction of a principle must be carried out by way of the principle itself, Adonis claimed a precedent for his modernist *Anthology* from within the classical *turath*. The ninth-century poet Abu Tammam, "Mallarmé of the Arabs," as Adonis calls him, edited a collection of pre-Islamic and early Islamic poetry, the *Diwan al-hamasa* [Anthology of Valor], which was a medieval *succès de scandale*. According to one count, it received at least thirty classical commentaries.[33] Abu Tammam also compiled a smaller anthology, the *Wahshiyat* [Wild Verses], known as "the lesser *Hamasa*." At the beginning of his introduction, Adonis names Abu Tammam's compilations as the sole models for his own efforts: "All anthologies that preceded this one, with the exception of Abu Tammam's two *Hamasa*, were conventional. They only confirmed the reigning standards and common taste" (I 9). In an interview published at the same time, Adonis repeated this boast and confession of influence: "What I can say about this work of mine is that it is the first poetic encyclopedia of its kind in the modern period, preceded by the great encyclopedia of Abu Tammam known as the *Diwan al-hamasa*."[34]

In naming Abu Tammam as a predecessor, Adonis asserts his place in a genealogy of nonconformism. Abu Tammam's editorial methods were notoriously idiosyncratic, not to say individualistic. Rather than arranging the poems, as was customary, *'ala-l-rijal* [by poet], Abu Tammam arranged them

ʿala-l-abwab [by topoi], with sections devoted to fortitude in battle, elegy, and the vituperation of women, among other subjects. He ignored chronology and tribal affiliation, and he juxtaposed poets of different eras and regions on the same page. Still more strangely, many poems are excerpted, their lines are rearranged, and sometimes two poems are combined into one.[35] Some commentators even suspected Abu Tammam of interpolating his own word choice where the poet's seemed to him questionable. Such procedures broke with the philological probity of court transmitters like al-Mufaddal al-Dabbi, anxious to preserve the original oral version of a poem before it fell into oblivion. In the medieval anecdotal tradition, Abu Tammam is reported to have compiled his anthologies in a friend's library while waiting out a snowstorm (a narrative explanation for the *Hamasa*'s eccentricities). Cocooned in his friend's library, Abu Tammam does not worry about origins or oblivion: in a scribal culture, poetry can be rearranged, rewritten, and even reattributed.

An eleventh-century critic, Ahmad ibn Muhammad al-Marzuqi, evokes the power of Abu Tammam's anthology with a memorable conceit: "If God brought them back to life, the poets [included in the *Hamasa*] might well follow Abu Tammam and submit to him" [i.e., submit to his editorial decisions].[36] This eschatological fantasy rhymes with the idea of the anthology we find in Adonis, who cites al-Marzuqi's commentary in his Rome lecture of 1961. In this fantasy, it is the present that will judge the past, not according to a philological standard of authenticity, but according to the needs and standards of the moment. It is in this sense that the poets of yesterday will paradoxically "follow" the poet of today. Like his later encyclopedia, Adonis's *Anthology* is a *taʾwil* of the *turath*, an allegorical interpretation of the classical tradition that promises to restore its authentic but heretofore hidden modernity, even if that means fracturing the very heritage it means to salvage.

Il Miglior Fabbro: The Poet as Editor

The worth of a critic is known not by his arguments but by the quality of his choice.

—EZRA POUND, "TOWARD A NEW PAIDEUMA"

The narrative argument of Adonis's *Anthology* results in a series of editorial principles as radical as they are comprehensive, affecting the look of the poems on the page as well as the criteria of selection. For Adonis, it is only by stripping away the mummy clothes of history and politics that the reader is put in contact with the poetic *turath* as such. This method of abstraction also explains the *Anthology*'s most notable typographical features. In contrast to medieval or nineteenth-century anthologies, invariably equipped with a bulky apparatus of philological commentary, the pages of Adonis's *Anthology*, like those of *Shiʿr* magazine, are remarkably clean. Vocalizations, the short vowel markings sometimes included in Arabic texts to clarify pronunciation and meaning, are kept to a minimum. There is no marginalia and no help given with difficult words. Nor does Adonis's edition provide any context, biographical, historical, or otherwise, for the poems he cites, whereas the classical critics often did supply a context for the occasion of the poem, typically anecdotal or legendary. This way of constructing the page serves as a corollary for Adonis's argument in favor of poetic autonomy: the exaggeratedly large blank spaces are allegories of the reader's solitude. Here, on the page, is where he or she confronts, without editorial intermediary, "the heritage itself."

In Adonis's telling, the transmission of this heritage is necessarily the work of individuals working in isolation. As he writes in the introduction to his *Anthology*, "In selecting these poems I have followed the thread that links us to the character of the poet—to his worries, joys, pains, and own individual life—without consideration for politics or reigning societal values: the thread that links us to the individual not the society; to creativity, not to the past" (I 14). How does this personalist principle get translated into editorial terms? What are the kinds of poems it selects for, and what kinds does it exclude? Adonis explains that it is chiefly a matter of genre:

> I must indicate that I am inclined to consider the poem of praise [*al-madh*] and the poem of blame [*al-hija'*], as well as things similar or somehow connected to them, a part of our political and social history, not part of our poetic history. I do not evaluate poetry by its topoi, but rather by its value as determined by its manner of expression and the extent to which it complies with contemporary poetic values and with my understanding of poetry. (I 14)

This exclusion of *hija'* and *madh* from an anthology that claims to represent the poetic heritage as such, whose criterion for inclusion is simply whether or not the poem is "poetic," is what makes Adonis's editorial principles so radical. An enormous amount of the classical corpus—perhaps the very core of it, from Ka'ab bin Zuhayr's "*Banat Su'ad*" to al-Mutanabbi's praise poems for his patron Sayf al-Dawla—belongs to these two genres. Even in the relatively unorthodox case of Abu Tammam's *Hamasa*, of the 261 selections there are 80 *hija'* poems and 32 *madh*, each of which is given a separate chapter. The motive for Adonis's exclusion is clear. It is meant to purify the poetic tradition of politics, a late modernist translation of the Mallarméan dictum, "*donner un sens plus pur aux mots de la tribu*," and it is yet another example of the movement's tendency to generate the new by way of negation. The three volumes of Adonis's *Anthology* are indeed devoid of *hija'* and *madh*. Even in the case of included poems that do belong to these genres, the sections of explicit praise have been edited out.

What is left of the *turath* when these genres have been removed, along with the classical tradition's anecdotal narratives and philological commentary? A poetics of melancholy. This is suggested first of all by the fact that the elegy or *marthiya* (pl. *marathi*) is the only classical genre that survives in Adonis's *Anthology*, which is strewn with laments for sons, brothers, friends, and heroes. This survival is somewhat surprising given modernism's vigorous resistance to all generic conventions. Adonis's own resistance to genre, and not just those of *madh* and *hija'*, is otherwise implacable. While the poems of his *Anthology* are arranged chronologically by author, each individual poem or excerpt is given a thematic title, none of which betray the genre to which the poem belongs: "Today and Yesterday," "Woman," "Confusion," "Rain," "Despair." The economy of genre is in this sense also an economy of repression, in which the repressed object—politics—becomes a motive for melancholy. It is precisely the same logic that governs *The Songs of Mihyar*, a way of thinking that originates in the modernists' common experience of defeat and disillusionment as members of the SSNP.

Elegy persists in Adonis's *Diwan* not merely as a genre but also as a mood. The *Anthology* is a collection almost exclusively interested in passing things. Here is one ninth-century poet's evocation of a rose: "A visitor, gliding toward us each year, / A handsome face, chastely perfumed, an intimate of wine, / Fifty days old, he goes in peace" ('Ali bin Jahm, II 266). In many cases, the worldly things of these poems—clouds, rain, women, settlements and cities—are only remembered, their sensual plenitude a function of being past. "My eye quivered and then I saw him, as if my eye had knowledge of absent things" (Ibrahim bin al-'Abbas al-Suli, II 260). The incipient tear of grief brings a visionary clarity, a knowledge of hidden or invisible events. In this way, the erotic nostalgia of the *nasib*, in which the poet laments the beloved's absence over the traces of her abandoned campsite, and the dry-eyed calm of the *zuhd*, in which the ascetic counsels equanimity in the face of life's brevity, merge into one structure of feeling. Under this Saturnine gaze, alternately tearful or stoic, history is transformed into a collection of *memento mori*: "Why do the graves not answer when the melancholic [*al-ka'ib*] calls out to them? / Holes roofed by stones and sand dunes, / Inside are parents, children, youths and old men. / So many lovers to whose parting my soul was unreconciled" (Abu al-'Atahiya, II 161). In the introduction to his anthology, writing of the pre-Islamic poets, Adonis takes this structure of feeling as a guiding principle, what he calls "the awareness of fate":

> What I mean by fate is an overwhelming power one cannot fight against. It takes away all things, transforms all things. Confronted by this power, the poet feels impotent, outmaneuvered. Fate is not the power of death, but a dynamic, leveling force that brings absence in its wake: absence of the beloved, of settlements, relatives, the tribe.... This explains the rooted melancholy [*al-ka'aba al-mujadhdhara*] in the Arab spirit and Arabic poetry. For the Arab, melancholy is an authentic and natural spring. (I 27)

Adonis's determination to see melancholy as a creative principle affects not only the general tone of his *Anthology* but also his presentation of particular poets. The case of Abu Tammam is especially noteworthy, both for its own sake as well as its importance to Adonis's larger revisionary project. I have already noted the importance of Abu Tammam's *Hamasa* for Adonis's notion of the modernist anthology. In his later encyclopedia, *The Fixed and the Dynamic*, the 'Abbasid poet plays a similarly pivotal role. There, he is described as the discoverer of obscurity [*al-ghumud*], a density of syntax and imagery that leads to misunderstanding and misinterpretation but also poetic newness. "If alchemy is, in the words of Jabir bin Hayyan, 'giving to physical bodies forms they did not possess,' then the beginning of alchemy in poetry is 'giving to the word meanings it did not possess,' and this was the achievement of Abu Tammam." Adonis goes on to characterize this *alchimie du verbe* as a poetics of metaphor (*al-majaz*), which he contrasts with what he considers the dominant, theological poetics centered on referential description (*al-wasf*). The polysemy of metaphor, which results from its semantic obscurity, is what connects *al-majaz* to the exegetical principle of *ta'wil*, the hermeneutical trope that governs the entire encyclopedia and aims at opening the tradition to its own multiplicity. In this way, Adonis places Abu Tammam at the origin of a modernist poetics of pluralism and transformation.[37]

In his *Anthology*, Adonis adopts a different though related strategy. In this earlier, seminal work, he seeks to reconceive the 'Abbasid poet as a modernist by virtue of being an elegist. The second volume of the *Anthology* includes 78 excerpts from Abu Tammam's oeuvre, second only to Abu Nuwas, who has 91. Seventeen of these excerpts, about one-fifth of the total, are *marathi*. Adonis's elegiac revision is especially ambitious because of Abu Tammam's reputation as the greatest of the 'Abbasid panegyrists. Most of these efforts are simply excluded from the *Anthology*. A more subtle approach is taken with what is perhaps Abu Tammam's most famous *madh*, his "Ode to Amorium," a poem that commemorates the caliph al-Muʿtasim's sack of the Byzantine stronghold Amorium in 838. Adonis cites ten lines of the poem (11–12; 25–33) (thereby excising its proverbial, thoroughly unmodernist opening hemistich, "The sword is more truthful than the pen"). The lines cited in the *Anthology* are drawn from the poet's description of the city, at the time the most prosperous in Asia Minor, before and after the Muslim armies attacked it and set it on fire. Abu Tammam figures the caliph's victory over the city as a rape of its inhabitants, "For on that day the sun did rise upon no man but chaste, nor set upon a virgin," and the last lines quoted by Adonis portray a scene of destruction:

> *The city in her ruins looked as lovely as Mayy's haunts, in their heyday, to Ghaylan.*
> *Her cheek, though streaked with grime, appeared as tempting as cheeks aflush with maiden modesty.*

Gazing on her disfigurement, no need had we of beauty nor of pleasing sights. (II 201-2)

The effect of Adonis's editorializing is to make a poem written in praise of the caliph into an elegy for the city he has destroyed. With a typical melancholy flourish, the beauty of that city, figured now as a woman, is only revealed in postbellum retrospect. The plausibility of this sleight of hand is heightened by the fact that the city elegy is an established genre in Arabic, the *ritha' al-mudun*, which stems from the Old Testament Lamentations and has its roots in even more ancient poems such as the Sumerian "Lament for Ur." Adonis's *Anthology* includes several examples of the genre from the classical tradition, including a generous selection of Abu Ya'qub al-Khuraymi's canonical "Elegy for Baghdad," a poem composed during the civil war that followed the death of caliph Harun al-Rashid in the early ninth century (II 175-78). After an opening section that remembers the city when it was "a paradise on earth," "surrounded by vineyards, palm trees, and basil," the bulk of the poem remembers the city's destruction and laments its present, in which Baghdad's inhabitants have turned on one another, widows' keening fills the streets, and the marketplaces are abandoned. The poem ends with a long section of praise for al-Ma'mun, son of al-Rashid, who was in fact responsible for besieging and sacking the city, becoming caliph after defeating his brother al-Amin. In accordance with his principles, Adonis excises this final *madh*, in which al-Khuraymi extols Baghdad's new ruler, "the rescuer and restorer," and looks forward to the rebuilding of the capital. In Adonis's truncated version, the elegy ends not with a vision of communal restoration but a fabled city in ruins, a melancholic tableau that is typical of the anthology as a whole.[38]

In one of his most explicitly modernist notations, Walter Benjamin dreamt of composing a work made entirely of others' words, a "literary montage" that "needn't say anything, merely show." This dream of a book constructed from citations, in which the collector would be present only in his chosen constellation of objects, stemmed from Benjamin's desire to devise a mode of cultural inheritance that would explode what he called the catastrophe of tradition. "From what are the phenomena to be rescued?" he asks in another of his methodological notes from *The Arcades Project*. "Not only, and not in the main, from the discredit and neglect into which they have fallen, but from the catastrophe represented very often by a certain strain in their dissemination, their 'enshrinement as heritage.'—They are saved through the exhibition of the fissure within them.—There is a tradition that is catastrophe."[39] Benjamin's principle of literary montage bears comparison with Adonis's own attempts to save the phenomena. The dream of a work composed of citations from the literary past, a dream that haunts any number of modernist projects from *The Waste Land* to *The Cantos*, is precisely the dream of an anthology. And Adonis's methods of abstraction and fragmentation, his uncanny feel for the "fissures" in the classical *turath*, have a formal resemblance to the juxtapositions and jagged discontinuities of Benjamin's work, which explicitly seeks "the places where the tradition breaks off."[40] It is their common perception of a crisis in the transmission of heritage—along with their interest in melancholy and the hermeneutics of allegory—that suggests a comparison between the two thinkers. But one also needs to make distinctions. Benjamin's search for a usable past with which to "blast open the continuum of history" was explicitly a technique of political pedagogy, an attempt to shock the present awake into an apprehension of its revolutionary potential. Adonis's work of collection and rearrangement, on the other hand, is meant to expunge all traces of political conflict—"the state, power struggles, and everything that accompanies them"—from the poetic *turath*. This liberal dream of literary purity would have made little sense to Benjamin, who recognized the "enshrinement of heritage" as a symptom of the very tradition he wanted to explode.

It is just this dream that marks Adonis's *Anthology* as a text of its own historical moment, when literary autonomy represented an emancipatory if not quite utopian ideology. In Lebanon and elsewhere in what was beginning to be called the Third World, the doctrines of late modernism allowed poets to free themselves from the constraints of parochialism and to perform a critical revision of their literary canon, one that had, they felt, for too long been subject to the dictates of state culture. For the modernists, the inherited *turath* was indeed a tradition of catastrophe, the legacy of a triumphant orthodoxy. This triumph was an ongoing crisis, a falsification of the heritage that rendered it unusable for future generations. Adonis's *Anthology* seeks to resolve this crisis through an internal translation of the literary past, one that wrests the archive of poetry away from its sinecured custodians and attempts to restore, through much textual violence, its original purity. Adonis's *Diwan* thus becomes a "heritage museum," a site for the translation—the preservation, transformation, and resurrection—of the authentic *turath*.

The anthologist's curatorial work finds its analogue within the pages of Adonis's *Anthology* in the figure of the elegist. The *marthiya* is central to Adonis's collection not only because the genre is ostensibly "personal" and "apolitical," but because the elegy at once memorializes the past and ensures its survival into the future, however fitfully and fragmentarily. Among the most moving texts of Adonis's *Anthology* is a fragment of Abu Tammam that Adonis calls "Elegy for a Son." In an anguished scene of life-in-death and death-in-life, the poet elegizes what was to have been the future but is now falling into the past. It is also a found allegory for Adonis's own modernist anxiety about the death of tradition and its struggle to communicate itself into the present:

The last time I saw him, Death had thrown him low, prostrate with sickness.
His choked plaints caught in his throat, his cries turning each around the other,
Echoes that turned the tongue on itself. Death would not let him speak clearly,
His eyes now turning fixedly upwards, his eyelids flickering closed.
   (II 228)

CHAPTER SIX

"He Sang New Sorrow"

ADONIS AND THE MODERNIST ELEGY

Ritha' *and Variations*

"Averroës' Search," the short story by Jorge Luis Borges, narrates a famous and arguably fateful instance of mistranslation between East and West, between the Arab-Islamic world and the tradition of classical Greece.[1] The story is set on the day when Ibn Rushd, composing his commentary on Aristotle's *Poetics*, decides to translate the Greek words for "tragedy" and "comedy" into "panegyrics" and "satires"—or, to use the Arabic terms that Borges does not, "*madh*" and "*hija*'." The tale, which is in large part a dialogue between the philosopher and his intimates, ends by suggesting that Ibn Rushd's error stems from his conviction that the Qur'an and the poetry of pre-Islamic Arabia had "already said all things," from which it follows that Greek words must have Arabic equivalents. Unfamiliar with the tradition of classical theater, Ibn Rushd writes, "There are many admirable tragedies and comedies in the Qur'an and the *muʿallaqat* of the mosque." In this way, Borges's story becomes a comedy, unless it is a tragedy, about the inability to think outside of a particular vocabulary, about how, in Wittgenstein's phrase, the limits of my language constitute the limits of my world.

The Arab modernists were aware of this topos of literary history, if not Borges's particular version of it, and they were eager to avoid Ibn Rushd's mistake. At the end of his lecture to the Cénacle libanais, Yusuf al-Khal urged Lebanese poets "to benefit from the poetic experiences of literary writers of the world. For the modern Lebanese poet must not fall prey to the danger of isolationism as the ancient Arab poets did with respect to Greek literature." Ibn Rushd's fault, under this reading, was his provincialism. The philosopher's mistranslation of Aristotle was the result of the narrowness of his intellectual experience, "bounded within the circle of Islam," as Borges writes. At the end of his story, Borges admits to experiencing a certain empathy with Ibn Rushd, based on a recognition of their common limitations: "I felt that Averroës, trying to imagine what a play is without ever having suspected what a theater is, was no more absurd than I, trying to imagine Averroës yet with no more material than a few snatches from Renan, Lane, and Asín Palacios." This sort of empathy is anathema to the Arab modernists (nor is it one that Borges himself was always comfortable with, anxious as he was about the marginality of the Argentine tradition). The modernists' project is instead a relentless effort of deprovincialization, a possibly quixotic attempt to make the limits of their language coincide with the limits of world literature.

What seems peculiarly comic about Ibn Rushd and makes him an especially difficult object of empathy is that the limits of his world are the limits of literary genre. *Madh*, poetry written in praise of the tribe, patron, or caliph, and *hija'*, invectives written against personal or communal enemies, were the primary genres of classical Arabic poetics, but they hardly stake out the frontiers of contemporary practice. On the contrary, as we have seen in the previous chapter, *madh* and *hija'* were precisely the two genres Adonis excluded from his *Anthology of Arabic Poetry*, arguing that they were "a part of our political and social history, not a part of our poetic history." So the genres that once defined the limits of poetry are now banished from the realm of poetry altogether. Adonis's exclusion of *madh* and *hija'* exemplifies modernism's traditional resistance to genre and its taboo on conventionalized poetry of all kinds—its method for producing novelty out of prohibition. As Fredric Jameson argues, "The reaction against genre theory in recent times is a strategic feature of what must be called *the ideology of modernism*"—an ideology that abstracts literature from those historical institutions, such as genre, that mediate between readers and authors in favor of an idealized or individualized conception of artistic production.[2] In the already cited words of Stephen Spender, "The poet is writing as one person for the reader reading as one person." But we have seen that Adonis does not uphold the taboo on genre in all cases. While poems of praise and blame are excluded from Adonis's *Anthology*, the presence of *marathi* is unmistakable. Indeed, his collection imposes a lyrical but more specifically elegiac modulation on the whole history of Arabic poetry, now arranged under the brooding gaze of the anthologist.

The *marthiya* is central not only to Adonis's revision of the classical corpus but also to his own poetry, which is full of a particular kind of elegy—those for fellow poets. It is by way of the elegy and its variations that Adonis negotiates his turn away from politics and seeks to establish a modernist countercanon, a series of imaginary filiations that provide him with a compensatory, nonpolitical authority. Even while bidding farewell, the elegist makes a claim upon his precursor, seeking to annex some of the previous poet's power. The elegy is in this sense another mode of translation, in which the poet asserts his right to a particular literary inheritance and projects its survival under unpropitious circumstances. As Rosanna Warren writes in a remarkable essay, "A poet's elegy for another poet is somehow a translation of that poet or at least of a tradition, and involves some kind of transfer of powers, perhaps aggressively asserted by the survivor."[3]

Without some sense for the tradition or institution of the Arabic *ritha'* as well as its varieties of contemporary practice, it is difficult to appreciate the strangeness and polemical charge of Adonis's *marathi*. In the medieval Arabic tradition, elegies were most often composed for relatives or patrons. Less frequently, they were written for cities or even—a parodic subgenre—domestic animals. The main lines of this practice survived through the early twentieth century and witnessed a significant rebirth at the hands of neoclassical poets such as Ahmad Shawqi. Adonis edited an anthology of Shawqi's poems in 1982 and wrote an introduction in which he censured the Egyptian, the so-called Prince of Poets, as the passive transmitter of outworn conventions: "The speaker of these poems," Adonis writes, "is the tradition, a tradition that does not make a new beginning, but rather shores up the authority of old words." In the same preface, he describes Shawqi's poetry as a mixture of pre-Islamic *lafz* [expression] and Islamic *ma'na* [meaning].[4] Adonis's rivalry with the Egyptian poet was of long standing. This was partly the result of the modernists' agon with the *Nahda*, which they attacked for being a false or merely formal renaissance. But it was also the result of Shawqi's reputation as an elegist. Nearly one-quarter of the Egyptian's poems were *marathi*, most of them for local pashas and politicians such as Mustafa Kamil and Sa'd Zaghlul—Shawqi's long elegy for the Wafdist prime minister is one of the texts included in Adonis's anthology—or Arab luminaries such as King Husayn and 'Umar al-Mukhtar. In one of these poems, Shawqi supplies a punning epigram for everything Adonis found objectionable in the classical tradition. Ventriloquizing the German emperor Wilhelm II, who paid homage to Salah ad-Din while visiting his grave in 1898, Shawqi writes: "The great man is he who weeps for the great ('*izam*) / and mourns them even when they be but bones ('*izam*)." For Adonis, as we have seen, it is this confusion of the poetical with the political, the assumption that literary greatness should be dependent on another kind of greatness, that vitiates so much of the canon. To a modernist sensibility, the neoclassical elegy is merely a praise poem that happens to be written in the past tense. (This is in fact a classical commonplace: as Abdelfattah Kilito has noted, summarizing the critical tradition, "[The elegy] differs from the panegyric only in one formal property: the use of the past instead of the present tense. Rather than 'He is . . .' or 'You are . . . ,' we have 'He was . . .' or 'You were . . .'")[5]

The second rival tradition of elegy is that of the collective *marthiya*. The origins of this poetry lie in the classical genre of the city elegy, or *ritha' al-mudun*. Adonis's *Anthology* includes a number of such poems—some of them, like Abu Tammam's "Ode to Amorium," of the editor's own fabrication. A more recent and relevant example, well known to Adonis, is Shawqi's elegy for Damascus, "*Nakbat Dimashq*," a poem composed on the occasion of the French shelling of Damascus to put down the Syrian Revolt of 1925–27.[6] Borrowing from a reserve of conventional tropes and figures, Shawqi's poem is a markedly anticolonial and pan-Arabist performance: "I have given you counsel and though our dwellings differ, in our cares we are all from the East. / Though our countries are separate, we are bound by one undivided tongue [*nutq*] and one eloquence [*bayan*]." Shawqi's elegy, one of his best-known poems, expresses the poet's sorrowful empathy for the suffering of his fellow Arabs and also mounts a thrilling invective against the French. Another contemporary strain of the collective *marthiya* was what Adina Hoffman has called "a bold new form of politically charged elegy," written by Palestinian poets in the wake of the massacre of Kafr Qasim in 1956. The most striking examples of these poems are Samih al-Qasim's "*Kafr Qasim*" and Mahmoud Darwish's later, Lorca-like series, "*Azhar al-Dam*" [Flowers of Blood], in which the poet speaks of his wish to assume "the power of the graveyard's silence." "The poetry of Kafr Qasim became, in a sense, a genre unto itself," Hoffman writes. "When a poet read his verse about the massacre aloud before a crowd it took on extra meaning, as though he were speaking not just for himself but for the group as a whole and as if the grisly event were not unique but the sum of so many others." And indeed, such collective elegies tapped into a long tradition of lamentation, reformulating it and reauthorizing it for specifically political, anticolonial purposes.[7]

Adonis's *marathi* are markedly distinct from the neoclassical and the collective elegy, his innovations spring from a refusal of their tropes and techniques. In contrast to the neoclassical elegies, directed at prominent political figures, Adonis's are addressed to individuals whose lack of political authority is explicitly marked by the poems themselves. Most of Adonis's *marathi* are in fact written for poets who were the victims of political power. The elegist's claim of affiliation is thus premised on a common experience of suffering and sometimes exile. Elegies written for fellow poets are hardly unknown in Arabic literature. Shawqi composed *marathi* for his compatriot Hafiz Ibrahim as well as Victor Hugo. But Adonis's single-mindedness in this respect is unusual if not unique. Moreover, the poets he elegizes are neither acquaintances nor contemporaries but classical precursors, figures for whom there can be no claim of affective bonds or pose of mourning. In the second portion of this chapter, I will argue that these two features of Adonis's elegies—that they are typically addressed to fellow poets and that they are affectively impoverished—suggest that his *marathi* are best read as translated *tombeaux*.

The most concentrated group of elegies in Adonis's oeuvre is the suite of seven *marathi* that comprise the final section of *The Songs of Mihyar the Damascene*. In chapter 2, I suggested that this series of elegies represents a climax of the collection's poetics of apostrophe, its constant alternation between address and evasion, turning toward and turning away. The addressees of these *marathi* are not always specified, but the subjects of the central four poems are named. The first, "Elegy for 'Umar ibn al-Khattab," sets the terms for Adonis's swerve away from the mainstream elegiac tradition, with its deference to figures of political power. 'Umar was the second caliph and therefore a fitting subject for praise and elegy. But Adonis's poem is actually a *hija'*: not a poem in praise of the caliph but a critique of his rule.

> A voice without promise, without justification [*ta'illa*],
> cries out, with the sun for an umbrella [*mazalla*],
> When will you be beaten, Jibilla?
>
> Friend of despair and hope,
> the green stone hangs over the fire
> and we await
> your appointment coming from the heavens.

The intertext for the opening tercet is a medieval tradition according to which a nobleman named Jabala—"Jibilla" in the Adonis's text, for reasons of rhyme—has his robe trampled on while circumambulating the Kaaba.[8] Jabala turns on the inadvertently offending party, a poor Bedouin, and beats him. 'Umar is asked to intercede and initially agrees to let the Bedouin answer Jabala blow for blow, in accordance with the Islamic stipulation that all worshippers are equal, but then lets the nobleman go, apparently out of deference to his status. The question at the heart of Adonis's elegy, "When are you beaten, Jibilla?" is effectively a demand for justice made in solidarity with the victim, whose solitary voice, exposed to the elements, is otherwise "without justification." As for 'Umar, the subject of the elegy, he is condemned as a failed caliph, an abuser of power.

This episode of unjustly suspended punishment stands in apposition to the other *marathi* of the series, addressed to Abu Nuwas, Bashshar ibn Burd, and al-Hallaj, not only because these three elegies are addressed to literary confreres but also because their scenes of punishment are explicitly represented or alluded to. The contrast is particularly apparent in the elegies for Bashshar, a blind poet of the eighth century, and al-Hallaj, a mystical exegete and poet of the ninth and tenth centuries as well as a consistent alter-ego for Adonis. In his elegy for Bashshar, the poet is figured as a victim of the state. The *marthiya* begins, "Do not weep for him, but leave him to the mad caliph's whip," an allusion to the flogging that caused the poet's death after he had composed a *hija'* against the caliph al-Mahdi (a gesture mimicked by Adonis's own invective against 'Umar). Al-Hallaj's crucifixion and dismemberment at the hands of the 'Abbasid regime is part of his legend, and Adonis's poem evokes al-Hallaj as a Christ-like figure of resurrection or indeed an Adonis-like figure of vegetal rebirth. Part of Adonis's affinity for *marathi* can be explained by his obsessional interest in myths of resurrection, which, as Peter Sacks has convincingly demonstrated, also lie behind the genre of elegy.[9]

In an enigmatic phrase from the *marthiya* for Abu Nuwas, the elegist asks the poet to "leave us to the beautiful torture" [*al-'adhab al-jamil*], a phrase that can bear several readings. One points toward Adonis's interest in the morbid eroticism of Yves Bonnefoy's early verse, which Adonis translated, and the French poet's inflection of what Bataille called "*la joie suppliciante*"—i.e., "the art of turning anguish into delight." Another points us toward traditions of Shiite martyrology, which Adonis became increasingly fascinated by over the next decade. Taken together, these readings suggest that the elegies' emphasis on suffering, their insistence on episodes in which poets are subjected to the violence of the state, is an early example of Adonis's effort to establish a modernist countercanon, a heterodox tradition of the anathematized. "The beautiful torture" evokes the necessary misery of aesthetic creation as well as its tradition of poetic martyrs. For Adonis, Arab modernists—whatever epoch they belong to—are indeed a persecuted sect, like the Shia, the Alawis, or the SSNP. The bonds that hold this sect together are not those of empathy or sentiment—nor a positive political doctrine—but rather a common experience of marginality and a specifically literary "commitment." The tradition of poetic martyrs is figured in the opening of the elegy for Abu Nuwas as a "pageant of stone" [*mawkib al-hajar*], a historical frieze in which the poet situates himself in the train of his precursor-poet: "You know that behind you, in the pageant of stones, / beyond our history of corpses, / there is me and poetry and the rain." The elegies of *The Songs of Mihyar* are not so much poems of mourning—"Do not weep" might even be their motto—so much as they are poems of canonical revision, claiming certain aspects of the poetic tradition while ignoring or repressing others. The rain, here as elsewhere in Adonis's work, is a promise of canonical cleansing: poetry washed clean of the blood of history.

In his *Anthology*, Adonis imagines this revision of the archive as a revival or rebirth. A similar idea animates his elegy for Bashshar:

> Do not weep for him, but leave him to the mad caliph's whip.
> Call him devil, call him plague,
> he is here, and still there,
> rumbling in the deaf [*samma'*] streets,
> rumbling in our mute [*kharsa'*] caverns,
> rumbling like an earthquake.
>
> He is here, and still there,
> blind, without land or city,
> he searches for a blue pearl
> that his poems will keep safe
> for a lean year.

Here, the rebirth of 'Abbasid modernism is figured through a present-tense evocation of the poet's voice, rumbling through the silent streets of Baghdad. The emphasis given by the rhyme *samma'-kharsa'* reminds us that the trope of a deaf or mute landscape is a family resemblance between the Western tradition of pastoral elegy ("Where were you, nymphs?") and the medieval Arabic canon, in which the poet is forever questioning the graves or abandoned campsites and never receiving an answer.[10] "I called you, O Kulayb, and you did not reply [*falam tujibni*]—and the wasteland, how will it answer me?" asks the pre-Islamic poet Muhalhil ibn Rabi'a in a famous elegy for his brother Kulayb, a poem cited by Adonis in the first volume of his *Anthology*. In the second stanza of "Elegy for Bashshar," the poet's blindness becomes the stigmata of mystical insight. Unable to see, he nevertheless searches for a *blue* pearl, a treasure for his poems to store up for "a lean year" (an idiom that exists in both English and Arabic). In the context of 'Abbasid court life, this might mean a year without caliphal commissions and their demand for a steady diet of praise and blame.

The tropes and structures of the *ritha'* remain crucial to Adonis's later poetry, oftentimes in texts not specified as elegies. *Kitab al-tahawwulat wa-l-hijra fi aqalim al-nahar wa-l-layl* [The Book of Transformations and Emigrations in the Regions of Night and Day] (1965) was Adonis's next collection following *The Songs of Mihyar*.[11] It was published at the same time as his *Anthology*, and its long central poem, "*al-Saqr*" [The Hawk], is another upshot of Adonis's dive into the archive of classical Arabic poetry and history. The protagonist of the poem is 'Abd al-Rahman (731–788), an Umayyad prince who fled from Damascus during the 'Abbasid revolt and eventually founded the emirate of Córdoba, the seed of seven centuries of Muslim rule in Andalusia. But 'Abd al-Rahman's success as a dynast is only briefly alluded to in Adonis's poem, which narrates his lonely journey west rather than his military triumph: "hawk" here bears connotations of migration and flight rather than martial prowess. 'Abd al-Rahman was also, fittingly, a poet (though hardly canonical) and Adonis's text is interspersed with citations from 'Abd al-Rahman's verse as well as autobiographical fragments.[12] "The Hawk" is thus a collage-like composition, "a poem including history" as Pound would say, a technique that becomes increasingly characteristic of Adonis's poetry and which can be read as a formal reflection in his poetry of his work as an anthologist. Reviewing the collection, Husayn Muruwwa criticized Adonis again for the "fragmentation of the work" as well as its methods of abstraction and obsessive focus on "the seashell of the self," the familiar watchwords of Marxist antimodernism. But Muruwwa singled out "The Hawk" as a poem that managed to hold its contradictions in a creative suspension, engineering a "mutual interaction" between "the interior self and the exterior topic," so that the poem represented "a great gift to Arabic literature."[13] The poem's itinerary follows the route laid out by *The Songs of Mihyar*: it narrates a flight westward from a violent "city of endings" toward a city of new beginnings, with its face turned out toward the world. 'Abd al-Rahman's is an exilic figure of cultural translation who rescues the literary heritage, or certain fragments of it, from the nightmare of history: "He builds, on a peak, in the depths' furthest reaches, / Andalusia of the depths, / al-Andalus risen from Damascus, / carrying for the West the harvest of the East."

"The Hawk" is also a modernist modulation of the city elegy. The genre is explicitly invoked in the opening passage of the poem's second section, "Season of Spring," which evokes the scene of departure:

> It falls quiet, the cry of the deserts [*al-barari*]:
> clouds scud over the palms
> and rosy masts [*al-sawari*] wing past the groves' verge.
>
> It falls quiet, the cry of return:
> I ask her—Damascus does not answer [*la tujib*],
> she does not come to aid the stranger.

The rhyme of *barari* and *sawari*, which we have already encountered in "The New Covenant," establishes a recognizably modernist topography: the interior wastes and the seacoasts of exile. It is the trope of questioning and receiving no answer that suggests an elegiac element, and the poem is indeed a *ritha'* for Damascus, though in a peculiar sense. Many city elegies, such as Shawqi's "*Nakbat Dimashq*," evoke a happy and prosperous past before lamenting the fallen present: "I entered you [the city] lit by sunset, all the lines of your face laughing and bright. / Streams flowed beneath your gardens, your hills were full of leaves and doves." This convention is found in the genre's earliest examples: "How doth the city sit solitary *that was* full of people! *how* is she become as a widow! She *that was* great among the nations, *and* princess among the provinces, *how* is she become tributary!" (Lamentations 1:1). Adonis's poem generally eschews this nostalgia. Although 'Abd al-Rahman's own quoted poetry does record Damascus's idyllic past, "The Hawk" is also strewn with elements of invective, a kind of *hija' al-mudun*. In this passage, the anathema rises from the graves:

> It falls quiet, the cry of return:
> Damascus, I dream
> of terror in the shade of Qassiyun
> of a time past with no eyes
> of a desiccated body, of wordless cemeteries
> crying out, Damascus,
> die here, burn your promises,
> crying out, no, die and do not return.

The naming of Damascus, here and throughout the poem, stands in contrast to Adonis's practice in *The Songs of Mihyar*, where the toponym is placed under taboo, its single occurrence qualified by a negative: "*la Dimashq*" [not Damascus]. But the elegy is in fact a variation of this strategy. The genre's characteristic gesture of address and farewell, *ave atque vale*, is another way for the poet to mark his distance from the city, a gesture of disaffection rather than nostalgia. For poets such as al-Shawqi, the *ritha'* provides an opportunity to express solidarity with a collective, to affirm communal ties at a moment of historical trauma and dispersion. The *marthiya* is thus an occasion of what Shawqi calls "eloquence" [*bayan*]: a performance that establishes the poet and audience as a community of "one tongue." For Adonis, by contrast, the elegy registers a state of solitude. The unanswering stones and wordless cemeteries are figures for the poet's exile; loss of place is not so much an occasion for eloquence as the experience of aphasia: "I own a choked language [*lugha makhnuqa*]," Adonis writes in "The Hawk" (echoing Unsi al-Hajj). We should also note that for Adonis the *ritha'* is explicitly a genre of writing rather than a species of oral performance. The elegies for Abu Nuwas and al-Hallaj both refer to the poets' "*risha*" [feather, pen], and the many citations scattered through "The Hawk" reinforce our sense of the text as a written document, a constellation of clippings. The written quality of the text and its self-conscious lack of "eloquence" are refusals of the affective solidarity found in other examples of the city elegy. For Adonis, the *marthiya* is a specifically archival genre. Its pathos is that of the melancholy collector rather than the impassioned orator or ritualized mourner. Rather than a speech of empathetic identification, it is a document of disaffiliation.

Another text in which Adonis's modernist program is refracted through the genre of elegy, though once again the poem is not specifically labeled a *marthiya*, is "*Mir'a li-Abi al-'Ala'*" [A Mirror for Abi al-'Ala'], a poem from the 1969 collection *al-Masrah wa-l-maraya* [Theater and Mirrors].[14] Approximately one-third of the poems in this book are called "mirrors," with predicates ranging from historical personages (the caliph al-Mu'awiya, al-Hajjaj, Ziryab), to places (the Hussein Mosque, Beirut), to abstract nouns (sleep, time, a certain instant). There are also several "mirrors" for classical or legendary poets: Waddah al-Yaman, Orpheus, and Abu al-'Ala' al-Ma'arri, a blind poet of the tenth and eleventh centuries. "Mirror" thus seems to name an emergent genre of poem, situated at the crossroads between historical reflection, elegy, ode, and invective, which are increasingly the compass points for Adonis's poetry as a whole. The *mir'a* is a genre born of the archive, but it reflects the evanescence of experience. The objects and persons under its purview are evoked only in passing, as they stray across the quicksilver of the poet's attention. We have already seen how all these connotations are present in "Elegy," a poem from *The Songs of Mihyar*, where the rhyme of *baqaya–maraya* [traces–mirrors] epitomizes a melancholy poetic in which people and things come and go and the poet pauses to mark the remains of their passage. The mirror is also an emblem of identification and differentiation, like the mask.[15] "A Mirror for Abi al-'Ala'" evokes a visit to the grave of the 'Abbasid poet, whose tomb—a tourist site before it was destroyed in the current conflict—lies just south of Aleppo:

> I recall that in al-Ma'arra I visited [*zurtu*]
> your eyes and heard your steps.
> I recall that the grave walked, mimicking your steps,
> while around the grave
> your voice, like a confused rumbling, slept
> in the body of days, or in the body of words,
> on the bed of poetry.
>
> And your parents were not there
> And al-Ma'arra was not.

The language of the opening line, "*adhkur anni zurtu fi-l-Ma'arra*," suggests the poet's visit is related to a type of religious pilgrimage, the *ziyarat al-qubur* or visiting of the graves. In Shia practice, these visits were typically made to the tombs of imams as well as other members of the Prophet's family, reputed to possess powers of intercession. *Theater and Mirrors* also contains the poem "A Mirror for the Mosque of Hussein," which suggests a related sort of pilgrimage. The tomb of Adonis's poem does not belong to an imam or saint, however, but to a skeptical poet who often expressed doubts about the afterlife. It is a scene of literary rather than religious piety. Al-Ma'arri, "the great Syrian poet," in Antun Sa'ada's words, is one of the fixtures in Adonis's heterodox canon. He comments on al-Ma'arri's verse at length in the introduction to the second volume of the *Anthology*, where he calls him, echoing Eliot, a "metaphysical" poet of disillusionment and death. Man, in al-Ma'arri's verse, "is dead before he is put in the grave, and life is no more than death in motion. The clothes man wears are his shroud, the home his grave."[16] The penultimate line of Adonis's poem seems to allude, complexly, to the epitaph al-Ma'arri is said to have written for his own tombstone: "*Hadha janahu abi 'alaya wa ma janaytu 'ala ahad*" [This wrong was by my father done to me, but never by me to anyone]. The "wrong" in this case is procreation—"man's birth is the original sin," as Adonis glosses it[17]—which al-Ma'arri took care not to commit, living a famously ascetic life and remaining childless on principle. Here then is another figure, like that of Artaud, for modernism's impossible inheritance. For how does one claim the legacy of a poet careful to have no heirs? "He did not leave an artistic tradition [*taqlid fanni*] that one might be influenced by," Adonis acknowledges in the *Anthology*, yet his poem of pilgrimage is an attempt to claim this un-inheritable heritage, to secure an intercessor on behalf of his own poetic afterlife. In the last line, "There was no al-Ma'arra," the whole theater of the poem falls away. This may suggest the visiting poet's ultimate identification with the poet's blindness, or else that the visit, like many mystical journeys, takes place in the poet's mind—a reading that gains plausibility in view of Adonis's reluctance to return physically to Syria, and in view of the self-consciously visionary character of the collection as a whole. The poem's opening verb, "*adhkur*," which might be translated as "I recall," "I state as a fact," or "I think of," is a gesture of defiance. Adonis's poetic "visit" crosses boundaries that political authorities have made otherwise uncrossable.

"Mirror for Abi al-'Ala'," like the elegies for Bashshar ibn Burd, al-Hallaj, and Abu Nuwas, is not a poem of mourning but one of genealogical revision. This function is not foreign to the history of elegy, though it has not always been a feature of the Arabic *ritha'*. As Peter Sacks writes of the tradition that stems from Theocritus, Moschus, and Bion, "In its earliest conflictual structures, as also in successive adaptations of the eclogue form, the elegy clarifies and dramatizes this emergence of the true heir."[18] For Adonis, the elegy is indeed a claim of inheritance and the right to transmission. It is also a genre that attempts to reimagine the relation between the institutions of literature (including genre) and the institutions of politics. For the modernists, the point of this rewriting was to wrest poetry away from the mobilizing power of the state, thereby freeing the transmission of culture from "the tradition of politics." In "Mirror for Abi al-'Ala'," a tenth-century poet returns to life as a voice attended to by a contemporary poet who visits his tomb. This scene of transmission takes place outside or beyond national boundaries—on "the bed of poetry," where one's forbears and place of birth no longer have any authority, or even existence.[19]

The Tombeau *in Translation*

In an interview on the subject of his long poem "*Qabr min ajli New York*," written in the spring and summer of 1971 while he visited the United States, Adonis acknowledged the text as "as important stage in my life as a poet." Whether the poem's importance was due to its status as a beginning or ending is difficult to say. "It was a shock," Adonis says. "And I suppose it had some influence on what I wrote subsequently. But the experience was unique, a kind of island in my poetry."[20] The singularity of "*Qabr*"—a title I leave untranslated for now—can be explained in several ways. In the same interview, Adonis draws attention to the poem's fractured language, its broken syntax and heterogeneous typography, including bullet points, mathematical equations, and words in Latin script, which distinguish it from his customary high rhetoric. Adonis suggests the fragmented style of the poem is partly a reflection of its setting, which is the shattered cityscape of New York: "The language of the poem is also cracked, with smashed and broken places."[21] The mere fact that the poem takes places in a city represents a departure for Adonis. His previous verse pointedly resisted such emplacements and the experience of "shock" they entail, a resistance typical of late modernism's turn away from the urban environment. The poetry Adonis composed in the late 1950s and 1960s is instead characterized by its placelessness. Its subjects are always on the move, and the grim, volatile landscapes they migrate through are uncompromisingly abstract. The most striking anomaly, however, is the poem's political content. Written in the midst of the Vietnam War, "*Qabr*" is expressly an antiwar poem. It contains quotations from Robert McNamara and William Calley (whose trial concluded as Adonis began writing his poem), invocations of Ho Chi Minh, and lines such as, "In the morning I woke up screaming: Nixon, how many children have you killed today?" Given Arabic modernism's stubborn differentiation of the poetic and the political as well as its resistance to historical occasions, "*Qabr*" seems to represent a dramatic departure from Adonis's earlier commitments.

In fact, much of Adonis's work in the late 1960s and early 1970s appears to revise if not repudiate his previous stances. Whereas Adonis, like all the modernists at *Shiʿr*, had held himself aloof from straightforwardly political polemics, his later work seems to exhibit an explicitly *engagé* spirit. In his study of post-1967 intellectual history, Fuad Ajami takes Adonis as the most articulate voice of the Arab intelligentsia's new "radical sensibility," a corrosive skepticism toward the pieties of the previous era:

> In the eyes of a large number of radical activists, the defeat [in the 1967 war] was an indictment of an entire way of life, proof not only that some deep realities had eluded yesterday's radicals but also that those radicals themselves were part of the problem. Thus, all facets of Arab life were subjected to a ruthless assault: Islam, the Arabic language, the capacity of the Arab as an individual, the record of the radical Arab states. Among those who wanted to get to the deep structure behind the defeat there was a consensus that the heroes of yesterday had made too many compromises with the past, that they had given in to that frustrating, hopeless body of attitudes and habits, that immutable thing called tradition.[22]

For the modernists, of course, the critique of tradition, as well as the critique of language, subjectivity, and statist nationalism, was hardly a new undertaking. Indeed, one might argue that for the modernists, the Arab defeat of 1967 was not the trauma it was for their peers—a trauma that led to self-criticism, disillusionment, and despair—precisely because it confirmed what they had been arguing for many years. The politics of pan-Arabism now seemed as bankrupt as the *Shiʿr* poets had always insisted, and the cultural tradition was shown to be in need of just the kind of systematic revision that Adonis had begun to give it through his work as poet and editor. It is therefore wrong to argue, as Ajami and others have done, that the *Naksa* of 1967 radicalized Adonis. The radicalism was always there—but what sort of radicalism was it? And to what extent did Adonis in fact repudiate his earlier positions?

There is certainly a shift in rhetoric as well as intellectual alliances. In 1968 Adonis founded his own magazine, *Mawaqif* [Positions], a bimonthly journal—later a quarterly—that he edited for the next twenty-five years, first in Beirut and then in Paris. The remit of *Mawaqif* was broader than that of *Shiʿr*, which dedicated itself "to poetry and to poetry only."[23] Although it included a great deal of verse, including verse from abroad, *Mawaqif* also featured essays on politics, religion, philosophy, and literary theory. It was a journal of cultural criticism rather than literature or poetry as such. In his opening manifesto for the new magazine, Adonis struck a tone that resonated through its early issues. "Culture [in this magazine] is struggle—the unity of thinking and doing. It is culture that does not intend to interpret the world, life, and the human person except for one purpose: to change the world, life, and the human person. It is, in other words, a culture-revolution [*al-thaqafa—al-thawra*]."[24] Adonis's explicit use of Marxist and even Maoist tropes—the Chinese Cultural Revolution was announced in the summer of 1966—indicate his self-conscious positioning of *Mawaqif* as an organ of the Arab New Left, even while he continued to publish a number of colleagues from his days at *Shiʿr*. This explains the ambivalent reactions his writings now provoked among former critics like Muruwwa, a pillar of the old left, whose analyses of Adonis's post-*Shiʿr* work recycle antimodernist arguments while also acknowledging his rival's poetry as "a great gift" to the Arab patrimony.

The rhetoric of revolution is pervasive in the early issues of *Mawaqif*. The second issue, published in the winter of 1969, included four essays on the theme: "Revolution and Revelation" (René Habachi); "Arabic Thought Confronting the Revolution" (Maxime Rodinson); "Man and Revolution" (László Gyurkó); and "From Authoritarian Revolution to Popular Revolution" (Haidar Haidar). The same issue includes Adonis's lecture, "Poetry and Revolution," delivered to a conference of Lebanese and Soviet writers in the company of his former rivals, Muruwwa and Suhayl Idris, editor in chief of *al-Adab*. Adonis's lecture is the sort of feature that often appeared in leftist organs of the region and that *Shiʿr* resolutely refused to publish. But the content of Adonis's lecture does not represent a substantive departure from his earlier positions. He argues that a truly revolutionary poet must undertake "a continual revision of the past" in order that his verse should not depend on traditional models but emerge "from the future, which is to say from adventure and the unknown." In addition, the revolutionary poet should adopt an uncompromising attitude toward "the regime" [*al-nizam*], which in the Arab world is essentially a dressed-up caliphate despite its self-declared progressivism. "We are confronted with the following irony," Adonis writes: "Societies heading toward liberation that nevertheless oppose, in the name of revolution, all truly revolutionary poetic tendencies." This is a retrofitting of Adonis's critique of the state. In the post-'67 era, following the defeat of Nasserism, such critiques became a commonplace on the Arab left, allowing a rapprochement between

Adonis and his rivals that was mostly on his terms. In the final part of his lecture, Adonis addresses the revolutionary poet's relation to the public or "the masses" [*al-jumhur*]. For the modernists of *Shiʿr*, this figure is often simply absent, or else it is present as a kind of anonymous background against which the lonely poet strikes his heroic poses. Adonis varies the theme by coloring it with a cultural elitism that is also a modernist and avant-gardist convention. Since the Arab public "can neither read nor write and is stuffed with parochial religious and cultural traditions that contradict the revolution," the revolutionary poet "cannot be led by the people, but must go on ahead of them."[25]

None of these positions are new for Adonis. A revisionary approach to the literary heritage, a mistrust of state culture, and a disdain for figures of collectivity are all characteristic of his pre-'67 writings. And though "revolution" is a relatively new addition to Adonis's vocabulary—certainly it receives a new emphasis—the trope already played an important role in the history of the modernist movement. We remember Charles Malik's call for "a Western revolution," whose protagonists were "cut for the highest heroism of the spirit." We might also recall Unsi al-Hajj's distinction between the surrealists' merely "political revolution" and the truly "human revolution" exemplified by Artaud. So it is not surprising that Adonis's own call for a revolution, though it bears the trappings of Marxist terminology, is centered on the originally liberal anti-Communist trope of man, Malik's most lasting contribution to the Arab modernists' lexicon. In his headnote to the second issue of *Mawaqif*, Adonis writes,

> After close to a half century of talk about the Arab revolution, and after the establishment of several Arab regimes that describe themselves as revolutionary, the model of Arab society is still one that does not think its own thought, but rather thinks in supernatural terms. In this society, man is not a free subject dependent on himself, but a follower dependent on others. Revolution is that which creates another model for Arab society—a society centered entirely on itself, a society in which "man is the god of man," as Feuerbach puts it.[26]

All this suggests that Adonis's work of the late sixties and early seventies does not represent the radical break that both he and many of his readers assert. Adonis's resignation from *Shiʿr* and his foundation of *Mawaqif* allowed him to broaden his editorial purview and, in the political realignment following the *Naksa*, to link himself with leftist intellectuals who had formerly been antagonists. His writing acquires a notably *engagé* tone; references to Lenin, Mao, and Ho Chi Minh edge out those to Nietzsche, Eliot, and Perse. But the continuities in Adonis's work are finally more revealing though sometimes less obvious than the breaks. Despite the various intellectual traditions he has at times made his own, from Marxism to Shiism to Sufism, Adonis's basic commitments as a poet and critic, even today, remain those of a late modernist liberal, which is one reason I have spent so much of this book analyzing that distinct and surprisingly resilient matrix of thought. In what follows, I want to trace out another line of resiliency—that of genre—between Adonis's early poetry and the apparently "unique" text that is *"Qabr min ajli New York,"* a major work in Adonis's oeuvre.

The poem's many translators and critics have universally ignored the question of its genre, although it imposes itself from the outset. For all its length and formal complexity, *"Qabr,"* has been translated into English four times (as well as French, Spanish, and Turkish). Three of the English translations use the title "A Grave for New York," while the fourth, by Samuel Hazo, is called "The Funeral of New York." *"Qabr"* does signify "grave" ("funeral" takes a few liberties), but Adonis's long-standing interest in the genre of the *marthiya* suggests the poem should be read as a translated *"tombeau"*—in English, "tomb," but in French, a type of elegy, as we will see.[27] This suggestion is corroborated by the September–October 1970 issue of *Mawaqif*, which includes Adonis's translation of a French poem by the Lebanese artist Etel Adnan, entitled *"Qabr thawri min ajli 'Amman"* [A revolutionary *qabr* for Amman]. Adnan's poem, which has never been published in French—though one presumes its original title was *"Tombeau révolutionnaire pour Amman"*—was written in response to the outbreak of the Jordanian civil war during what has become known as Black September. Given that Adonis's poem was begun the following spring and its title echoes that of Adnan, it seems justifiable to consider Adonis's *qabr* a genre translated from the French.[28]

What difference does it make to our reading of the poem if we know, or think we know, the genre to which it belongs? And if the genre itself is translated, as so many Arabic modernist genres are? In technical terms, the *tombeau* is a subspecies of elegy. In Renaissance France, it named a collective volume published on behalf of a prominent social figure, in which the individual elegies typically functioned as poems of learned praise. The genre suffered a long eclipse during the baroque and Enlightenment periods and was revived in the middle of the nineteenth century. Gautier, Debussy, and Baudelaire were all presented with collective *tombeaux*, but it was Mallarmé who transformed the genre (in music it was Ravel) by giving the name *"tombeau"* to individual texts rather than anthologies, and by making poets his exclusive subject: Poe, Baudelaire, and Verlaine (leaving aside *Pour un tombeau d'Anatole*, the unfinished elegy for Mallarmé's son). Dominique Moncond'huy describes Mallarmé's resuscitation of the genre as a step toward literary professionalization:

> Mallarmé made the poetic *tombeau* more than a commonplace commemoration or homage but rather the affirmation of the poet's special status—of his place outside the social world, a place on the margins, both because he was ignored and because he refused to belong. In this sense, we are truly at the antipodes of the collective *tombeau* as it was conceived in the sixteenth century. Instead of figuring an exchange

between the poet and social authority, in Mallarmé's *tombeau* what gets affirmed is the existence of a literary milieu, detached from the social ensemble and characterized by definite individuals. It is an affirmation, albeit a melancholic one, of autonomy, of a new status for the poet, who no longer seeks recognition except by his peers.[29]

Conceived in these terms, Mallarmé's project for the *tombeau* is strikingly similar to Adonis's project for the *marthiya*. Rather than a genre of posthumous eulogy or harmonious exchange between poet and collective, Adonis's elegies fabricate a countertradition of poets, whose autonomy from the workings of power confers on them an unsponsored legitimacy, even as this new freedom is also experienced as a painful species of exile. The translation of *qabr* as *grave* by Adonis's English collaborators is less momentous than Ibn Rushd's mistranslation of Aristotle (and rather than being imprisoned by the limits of genre, Adonis's translators seem, symptomatically, to be unaware that a genre exists). But this misrecognition does make it difficult to note the connections between "*Qabr*" and Adonis's earlier elegies, which are suddenly revealed, in retrospect, to have been versions of *tombeaux* themselves: poems about poets, which are not so much works of mourning as works of revision and selective transmission. To read Adonis's poems as *tombeaux* also helps make sense of their "affective impoverishment," a phrase I borrow from Leo Bersani's reading of Mallarmé's elegies. Bersani writes, "The poetic *hommage* provides the occasion for an emotionally and intellectually neutral moving away from the poets being honored," so that "The *Tombeaux* poems are, by virtue of the very project which inspires them, *hommages manqués*."[30] Similarly, in Adonis's *marathi* for his ʿAbbasid precursors, the claim of filiation is made on the basis of a common exclusion rather than empathy. "Do not weep for him" and "leave us to the beautiful torture" are directives that mark the fact of suffering in the absence of any affective bond. The elegy is the occasion for a ritual visit to the grave, but the community it imagines is textual and canonical rather than one bound by affect.

The poet at the center of the New York *tombeau* is explicitly Walt Whitman. Adonis knew the American bard's work from Roger Asselineau's French translations, published in 1956, as well as those undertaken by Yusuf al-Khal for *Shiʿr*.[31] "Tombeau for New York" is in fact a dense tissue of translations and transmissions, not only from Whitman but from the pre-Islamic poet ʿUrwa ibn al-Ward ("I divide my body into many bodies"); Tacitus ("*ubi solitudinem faciunt, pacem appellant*"); Mao ("Weapons are a very important element in war, but they are not decisive"); Robert McNamara ("We will replace men with fire"); and Adonis himself, in a line from the opening psalm of *The Songs of Mihyar*: "He has no ancestors and in his footsteps are his roots." This last quotation acquires an ironic cast when set in the midst of so many literary ancestors, but we have already noted how Adonis's conception of the poem-anthology or poem-museum reimagines the relation between innovation and citation. In Whitman, Adonis seems to have found a fellow spirit. "These are the thoughts of all men in all ages and lands," the American poet writes in "Song of Myself," "they are not original with me." And as he later admits, "I resist anything better than my own diversity."

"Tombeau for New York" is divided into ten parts.[32] The first is set, as so many *mahjari* narratives of emigration are, in New York Harbor.[33] In Adonis's version, the Statue of Liberty presents itself as an icon of imperialism. The statue smothers a child with one hand while the other holds "a rag, which one document calls 'liberty' and which we call 'history'" (71). The "we" of this passage, as elsewhere in the poem, is a vaguely Third Worldist collective, though it articulates a markedly Arab version of history. Adonis's rhetoric of solidarity with the marginalized figures he encounters in New York, and imagines in Southeast Asia, is often tempered by a sense of rival historical experiences. "The Blacks hate the Jews," the poet thinks, racing through the streets of Harlem, but "when they remember the slave trade, they do not love the Arabs" (82). In the next section, however, his solidarity is forcefully reasserted: "Harlem, I do not come from the outside: I know your hatred, I know its sweet bread" (83). The narrative of "Tombeau" is made up in large part of these gestures of affiliation and disaffiliation, as the poet negotiates his way through the uneven physical and social landscape of New York. He walks up Wall Street, along Madison and Park Avenues, and into Harlem: "I advance like a number, lost in the desert, clenched in the black dawn's teeth. There was no snow, there was no wind. I was like one who trails after a ghost" (84–85). The ghost is Whitman—"Is he a woman? a man? a woman-man?"—and Adonis's *tombeau* is an attempt to claim the American poet for the "we" of the poem, to rescue him from his native city now transformed into the metropole of Empire.

Returning to the opening tableau, the Statue of Liberty is described as having "a face that is a closed window." "Walt Whitman will open it," the poet exclaims: "I speak the password primeval—but no one hears it" (71–72). What follows, over the next six sections of the poem, is another version of the modernist katabasis: a descent into the underworld that is New York City in the early 1970s. But here, in a hell that Adonis calls "the mossy-side of the Earth," the poet has no spiritual guide. Whitman is nowhere to be found in the city he mapped for future flâneurs. The poet's password, like the elegist's question, echoes in an empty cityscape: "Whitman, I did not see you in Manhattan and yet I saw everything." In this middle portion of the text, the poet is witness to a surrealist catalog of horrors. Wall Street is "A market with slaves of every race, humanity living like plants in glass gardens" (73), where "Arab rivers [of gold] carry millions of corpses, victims and sacrifices to the great idol" (80). In Harlem and Bedford-Stuyvesant, "The trash is a banquet for the children and the children are a banquet for the rats." Meanwhile, "Fire creeps forward under the asphalt, in the pipes of the sewer" (83). This is a more or less familiar inferno of modernity, an urban nightmare of alienation, antagonism, and disenchantment.

At the end of the eighth section, with the poet preparing for his flight back to Beirut, Adonis writes, "I rose before the dawn and woke up Whitman." There follows an extended apostrophe to the American poet, borrowing extensively from his verse. "Walt Whitman," it begins, "I see letters to you flying in the streets of Manhattan." And again, "Whitman, 'the clock indicates the moment' and I, / 'I see what you do not—I know what you do not'" (the citations are from "Song of Myself" and "You Felons on Trial in Courts"). Finally, in a passage that brings the poem to a visionary close, the speaker claims a poetic inheritance based on a shared history of exile. The anaphora in particular are reminiscent of Whitman's odes:

> Criminal, exile, emigrant [a trinity from "The Sleepers"], you are nothing but a cap worn by birds unknown to American skies! Whitman, let it be our turn now. Of my gaze, I make a ladder. Of my steps, I make a pillow. We will wait. Man dies, but he lasts longer than the grave. Let it be our turn now. I wait for the Volga to flow through Manhattan and Queens. I wait for the Hwang Ho and the Hudson to debouch as one. You find this strange? Did the Orontes not flow into the Tiber? Let it be our turn now. (93)

The Orontes arises in eastern Lebanon, not far from the ancient Heliopolis, flows north through Syria and eventually into the Mediterranean basin, where it might be said to meet the Tiber. The idea of the Levant as a source or spring for Mediterranean civilization may be a leftover from Saʿada's vision of Syrian and world history. "Tombeau" takes this vision a step further. Its concluding apocalyptic vision of the inflowing of all rivers is a figure for the globalist ambition at the heart of Arab modernism, an omnium-gatherum of voices and languages. The internationalist intention of "Tombeau" is explicit, and it explains why Adonis's Whitman is not the omnivorous bard, "Stuffed with the stuff that is coarse, and stuffed with the stuff that is fine," nor the sexual martyr of Lorca's ode, with a beard full of butterflies, nor even Pessoa's great cosmic liberator. In Adonis's poem, Whitman is a friend of the emigrant and exile, "a southerner as soon as a northerner," as Whitman writes in "Song of Myself," "Not merely of the New World but of Africa Europe or Asia . . . a wandering savage." In "Tombeau," the wanderer has been chased from his own city by the uprooting forces of modernity. But it is precisely this deracination that suits him for Adonis's countercanon, in which ʿAbbasid libertines and mystics, French diplomats, and American loafers make an unlikely company. As in his previous *marathi*, Adonis's *tombeau* extracts a precursor poet from his own history in order to rescue him for a literary genealogy.

Adonis's *tombeau* is an extreme case, in formal and historical terms, for Arabic modernism. Rather than explain the text's singularity by reference to its subject matter—the shock of the poet's encounter with New York—or its newly discovered political commitments, I suggest that its unruly energies are the signs of a modernist poetic coming in contact with its own limitations. The political solidarities imagined by the poem as well as its urban setting, whose social density the writing struggles to register and distribute, do distinguish this poem from Adonis's prior or subsequent work, in which the city exists as an abstract topos or blurred backdrop rather than a concrete setting. But these anomalous tendencies in "Tombeau" are reined in by the poem's formal and ideological continuities with earlier texts. Adonis consistently uses the *marthiya* as a vehicle of revision, one that invests the *turath* of Arabic poetry with a Babel of competing voices, some from within the tradition and some from without. In the *tombeau*, the poet's claim to an inheritance of Whitman—"Let it be our turn now"—stakes out a common terrain of exile from the forces of history. It is in this nonplace, a kind of international zone, that Adonis erects his modernist "pageant of stones."

I will conclude by noting that this pageant has not ended. Adonis's generic experiments and innovations have provoked further translations, such as the Tunisian poet and novelist Abdelwahab Meddeb's *Tombeau d'Ibn Arabi*. Meddeb's *tombeau* was written in French but can hardly be imagined without the precedent of Adonis's "*Qabr*." In the first place, the French text is a particular kind of *poème en prose*, "a prose haunted by alexandrines hidden between commas," as Meddeb explains in his preface.[34] The rhythm established by these hidden alexandrines is not the Khalilian rhythm of the metronome nor the expressive harmonies of *tarab*: "The twelve syllables that form the alexandrine get thrown off track, going under, or over, for no other reason than to outwit the fixed count of syllables and to welcome the rule of the odd number. . . . [These pages] ought to be heard according to listening to the discontinuous and to the discordant, as if to keep from glossing over whatever does not run smoothly in this world that absorbs us." Meddeb's text is also, like Adonis's *tombeaux*, a work of inheritance and genealogical transformation rather than affective eulogy. (As Jean-Luc Nancy notes in his afterword, "Of the funerary monument, the poetic genre retains the monument more than the funerary.")[35] Meddeb's poem claims the authority of an illustrious though arguably heterodox precursor, the itinerant Andalusian mystic and poet Ibn ʿArabi, as well as more indisputably canonical authorities: "This *Tombeau* is not a question of praise or homage. It means to show how a text that maintains a link with the dead can be written at the present day. Of those dead, the living remember Ibn Arabi, who has never stopped speaking to us through the words that weave his phrases. From this privilege I draw another: his surprising closeness to Dante. They are the two symbolic figures who through history confirm my twofold spiritual genealogy, Arab and European, Eastern-Western."[36] Finally, Meddeb suggests that his poem charts a nomadic course among certain "pilgrimage sites"—including Carthage, Rome, Ronda, and the

Atlas Mountains of Morocco—although these journeys are, as with Adonis, gestures of literary rather than religious piety. In all these senses, the French genre of *tombeau* has been retranslated from the Arabic *qabr*.[37] The opening lines of Meddeb's poem suggest how Adonis's modulation of the *marthiya* has survived yet further modulations:

> Ruins, remember, neglected grounds, dust, wanderers' refuge, the voice blends with its echo, look at the man in the cave, the rock is a mirror, everything is deserted, I wait for the clouds to shed their tears, I wait for the flowers to speak, I call out, no one answers, the stones hear my excitement, how many moons thrown in the well, how many suns come out of oblivion, the tree touches the sky, and the spark spells out a star, lightning flashes a carpet in the shadows, on the headlands in the south, winds brush against the thunder, on the path, I say a rosary of pearls, black camels double the mounts and hills, sand covers the tracks in the dunes, seers wandering in the shade of gardens, the summer heat is a woman's smile that unearths the custom of the dolls, so many vague paths, oh memory, oh mystery.[38]

The host of echoes heard in this passage—echoes from the pre-Islamic desert, from Moorish Spain, Beirut, and Paris—suggest how the genealogy of Arab modernism keeps reaching back to include new eras of the past while simultaneously reaching forward into the present. The imaginative space cleared at great cost by Adonis and his fellow modernists at *Shiʿr* helped make possible the border-crossing, transhistorical poetics of Meddeb—a poet who does not write in Arabic and for whom the peculiar rhetoric of late modernism is, one presumes, at best a historical curiosity.[39] Has Arabic literature, through the works of the *Shiʿr* poets and their literary progeny, finally joined the ranks of world literature? Will the maps of modernism make room for these "heretics" from Beirut? Perhaps the greatest benefit of historical criticism is its reminder that such questions only stake out the limits, more or less comical and contingent, expanding and then contracting, of our language and our world.

EPILOGUE

Tehran 1979—Damascus 2011

ON FEBRUARY 12, 1979, Adonis published a twelve-line poem on the front page of the Lebanese daily *al-Safir* entitled "Salutation to the Iranian Revolution." Eleven days earlier, Ayatollah Ruhollah Khomeini returned after fourteen years of exile to Iran, where he was greeted by millions of supporters on the streets of the capital. Mohammad Reza Shah had fled the country two weeks earlier, leaving in his place a government with minimal popular support. Adonis has never reprinted his poem (nor has it ever been translated):

*A horizon, a revolution, the tyrants scattered—
how shall I tell Iran of my love
of what is in my sighing
of what is in my sobbing
when words cannot say it?*

*I will sing for Qom and my passion will make it
a raging fire that spreads across the Gulf.
So I say: distance and weeping
        are my Arab earth—and here is its thunder
storming, creating,
aflame,
tracing a new East, standing sentinel.*

*For the East, the people of Iran write a prologue of possibilities.
For the West, the people of Iran write Your face, O West, is dead.
The people of Iran are an East rooting itself [ta'assala] in our earth, a
    prophet.
They are our foundational refusal, a covenant for Arabs.*[1]

During the month that followed, as the ayatollah began to consolidate the new system of governance he called "custodianship of the jurist" [*velayat-e faqeh*], Adonis published two essays in Lebanon's *al-Nahar* newspaper. These

FIGURE 8. Front page of *al-Safir* newspaper, February 12, 1979. Headline: "Tehran in the Grip of Revolution." Adonis's poem is the boxed text at lower right. Courtesy of the Nami Jafet Memorial Library, American University of Beirut.

prose texts were less rapturous than his poem but unambiguous in their enthusiasm for developments in Tehran. Adonis called the revolution "a singular event," which was "not merely a protest movement, but rather a radiant opening in a long, stagnant, and repressive history." Working from Arabic translations of the ayatollah's writings, Adonis described Khomeini as a pro-Palestinian, anti-imperialist rebel who fought "for freedom and against tyranny, and who had struggled against the enslavement of man."[2]

Thirty-two years later, in March 2011, demonstrations against the Baathist regime of Bashar al-Assad broke out across Syria. This time, Adonis was notably slower and more ambivalent in his response, and he wrote no poems. The demonstrations came on the heels of similar uprisings in Tunisia and Egypt, which Adonis had warmly welcomed. For him, "the spark of Bouazizi"—the Tunisian fruit vendor whose self-immolation lit the fuse of the revolts—cast a pitiless light on the region's autocracies. But when the spark landed in Syria, Adonis's ardor cooled. For several weeks, he wrote very little about the protest movement, though he criticized the Baathist regime as despotic and unfit to govern a pluralistic society such as Syria's. Adonis seems to have been especially troubled by what he saw as the opposition's lack of commitment to secular values. Finally, in an editorial published in late May, by which time over a thousand protesters were dead and Syrian tanks had shelled several cities, he declared, "I will never agree to participate in a demonstration that comes out of the mosque."[3]

Many of Adonis's critics saw a double standard at work in his responses to the two uprisings. Why did he support the Iranian revolution, whose religious character Adonis fully acknowledged and even emphasized, while holding himself aloof from the Syrian protesters (who arguably came out of the mosques only because these were among the few spaces not entirely controlled by the regime)? Several critics accused Adonis, raised in an ʿAlawite family, of harboring a sectarian agenda. The reason he backed the Iranian revolution, they reasoned, was because it had come out of Shiite mosques. The Syrian opposition, on the other hand, was primarily led by Sunnis (who form a majority of the population). For Adonis's critics, the ironies were clear: the poet who styled himself as a cosmopolitan champion of modernist ideals had revealed himself to be merely another tribalist. "It is well known that Adonis is a Shia ʿAlawite," opined Egyptian poet Hasan Tilib in an interview with the weekly *Akhbar al-adab*. "And it has been clear to us since Khomeini's revolution in the seventies that Adonis's Shiite identity has acquired the upper hand, winning out over Adonis the modernist and man of enlightenment."[4] Adonis's most tenacious critic, both in 1979 and 2011, was the Syrian Marxist Sadiq Jalal al-ʿAzm, professor of philosophy at the University of Damascus and the poet's former colleague at *Mawaqif* magazine. In the wake of the Syrian uprisings, al-ʿAzm expressed his bewilderment that Adonis, "the man of freedom, transformation, revolution, progress, and modernity," could have subscribed to the "medievalist" ideas of Khomeini while "disparaging, if not condemning the Syrian revolution from its outset."[5] In an earlier critique, al-ʿAzm implied that Adonis's support for the clerics of Qom signaled a deep incoherence in his intellectual career, which al-ʿAzm described as a series of ideological pit stops.

Was Adonis's journey from nationalism to Islamism, passing by way of Nasserism, socialism, and extreme leftism, a matter of organic and systematic progress (which one might explicate) in his intellectual convictions, his political positions, and his ideological outlook? Or was it merely a matter of his adapting to historical occasions as they arose—a matter of conforming to the strongest cultural and political winds of the moment?[6]

The rest of this epilogue tries to provide a response to this question, which al-ʿAzm did not answer. It does so by presenting a short but detailed narrative about Adonis's writings on the Iranian and Syrian revolutions. My intent in relating this history is to bring the story of Arabic modernism as close as possible up to the present—in an admittedly schematic fashion—as well as to investigate its afterlives, its ability to adapt itself to new conjunctions. A consistent aim of this book has been to provide the texts of Arabic modernism with their historical occasions, even or especially when the texts deny them. In this case, where the writings are topical, I try to extract general principles. I believe Adonis's modernist commitments do survive beyond the parameters of this study and are ultimately more important than sectarian considerations. It is true that his writings of the 1970s exhibit a drift away from these commitments. The drift culminated in his support for the Iranian revolution, which he eventually recanted. The emergence of a populist, theocratic police state in Tehran ended his engagement with radical Shiite politics. In the aftermath of this episode, I will argue, a chastened Adonis returned to the principal tenets of his intellectual project, including his skepticism toward all forms of political involvement, a fierce repudiation of leftism, and an insistence on autonomy as the condition for literary "revolution." All these long-standing habits of thought were notable in his writings on Syria in 2011. His wariness toward the protesters, which so bitterly disappointed many of his peers, was consistent with the ideas about poetry and politics he espoused for most of his career. His writings on Iran are in this sense the exception that clarifies the rule.

Political Islam

In the two articles he published in *al-Nahar* in February 1979, while Khomeini was tightening his hold on the Iranian state, Adonis argued that the uprising disproved leftist shibboleths and confirmed his own reading of history. In the first article, published the day after Khomeini appointed Mehdi Bazargan as prime minister of the provisional government, Adonis teased Marxist intellectuals who had come around to supporting the revolution (he singled out Egyptian historian Anouar Abdel-Malek) for their previous dismissals of religion as an irremediably reactionary element in Arab life. "Here is the thing that some of us considered to be outside history, now entering into history through the front door," Adonis wrote. "Here is the thing that some of us believed to be a tradition on its last legs, now looking singularly modern [*hadith*], revolutionary, and enduring." Although Marxists often referred to Khomeini's movement as an example of "political Islam," thereby highlighting its progressive character in their eyes, Adonis argued that they were ignoring the truly novel aspect of the uprisings: "Let us clearly acknowledge that what is happening today in Iran is not merely 'political Islam,' but precisely Islam as such." Khomeini's movement was neither a reactionary traditionalism nor an expression of class consciousness. Instead, it was a "total revolution," a mixture of the spiritual and the worldly, the cultural and the economic. A materialist analysis of the revolution was therefore insufficient; intellectuals had to grapple with the fact that Islam *as such*, the "ideological-religious element," had become "the prime mover" of historical events.[7]

In Adonis's view, the holistic nature of Khomeini's revolution lent it a deep historical authenticity. In its antagonism toward the state and its rejection of traditionalism, the Iranian uprising represented a return to the first principles (*al-usul*) of Islam itself. In a résumé of the argument he published six years earlier in his critical encyclopedia, *The Fixed and the Dynamic*, Adonis reminded his readers that Islam was originally a movement of rebellion:

> In its period of consolidation, Islam was a radical and total transformation of Arab society: it was a revolution. We know that this movement of transformation and revolution ceased, or went into retreat, as soon as the institution of the caliphate—i.e., state power—began to oppose the dynamism of Islam. We also know that the revolutionary impulse within Islam—i.e., the idea and practice of the religion according to the conditions of contemporary Muslims and their continuously changing needs—we know this impulse emerged during the caliphate of 'Uthman, then rooted itself [*ta'assul*] and expanded with the establishment of the Umayyad caliphate. This revolutionary impulse derived legitimacy from its certainty that it represented the true Islam [*al-islam al-haqq*], and from its adherence to first principles [*al-usul*] as the revolutionaries understood them: Islam was justice, equality, and freedom; it was on the side of the oppressed, the abused, the persecuted, the impoverished, and the outcast; it was not on the side of power and tyranny.[8]

Adonis went on to say, still summarizing the theses of his encyclopedia, that Islam's revolutionary, modernist impulse had been latent for the previous thirteen hundred years. Despite the efforts of heroic individuals and isolated social movements, the mainstream of Islamo-Arabic history was one of political repression and intellectual orthodoxy. Caliphs and their followers co-opted the faith's radical energies and converted them into instruments of the status quo. It is in this light that the Iranian revolution represented a "brilliant opening." In *The Fixed and the Dynamic*, Adonis claimed that "The destruction of a principle [*asl*] must be carried out by way of the principle itself," and he believed that Khomeini's uprising was engaged in just this type of self-criticism. The revolution was an innovation that was also a return to origins—an act, in other words, of political *ta'wil*.

For Adonis, the modernist countercurrent within Islam was primarily Shiite. Islam's "revolutionary impulse" emerged and expanded during the Umayyad period (661–750) due to the early caliphate's antagonism toward the partisans of 'Ali, whom Adonis characterized as torchbearers of the faith's revolutionary beginnings. This Umayyad history is examined at length in his encyclopedia, where it is clear that the grand antitheses structuring Adonis's work (viz., the Fixed and the Dynamic) have their historical origins in the conflict over the foundation of the first dynasty and the civil wars that ultimately divided Sunni and Shiite sects.[9] The Shiites are not the only group in Adonis's account to keep alive the flame of "the true Islam," but their primacy is evident both from his historical narrative as well as the significance he gives to the operation of *ta'wil*, an invention of Shiite imams that allows for the reinterpretation of authoritative texts according to the needs of the present, what Adonis calls "the putting-into-time of religion [*tazmin al-din*]."[10] In his writings on Iran, Adonis does not emphasize the Shiite nature of the revolution, though he uses a number of terms specific to its political theology (for example, the notion of *wilaya* [governance], which was also fundamental to Khomeini's political writings). But it is clear that for Adonis the Iranian revolution was appealing not only for its anti-imperialism but for its rootedness in a specifically Islamic genealogy: a "true" yet "modern" Islam whose sudden reemergence proved the Marxists wrong.

Many Arab intellectuals backed the Iranian revolution, but Adonis may have been unique in suggesting that it corroborated his peculiar philosophy of history. The poet's analyses of events in Tehran cast themselves as the culmination of his researches in *The Fixed and the Dynamic* (later editions of the encyclopedia include the Iran texts as an addendum). Perhaps the only other intellectual who staked as much on the revolution, and who strayed as far from the consensus of his peers, was the French philosopher and historian Michel Foucault. Foucault also hoped the Iranian uprising would signal a new kind of "spiritual politics," and he suggested that what was ultimately at issue in Tehran was nothing less than the fate of modernity itself. He called the Iranian revolution "Perhaps the first great insurrection against global systems, the form of revolt that is the most modern and the most insane."[11] It is instructive, therefore, to briefly compare Foucault's writings on Iran with those of Adonis. In this strictly limited case, the two thinkers, who never met and did not know each other's work, have enough in common to make their differences illuminating.

Foucault made two trips to Iran in the fall of 1978 as a correspondent for the Italian daily *Corriere della sera*. Like Adonis, Foucault saw the Iranian revolution as a refutation of Marxist ideas about religion. "Do you know the phrase that makes the Iranians sneer the most," he asked his European readers, "the one that seems to them the stupidest, the shallowest? 'Religion is the opium of the people.'" The Iranian uprising, in its mass character, did not exhibit any signs of class consciousness, nor did the Shiite clerics act as a vanguard of the Bolshevist type. This made it hard for foreign observers to recognize what was taking place. But it was precisely this unclassifiable character of the Iranian revolt that excited Foucault. He viewed the demonstrations as gestures of pure revolt, and he admired the protesters' willingness to throw a wrench in the machine of history. "Uprisings belong to history, but in a certain way, they escape it," Foucault wrote in his last article on Iran, in which he maintained a qualified support for the revolution. "The man in revolt is ultimately inexplicable. There must be an uprooting that interrupts the unfolding of history and its long chains of reasons for a man 'really' to prefer the risk of death over the certainty of having to obey."[12]

Foucault's fascination with such nonhistorical and ultimately inexplicable moments of rupture—moments that bear more than a passing resemblance to the epistemological breaks analyzed in *The Order of Things*—was reflected in his admiration for Khomeini's role in this revolutionary drama. The ayatollah's authority, for Foucault, had little to do with his political program, about which Foucault evinced little curiosity. Instead, Foucault ascribed the ayatollah's power to his "inflexibility," his "unwavering intransigence," and his sovereign refusal to engage in normal political behavior. In the fall of 1978 Khomeini declined to negotiate with the shah and summarily rejected the nationalist opposition's last-minute proposal to liberalize the structures of the state. "Khomeini *says nothing*," writes Foucault, "nothing other than no—to the shah, to the regime, to dependency." Foucault understood the ayatollah's uncompromising stance to be a refusal of politics as such, or at least the rationalized politics of liberalism as well as the class- and party-based politics of the left. He called the Iranian revolution "a strike against politics" and averred that "Khomeini *is not a politician*. There will not be a Khomeini party; there will not be a Khomeini government." Foucault often insisted on this point, which reflected Khomeini's public declarations at the time: "By 'Islamic government,' nobody in Iran means a political regime would have a role of supervision or control." The analyses of Foucault and Adonis converge in regarding the Iranian uprising as an event that transcended politics in its familiar forms. In writing, as Foucault did, of a "spiritual politics" or, as Adonis called it, "a total revolution," both thinkers were attempting to pick out what was truly novel in the uprising and exceeded contemporary methods of theorization.[13]

Foucault's interest in Iran's revolution was also the result of his desire to identify the roots and strategies of modern governance. It was clear to him that the demonstrators in Tehran were not simply rejecting a corrupt ruler but also the historical logic of modernity itself—or at least modernity conceived, as Foucault had come to think of it during the 1970s, as a regime of disciplinary administration and technocratic statism. In Foucault's account, modernization was the shah's *raison d'être*, "something that is the basis not only of his government, but also of his dynasty." Iran's state-led effort to centralize the security apparatus, secularize society, and industrialize the economy began with Reza Khan in the 1920s. It had failed, but not because the regime had gotten out in front of its retrograde subjects, as the shah's apologists in the West liked to claim. Quite the reverse, Foucault argued, the revolutionary collective was way ahead of the regime: "Recent events did not signify a shrinking back in the face of modernization by extremely retrograde elements, but the rejection, by a whole culture and a whole people, of a *modernization* that is in itself an *archaism*." This battle between an administrative state and a rebellious populace was not a new phenomenon. Instead, it was a conflict embedded in the deepest strata of Iranian history. In a dispatch written in October 1978, Foucault wrote of the country's "surprising destiny," which placed it at the confluence of two ancient and antithetical streams of history, one from Sassanid Persia and the other from the earliest epoch of Islam:

> At the dawn of history, [Persia] invented the state and government. It conferred its models of state and government on Islam, and its administrators staffed the Arab Empire. But from this same Islam, it derived a religion that, throughout the centuries, never ceased to give an irreducible strength to everything from the depths of a people that can oppose state power.[14]

This bold claim, which Foucault made more than once, mirrors Adonis's equally sweeping characterization of a perpetual conflict between the caliphate and its prototypically Shiite antagonists, between static orthodoxy and dynamic modernity. Foucault viewed the regime of the shah and its modernizing bureaucrats—a Persian mirror of Giscard d'Estaing's technocracy—as an heir to the Sassanid inventors of the state, just as he viewed the Shiite masses of Tehran as heirs to the 'Alid enemies of the caliphate.[15] For Foucault, the "spiritual politics" of the demonstrators was an *anti*politics. The long history of Shia dissidence had given the protesters in Tehran a unique and "irreducible strength" to oppose the disciplinary powers of the modern state.[16] The depth of their opposition was not expressed through a rival political program—whatever "Islamic governance" meant, Foucault was sure it was not that—but through their inexplicable, uncompromising disobedience. Their uprising was a gesture of apophatic politics: "Khomeini says nothing, nothing other than no." In this way, Tehran represented a magical site for the philosopher, a place suddenly charged with millenarian energies where the destiny of modernity—and the definition of politics itself—was at stake.

For all his points of agreement with Foucault, Adonis's support for the revolution went beyond an attraction to its rhetoric of refusal and postures of anarchic revolt. Instead, it was grounded in a reading of the Islamic past that claimed to have identified the deepest currents and countercurrents of that history. Foucault's analysis certainly did rely on a specific understanding of Shiism's role in the revolution, but that role had nothing to do with Shia doctrine. Foucault did not pose as an exegete of Islam, nor was his support for the protesters based on any positive notion of what "spiritual politics" might entail after the properly revolutionary phase was over. He was one of those, as he wrote in his last article on the subject, "who sought in Iran not the 'deep reasons' for the movement, but the manner in which it was lived." Adonis, on the contrary, sought the deep reasons. For him, the force of the revolution was inseparable from its roots in a long history of political and intellectual heterodoxy, whose heroes were paradigmatically though not exclusively Shiite. It was Shiism that maintained a connection to the original impulses of Islam as a revolutionary praxis, "a continual refusal of the dominant regime," while also adapting itself to the conditions of contemporary Muslims (in this respect, Adonis's thought echoes that of the Iranian Ali Shariati). Foucault interpreted events in Tehran as a revolt against modernity, while Adonis interpreted them as the beginning of an alternative modernity, one that would not only make things new, but also make them authentic.[17]

Adonis was understandably reluctant to identify the specific elements of this alternate modernity. Khomeini had yet to show his hand; the revolution was still "a prologue of possibilities," as Adonis writes in his "Salutation." The poet was impressed, as we have seen, by Khomeini's anti-Western credentials, but also by the fact that his revolution "aimed not merely to achieve liberation from external agents, by insisting on self-determination, but to achieve liberation from within: justice, equality, and the freedom and dignity of man, so that he might take charge of himself and his destiny."[18] What Adonis wanted from the revolution, and what he convinced himself it might actually bring about, was more than a politics of liberal anti-imperialism. It was a transformation of the nature of politics itself. The "total" nature of Khomeini's revolt would combine what had previously seemed autonomous spheres of activity. It is in this light that we must read what is perhaps Adonis's most surprising declaration, made at the end of his second essay for *al-Nahar*. Adonis argued, not for the first time, that the region was undergoing a "cultural crisis," the result of a widening gap between words and things, between the sclerotic ideal of tradition promoted by the regimes and the dynamic conditions of modern life:

> In this way, the Islamic revolution in Iran reveals two related things: first, the necessity of revising the meaning of inherited culture; and second, the necessity of revising the relation between culture and politics on the one hand, and culture and the ever-changing world on the other. As to the first necessity, I must insist that culture, understood as a creative act, is a society's power to continually renew itself. And as to the second necessity, I must insist that cultural work is inseparable from political work, and that cultural struggle is, in its essence, a political struggle.[19]

It is difficult to reconcile the final claim of this passage with Adonis's earlier modernist rhetoric (the necessity of revision is, on the other hand, entirely consistent). The autonomy of cultural work, and poetry in particular, was a central pillar of the *Shiʿr* group's program. The alternate, authentic modernity Adonis hoped for in Tehran was in this sense startlingly different from the version he once espoused in Beirut. And so it seems fair to wonder with Sadiq Jalal al-ʿAzm whether in the winter of 1979 Adonis was not merely riding the strongest political winds of the moment—which happened in this case to be raging from the East.

The Return to Roots

Adonis's reevaluation of his position on Iran began in the summer of 1979, with a disavowal of his poem "Salutation to the Iranian Revolution"—or at least a disavowal of the poem *as a poem*. Asked by an interviewer with *al-Safir*, the same newspaper that published "Salutation" six months earlier, to parse what he meant by writing, "Your face, O West, is dead," Adonis explained, "I don't look at the poem from an artistic point of view. I look at it, instead, as an act of testimony [*shahada*] spoken from a sense of moral sympathy with the Iranian revolution." It was not so much a poem, he emphasized, as "a testimony, albeit in a poetic form." The interviewer astutely noted that Adonis had always dismissed merely formal definitions of poetry and suggested that he must therefore not regard the "Salutation" as a poem at all, a suggestion that Adonis did not challenge—and indeed he never included the poem in any subsequent collection of verse.[20] It would be wrong to make too much of this brief exchange, or the poem that is its subject, but it suggests how quickly Adonis moved to re-erect some old distinctions in the wake of Khomeini's revolution. If one has to differentiate between poems proper and works of "moral sympathy" (or solidarity), what becomes of the inseparability of cultural and political struggle?

A more significant step in this process of reorientation is Adonis's "*Bayan al-hadatha*" [Manifesto for Modernity], published a year after his first two essays on Iran.[21] Perhaps because of its title, the essay is often read as Adonis's mature or definitive statement on the subject of *al-hadatha*. But the essay is better understood as a restatement of Adonis's earlier principles in the aftermath of the revolution. Although Khomeini is never mentioned, he hovers in the background of the text, like a finger raised in warning against the temptations of *engagement*. Whereas Adonis's writings in the 1970s discovered modernist precursors in all fields of Arab life—its mystics, philosophers, poets, and social movements—the manifesto recenters the question of *al-hadatha* firmly within poetic territory. The essay begins by taking up the question of whether modernism is indigenous to Arab history or else, as its many critics claimed, a foreign import and for that reason "inauthentic" [*ghayr asila*]. But even French modernism took its cues from Edgar Allan Poe, notes Adonis, and in fact all modernist poets, from Rimbaud to Eliot, took their ideas from elsewhere. Modernism, in other words, has always emerged out of acts of translation. Yet Adonis then goes on to revisit the argument of his *Anthology*, namely, that Arabic poetry does indeed have its own "deep and authentic [*asila*]" *hadatha*—namely, the modernism of the ʿAbbasid era, which predates the French version by a millennium. It was in the eighth and ninth centuries, Adonis reminds us, that Arab poets formulated a cosmopolitan poetics, with borrowings from India, Persia, and Greece, which marked a radical departure from the parochial purity of Bedouin verse. In other words, ʿAbbasid modernism was authentic insofar as it had roots in many different traditions. In this way, the discourse of politico-religious authenticity that characterizes Adonis's writings on Iran is recoded by the "Manifesto" into aesthetic terms, while his concern with origins [*usul*] and genealogies is displaced by a more familiar rhetoric of cultural borrowings.

The attempt to reclaim *al-hadatha* for poetry comes to a climax in the closing passages of the essay. There, Adonis defines the modernist "poem-text"—the sort of open-work verse that he began to write in the mid-1970s—in just those terms he had used the previous year to analyze the Iranian uprising. A modernist poem's rhythm, Adonis writes, "Is a creative rhythm that tends, essentially and necessarily, toward a total transformation, that is to say, toward the heart of a total and revolutionary praxis [*al-mumarasa al-thawriyya al-shamila*]." In this way, a rhetoric of revolution is reincorporated into the modernist poem itself, which becomes once again a figure of totality. Adonis's final peroration equates modernism with the work of creativity, or *ibdaʿ*: "The essential thing is creativity, in order to illuminate and reveal more of man and the world. Creativity has no age and never grows old. Poetry should therefore not be judged by its modernity, but by its creativity. Not every modernity is creative; but creativity is eternally modern." In a critique of Adonis's manifesto, Sadiq Jalal al-ʿAzm suggests that Adonis's rhetoric here is patently theological. "Creativity" is a purely metaphysical category, and the same might be said of "Islam as such." "What is the truth of modernism?" Al-ʿAzm asks. "Adonis responds: Modernism, in its true and profound meaning, is creativity. And what is creativity? Creativity is creativity."[22] The tautology is as empty as al-ʿAzm suggests, but it is important to remember that *ibdaʿ* is a keyword in Adonis's late modernist poetics. Throughout his writings of the 1950s and 1960s, the idealization of creativity and its corollary sublimation of "man" served to wall off poetry—"the original creative force in Arab life," as Adonis asserts in the *Anthology*—from historical pressures. With this background in mind, we can read the manifesto not as a theological tract disguised as an essay on poetics, as al-ʿAzm suggests, but instead as a reaffirmation of the split between literary and political history, in which the language of revolution is reserved for literature.

Adonis's last act of disavowal and retrenchment came a year later, in the summer of 1980, when he published his third and final essay on Iran in *al-Nahar*. By this time, Khomeini had used the US hostage crisis to purge oppositional elements from his regime, he had shuttered many newspapers, and the crackdown on leftists had begun. Adonis begins his article by reviewing the historical conditions for political Islam's success, the most important of which was the bankruptcy of secular Arab nationalism in 1967. In the absence of a legitimate anti-imperialist movement, Islamists stepped into the breach, promising a unified front that would surpass Nasserism in its mass appeal as well as its intransigence toward the West. Adonis acknowledged the logic of this position but ended his article by suggesting that Islamism was only Arab nationalism dressed in new robes—a reprise of antiliberal, state-centered authoritarianism. Like Nasserism, Islamist politics was fierce in the face of foreign threats but failed to look critically at its own traditions—that project of "liberation from within" Adonis had once ascribed to Khomeini's revolution. Political Islam did not criticize the notion of unity, nor did it offer to rethink the notion of the state (*al-dawla*); if anything, it merely confirmed Adonis's worry that the theory and practice of the caliphate remained in force, thirteen hundred years after their foundation. Adonis ended his article with a fearful prophecy: "the armed jurist" [*al-faqih al-'askari*] would take the place of "the armed man-of-letters."[23]

More explicitly than his "Manifesto," Adonis's last article on Iran puts politics back in its place. In his earlier pieces, Adonis had rejected the idea of "political Islam" and insisted on speaking of "Islam as such." He argued that the Iranian revolution was not merely political, did not just aim at overthrowing the regime, but represented a "total" reversal of the status quo. In the last article, by contrast, Islamism reveals itself as simply another movement fascinated by state power. In Iran, Islam became nothing more than the official ideology of the regime; Khomeini turned out to be a politician after all.

This lesson, and Adonis's subsequent recalibration, had lasting effects. The aftermath of Tehran reanimated the poet's ingrained suspicion that all political movements were basically alike in their brute will to power. This skepticism would become a leitmotif in his pronouncements on the Syrian uprising. In a rare moment of self-criticism, included in an open letter to the opposition in the summer of 2011, Adonis repented of his support for the Iranian revolution in exactly these terms:

> Putting an end to the dictatorial [Baathist] regime is necessary, but will not solve the whole problem. How did Iran benefit, for example, by replacing the dictatorial regime of the shah, which ruled in the name of liberalism, with an equally dictatorial regime, which ruled in the name of religion? Religious despotism is worse because it is total: corporeal and spiritual at once. Perhaps all of us who stood with the Iranian revolution made an error in thinking it would work toward real freedoms.

For Adonis, the obsession with political power is the major fault of postwar Arab politics, particularly those of the left. And he thought he detected this same obsession among the Syrian rebels: "The discourse of 'the Arab Spring' does not revolt against the corruption of Arab society, but instead against political power. This is the 'revolutionary tradition' in our History, then as now. Particularly since the Nasserist revolution, we have seen how all things that depend on state power change—new leaders replace the old discredited ones— and yet nothing essential is altered." Adonis may have made a mistake in supporting the Islamic revolution, but this mistake ended up confirming the wisdom of his liberal disdain for politics as practiced by nationalists, Marxists, and Islamists alike.[24]

In his writings about Syria, Adonis's suspicion of state-centered politics is matched by his privileging of culture—what he sometimes calls the domain of "mentalities." In an early article published in May 2011, Adonis acknowledged, as he often did, the necessity of regime change all across the region as a general principle. And yet, he cautioned, "Such a change, if limited to its politico-authoritarian aspect, means nothing. It is evident that any change, in order to be total and categorical, must engage in rebuilding the social and cultural structures on which these regimes are founded." He made the same argument in an article published that fall: "Society does not necessarily change merely because the regime does. One must therefore change its institutions—which, in turn, will never be altered except through a total rupture with the antiquated bases of the reigning mode of thought."[25] Again and again in his writings on Syria, as in his "Manifesto of Modernism," Adonis argues that the true ground for revolution is culture, or what we might call the realm of social reproduction. "Politics" is, by contrast, the barren realm of an eternal and unchanging struggle for power. Paradoxically, the only way to maintain the possibility of a true revolution is by distancing oneself from any actually existing revolutionaries—precisely because they are not revolutionary enough. Such are the ironies of radical liberalism in Tehran and Damascus.

Adonis's critics were right to see an inconsistency between the enthusiasm he showed for the Iranian uprising and the skepticism with which he greeted the Syrian protests. In a response to al-ʿAzm's early charge of inconstancy and opportunism, Adonis cited an aphorism from Nietzsche's *Daybreak*: "The snake that cannot shed its skin perishes. So it is with men who cannot change their mind: they are no longer men."[26] I believe the discrepancy between Adonis's positions has less to do with sectarian considerations and more to do with his recovery and reassertion, after 1979, of the liberal, late modernist scruples developed during the early years in Lebanon. In the story he tells of his emigration from Syria in 1956, Adonis describes it as an escape from "the hegemony of the political," a flight from the internecine battles of Damascus to the refuge of Beirut, "city of beginnings." There, among other migrants and misfits, Adonis and his fellow modernists dreamt of establishing a culture that would be revolutionary by virtue of its distance from any state or party apparatus. It was a dream they shared with many other liberal modernists at the time, a fantasy of escaping the coils of ideology into the open waters of world literature. This fantasy produced some of the greatest Arabic poems of the century, but it could not survive the *Naksa*, the outbreak of the Lebanese Civil War, and Khomeini's revolution unscathed. Viewed against this turbulent background, the inconsistencies of Adonis's thought are less remarkable than its continuities. In the aftermath of his Iranian adventure, Adonis began to resurrect old distinctions and put things back in their respective places. Those disappointed by Adonis's position on Syria professed shock that a revolutionary modernist should shy away from the uprising. But this is to have misunderstood what sort of revolution and what sort of modernity Adonis has been writing about for more than half a century.

NOTES

Introduction: Modernism in Translation

1. "Greenwich Village": Samir Khalaf, *Lebanon's Predicament* (New York: Columbia University Press, 1987), 262. The figures for the construction boom are from Samir Kassir, *Beirut*, trans. M. B. DeBevoise (Berkeley: University of California Press, 2010), 412. Roger Shattuck, *The Banquet Years: The Origins of the Avant-Garde in France, 1885 to World War I* (New York: Vintage, 1968), 30.

2. Franck Mermier, *Le livre et la ville: Beyrouth et l'édition arabe* (Paris: Sindbad, 2005), 52 [my translation]; Fuad Ajami, *Beirut: City of Regrets* (New York: W.W. Norton, 1988), 27–28; Adonis, *Ha anta ayyuha al-waqt* [Here You Are, O Time] (Beirut: Dar al-Adab, 1993), 10. All translations from the Arabic are my own. For transliteration, I have simplified the system used by the *International Journal of Middle East Studies*, excluding diacritical marks except for the 'ayn (') and the hamza (').

3. Muhammad Jamal Barut, *al-Hadatha al-ula* (Sharjah: Manshurat Ittihad Kuttab wa-Udaba' al-Imarat, 1991), 10.

4. Scholars have often reproduced this loose terminology, with confusing results. In much English-language scholarship, for example, "modernist" is an umbrella term for any twentieth-century poetry in Arabic that does not employ conventional meters or an obviously classicizing diction. See, for example, M. M. Badawi, *A Critical Introduction to Modern Arabic Poetry* (Cambridge: Cambridge University Press, 1976), in which "new" or "modern" poetry (both words translate the Arabic *hadith*) is essentially a generational category, including all Arab poets who reacted against the "romantic" poetry of the interwar years. The same is true of Salma Khadra Jayyusi's *Trends and Movements in Modern Arabic Poetry*, 2 vols. (Leiden: Brill, 1977). It is symptomatic that Jayyusi's chapter on post-1948 poetry in *The Cambridge History of Arabic Literature* is simply titled "Modernist Poetry in Arabic." In that essay, as elsewhere, she uses "modernist" as both a periodizing term and a description of formal or thematic innovations, but not as the name for a particular historical movement, as I do here. See *Modern Arabic Literature*, ed. M. M. Badawi (Cambridge: Cambridge University Press, 1992), 132–79. In Shmuel Moreh's collection of essays, *Studies in Modern Arabic Prose and Poetry* (Leiden: Brill, 1988), "modernist" is used to describe any twentieth-century poetry written by "a new class of secular educated [Arabs] who had received a Western education, had learned foreign languages, and had come into close contact with European literature" (70).

5. In *Metapoesis in the Arabic Tradition: From Modernists to Muḥdathūn* (Leiden and Boston: Brill, 2015), Huda J. Fakhreddine criticizes the use of "modernist" as a historical term in studies of Arabic poetry, suggesting that its exclusive application to twentieth-century literature has obscured the innovative qualities of classical writers such as the 'Abbasid poets of the eighth and ninth centuries. Fakhreddine argues, "The term 'modern' should be understood as a literary term rather than an historical one" [2], i.e., it should be understood as a trope of critical self-reflection (metapoesis) rather than as a periodizing category. This suggestion mirrors Adonis's own avowedly idealist and "literary" conception of *al-hadatha*. Such antihistorical arguments may be useful in provoking revisionary readings of classical poetry, but they are less satisfying when applied to the poetry and poetics of the *Shi'r* group.

6. Nazik al-Malaʾika, *Qadaya al-Shiʿr al-muʿasir*, 2nd ed. (Baghdad: Manshurat Maktabat al-Nahda, 1964), 182. I examine al-Malaʾika's own poetics in chapter 4.

7. Adonis, *Ha anta*, 189.

8. Malcolm Bradbury and James McFarlane, eds. *Modernism, 1890–1930* (New Jersey: Humanities Press, 1978); Marshall Berman, *All That Is Solid Melts into Air* (Penguin: New York, 1988). On the "transnational turn," see Douglas Mao and Rebecca L. Walkowitz, "The New Modernist Studies," *PMLA*, 123:3 (2008), 738–42.

9. The best critical works on the *Shiʿr* group are those of Kamal Kheir Beik, *Mouvement moderniste de la poésie arabe contemporaine* (Paris: Publications orientalistes de France, 1978); Barut, *al-Hadatha al-ula*; and Dounia Badini, *La Revue* Shiʿr / *Poésie et la modernité poétique arabe: Beyrouth (1957–70)* (Paris: Sindbad, 2009).

10. For a pair of recent attempts to drastically expand the boundaries of modernism, see Susan Stanford Friedman, *Planetary Modernisms: Provocations on Modernity across Time* (New York: Columbia University Press, 2015), and *Modernism*, 2 vols., ed. Astradur Eysteinsson and Vivian Liska (Amsterdam: John Benjamins, 2007). It is symptomatic that Eysteinsson and Liska's massive anthology includes essays on the modernisms of Norway, Catalonia, and the Faroe Islands but makes no mention of the Arab world.

11. Gregory Barnhisel, *Cold War Modernists: Art, Literature, and American Cultural Diplomacy* (New York: Columbia University Press, 2015), 23.

12. Samir Kassir, *Beirut*, trans. M. B. DeBevoise (Berkeley: University of California Press, 2010), 347.

13. George Steiner, *After Babel* (Oxford: Oxford University Press, 1975), 466.

14. Clement Greenberg, "Modernist Painting," in *The Collected Essays and Criticism*, ed. John O'Brian (Chicago: University of Chicago Press, 1960), 4:85.

15. Theodor Adorno, "Cultural Criticism and Society," in *Prisms*, trans. Samuel and Sherry Weber (Cambridge: MIT Press, 1981), 24.

16. *Shiʿr* 7:25 (Winter 1963), 141.

17. Pierre Bourdieu, *The Rules of Art: Genesis and Structure of the Literary Field*, trans. Susan Emanuel (Stanford: Stanford University Press, 1996). In his chapter on "the conquest of autonomy," Bourdieu writes, in terms that invite comparison with the Arab modernists' project, "Rather than a ready-made position which only has to be taken up . . . 'art for art's sake' is a *position to be made*. . . . Those who would take up that position cannot make it exist except by making the field in which a place could be found for it, that is, by revolutionizing an art world that excludes it, in fact and in law" (76).

18. Franco Moretti, *Modern Epic* (London: Verso, 1996), 200 [emphasis in the original].

19. See Serge Guilbaut, *How New York Stole the Idea of Modern Art: Abstract Expressionism, Freedom, and the Cold War*, trans. Arthur Goldhammer (Chicago: University of Chicago, 1983); Peter Coleman, *The Liberal Conspiracy: The Congress for Cultural Freedom and the Struggle for the Mind of Postwar Europe* (New York: Free Press, 1989); Frances Stonor Saunders, *The Cultural Cold War: The CIA and the World of Arts and Letters* (New York: New Press, 2000); Giles Scott-Smith, *The Politics of Apolitical Culture: The Congress for Cultural Freedom, the CIA and Post-war American Hegemony* (London and New York: Routledge, 2002); Gregory Barnhisel, *James Laughlin, New Directions, and the Remaking of Ezra Pound* (Amherst and Boston: University of Massachusetts Press, 2005); Andrew N. Rubin, *Archives of Authority: Empire, Culture, and the Cold War* (Princeton: Princeton University Press, 2012); and Barnhisel, *Cold War Modernists*. As Barnhisel writes in this last work, "The term *Cold War modernism*, as I use it in this book, does not describe new works in the modernist tradition produced during the Cold War years. Instead, it refers to the deployment of Modernist art as a weapon of Cold War propaganda by both governmental and unofficial actors as well as to the implicit and explicit understanding of modernism underpinning that

deployment" (28). This definition, which makes cultural products the epiphenomena of propaganda efforts, seems to exclude any formal examination of the works in question, and indeed Barnhisel—like the other cited scholars in this respect—is mostly silent on such matters.

20. Cf. Penny M. Von Eschen, *Satchmo Blows Up the World: Jazz Ambassadors Play the Cold War* (Cambridge: Harvard University Press, 2006).

21. On Cold War culture in Latin America, see Jean Franco, *The Decline and Fall of the Lettered City: Latin America in the Cold War* (Cambridge: Harvard University Press, 2002), as well as Patrick Iber, *Neither Peace nor Freedom: The Cultural Cold War in Latin America* (Cambridge: Harvard University Press, 2015). On the African context, see Peter Kalliney, "Modernism, African Literature, and the Cold War," *Modern Language Quarterly* 76:3 (September 2015) 333–68; and Nathan Suhr-Sytsma, "Ibadan Modernism: Poetry and the Literary Present in Mid-century Nigeria," *Journal of Commonwealth Literature* 48:1 (March 2013), 41–59.

22. Amanda Anderson, *Bleak Liberalism* (Chicago: University of Chicago Press, 2016), 100.

23. There is a small but growing body of scholarship on Cold War culture in the Arab world and the role of the CCF. See in particular Elizabeth M. Holt, "'Bread or Freedom': The Congress for Cultural Freedom, the CIA, and the Arabic Literary Journal *Ḥiwār*," *Journal of Arabic Literature*, 44 (2013), 83–102; and Elliott Colla, "Badr Shākir al-Sayyāb, Cold War Poet," *Middle Eastern Literatures* 18:3 (2015), 247–63. Here too, the focus has been on institutional history, the oxymoron of literary autonomy with governmental support, and the restricted field of play offered by Cold War binarisms. How these factors affected literary forms is left mostly unexamined.

24. *Shiʿr* 2:6 (Spring 1958), 7–9. The poem was included without modification in Adonis's collection *Awraq fi-l-rih* [Leaves in the Wind] (Beirut: Dar Majallat Shiʿr, 1958), 128–31. A revised version was published in his next collection, *Aghani Mihyar al-Dimashqi* [The Songs of Mihyar of Damascus] (Beirut: Dar Majallat Shiʿr, 1961) 224–27.

25. Edward Said, *The World, the Text, and the Critic* (Cambridge: Harvard University Press, 1983), 17.

26. Octavio Paz, *Los Hijos del limo: del romanticismo a la vanguardia*, 3rd ed. (Barcelona: Editorial Seix-Barral, 1981), 17.

27. *Al-Adab al-ʿarabi al-muʿasir: aʿmal muʾtamar Ruma al-munʿaqad fi tishrin al-awwal sanat 1961* (Paris: Manshurat Adwaʾ, n.d. [1962]), 47–49. It is because of this methodological focus on translation that I have so little to say about the work of Muhammad al-Maghout, whose early poetry would necessarily figure in any comprehensive study of the Beiruti modernists.

28. Hans Wehr, *A Dictionary of Modern Written Arabic*, 3rd ed., (Beirut: Librairie de Liban, 1974).

29. There are a number of recent and sophisticated works on translation in the *Nahda*. See in particular Kamran Rastegar, *Literary Modernity between the Middle East and Europe: Textual Transactions in Nineteenth-Century Arabic, English, and Persian Literatures* (London and New York: Routledge, 2007); Shaden M. Tageldin, *Disarming Words: Empire and the Seductions of Translation in Egypt* (Berkeley and Los Angeles: University of California Press, 2011); and Marwa Elshakry, *Reading Darwin in Arabic, 1860–1950* (Chicago: University of Chicago Press, 2013).

30. Fakhreddine, *Metapoesis*, 22.

31. Pascal Casanova, *The World Republic of Letters* (Cambridge: Harvard University Press, 2004), 238. One of the earliest uses of "*naql*" in Arabic was in reference to the intralinguistic transmission of prophetic *hadith*, as in the phrase "*naqala al-hadith ʿanhu*" [he transmitted the saying from him].

32. Yusuf al-Khal, trans. and ed., *Diwan al-shiʿr al-amriki* (Beirut: Dar Majallat Shiʿr, 1958), 7.

33. Yusuf al-Khal, trans. and ed., *Qasaʾid mukhtara* (Beirut: Dar Majallat Shiʿr, 1962); and Yusuf al-Khal, Adonis, Buland Haydari, Desmond Stewart, Munir Bashshur, and Ibrahim Shukrallah, trans., *T. S. Eliot, Tarjamat min al-shiʿr al-hadith* [T. S. Eliot, translations of modern poetry] (Beirut: Dar Majallat Shiʿr, 1959). Dounia Badini has compiled a comprehensive table of the magazine's translations, *La Revue* Shiʿr, 455–60.

34. *Shiʿr* 4:14 (Spring 1960), 83.

35. *Shiʿr* 7:25 (Winter 1963). The trope is repeated in the opening editorial of *Shiʿr* 5:18 (Spring 1961), 7: "From its beginning, *Shiʿr* magazine aimed to establish a creative relation to world poetry. It takes and at the same time it gives, placing Arabic poetry on the map."

36. Erich Auerbach, *Time, History, and Literature: Selected Essays*, ed. James I. Porter (Princeton: Princeton University Press, 2014), 253. See also Emily Apter, "On Translation in a Global Market," *Public Culture* 13 (2001), 1–12; and Jonathan Arac, "Anglo-Globalism?" *New Left Review* 16 (July–August 2002), 35–45.

37. Aamir R. Mufti, *Forget English! Orientalisms and World Literature* (Cambridge: Harvard University Press, 2016), 38.

38. Lamartine visited Lebanon in 1832, a trip he recounts in *Voyage en Orient*, and lent his name to a room in the Shihabist palace of Beiteddine. The Lebanese poet Abdo Wazen claims "Le Lac" has had more than twenty translations into Arabic ("Kharitat al-shiʿr al-amriki bi-l-ʿarabiyya ma zalat tattasiʾ," *al-Hayat*, July 7, 2009). Shawqi Abi Shaqra's translation of "Le Bateau ivre" was published in *Shiʿr* 3:11 (Summer 1959), 32–37 (the same number includes a translation of Yeats's "Sailing to Byzantium"). I discuss Adonis's version of Saint-John Perse's *Amers* in chapter 3.

39. Yusuf al-Khal, *Al-aʿmal al-shiʿriyya al-kamila, 1938–1968*, 2nd ed. (Beirut: al-Taʿawuniyya al-Lubnaniyya lil-Taʾlif wa-l-Nashr, 1979), 232–35.

40. This feeling for the sea, as well as the Noah myth, was not shared by the modernists' contemporaries, nor even by all those associated with the movement itself. The Palestinian polymath Jabra Ibrahim Jabra, a frequent contributor to *Shiʿr*, set his melodrama of ideas, *al-Safina* [The Ship] (1970), on a Mediterranean cruise boat. The novel rehearses all the mythic and historical themes of the modernist genre, which it finally rejects in favor of a specifically Palestinian longing for the land. Similarly, at the close of the poet Mahmoud Darwish's memoir of the Israeli bombardment of Beirut in 1982, an allusion to the Noah myth bears very different connotations than it does for Adonis. Anticipating the PLO's expulsion from Lebanon, Darwish admits to his hatred of the sea and refers bitterly to "Noah's modern arks" [*sufun nuh al-haditha*], which are for him the emblems of exile. Mahmoud Darwish, *Dhakira lil-nisyan* (Beirut: Riad el-Rayyes, 2007), 187; cf. *Memory for Forgetfulness*, trans. Ibrahim Muhawi (Berkeley: University of California Press, 1995), 180–81.

41. Albert Hourani, "Visions of Lebanon," in *Toward a Viable Lebanon*, ed. Halim Barakat (Washington, DC: Center for Contemporary Arab Studies, 1988), 5. An exception to the modernists' avoidance of the city is Khalil Hawi's "Layali Beirut" [Beirut Evenings], from his 1957 collection, *Nahar al-ramad* [River of Ashes], which turns the capital into a phantasmagory of sexual temptation and spiritual travail. Another exception is the early work of Muhammad al-Maghout, especially his 1959 collection *Huzn fi dawʾ al-qamar* [Sadness in the Moonlight] (1959), much of which is set in the streets and cafés of Damascus. Hawi and al-Maghout were atypical of the modernist group in many respects, and neither remained with the movement for long (or expressed much loyalty toward it afterward).

42. Berman, *All That Is Solid*, 309.

43. Adonis, *al-Hiwarat al-kamila, v.1 (1960–1980)* [The Complete Interviews, vol. 1 (1960–1980)] (Damascus: Bidayat lil-nashr wa-l-tawziʿ, 2010), 8.

44. *Shiʿr* 6:22 (Spring 1962), 10.

45. Samuel Moyn, "Jacques Maritain, Christian New Order, and the Birth of Human Rights," SSRN Working Paper (May 1, 2008), http://ssrn.com/abstract=1134345.

46. The history of this figure in midcentury American intellectual life has been thoroughly analyzed by Mark Greif, *The Age of the Crisis of Man* (Princeton: Princeton University Press, 2014). Stefanos Geroulanos emphasizes the prewar roots of the French discourse on "the death of man" in *An Atheism That Is Not Humanist Emerges in French Thought* (Stanford: Stanford University Press, 2010). Kristin Ross provides an acute reading of the French situation in the 1960s in her chapter "New Men," in *Fast Cars, Clean Bodies* (Cambridge: MIT Press, 1996).

47. We can also see this heroization at work in the convoluted textual history of the poem. In the original version, which I have translated, a poet and a "rebel for freedom" accompany Noah on his dive into the mud of creation. These figures were edited out of later versions, in which it is Noah alone who performs the ritual of resurrection. In these later rewrites, beginning with the version printed in Adonis's *Songs of Mihyar* (1961), the poem is divided into two numbered parts, with the "we" of the opening section giving way in the second section to the new Noah's lyrical "I." This move away from figures of collectivity happens over and again in the history of Arabic modernism.

Chapter 1: Lebanon and Late Modernism

1. Adonis, *Ha anta*, 31–33. Emphases in the original.

2. Khalida Saʿid, *Yutubiya al-madina al-muthaqqafa* (Beirut: Dar al-Saqi, 2012), 9. The five institutions examined by Saʿid are the Cénacle libanais, the Rahbani musical family, *Shiʿr* and *Mawaqif* magazines, and Janine Rubeiz's art gallery, Dar el Fan wal Adab.

3. Khalaf, *Lebanon's Predicament*, 263–65.

4. See Khalaf, *Civil and Uncivil Violence* (New York: Columbia University Press, 2002), 196–203. In his long essay on the city, Fuad Ajami employs the same metaphor: "The wealthy Arabs—puritanical at home—needed a place to play. Beirut became the playground." Ajami, *Beirut: City of Regrets*, 25.

5. Adonis, *Ha anta*, 13.

6. *Ibid.*, 96.

7. Robert Scholes and Clifford Wulfman, *Modernism in the Magazines: An Introduction* (New Haven: Yale University Press, 2010).

8. My characterization of Lebanon in this period is primarily indebted to Fawwaz Traboulsi, *A History of Modern Lebanon* (London: Pluto Press, 2007), esp. 109–27, and Carolyn L. Gates, *The Merchant Republic of Lebanon: Rise of an Open Economy* (London: I. B. Taurus, 1998).

9. Hanna Batatu, *The Egyptian, Syrian, and Iraqi Revolutions: Some Observations on Their Underlying Causes and Social Character* (Washington, DC: The Center for Contemporary Arab Studies, 1984), 12. Batatu notes that in Egypt, during the period 1952–76, the number of state employees rose from 325,000 to approximately 2.9 million; in Syria, between 1960 and 1979, the number rose from 34,000 to 331,000; and in Iraq between 1958 and 1978, the number went from 85,000 to 662,000. For further details, see Roger Owen, *State, Power and Politics in the Making of the Modern Middle East*, 2nd ed. (Routledge: London and New York, 2002), 27–44. Owen offers a useful caution against what he calls "the reification of the state," i.e., the assumption that the state is "a single actor with a systematic program of social transformation." This sort of reification is common to many of the modernists—particularly Adonis—whose antipathy toward the state often leads them to exaggerate its power and uniformity.

10. Anouar Abdel-Malek, *Égypte, Société Militaire* (Paris: Éditions du Seuil, 1962), 199.

11. Richard Jacquemond, *Conscience of the Nation: Writers, State, and Society in Modern Egypt* (Cairo: American University in Cairo Press, 2008), 15-16. On Iraq, see Orit Bashkin, *The Other Iraq: Pluralism and Culture in Hashemite Iraq* (Stanford: Stanford University Press, 2009). Bashkin argues for the existence of "vibrant, pluralistic public spheres" in Iraq prior to the 1958 revolution. On Syria, see Miriam Cooke, *Dissident Syria: Making Oppositional Arts Official* (Durham: Duke University Press, 2007). Cooke notes that the imposition of martial law in 1963 gave "the state absolute control over the production of culture and the distribution of information" (8).

12. *Shiʿr* 1:4 (Fall 1957), 123. The study of myth is *al-Ustura fi-l-shiʿr al-muʿasir: al-shuʿaraʾ al-tammuziyyun* (Beirut: Manshurat Majallat Afaq, 1959). Manshurat Majallat Afaq was a publishing house attached to Dar Majallat Shiʿr.

13. T. S. Eliot, "The Man of Letters and the Future of Europe," *Sewanee Review* 53:3 (1945), 341.

14. *Ha anta*, 180.

15. Naguib Mahfouz, *Respected Sir* (1975), trans. Rasheed El-Enany (Cairo: American University Press, 1987), 110-11. For a detailed analysis of this history, see Alain Roussillon, "Sociologie et Société en Égypte: le contournement des intellectuels par l'État," in *Les Intellectuels et le pouvoir: Syrie, Égypte, Tunisie, Algérie*, ed. Gilbert Delanoue (Cairo: Centre d'études et de documentation économique, juridique et sociale, 1986), 95-138.

16. Gabriel Ménassa, "Réconstruction de l'économie libanaise," *ʿAhd al-nadwa al-lubnaniyya* (Beirut: Dar al-Nahar, 1997), 168, 170. "*Laissez-aller*," Nadim Shehadeh, *The Idea of Lebanon: Economy and State in the Cénacle Libanais, 1946-54* (Oxford: Centre for Lebanese Studies, 1987), 8. A full study of the Cénacle is a desideratum.

17. See Gates, *The Merchant Republic*, 86-93.

18. For a vivid characterization of this new consumer society, see Kassir, *Beirut*, 371-84. On gold shipments, *ibid.*, 357; on the oil surplus, Samir Khalaf, *Civil and Uncivil Violence in Lebanon* (New York: Columbia University, 2002), 163.

19. Samir Amin, *Delinking* (London: Zed Books, 1990); for tourism numbers, see Gates, *The Merchant Republic*, 118.

20. Shehadeh writes, "The vision of the Cénacle was essentially the Christian Lebanese nationalist vision but one which favored a dialogue with Islam through which it was hoped Arabist ideologues could be convinced that Lebanon was also theirs and that it served as a conduit for modernisation and progress" (*The Idea of Lebanon*, 17).

21. Charles Malik, "The Near East: The Search for Truth," *Foreign Affairs* 30:2 (January 1952), 239-40.

22. *Shiʿr* 1:4 (Fall 1957), 86.

23. On *al-Adab*, see Monica Ruocco, *L'intellettuale arabo tra impegno e dissenso: analisi della rivista libanese al-Ādāb* (Rome: Jouvence, 1999). There is less scholarship on *al-Thaqafa al-Wataniyya*, but see Barut, *al-Hadatha*, 45-53.

24. *Al-Thaqafa al-Wataniyya* 6:2 (February 1957), 9. For an analysis of Muruwwa's intellectual career, from his early days as a Shiite cleric in Najaf to his mature Marxist studies, see Yoav Di-Capua, "Homeward Bound: Ḥusayn Muruwwah's Integrative Quest for Authenticity," *Journal of Arabic Literature* 44 (2013), 21-52.

25. *Al-Adab al-ʿarabi al-muʿasir*, 45-51.

26. For an analysis of the conference proceedings, viewed as an example of the crisis of tradition, see Muhsin J. al-Musawi, *Arabic Poetry: Trajectories of Modernity and Tradition* (London and New York: Routledge, 2006), 54-64.

27. *Al-Adab al-ʿarabi*, 160-78.

28. Saunders, *The Cultural Cold War*, 1.

29. Frank Kermode, *Not Entitled* (New York: Farrar, Straus and Giroux, 1999), 225.

30. On CCF magazines, including those outside Europe, see *Campaigning Culture and the Global Cold War: The Journals of the Congress for Cultural Freedom*, ed. Giles Scott-Smith and Charlotte A. Lerg (London: Palgrave Macmillan, 2017).

31. Rubin, *Archives of Authority*, 56.

32. The entire manifesto is reprinted in Scott-Smith, *The Politics of Apolitical Culture*, 167–68.

33. *Ibid.*, 2.

34. Scott-Smith dates this turn away from Europe to a conference held in Milan in 1955, "probably the first time that [CCF-affiliated] Western intellectuals had been confronted by critics of colonialism from the lands themselves." The Milan conference took place just months after Bandung had signaled the entrance of newly independent and still colonized Afro-Asian nations into the realm of international politics. Scott-Smith argues that Milan also marked a turn from the militant anticommunism of the CCF's first five years to a new consensus based on the technocratic, end-of-ideology thesis later popularized by Daniel Bell. But as Scott-Smith remarks, "Exporting the 'end of ideology' position to regions that did not experience the conditions of prosperity in the West was an almost insurmountable problem" (*The Politics of Apolitical Culture*, 153–59).

35. "Remarks by Mr. W. Z. Laqueur," undated (probably 1953 or 1954), Series II, Box 229, IACF (International Association for Cultural Freedom). Walter Laqueur, a Middle East expert who specialized at the time in Soviet-Arab relations, was also the editor of *Soviet Survey*, a CCF-sponsored journal. In his writings, Laqueur often emphasized the high regard Arabs supposedly feel toward intellectuals: "In Arab society the influence of writers and poets on public opinion has traditionally been much greater than that of their colleagues in the West." Laqueur suggests that this esteem is a symptom of the region's backwardness and results in the native population's susceptibility to propaganda. Walter Z. Laqueur, *The Soviet Union and the Middle East* (New York: Frederick A. Praeger, 1959), 284.

36. Miles Copeland, *The Game of Nations* (London: Weidenfeld and Nicolson, 1969), 195.

37. "Interview with Daniel Lerner," April 30 [1953 or 1954?], Series II, Box 229, IACF.

38. Silone to Hunt, February 26, 1962, Series II, Box 292, IACF. All Silone's correspondence with the CCF is written in French. The translations are my own.

39. *Generations of Men* belongs to that midcentury corpus of novels and philosophical works Greif has called "the discourse of man." Hunt's story opens in the grasslands of fictional Chetopa County, a Faulknerian landscape peopled by Hemingwayesque loners: "The earth was silent, deeply and intensely still, prostrate before the black violence of tornadic winds or stunned by the heat that hammered against the surface of the yellow roads. In this place a man stood close to himself, carved out in isolation against the sky, and there was a nearness to the land and all its seasons which once felt could rarely be satisfied elsewhere" (Boston: Little, Brown, 1956), 3. On Hunt's role in the CCF, see Stonors, *The Cultural Cold War*, 241–43.

40. Hunt to Silone, October 26, 1961, Series II, Box 292, IACF.

41. Al-Khal to Simon Jargy, May 1960, Series I, Box 55, IACF.

42. See the two letters from Hunt to al-Khal, August 25 and September 19, 1961, Series I, Box 26, IACF. The two men's entire correspondence is in English.

43. "Indonesian Notebook," *Encounter* 23 (August 1955), 24–31. Wright's account was first published a month earlier in the CCF's French publication: "Vers Bandoeng, via Séville," *Preuves* 53 (July 1955), 6–15.

44. *The God That Failed*, ed. Richard Crossman (New York: Columbia University Press, 2001), 270–71.

45. Stephen Spender, *The Struggle of the Modern* (Berkeley: University of California Press, 1963), 54.

46. On February 27, 1961, the Paris office sent al-Khal a telegram notifying him that Spender was coming to Lebanon and was "WILLING LECTURE BEHALF CONGRESS TOPICS NEW POETS AND PLAYWRIGHTS IN ENGLAND OR SOME THOUGHTS ON COMMUNISM AND ANTI-COMMUNISM STOP WOULD APPRECIATE YOU ORGANIZE LECTURE." Series I, Box 26, IACF.

47. *Shi'r* 5:18 (Spring 1961), 187–89.

48. Spender, *The Struggle of the Modern*, 96. Spender's estimate of contemporary modernists was echoed by his successor at *Encounter*. In some of the first criticism he published in the magazine after becoming co-editor, Frank Kermode compared "paleomodernists" of the early twentieth century with "neomodernists" of the present, concluding "there has been only one Modernist Revolution, and . . . it happened a long time ago. So far as I can see there has been little radical change in modernist thinking since then. More muddle, certainly, and almost certainly more jokes, but no revolution, and much less talent" (April 1966), 73.

49. *Al-Adab al-'arabi al-mu'asir*, 30. Newspaper clippings related to the conference, many generated by participants after their return home to the region, show that the aim of suturing Arabic letters to world literature was a conscious press strategy (the clippings are archived in IACF files, Series III, Box 433). A report in the Baghdad newspaper *al-Watan* was titled "Arabic Literature Becomes World Literature" (December 31, 1961). An interview with Jargy in *L'Orient Littéraire* suggested the same thing: "Simon Jargy says: 'Middle Eastern writers will make a tremendous entrance into universal letters'" (December 2, 1961). The Lebanese daily *al-Nahar* reported, "The essential goal of the conference was to allow contemporary Arabic and European literatures to interact and to put Arabic literature at the level of world literature" (October 27, 1961).

50. Silone to Adonis, July 1, 1961, Series III, Box 432, IACF.

51. *Al-Adab al-'arabi al-mu'asir*, 30.

52. Crossman, *The God That Failed*, 102. Silone's anecdote echoes the second item in the CCF's Freedom Manifesto: "Freedom is defined first and foremost by [man's] right to hold and express his own opinions, and particularly opinions which differ from those of his rulers. Deprived of the right to say 'no,' man becomes a slave." Cf. Scott-Smith, *The Politics of Apolitical Culture*, 167.

53. Jean-Paul Sartre, *"What Is Literature?" and Other Essays* (Cambridge: Harvard University Press, 1988), 249, 237. *Engagement* was constantly derided in the pages of *Preuves*. See, for example, the two articles by Aimé Patri, "De l'opium des intellectuels à la cure de désintoxication," 5:53 (July 1955), 81–85; and "Les années d'apprentissage de Sartre," 11:122 (April 1961), 70–75. In its June 1952 issue (2:16), *Preuves* published George Orwell's 1945 essay, "The Prevention of Literature," under the punning title "La littérature encagée." Orwell's conclusion encapsulates what would become the standard liberal critique of Sartre: "Literature is doomed if liberty of thought perishes. Not only is it doomed in any country which retains a totalitarian structure; but any writer who adopts the totalitarian outlook, who finds excuses for persecution and the falsification of reality, thereby destroys himself as a writer. There is no way out of this. No tirades against 'individualism' and the 'ivory tower,' no pious platitudes to the effect that 'true individuality is only attained through identification with the community,' can get over the fact that a bought mind is a spoiled mind."

54. For a comprehensive history, see Yoav Di-Capua, *No Exit: Arab Existentialism, Jean-Paul Sartre, and Decolonization* (Chicago: Chicago University Press, 2018).

55. *Al-Adab* 1:1 (January 1953), 1.

56. Mahmud Amin al-'Alim and 'Abd al-'Azim Anis, *Fi-l-thaqafa al-misriyya* (Beirut: Dar al-Fikr al-Jadid, 1955). For a history of *iltizam*'s reception among Arab intellectuals,

see Verena Klemm, "Different Notions of Commitment (*Iltizām*) and Committed Literature (*al-adab al-multazim*) in the Literary Circles of the Mashriq," *Arabic and Middle Eastern Literatures* 3:1 (2000), 51–62.

57. *Al-Adab al-ʿarabi al-muʿasir*, 220–34.

58. On the memoir, see Colla, "Badr Shākir al-Sayyāb." The anthology has been republished as *Mukhtarat min al-shiʿr al-ʿalami al-hadith*, 2nd ed. (Abu Dhabi: Cultural Foundation Productions, 1998).

59. *Qasaʾid Badr Shakir al-Sayyab*, ed. Adonis (Beirut: Dar al-Adab, 1967); "the real beginning of modernity": *Violence et Islam: Entretiens avec Houria Abdelouahed* (Paris: Éditions du Seuil, 2015), 146.

60. *Thalathat shuʿaraʾ wa sahafi: rasaʾil min Jabra Ibrahim Jabra, Yusuf al-Khal, wa Tawfiq Sayigh ila Riad al-Rayyes*, ed. Riad El-Rayyes (Beirut: Riad El-Rayyes, 1996), 202.

61. For a biography of al-Sayyab, see Ihsan ʿAbbas, *Badr Shakir al-Sayyab: Dirasa fi hayatihi wa shiʿrihi* (Beirut: Dar al-Thaqafa, 1969). Adonis evokes al-Sayyab's visit to Beirut in 1957 in *Ha anta*, 124–31. For the magazine's contemporary account of the visit, see *Shiʿr* 1:3 (Summer 1957), 111–13. On the Franklin Books Program, see Amanda Laugesen, "Books for the World: American Book Programs in the Developing World, 1948–1968," in *Pressing the Fight: Print, Propaganda and the Cold War* (Amherst: University of Massachusetts Press, 2010), 126–44.

62. *Al-Adab al-ʿarabi al-muʿasir*, 235.

63. *The God That Failed*, 113–14. Silone is not the only contributor to round off his essay in this way. In Richard Wright's version, "I headed toward home alone, really alone now, telling myself that in all the sprawling immensity of our mighty continent the least-known factor of living was the human heart." He goes on to promise himself, "To fight, to create a sense of the hunger for life that gnaws in us all, to keep alive in our hearts a sense of the inexpressibly human" (162). The other American contributor, journalist Louis Fischer, concludes on a similar note: "I thought, in my Soviet phase, that I was serving humanity. But it is only since then that I have discovered the human being" (228). In fact, the rhetoric of man provided writers all over the world a way of bringing essays and prize acceptance speeches to an orotund close. For an especially turgid example, see William Faulkner's Nobel Prize speech of 1950, "I Decline to Accept the End of Man," as well as Greif's pertinent comments in *The Age of Man*, 116–21.

64. Guilbaut, *How New York*, 143.

65. Frederic Jameson, *A Singular Modernity* (London and New York: Verso, 2002), 166. Peter Kalliney has shown how the rhetoric of literary autonomy was used by African modernists such as Christopher Okigbo and Wole Soyinka, who edited and published in magazines funded by the CCF, to declare their independence of both colonial culture and the new postcolonial states. See Kalliney, "Modernism, African Literature, and the Cold War." In Latin America, late modernism in poetry is preeminently the work of Octavio Paz. As Jean Franco writes, "In his essays on poetry, especially *El arco y la lira*, Paz put poetry outside exchange value and outside history: 'poetry has not yet been incarnated in history, the poetic experience is a state of exception'" (*The Lettered City*, 52). "La consagración del instante," a chapter from *El arco y la lira* (1956)—Paz's most systematic work of poetics, which defines poetry as "nothing but the revelation of the human condition"—was translated and published in *Shiʿr* 7:28 (Fall 1963), 81–88.

66. *Al-Adab al-ʿarabi al-muʿasir*, 179–80.

67. Spender, *The Struggle of the Modern*, 238.

68. Erich Auerbach, *Time, History, and Literature*, 253–54.

69. "Letter to a Young Writer," *Encounter* 2:3 (March 1954), 5.

70. Cited in Mufti, *Forget English!*, 213.

71. This is one explanation for *Encounter*'s editorial policy toward African writers such as the Nigerian Wole Soyinka and the Sudanese Tayeb Salih, whose early short stories, "The Doum-Tree of Wad Hamid" (November 1962, 15–21) and "A Handful of Dates" (January 1966, 22–24), were the only Arabic fictions to appear in *Encounter* before the *Times* revelations. Both writers' interest in local myth and, in Salih's case, village life may well have appealed to the magazine's European editors. In the same vein, one might examine the attractions of Latin American magical realism—similarly invested in local myth and rural settings, and with its roots in CCF-sponsored magazines—to readers in the metropole. For a narrative of how "magical realism goes global as a particularistic aesthetic that satisfies a demand for *local color* from marginal cultures in the global field of world literature," see Mariano Siskind, *Cosmopolitan Desires: Global Modernity and World Literature in Latin America* (Evanston: Northwestern University Press, 2014), 59–100.

72. Cf. Husayn Muruwwah, "Min jama'at *Shi'r* ila majjalat *Hiwar*" [From the *Shi'r* Group to *Hiwar* Magazine], *al-Tariq* 11:21 (November 1962), 9. A year after the Rome conference, Muruwwah cocked an eyebrow at "the opulence and elegance bestowed on these *hommes des lettres* from invisible sources."

73. Hunt to al-Khal, November 2, 1961, Series I, Box 26, IACF.

74. In his memoir of the period, the translator Denys Johnson-Davies claims it was he who suggested to Hunt that Sayigh would be preferable to al-Khal as editor of the magazine. See *Memories in Translation: A Life between the Lines of Arabic Literature* (Cairo: American University in Cairo Press, 2006), 70. I owe this reference to Michael Vasquez.

75. Al-Khal to Hunt, November 7, 1961, Series II, Box 228, IACF.

76. Quoted in Matthew F. Jacobs, *Imagining the Middle East: The Building of an American Foreign Policy, 1918–1967* (Chapel Hill: University of North Carolina Press, 2011), 125.

77. See Salim Yaqub, *Containing Arab Nationalism* (Chapel Hill: University of North Carolina Press, 2003), especially chapter 8. Eisenhower's opinion of Nasser is quoted on p. 2.

78. This is the gist of Hunt's letter to Silone on March 28, 1961. The novelist seems to have been worried that a meeting of Arab intellectuals from across the region, such as the one planned in Rome, would be a boon to Nasserists. Hunt wrote back: "The popularity of Nasser in the Middle East is very great, particularly among the masses and leftist intellectuals. But pan-Arabism has its own roots and meaning in the Middle East, independently of Nasser. He has appropriated the idea in part for its inherent attractiveness, and in part to beef up his own ideological position, which is actually quite weak.... In fact, the participants in our seminar will have extremely varied opinions about Nasser and pan-Arabism, as well as all other topics now debated in the Middle East. My principal concern is thus to make sure that those who belong to our own intellectual community do not lose their connections with real or potential friends in the region—either out of negligence or because of their opposition to certain of its unpleasant political regimes." Series I, Box 30, IACF.

79. This is why Lebanon, for all its convenience, was not the CCF's preferred site for a regional office. As one internal memorandum put it, summarizing a consultation with Daniel Lerner (Turkey expert and author of *The Passing of Traditional Society*), "Branch would be most easily established in Lebanon, but least worth while. Branch would be hardest to establish in Egypt, but most worth while." Interview with Daniel Lerner, April 30 [1953 or 1954?], Series II, Box 229, IACF. The CCF did establish a Cairene branch, but it was never very active—a continual disappointment to the Paris office.

80. Edward Said, *The Question of Palestine* (New York: Vintage Books, 1992), 145.

81. Hunt to Silone, December 12, 1961, Series II, Box 292, IACF.

82. Hunt to al-Khal, November 13, 1961, Series I, Box 26, IACF.

83. Spender to Hunt, n.d. (spring 1961), Series II, Box 297, IACF.

84. Al-Khal to Hunt, November 23, 1961, Series II, Box 228, IACF.

85. Jargy to Jamil Jabre, May 28, 1962, Series II, Box 228, IACF.

86. Sayigh's diary during the period of his negotiations with the CCF have been published as *Mudhakkirat Tawfiq Sayigh bi-khatt yadihi wa-huwa yastaʿidd li-isdar majallat Hiwar* [The Memoirs of Tawfiq Sayigh in His Own Hand as He Prepared to Publish the Journal *Hiwar*] (Beirut: Dar Nelson, 2011). Sayigh records a conversation during the spring of 1962 in which Jargy mentions that Hunt is very eager to have al-Sayyab on the new magazine's masthead, since "the Arab nationalists love him" (19). On the history of *Hiwar*, see Holt, "Bread or Freedom."

87. Siskind, *Cosmopolitan Desires*, 3.

88. Berman, *All That Is Solid*, 232.

Chapter 2: The Genealogy of Arabic Modernism

1. For a succinct account, see Labib Zuwiyya Yamak, *The Syrian Social Nationalist Party: An Ideological Analysis* (Cambridge: Harvard University Press, 1966), 72–75. For a more thorough, if partisan analysis, see Adel Beshara, *Lebanon: The Politics of Frustration—the Failed Coup of 1961* (New York: RoutledgeCurzon, 2005).

2. *Al-Adab*, "*Lubnanuna*" [Our Lebanon], 10:2 (February 1962), 1.

3. Hunt to Hourani, January 17, 1962, Series I, Box 32. In his response, Hourani wrote, "I think on balance you are right about the Arabic periodical. I was always in two minds about Yussuf and his group. On the one hand, I suspected, without actually knowing, that they were more closely linked with the P.P.S. than they cared to admit; but on the other, Yussuf is an editor of great and proved abilities and the periodical would start with a group of writers who are really concerned to make it a success. However, in view of recent events in Lebanon, the first factor seems to me more important than the second." Hourani to Hunt, January 23, 1962, Series I, Box 32.

4. *Al-Tariq* 21:11 (November 1962), 10.

5. *Shiʿr* 6:22 (Spring 1962), 6–7.

6. *Al-Adab* 9:2 (February 1961), 65–66. This was not the first time the *Shiʿr* poets were accused of having undeclared political motivations. See, for example, the interview in *al-Nahar* with Yusuf al-Khal, reported in *Shiʿr* 3:9 (Winter 1959), 135–36, where the editor in chief denies accusations that the magazine was a front for the SSNP. Al-Khal protests, "[The magazine] belongs to no party, neither sectarian nor political. It is for poetry only."

7. It was common for pan-Arabists to describe the SSNP as a party for Greek Orthodoxy, the sect to which Saʿada belonged. The editorialists' use of the word "*daʿwa*," often employed in the religious sense of a "call," hints at this critique. For a more detailed account of Hawi's relation to Saʿada, see Mahmud Shurayh, *Khalil Hawi wa Antun Saʿada* (Beirut: Dar Nilsun, 1995). For a vivid if speculative account of Hawi's life, work, and suicide in 1982, see Fuad Ajami, *The Dream Palace of the Arabs* (New York: Random House, 1999), 26–100.

8. *Al-Adab* 9:3 (March 1961), 67–68.

9. *Shiʿr* 5:18 (Spring 1961), 175–81.

10. In the chapter he dedicates to al-Ghazali in *al-Thabit wa-l-mutahawwil* [The Fixed and the Dynamic] (1973), Adonis censures the eleventh-century theologian for limiting philosophical speculation by Qur'anic precept (Beirut: Dar al-Saqi, 2002), 3:49–55. Adonis's major text on the Egyptian poet Ahmed Shawqi is the introduction to *Diwan al-nahda* [Renaissance Anthology] (Beirut: Dar ʿIlm al-Malayyin, 1982), 5–19, where Adonis criticizes Shawqi as a derivative poet who recycled orthodox forms and rhetoric.

11. *Al-Adab* 9:7 (July 1961), 1–3. The title is from Khalil Hawi's poem "*Al-Majus fi urubba*" [The Magus in Europe]: "We are from Beirut, unfortunately, born / with borrowed

faces and borrowed minds. / Our thoughts are born as whores in the market / then spend their lives pretending to be virgins" (*Diwan*, 112–13).

12. *Shiʿr* 6:22 (Spring 1962), 5–16.

13. On these networks, see Steven Hyland, "'Arisen from Deep Slumber': Transnational Politics and Competing Nationalisms among Syrian Immigrants in Argentina, 1900–1922," *Journal of Latin American Studies* 43 (2011), 547–74; and Ilham Khuri-Makdisi, *The Eastern Mediterranean and the Making of Global Radicalism, 1860–1914* (Berkeley: University of California Press, 2010), 51–54.

14. Patrick Seale, *The Struggle for Syria: A Study of Post-war Arab Politics, 1945–1958* (New York: Oxford University Press, 1965), 68. ʿAflaq goes on to assert, "Among the many movements of Arab rebirth, this was one which aborted and lost itself in an unhealthy romanticism."

15. Albert Hourani notes that after Versailles, adherents of Syrian nationalism, unlike Iraqi or Egyptian nationalists, had no single state to focus their efforts on, and so the doctrine went into eclipse beginning around 1918. He also suggests that Saʿada's untimely revival of this ideology in the 1930s might be partly explained by his sojourn in South America during the intervening decade: "He may well have imbibed there the kind of Syrian patriotism which had been common among the educated class of Lebanon in the late nineteenth century, and which was preserved among the fossil communities of the Lebanese dispersion when it was tending to die out in the mother country itself." *Arabic Thought in the Liberal Age: 1878–1939* (Cambridge: Cambridge University Press, 1983), 317.

16. Antun Saʿada, *Al-Athar al-kamila*, 5:155.

17. For a discussion of Samné's and Lammens's work, including the latter's influence on Saʿada, see Kamal Salibi, *A House of Many Mansions: The History of Lebanon Reconsidered* (Berkeley: University of California Press, 1988), 130–50.

18. *Al-Athar al-kamila*, 5:153–54.

19. Yamak, *The Syrian Social Nationalist Party*, 144.

20. Adonis, *Ha anta*, 107, 70.

21. I will use the third edition (Beirut: al-Matbaʿa al-Tijariyya, 1955). Further references will be made in parentheses in the main text.

22. There are few studies of the southern *mahjar* group in English. See the two articles by C. Nijland, "A 'New Andalusian' Poem," *Journal of Arabic Literature* 17 (1987), 102–20; and "The Fatherland in Arab Emigrant Poetry," *Journal of Arabic Literature* 20:1 (March 1989), 57–68. A comprehensive resource is Salah al-Din Hawwari, *Shuʿaraʾ al-mahjar al-janubi* [Poets of the Southern Mahjar] (Beirut: Dar wa Maktabat al-Hilal, 2009).

23. *Shiʿr* 1:2 (Spring 1957), 2. The *jeudi* gathering is written up in *Shiʿr*'s fall issue of 1962, 157–58 (another guest at the salon was Charles Malik). Khalil Hawi, *Kahlil Gibran, His Background, Character and Works* (Beirut: Arab Institute for Research and Publishing, 1963); and *al-Nabi*, trans. Yusuf al-Khal (Beirut: Dar al-Nahar lil-Nashr, 1968).

24. *Nushuʾ al-umam*, 164; al-Khal's editorial, published in 1937, is cited in Jacques Amateis's biography, *Yusuf al-Khal wa majallatuhu 'Shiʿr'* (Beirut: Dar al-Nahar, 2004), 47.

25. For a discussion of the poem, a partial translation into English, and an analysis of its reception in Arab literary circles (Saʿada's contribution is mentioned en passant), see Nijland, "A 'New Andalusian' Poem."

26. *National Geographic* 64:1 (July 1933), 96–126.

27. James F. Goode, *Negotiating for the Past: Archaeology, Nationalism, and Diplomacy in the Middle East, 1919–1941* (Austin: University of Texas Press, 2017), 11.

28. The earliest and most influential of these studies is Asʿad Razzuq, *al-Ustura fi-l-shiʿr al-muʿasir* (op. cit.). See also Rita Awad, *Usturat al-mawt wa-l-inbiʿath fi-l-shiʿr al-ʿarabi al-hadith* (Beirut: al-Muʾassasa al-ʿArabiyya lil-Dirasat wa-l-Nashr, 1974); Barut,

al-Hadatha, 109–70; and Terri Lynn DeYoung, "And Thereby Hangs a Tale: A Study of Myth in Modern Arabic Poetry" (PhD diss., University of California, Berkeley, 1988), esp. chapter 4.

29. *Shiʿr* 2:7–8 (Summer–Fall 1958) 57–67. See Jabra Ibrahim Jabra, *Adunis: dirasa fi-l-asatir wa-l-adyan al-sharqiyya al-qadima* [Adonis: A Study of Ancient Eastern Myths and Religions] (Beirut: Dar al-Siraʿ al-Fikri, 1957).

30. Cf. Razzuq, *al-Ustura*, 9–17. On the reception of Eliot in Arabic, see Terri DeYoung, "T. S. Eliot and Modern Arabic Literature," *Yearbook of Comparative and General Literature* 48 (2000), 3–21; and al-Musawi, *Arabic Poetry*, 218–36.

31. The first serious study of the importance of Saʿada's mythological writings to the *Shiʿr* poets is Joseph Zeidan, "Myth and Symbol in the Poetry of Adūnis and Yūsuf al-Khāl," *Journal of Arabic Literature* 10 (1979), 70–94. The best study of Adonis's early nationalist poetry, which in most cases was never reprinted, is Sharbil Daghir, "Tawashujat al-idiyulujiya wa-l-hadatha: Antun Saʿada wa Adunis" [The Entanglements of Ideology and Modernity: Antun Saʿada and Adonis], *Fusul* (1997), 145–72.

32. *Al-Siraʿ al-Fikri*, 40.

33. See, for example, Adonis's essay "Muhawala li-taʿrif al-shiʿr al-hadith" [An Attempt to Define Modern Poetry], *Shiʿr* 3:11 (Summer 1959), 79–90.

34. Khalaf, *Lebanon's Predicament*, 247; Samir Kassir, *Beirut*, 461.

35. Samuel Weber, *Institution and Interpretation* (Minneapolis: University of Minnesota Press, 1987), 26–27; Franco Moretti, *Distant Reading* (London: Verso, 2013), 34.

36. Edward Said, *Out of Place* (New York: Knopf, 1999), 263–69. There is no monograph in any language on Malik's career as a professor, diplomat, and ideologue, though several scholars have focused on his role as a framer of the Universal Declaration of Human Rights. See Samuel Moyn, *The Last Utopia: Human Rights in History* (Cambridge: Harvard University Press, 2010), esp. 62–68; and Lydia Liu, "Shadows of Universalism: The Untold Story of Human Rights around 1948," *Critical Inquiry* 40:4 (Summer 2014), 385–417.

37. In the introduction to *Man in the Struggle for Peace*, Malik attempts to ground Heideggerian ontology in the tradition of Judeo-Christian humanism, in opposition to Sartre whose atheistic philosophy Malik brands as a version of "radical existential pride" (New York: Harper & Row, 1963), ix–xix. Traces of Heidegger's style of exposition are evident in Malik's 1956 address to the Cénacle libanais, "al-Wujud bil-fiʿl" [Actual Existence], a meditation on Lebanon's historical identity couched in an etymology of the Arabic verbs *"wajada"* [to exist, to find] and *"faʿala"* [to do, to make actual]. *ʿAhd al-Nadwa*, 311–19. Another Heideggerian tic, only apparent in Malik's English writings, is his penchant for hyphenated phrases: "existence-as-usual," "going-on-ness," "being-won-over," etc.

38. According to al-Khal, the focus of instruction was on the Arab and Western rationalist tradition. See *al-Nahar*, October 6, 1955, 4.

39. Al-Khal, *Dafatir al-ayyam*, 378, 370.

40. "From the Leader to Doctor Charles Malik," *al-Nizam al-jadid* 1:1 (March 1948), 61–65.

41. Quoted in Glenn Mitoma, "Charles H. Malik and Human Rights: Notes on a Biography," *Biography* 33:1 (Winter 2010), 232–33.

42. Hisham Sharabi, *Embers and Ashes: Memoirs of an Arab Intellectual*, trans. Issa J. Boullata (Massachusetts: Olive Branch Press, 2008), 17–25. Malik's son, Habib C. Malik, discusses his father's academic writings, with an emphasis on his relation to Kierkegaard, in "The Reception of Kierkegaard in the Arab World," in *Kierkegaard's International Reception, Volume 8, Tome III: The Near East, Asia, Australia and the Americas*, ed. Jon Stewart (Burlington: Ashgate, 2009), 41–49.

43. "Readings in Philosophy, Volume I," compiled and edited with an introduction by Malik (Beirut: n.p, 1939), 20

44. In this précis of his thought, I will rely on the following texts by Malik: "The Communist Doctrine of War and Revolution," *World Affairs* 113:3 (Fall 1950), 76-79; "Human Rights in the United Nations," *International Journal* 6:4 (Autumn 1951), 275-80; "The Near East: The Search for Truth," *Foreign Affairs* 30:2 (January 1952), 231-64; "The Relations of East and West," *Proceedings of the American Philosophical Society* 97:1 (February 1953), 1-7; "Call to Action in the Near East," *Foreign Affairs* 34:4 (July 1956), 637-54; "Some Urgent Tasks," *World Affairs* 124:4 (Winter 1961), 103-5; *The Individual in Modern Society* (Corning: Corning Glass Foundation, 1961); and *Man in the Struggle for Peace*.

45. *The Individual in Modern Society*, 14.

46. "Some Urgent Tasks," 105.

47. "The Relations of East and West," 6.

48. *Man in the Struggle for Peace*, 229 [emphasis in the original].

49. It is typical, too, of a much wider spectrum of postwar discourse. See William Inboden, *Religion and American Foreign Policy, 1945-1960: The Soul of Containment* (Cambridge: Cambridge University Press, 2008). Malik's participation in this stream of American religious and intellectual life predates World War II. In 1934, while a doctoral student at Harvard, he joined the Cambridge branch of Frank Buchman's Oxford Group, a precursor to the Moral Re-Armament movement (see Indoben's discussion, 191-97). Malik's belief that "the ultimate crisis" in world affairs was "entirely spiritual" echoes Buchman's thoughts on European rearmament: "The crisis is fundamentally a moral one. The nations must rearm morally. Moral recovery is essentially the forerunner of economic recovery." *Remaking the World: The Speeches of Frank N. D. Buchman* (London: Blanford Press, 1955), 46.

50. "The Relations of East and West," 7.

51. "The Near East: The Search for Truth," 239. Malik argued against the idea that Israel could play this role precisely because it was not "grounded" in either the Christian or the Muslim traditions.

52. "Call to Action in the Near East," 647-48. Given Malik's consistently spiritualist emphasis, it is somewhat surprising to find "freedom of enterprise" on this list of liberties. Malik argues in his Cénacle address that for Lebanon to achieve "real existence," it must institute "a regime that destroys economic injustice without infringing on personal liberty [al-hurriyya al-shakhsiyya]" (318). This tension is found throughout the corpus of Arabic modernist poetry, where Phoenician tropes of commercial "give and take" lie uneasily in a discourse that is profoundly antimaterialist.

53. "The Near East: The Search for Truth," 240.

54. "Lubnan al-wasit" [Lebanon the Middleman], *al-Huda* 57:2 (February 24, 1954). The cause Lebanon does not "betray" is presumably that of the Palestinians, whom Chamoun was often criticized for not supporting more strongly.

55. "Human Rights in the United Nations," 278. For Malik, the ideal person is Christ, "the supreme man and the supreme reality." But he recognized "man" as an ecumenical figure. See his introduction to *God and Man in Contemporary Islamic Thought*, ed. Charles Malik (Beirut: American University of Beirut, 1972), 1-100. Malik's interest in this figure can be traced back to his doctoral dissertation. In chapter 7, "Heidegger's Analysis of Man," Malik characteristically interprets Heidegger's ontology as a species of humanism, going so far as to translate *Dasein* as "man": "In this work I shall speak of man or Dasein interchangeably, meaning in either case the actual, living man in his personal, total, moral existence." "The Metaphysics of Time" (PhD diss., Harvard University, 1937), 267.

56. See Samuel Moyn, "Jacques Maritain, Christian New Order, and the Birth of Human Rights" (http://papers.ssrn.com/sol3/papers.cfm?abstract_id=1134345 [accessed

3/21/11]); and, more generally, his "Personalism, Community, and the Origins of Human Rights," in *Human Rights in the Twentieth Century*, ed. Stefan-Ludwig Hoffmann (Cambridge: Cambridge University Press, 2011). The most prominent spokesman for personalism in Lebanon was the philosopher René Habachi. See his 1960 lecture to the Cénacle libanais, "Un personnalisme de chez nous," '*Ahd al-nadwa al-lubnaniyya*, 377–87. Habachi's essay "Al-Shiʿr fi maʿrakat al-wujud" [Poetry in the Struggle for Existence] appeared in *Shiʿr*'s inaugural issue. *Shiʿr* 1:1 (Winter 1957), 88–95.

57. Moyn, *The Last Utopia*, 64–65.
58. "The Relations of East and West," 1.
59. "The Individual in Modern Society," 24. By his own account, Malik's most significant contribution to the Universal Declaration of Human Rights was Article 18's specification of "the right to freedom of thought, conscience, and religion," a phrasing that emphasized the right to inner freedoms rather than a religious minority's right to freedom of worship, which had been the overriding concern of previous international rights law. See Linde Lindkvist, "The Politics of Article 18: Religious Liberty in the Universal Declaration of Human Rights," *Humanity* 4:3 (Winter 2013), 429–47.
60. Jacques Maritain, *The Person and the Common Good*, trans. John J. Fitzgerald (Notre Dame: University of Notre Dame Press, 1966), 47.
61. "Some Urgent Tasks," 104.
62. *Man in the Struggle for Peace*, xl–xli. At the end of his book, Malik is more concrete in imagining this cohort of heroes: "If there are a hundred men, *well placed* in government, in the press, in industry, in labor, in the universities, and in the churches . . . who really believe that there is nothing like the values of the mind and spirit and man and God which have come down to Mediterranean-Western civilization from the last four thousand years—if there are one hundred such men, well placed and working as a team, then I believe we can rest" (230) [emphasis in the original].
63. Quoted in Amateis, *Yusuf al-Khal*, 55.
64. The lecture was reprinted a few months before the publication of *Shiʿr*'s first issue as "Fi mahiyyat al-shiʿr" [On the Essence of Poetry], *al-Adib* 11:15 (November 1956), 3–4.
65. Jacques Maritain, *Art and Scholasticism and The Frontiers of Poetry*, trans. Joseph W. Evans (New York: Charles Scribner's Sons, 1962); and *Khawatir ʿan amrika* [Thoughts on America], trans. Yusuf al-Khal (Beirut: Dar Majallat Shiʿr), 1958.
66. *Ibid.*, 53 [emphasis in the original], 9. This is one of the passages translated without acknowledgment by al-Khal. He renders "it delivers one from the human" as "*al-shiʿr yuharrir al-shaʿir min al-ihtimamat al-hayatiyya kullaha*" [poetry liberates the poet from all worldly cares].
67. *Ibid.*, 78, 37.
68. Yusuf al-Khal, *Al-aʿmal al-shiʿriyya al-kamila*, 19.
69. "Fi mahiyyat al-Shiʿr," 3.
70. *Al-Nahar*, Dec. 11, 1947, v. 3756, p. 1. The statement was also signed by Ghassan Tueni, publisher of *al-Nahar*. The immediate motive for their resignation was a purge of the party's upper echelons shortly after Saʿada's return from South America. In statements published in SSNP organs between December 1947 and January 1948, Saʿada accused the party's chief propagandist, Palestinian Fayez Sayegh, of spreading the doctrines of Nikolai Berdyaev (a lodestar in Malik's philosophical constellation), whose philosophy Saʿada characterized as "egotistical anarchism" and "personal individualism" [*al-shakhsiyya al-fardiyya*]. Against this creed, Saʿada argued for the primacy of the social and the national. See "al-Majmuʿ wa-l-mujtamaʿ" [The Group and Society] and "Madrasat al-ananiyya wa mahabbat al-dhat" [The School of Egotism and Self-Love] in *al-Athar al-kamila*, 14:184–87, 194–99.

71. Twenty years later, Malik's rhetoric of dignity, man, and Lebanese singularity acquired new uses. In January 1976, weeks after the massacre of Palestinians in the slum of Karantina in East Beirut, Malik helped found of a coalition of Christian groups called "The Front for Freedom and Man in Lebanon," later renamed the "Lebanese Front." This later history is presumably the cause for Edward Said's "bottomless disappointment" in his uncle by marriage.

72. The article begins, "Everyone has the right to freedom of thought, conscience and religion; this right includes freedom to change his religion or belief." See Lindkvist, "The Politics of Article 18."

73. The news service was the Middle East Service Bureau. In his biography, Amateis reproduces a page of publicity material that describes the company as "a non-political, non-governmental organization," with "no connection with any official institution." The services it offered included translation from Arabic to English and English to Arabic, publishing and printing, and advertising in the Middle East (see *Yusuf al-Khal*, appendix #10). Except that it published no poetry, this sounds like a trial run for *Shi'r*.

74. Quoted in Amateis, *Yusuf al-Khal*, 60.

75. "*Mustaqbal al-shi'r fi lubnan*" [The Future of Poetry in Lebanon], *'Ahd al-nadwa*, 337–44. Adonis calls al-Khal's lecture "the first theoretical manifesto for modernism in Arabic poetry" and quotes the ten principles in full (*Ha anta*, 61). The talk was summarized in the second issue of *Shi'r*, which also quotes the ten principles in full: 1:2 (Spring 1957), 96–99. For an English translation of the principles, see Jayyusi, *Trends and Movements*, 1:570–72.

76. Hunt was in correspondence with Asmar beginning in the summer of 1960 (see his letter of August 10, 1960, Series I, Box 164, IACF). Prior to his negotiations with Yusuf al-Khal, Hunt asked the French poet René Tavernier, a friend of the Congress on his way to Beirut, to determine whether the Congress's best option in Lebanon was to "affiliate ourselves with an already existing institution such as Michel Asmar's Cénacle." Hunt to Tavernier, June 12, 1961, Series I, Box 165, IACF.

77. *'Ahd al-nadwa*, 9.

78. Sa'ada, *al-Sira' al-fikri*, 61.

79. *'Ahd al-nadwa al-lubnaniyya*, 244 [my translation].

80. See Asher Kaufman, *Reviving Phoenicia: The Search for Identity in Lebanon* (New York: I. B. Tauris), 141–59. It was Sa'id 'Aql who translated Corm's poem into Arabic.

81. Michelle Hartman and Alessandro Olsaretti, "'The First Boat and the First Oar': Inventions of Lebanon in the Writings of Michel Chiha," *Radical History Review* 86 (Spring 2003), 45–46.

82. Antun Sa'ada, *al-Athar al-kamila*, vol. 5: *Nushu' al-umam* (Beirut: 'Umdat al-Thaqafa fi al-Hizb al-Suri al-Qawmi al-Ijtima'i, 1975), 111.

83. Elsewhere, al-Khal denied that "thought" [*al-fikr*] was a commercial good. In one of the columns he wrote for *al-Nahar* in the mid-1950s under the pen name "*Luqyan*" (after Lucian of Samosata, the Syrio-Grecian satirist), al-Khal derided the Lebanese mania for merchandise: "We have been traders since Plato, there is nothing new in that, nor is there anything shameful. What is shameful is that we should be traders even in thought. For thought and its content, which is knowledge, is not a commercial good." *Al-Nahar*, February 3, 1956. This is another example (cf. n.182) of that tension between entrepreneurialism and antimaterialism that runs through so many texts of Arabic modernism.

84. Malik delivered his lecture to the Cénacle in June 1956. *'Ahd al-Nadwa*, 314.

85. "*Sha'b*" is also the word al-Khal uses in the epigraph to his collection *Freedom*, which translates a passage from book 10 of *The Odyssey*. In al-Khal's version, Hermes' encouragement of Odysseus to rescue his companions [*hetairos*] from the prison of Circe

becomes a patriotic exhortation to liberate "your people" [shaʿbuka] from bondage. Additionally, the tenth and final principle of al-Khal's Cénacle speech was the admonition "to mix with the spirit of the people, not with nature."

86. Robinson Jeffers, *The Double Axe* (New York: Liveright, 1948), vii.

87. Perhaps it is not so unintuitive. I am reminded of Randall Jarrell's withering remarks in his essay "The End of the Line": "How could anyone fail to realize that the excesses of modernist poetry are the necessary concomitants of the excesses of late-capitalist society? (An example too pure and too absurd even for allegory is Robinson Jeffers, who must prefer a hawk to a man, a stone to a hawk, because of an individualism so exaggerated that it contemptuously rejects affections, obligations, relations of any kind whatsoever, and sets up as a nostalgically awaited goal the war of all against all. Old Rocky Face, perched on his sea crag, is the last of the *laissez faire*; Free Economic Man at the end of his rope.)" *Kipling, Auden and Co.* (New York: Farrar, Straus and Giroux, 1980), 82.

88. Yvor Winters, "Robinson Jeffers," *Poetry* (February 1930).

89. ʿAhd al-nadwa, 344.

90. *Al-Adab* 3:4 (March 1956), 1–2.

91. *Shiʿr* 6:2 (Spring 1962), 132.

92. Amateis, *Yusuf al-Khal*, 59.

93. *Shiʿr* 1:1 (Winter 1957), 73–81.

94. T. S. Eliot, *Tarjamat*, 3–4. Al-Khal notes that only in the case of Desmond Stewart and Buland Haydari's version of "Prufrock" does the translation "take a few liberties" [yatasarraf qalilan].

95. For a succinct characterization of nineteenth- and early twentieth-century Arabic attitudes toward translation, see Kadhim Jihad Hassan, *La part de l'étranger: la traduction de la poésie dans la culture arabe* (Paris: Sindbad, 2007), 142–53.

96. The same combination of fidelity and estrangement is at work in al-Khal and Adonis's translation of *The Waste Land*, where the German, French, Italian, and Latin phrases are reproduced in their original languages—that is, with Latin characters. In this case, as with Pound's extensive use of foreign phrases in the *Cantos*, the fidelity is exact and the estrangement effect comes from the juxtaposition of two different alphabets.

97. Al-Khal takes much of this biographical material from Hayden Carruth's essay "The Poetry of Ezra Pound," which al-Khal recommends at the end of his commentary. Significantly, Carruth begins by distinguishing between "expressionistic" poetry, in which the poem is "an instrument which conveys and arouses ... ideas or emotions," and "autonomistic" poetry, such as Pound's, whose texts are "self-sufficient." *Perspectives USA*, 16 (Summer 1956), 129–59. On the historical and political context for Carruth's essay, see Barnhisel, *The Remaking of Ezra Pound*, chapter 4, "Prying Apart Poetry and Politics."

98. Al-Khal, *Al-Aʿmal al-shiʿriyya al-kamila*, 198. Cf. Al-Musawi's comments in *Arabic Poetry*, 143, and Fakhreddine, *Metapoesis*, 32–34. Neither scholar quotes the final two lines, presumably because of their blatant anti-Jewish animus.

99. The multiple apostrophes of al-Khal's trilogy—"*Ayyuha-l-bahr, ayyuha-l-amal al-bahr*" [O sea, O hope-sea]—echo the famous cry of Grecian troops in Xenophon's *Anabasis*, "*Thalatta, Thalatta!*" As Amateis notes (*Yusuf al-Khal*, 66–67), al-Khal used this refrain as the title for an article written in 1955 for *al-Nahar*, which retells the story of the military retreat and ends with these remarks: "Those Greeks saw the sea as their salvation. And we, we who lived next to the sea before the Greeks, how many times have we turned our faces away from it, disbelieving it, forsaking its divine grace? ... Is the sea not our sole window on civilization?" In the original edition of *The Abandoned Well*, al-Khal used the article as a preface to "Call of the Sea," replacing the article's final line with a more pointed version of the question: "Is it not time for us to return?"

100. Al-Khal would have known, if only indirectly, of the maverick classicist Victor Bérard's *Les Phéniciens et l'Odyssée* (1902), which attempts to map a Phoenician Mediterranean *behind* the more familiar Homeric version: "Inventors of the alphabet, teachers of the Hellenes in astronomy, arithmetic, and navigation, the men of Tyre, according to Strabo, sailed the western seas beyond the columns of Hercules, where they founded cities shortly after the Trojan War; it is from them that Homer acquired his knowledge of the Occident." *Les Phéniciens et l'Odyssée* (Paris: Librairie Armand Colin, 1927), 1:18 [my translation]. Bérard, who translated *The Odyssey* into French, was a significant influence on the Lebanese neo-Phoenicians. It was to him that Charles Corm dedicated *La Montagne inspirée*. See Kaufman, *Reviving Phoenicia*, 144, 163, 212–13.

101. *Shiʿr* 1:1 (Winter 1957), 3–4. I have translated the text as an appendix to this chapter. No scholar so far as I am aware has tracked down a source for it in MacLeish's papers. His published correspondence makes no mention of *Shiʿr*, and there is nothing in the text to suggest he wrote it specifically for the magazine.

102. Evan Kindley, *Poet-Critics and the Administration of Culture* (Harvard: Harvard University Press, 2017), esp. 73–85.

103. For a more detailed account of this episode, see A. David Moody, *The Tragic Years, 1939–1972*, vol. 3 of *Ezra Pound: Poet* (Oxford: Oxford University Press, 2015), 376–77.

104. Adonis, *Ha anta*, 132.

105. See Peter Bürger, *Theory of the Avant-Garde* (Minneapolis: University of Minnesota Press, 1984).

Chapter 3: Figuration and Disfiguration in The Songs of Mihyar the Damascene

1. I will refer to the original edition of the poems, published in Beirut by Dar Majallat Shiʿr. The English translation is *Mihyar of Damascus, His Songs*, trans. Adnan Haydar and Michael Beard (Rochester: BOA Editions, 2008), 12. Here as elsewhere I use my own translations.

2. DeYoung suggests that in *Mihyar* we see "Adūnis creating a new myth, one not wholly dependent on just the mythopoetic reshaping of previously existing models" ("And Thereby Hangs a Tale," 262). Adel Daher, "al-Tashakhsun wa-l-takhatti" [Personalization and Transcendence in *The Songs of Mihyar the Damascene*], *Shiʿr* 6:24 (Spring 1962), 108–37. Thirty-five years later, Daher's article was republished in a slightly different form for a special number devoted to Adonis of the Cairene journal *Fusul* (1997), 199–217. As if to acknowledge the desuetude of the discourse of man, the quoted sentence in the revised version reads, "*tajriba jadida fi-l-khalq al-dhati*" [a new experiment in self-creation]. The article forms the basis for Daher's book-length study of Adonis, *al-Shiʿr wa-l-wujud* [Poetry and existence] (Damascus: Dar al-Mada lil-Thaqafa wa-l-Nashr, 2000).

3. *ʿAhd al-Nadwa*, 383.

4. First published in *Shiʿr* 5:20 (Fall 1961), 10.

5. Cf. Badawi, *A Critical Introduction*, 237. The use of Poundian personae was rampant among Arab poets in the 1950s, and many critics refer to Mihyar as a *qinaʿ*. See Jabir ʿAsfur, "Aqniʿat al-Shiʿr al-Muʿasir" [The Masks of Modern Poetry], *Fusul*, 1:4 (July 1981), 123–48.

6. "*Al-dakhil*" can also be translated as "the immigrant" (literally, "one who goes inside"). It is in this sense that the word is used as an epithet for ʿAbd al-Rahman (731–788), the Umayyad prince who fled Damascus during the ʿAbbasid revolt and "immigrated" to al-Andalus, where he founded the Emirate of Córdoba. As I will suggest, the emigration from Damascus is an important underlying narrative for the poems of *Aghani Mihyar*, although the ambiguity of "*al-dakhil*" also suggests a kind of "interior immigration" or katabasis of the self.

7. *Shiʿr* 6:23 (Summer 1962), 109–24. Barakat, who came from a Greek Orthodox family, had been a member of the SSNP and was friendly with the *Shiʿr* poets. His memoir of the 1950s and early 1960s in Beirut, which covers his relations with Adonis, Yusuf al-Khal, and Charles Malik, along with his experience in Saʿada's party, is *al-Madina al-mulawwana* (Beirut: Dar al-Saqi, 2006).

8. "Al-Tashakhsun wa-l-takhatti," 116. In his comments on Husserl, Daher is citing the essay of Hans Meyerhoff, "The Return to the Concrete," *Chicago Review* 13:2 (Summer 1959), 27–38, from which Daher borrows several formulations. Daher attributes the notion of "*l'homme-masse*" to the Christian existentialist Gabriel Marcel, but this seems to be a mistake.

9. *La Revue* Shiʿr, 302. Emphasis and capitalization in the original. I have discussed the merits and shortcomings of Badini's book more extensively in a review for *The Journal of Arabic Literature*, 44 (2013), 103–7.

10. *A Singular Modernity*, 131–36. This trope of the inward turn also survives in recent accounts of Arabic modernism such as Fakhreddine's, who understands poetic modernism—whether of the eighth or the twentieth century—to be centered on the figure of metapoesis, a trope of self-reflexivity and "poetic introspection" (*Metapoesis*, 15).

11. This is the date provided by Adonis in an interview with *Al-Nahar*, March 21, 2010 (http://international.daralhayat.com/internationalarticle/121365 [retrieved 3/24/10]). *Shiʿr*'s editorial in the spring issue of 1962 suggests an earlier date of 1958, though it is unclear whether an official resignation is implied. *Shiʿr* 6:22 (Spring 1962), 9. For a brief biography of Adonis by his primary French translator, see Anne Wade Minkowski, "Biographie d'Adonis," in *Adonis, Un poète dans le monde d'aujourd'hui, 1950–2000* (Paris: Institut du monde arabe, 2000), 202–86.

12. Adonis, *Le regard d'Orphée, conversations avec Houria Abdelouahed* (Paris: Fayard, 2009), 20 [my translation].

13. The poem has never been republished. I borrow my summary from Daghir's "Tawashujat al-Idiyulujiya," 156–58.

14. Adonis, *al-Aʿmal al-shiʿriyya al-kamila* [The Complete Works of Poetry], 1949–1961 (Beirut: Dar al-Saqi, 2012), 1:7.

15. Yamak, *The Syrian Social Nationalist Party*, 70.

16. Adonis, *Le regard d'Orphée*, 26–27. Adonis's experience in prison is the subject of his short verse play "al-Sadim" [The Mist], published in *Awraq fi-l-rih*, 107–18.

17. Hélène Cixous, in her suggestive preface to the French translation of *Aghani Mihyar*, wonders, "Who is this Mihyar? Who is the one called 'Damascene'?" Cixous's answer has Rimbaldian overtones (and is in this sense influenced by Adonis's efforts at self-canonization): "It isn't this Mihyar, nor that one. . . . Mihyar, *someone else*. Someone immediately Other." [*Ce n'est pas ce Mihyar-ci ni ce Mihyar-là. . . . Mihyar*, quelqu'un d'Autre. *Quelqu'un immédiatement d'Autre.*] *Chants de Mihyar le Damascène*, trans. Anne Wade Minkowski and Jacques Berque (Paris: Gallimard, 2002), 11.

18. *Shiʿr* 2:7–8 (Summer–Fall 1958), 10–23.

19. In the "definitive" Dar al-Adab texts of 1988, Adonis removed "Elegy" from *The Songs of Mihyar* but reprinted that version (with still further abbreviations) among the poems of *Leaves in the Wind* (Beirut: Dar al-Adab, 1988), 111–17.

20. This translation was first published in *The Paris Review* 217 (Summer 2016), 162, as "Elegy for the Times."

21. For Perse's translation, printed in the magazine *Commerce* in 1924, see his *Œuvres complètes* (Paris: Gallimard, 1972), 465. All citations of Perse are from this edition; the translations are my own.

22. *Ibid.*, 128.

23. Saint-John Perse, *On Poetry*, trans. W. H. Auden (New York: Bollingen Foundation, 1961), 10.

24. *Shiʿr* 1:4 (Fall 1957), 38–89. This is a year before Wallace Fowlie's English translation of the first four sections in *Encounter*, September 1958.

25. *Œuvres complètes*, 264, 330.

26. Perse, *al-Aʿmal al-shiʿriyya al-kamila*, trans. Adonis, 2 vols. (Damascus: Wizarat al-Thaqafa wa-l-Irshad al-Qawmi, 1976, 1978). The debate was inadvertently set off by the Palestinian critic Ihsan ʿAbbas, who noted that "Elegy for the Present Days" includes at least one phrase that is "almost a literal translation" from Perse. ʿAbbas, who did not believe the translation was in any way illicit, pointed to the phrase "*Al-layl yatakhaththar wa fawqa juthath al-ʿasafir tadubb tufulat al-nahar*" [Night thickens and day's infancy creeps over the corpses of sparrows], which rewrites a phrase from the fifth section of Perse's *Exil*, "*Sur des squelettes d'oiseaux nains s'en va l'enfance de ce jour.*" ʿAbbas, *Ittijahat al-shiʿr al-muʿasir* (Kuwait: al-Majlis al-Watani lil-Thaqafa wa-l-Funun wa-l-Adab, 1978), 141. In subsequent editions of the poem, beginning with the 1988 Dar al-ʿAwda edition, Adonis placed this phrase, along with two others, between parentheses, and he added a note acknowledging they were cited from Perse. Al-Munsif al-Wahhayibi's study, *al-Jasad al-marʾi wa-l-jasad al-mutakhayyal fi shiʿr Adunis* (1987), uncovered further unacknowledged borrowings from Perse, both in this poem and subsequent ones. Al-Wahhayibi's researches were extended by the Iraqi poet and scholar Kadhim Jihad in his now notorious book, *Adunis muntahilan* [Adonis as Plagiarist] (Cairo: Maktabat Madbuli, 1993). Jihad argues that Adonis's use of Perse was not a legitimate case of *tanas* [intertextuality] but rather deserves the term *intihal* [plagiarism], a word with its own long history in classical Arabic poetics. The Tunisian critic ʿAli al-Lawati, himself a translator of Perse into Arabic, mounted a second polemic. In the preface to his own version, al-Lawati detailed Adonis's errors of translation, some of them quite blatant, which he blamed on a faulty knowledge of French language and culture. See *Jinayat Adunis ʿala San Jun Birs* [Adonis's Crimes against Saint-John Perse] (Paris: Manshurat al-Nuqta, 1990). A reprise of these debates is provided by Nebil Radhouane, "Adonis Descendant de Saint-John Perse," in *Modernité de Saint-John Perse? Actes du colloque de Besançon des 14, 15 et 16 mai 1998*, ed. Catherine Mayaux (Besançon: Presses universitaires franc-comtoises, 2001), 401–13. All these controversies suppose that questions of literary authority can be decided by appeals to settled categories (accuracy, intertextuality, plagiarism) when it is precisely such categories that are at stake in modernist poetics. All quotations, even the unacknowledged kind, are translations. What distinguishes the *Shiʿr* group from their rivals is the argument that literary authority can be established by translation. For them, the institution of modernism is founded on such acts.

27. Saint-John Perse, *Anabasis*, trans. T. S. Eliot (New York: Harcourt Brace, 1949). The Bollingen editions of Perse's poetry include similarly detailed bibliographies of translations.

28. See Hugo Verani, "Octavio Paz y el primer poema," *Revista de la Universidad de Mexico* 12 (April 1982), 3. For Seferis's partial translation of *Amers*, unpublished during his lifetime, see Saint-John Perse, *Amers (apospasma)*, trans. Giorgos Seferis, ed. May Chehab (Athens: Ekdoseis Gavrielides, 2011).

29. *Shiʿr* 1:4 (Fall 1957), 83–89.

30. Perse, *Anabasis*, trans. T. S. Eliot, 9. The prefaces by Larbaud (trans. Jacques Le Clerq) and Hofmannsthal (trans. James Stern) are included in Eliot's edition, 101–7. These deracinated interpretations of Perse are of course rejected by the poet's Caribbean readers, who often pit Perse against Aimé Césaire in an agon of white and black poetic fathers. For Derek Walcott, it is precisely the rootedness of Perse's early poetry in its local landscape that makes it preferable to the "hammered and artificial" rhetoric of the later epics. Cf. *What the Twilight Said* (New York: Farrar, Straus and Giroux, 1998), 50–54.

31. "Saint-John Perse and I," *Mawaqif* 29 (Fall 1974), 164.

32. "Conférence d'Adonis donnée à la Fondation Saint-John Perse le 9 octobre 1993," *Souffle de Perse* 4 (1994), trans. Anne Wade-Minkowski, 4–9. In the same lecture, Adonis responds to the criticisms of his translations made by ʿAli al-Lawati (cf. n. 26). Adonis acknowledges some errors but argues that in general "the translator must follow the genius of the language of arrival rather than the laws of the language of departure."

33. The extracts from Lautréamont are precisely those portions that begin with an apostrophe to the sea: *"Vieil océan, tu es le symbole de l'identité: toujours égal à toi-même"* [Old ocean, you are the symbol of identity: always equal to yourself]. To highlight the mythic, Mediterranean atmospheres of this invocation, the translator Shawqi Abu Shaqra renders *"océan"* as *"Uqianus"* [Oceanus] as though it were the proper name of a divinity. *Shiʿr* 3:10 (Spring 1959), 74–86.

34. An antithetical use of this pun occurs at the end of Mahmoud Darwish's Beirut memoir, *Memory for Forgetfulness*. Waiting to embark on the boats that will take the PLO to Tunis, Darwish encounters a soldier who asks about the meaning of *"al-bahr"* in poetry. "Is *al-bahr* in poetry the same as *al-bahr* in *al-bahr*?" he asks. "Yes," the poet responds, *"al-bahr* is *al-bahr*, in poetry and in prose, and at the edge of the land." The soldier is sure there is some "symbolic" meaning to *"al-bahr"* in poetry, but Darwish assures him, "My *bahr* is your *bahr*—it's the same *bahr*. We are from one *bahr* and we are going to one *bahr*" (*Dhakira lil-nisyan*, 186). Darwish's insistence on the nonsymbolic character of *"al-bahr"* is partly a gibe at the modernists, whose valorization of the sea-voyage is so at odds with Darwish's own poetic and political experience of exile.

35. Adonis makes a similar claim in a note to his second prose poem, "Arwad, Princess of Illusion," where he suggests rather vaguely that his prosodic innovations are indebted to "several European poets," but also writes that, "For the style [*uslub*] of this poem, as for 'Only Despair,' I have relied on the old poetic style of Phoenicia and the Fertile Crescent." *Shiʿr* 3:10 (Spring 1959), 7–8. The prose poem is thereby figured as a bequeathal of ancient Near Eastern literature as well as modern French. On the prayer for rain, see the entry "Istiskāʾ," *Encyclopaedia of Islam*, 2nd ed., ed. T. Fahd. Fahd notes that the rogatory rite dates back to the earliest period of Arab history.

36. Roger Little, "The Image of the Threshold in the Poetry of Saint-John Perse," *Modern Language Review* 64:4 (October 1969), 777–92. And see Little's *Word Index of the Complete Poetry and Prose of Saint-John Perse* (Durham: Durham University, 1965).

37. Little suggests the *"portes ouvertes"* of the first line allude to the Roman practice of closing the gates of the temple of Janus during times of peace and opening them in times of war. He also examines the many connotations of *"l'astre roué vif,"* in which early critics discerned an allusion to the swastika (an interpretation Perse characteristically rejected).

38. "Who Are You?" is also the title of a short poem, another dialogue, at the end of the collection. The question is posed again in the first line of the poem "Odysseus": "Who are you? From what peak have you come, / O virgin tongue unknown to any but yourself, / What is your name?" This rewrites the close of book 8 of Homer's epic, in which Odysseus is confronted by Alkínoös after the king observes him weeping at the song of the minstrel: "Friend, you must not be / secretive any longer! Come, in fairness, / tell me the name you bore in that far country; / how were you known to family, and neighbors? / No man is nameless" (Fitzgerald's translation). *"Udis,"* Adonis's idiosyncratic spelling of "Odysseus," is a near anagram of *"Adunis"* (it is only missing the letter *nun*), and questions about names are obviously pertinent for a poet with such a flamboyant alias. In *Mufrad bi-sighat al-jamʿ* [Singular in Plural Form] (1975), a long poem full of cabalistic sleights, Adonis juxtaposes the letters of his own name with those of Orpheus [*Urfiyus*].

39. *Diwan al-shiʿr al-ʿarabi*, 3 vols. (Beirut: al-Maktaba al-ʿAsriyya, 1964), 2:11. In the same vein, see his essay "An Attempt to Define Modern Poetry," 86–89, as well as the later

essay, "Al-Ghumud wa-l-Wuduh" [Obscurity and Clarity], in *Zaman al-shiʿr*, 2nd ed. (Beirut: Dar al-ʿAwda, 1987), 275–84.

40. For classical critics' writings on *iltifat*, see Geert Jan Van Gelder, "The Abstracted Self in Arabic Poetry," *Journal of Arabic Literature* 14 (1983), 22–30.

41. Jonathan Culler, "Apostrophe," *diacritics* 7 (1977), 62.

42. Adonis's apostrophic technique may stem in part from his encounter with Perse. In his appendix to the translation of "Étroits sont les vaisseaux," Adonis makes special note of Perse's habit of "changing the grammatical person [*al-shakhs*] within the same dialogue," a practice that Adonis claims "animates the poem" [*yuhyi al-qasida*]. (This echoes the canonical justification for the *iltifat* by the twelfth-century critic al-Zamakhshari, who writes that the ancient Arabs "were wont to diversify their speech, for when one passes from one mode to another, this refreshes the mental energy of the listener." Cited in Van Gelder, "The Abstracted Self," 24.) Another of Adonis's models for the technique of multiplying voices is Yves Bonnefoy's *Du mouvement et de l'immobilité de Douve*, seven poems of which were anonymously translated—presumably by Adonis—for the second issue of *Shiʿr* 1:2 (Spring 1957), 67–74. In the section entitled "Douve Speaks," poems spoken by the dead heroine are interpolated with a series of other voices, whose poems are titled "*Une voix*" [A Voice], or "*Une autre voix*" [Another Voice], just as several of the poems in *Songs of Mihyar* are subtitled "*Aswat*" [Voices].

43. Michael Beard and Adnan Haydar, "Making Mihyar: The Familiarization of Adunis's Knight of Strange Words," *Literature East and West* 25 (1989), 87.

44. *Modern Epic*, 16. At the end of his chapter, Moretti qualifies this ascription of universality. "'Universal individual of mankind' Faust has been called: true, and false. False, if this is taken to mean that his person combines within it all that is significant in modern humankind. True, if it means that Goethe put Faust in a position to desire, and obtain, the advantages of an entire world" (34). Moretti, like Berman in *All That Is Solid*, reads Faust as a figure of Western imperial domination: his taste for totality is the ambition of hegemonic capital itself. But it is worth noting that this desire for "the advantages of an entire world" is also a feature of so-called peripheral modernisms, where the desire is not so much for domination as for inclusion.

45. Richard Poirier, "Modernism and Its Difficulties," in *The Renewal of Literature* (New Haven: Yale University Press, 1987), 107.

46. *Ibid.*, 108. I have focused on the displacements of *iltifat*, what linguists call pronominal shifters, but there are other examples. One example is Adonis's fondness for the metagram, in which a word is transformed by the displacement of individual letters. Here is an example from the final stanza of "Ard al-Sihr" [Land of Enchantment], from *The Songs of Mihyar*: "*Wa-lam tazal ardi ard al-sihr: / Ughalitu al-hawaʾ / Ajrahu wajh al-maʾ / Akhruju min qinnina fi-l-bahr*" [My land remains the land of enchantment: / I beguile the wind / I wound the face of the water / I emerge from a bottle in the sea]. "*Ajrahu*" and "*akhruju*," "*sihr*" and "*bahr*," "*hawa*" and "*wajh*" are metagrams. These are local examples, but the principle of the metagram might be expanded. The keywords of *Songs of Mihyar* are themselves a kind of *alchimie du verbe*: *baʿth* [rebirth], *bahth* [search], *bahr* [sea], *jurh* [wound], *hajar* [stone], *hibr* [ink], *ghubar* [dust], *qabr* [tomb], *barq* [lightning flash]. These games of word golf suggest the poet is being guided by vagaries of sound and orthography rather than semantics.

It was Roger Caillois who first pointed out the frequent use Saint-John Perse makes of metagram ("Une poésie encyclopédique," *Les Cahiers de la Pléiade*, Summer–Fall 1950, 101). For example, in *Vents*: "*Le vin nouveau n'est pas plus vrai, le lin nouveau n'est pas plus frais*"; or, in *Amers*, "*couvées de cailles et coulées d'ailes.*" Suzanne Bernard, whose study of the prose poem heavily influenced the modernists' theorization of the form, cites Caillois's discussion of this figure in detail. Suzanne Bernard, *Le Poème en prose de Baudelaire jusqu'à nos jours* (Paris: Librairie Nizet, 1959), 756–57. I will say more about the modernists' encounter with Bernard in the following chapter.

47. "Apostrophe," 67.

48. In the definitive edition of *Aghani Mihyar* (1988), these are the last two poems of the volume. In the original 1961 edition, they are followed by two long prose poems, "Elegy for the Present Days" and "Elegy for the First Century."

49. For *"rasama al-dar,"* Lane translates, *"It* (the rain) *rased the house* or *dwelling,* or *the houses* or *dwellings, leaving a relic,* or *relics, thereof cleaving to the ground."* Edward Lane, *An Arabic-English Lexicon* (Beirut: Librairie du Liban, 1997), 3:1084.

50. The rhetoric and themes of these last two poems, their elegiac apostrophes and images of burial and disfigurement, read again like condensed translations of Bonnefoy's *Du mouvement et de l'immobilité de Douve* (cf. note 43), a series of love poems set in the inamorata's grave, which were anonymously translated for the second issue of *Shiʿr*. One of the seven translated texts is poem XIII from the opening section, "Théâtre," which is particularly suggestive: *"Ton visage ce soir éclairé par la terre, / mais je vois tes yeux se corrompre / et le mot visage n'a plus de sens."* The "figure" of a face being disfigured, or rendered meaningless, is repeated many times. In "Vrai Nom," another of the poems translated for *Shiʿr*: *"Je nommerai désert ce château que tu fus, / Nuit cette voix, absence ton visage."* And elsewhere in the collection: *"Es-tu vraiment morte ou joues-tu / Encore en tout miroir / A perdre ton reflet, ta chaleur et ton sang / Dans l'obscurcissement d'un visage immobile?"* ("Le Seul Témoin"); *"O douée d'un profil où s'acharne la terre, / Je te vois disparaître"* ("Théâtre, XV"). Bonnefoy's early poetry attracted the attention of Arab modernists for many reasons, but especially for its mythic structures of death and rebirth, allegorized by animals such as the salamander and phoenix ("Lieu de la Salamandre" was another of the seven poems selected by *Shiʿr*). Khalida Saʿid notes the similarity between the bestiaries of Adonis and Bonnefoy in her article on "Resurrection and Ashes" (*Shiʿr* 2:5 [Winter 1958], 92–109). Later in his career, Adonis translated four volumes of Bonnefoy: *al-Aʿmal al-shiʿriyya al-kamila* [The Complete Poems] (Damascus: Manshurat Wizarat al-Thaqafa, 1986). Contrary to the title, this is not a translation of Bonnefoy's complete works but of *Poèmes* (Paris: Gallimard, 1982), including the preface by Jean Starobinski. The versions of *Douve* in this edition are distinct from those published in *Shiʿr* in 1958, though they may well be revisions.

51. See, for example, Margot and Rudolf Wittkower, *Born under Saturn* (New York: New York Review Books, 2007), which examines how Renaissance painters in Italy and northern Europe used the discourse of melancholia, interpreted as a symptom of genius, creativity, and alienation, to differentiate themselves from medieval craftsmen. What I am proposing, in a similar vein, is not a psychoanalysis of art or of artists but an attempt to explain how this self-diagnosis became useful to certain artists during a period of historical transition.

52. Sigmund Freud, "Mourning and Melancholia" (1917), in *The Standard Edition of the Complete Psychological Works of Sigmund Freud*, ed. and trans. James Strachey (London: Hogarth Press, 1953–74), 14:244.

53. Julia Kristeva, *Black Sun: Depression and Melancholia*, trans. Leon S. Roudiez (New York: Columbia University Press, 1989), 99, 164.

54. I am thinking of the dynamic famously elaborated by Adorno in *Aesthetic Theory*. The experience of the modern, Adorno writes, "Is more the negation of what no longer holds than a positive slogan. It does not, however, negate previous artistic practices, as

styles have done throughout the ages, but rather tradition itself.... This is why the modern when it was first theoretically articulated—in Baudelaire—bore an ominous aspect. The new is akin to death." *Aesthetic Theory*, trans. Robert Hullot-Kentor (Minneapolis: University of Minnesota Press, 1998), 21.

Chapter 4: The Origins of the Arabic Prose Poem

1. Nazik al-Mala'ika, *Qadaya al-shi'r al-mu'asir*, 2nd ed. (Baghdad: Manshurat Maktabat al-Nahda, 1964), 182, 185. Her chapter on the prose poem is based on an earlier essay, "Qasidat al-Nathr," published in *al-Adab* 10:4 (April 1962), 5–9. In addition to the studies by Moreh, Jayyusi, and Barut, three works I have found helpful on the subject of *qasidat al-nathr* are Ahmad Bazzun, *Qasidat al-nathr al-'arabiyya: al-itar al-nazari* (Beirut: Dar al-Fikr al-Jadid, 1996); Sami Mahdi, *Ufuq al-hadatha wa hadathat al-namat* (Baghdad: Dar al-Shu'un al-Thaqafiyya al-'Ama, 1988); and 'Abd al-Karim Hasan, *Qasidat al-nathr wa intaj al-dalala* (Beirut: Dar al-Saqi, 2008).

2. Moreh and Barut, among others, have noted formal precedents for the *qasidat al-nathr* in the unmetered *al-shi'r al-manthur* [prosified poetry] of *mahjar* writers such as Ameen Rihani and Khalil Gibran as well as the mixed meters of the Egyptian poet Abu Shadi in the 1930s. This suggests that the dissociation of metrical forms is a consistent trend in Arabic poetry—as with so many other poetries—of the twentieth century. In metrical terms, there is no difference between *al-shi'r al-manthur*, for which Rihani claimed a specifically Whitmanian precedent, and the *qasidat al-nathr*; the modernists simply removed the line breaks maintained by *mahjari* poets. Such considerations certainly cast doubt on the modernists' assertions of novelty, and yet the identification of precedents makes it less rather than more evident why so much attention and outrage should have centered on the *qasidat al-nathr* in the first place.

3. *Shi'r* 6:24 (Fall 1962), 146.

4. *Sea-Marks*, 122. It is typical of Perse's classicism that this phrase is itself an alexandrine with an emphatic caesura.

5. Khaled Furani has analyzed the development of *al-shi'r al-hurr* and the *qasidat al-nathr* within a narrative of secular modernity. For Furani, the chief symptoms of this modernity are its tendency to "compartmentalize"—that is, to separate not just religion from politics but also poetry from politics and poetry from orality—and its production of "self-sovereignty," a form of autonomy that keeps itself aloof from the "corrosive effects of the public or the authority of traditional meters." Khaled Furani, *Silencing the Sea: Secular Rhythms in Palestinian Poetry* (Stanford: Stanford University Press, 2012), 20. I agree with Furani regarding the importance of these two interrelated phenomena—specialization and autonomy—to Arabic modernism, but "the secular" strikes me as the wrong category for understanding them. The tempo of secularization is that of the longue durée, and it cannot give a satisfying account of why free poetry developed when and where it did, nor for why the prose poem—a quantum leap in the separation of poetry from orality as well the discourse of autonomy—succeeded it a mere decade afterward. I believe the modernists' emphasis on autonomy and their ethos of professionalism are better understood as symptoms of late modernism in its peculiarly Lebanese variant.

6. Adonis, "On the Prose Poem," *Shi'r* 4:14 (Spring 1960), 77. Suzanne Bernard, *Le Poème en prose de Baudelaire jusqu'à nos jours* (Paris: Librairie Nizet, 1959), 11, 764, 773 (emphases in the original). Significantly for Adonis, Bernard's historical narrative culminates with a reading of Perse, a poet she describes as "outside of time" with "few real disciples" (762). For discussions of the *Shi'r* poets' extensive use of Bernard, see Mahdi, *Ufuq al-hadatha*, 137–48, and Badini, *La Revue* Shi'r, 318–25.

7. al-Malaʾika, *Qadaya al-shiʿr*, 193–95. Al-Malaʾika's belief that meter is the essence of poetry affects her practice of translation and differentiates it from that of the modernists. The Iraqi poet's most consequential translation was a rhyming and metered Arabic version of Thomas Gray's "Elegy Written in a Country Churchyard," included in her first collection of poems, *ʿAshiqat al-layl* (1947). On this text, see the sensitive comments by Muhammad Abdul-Hai, *Tradition and English and American Influence in Arabic Romantic Poetry* (London: Ithaca Press, 1982), 27–29. The modernists, by contrast, produced no metrical translations. Mustafa al-Khatib's version of Paul Valéry's "Le Cimetière Marin" is one of the few published in *Shiʿr* (its rhyme scheme is also identical to the original). Al-Khatib's translation is prefaced with an editorial note, likely by Yusuf al-Khal, that wonders skeptically "whether the translator has succeeded, using this method, in conveying the translated poem's meanings and its poetic atmosphere? Is this method always the right one for poetic translation, or shall we prefer a poetic translation liberated from the chains of inherited meters?" *Shiʿr* 3:12 (Fall 1959), 75.

8. *Ibid.*, 193. The link between poetry and *tarab* was a classical commonplace. As the eleventh-century critic Ibn Rashiq writes in *al-ʿUmda*, "There is no doubt that poetry is what provokes *tarab* [*al-shiʿr ma atraba*], moving the soul and stirring the senses." Rashiq believed this virtue was unique to Arabic poetry. Quoted in Abdelfattah Kilito, *La langue d'Adam* (Casablanca: Toubkal, 1995), 39–40. Kilito goes on to note that for many classical critics, including al-Jahiz in the ninth century, *wazn* was the fundamental constituent of Arabic poetry and also what made that poetry strictly "untranslatable."

9. Cf. "Tarab," *Encyclopaedia of Islam*, 2nd ed., ed. J. Lambert. The fullest work on *tarab* is Ali Jihad Racy, *Making Music in the Arab World: The Culture and Artistry of Ṭarab* (Cambridge: Cambridge University Press, 2003). On the Egyptian singers and their role in midcentury politics, see Virginia Danielson, *The Voice of Egypt: Umm Kulthūm, Arabic Song, and Egyptian Society in the Twentieth Century* (Chicago: University of Chicago Press, 1997), 198.

10. Adonis, "On the Prose Poem," 75. Unsi al-Hajj, *Lan* (Beirut: Dar Majallat Shiʿr, 1960), 10. Khalida Saʿid's review was published in *Shiʿr* 5:18 (Spring 1961), 149–61. Baudelaire, *Oeuvres complètes I*, ed. Claude Pichois (Paris: Gallimard, 1975), 275–76 [my translation].

11. See Harden, *Saʿada fi-l-mahjar*, 1:133–34.

12. *al-Siraʿ al-Fikri*, 44–45, 54–55.

13. For a relevant discussion of the debates over *tarab*, modernism, and tradition among contemporary Syrian musicians, see Jonathan Shannon, *Among the Jasmine Trees: Music and Modernity in Contemporary Syria* (Middletown, Conn.: Wesleyan University Press, 2006), esp. chapter 5, "*Tarab*, Sentiment, and Authenticity," 158–87.

14. Yusuf al-Khal, *Thamrat al-funun* 1:3 (January 25, 1941), 1; cited in Amateis, *Yusuf al-Khal*, 43. Al-Hajj's articles appeared in *Al-Adib* 14:3 (March 1955), 29–32; 14:7 (July 1955), 25–31. See the commentary by Dounia al-Badini in *Une figure de la modernité poétique libanaise: Ounsi el-Hage* (Beirut: Université Saint-Joseph, 2007), 34–41. Jabra Ibrahim Jabra, *Tammuz fi-l-madina* (Beirut: Dar Majallat Shiʿr, 1959), 7. In the same passage, Jabra speaks of himself as "musicifying thought" [*umawsiq al-fikr*], a neologism Adonis borrows in *Aghani Mihyar*, where his protagonist, with Orphic overtones, claims to "musicify the depths" [103]. "Symphonic construction": Adonis, "An Attempt to Define Modern Poetry," 89.

15. *Shiʿr* 4:14 (Spring 1960), 80.

16. *Lan*, 7, 13.

17. Carl Dahlhaus, *The Idea of Absolute Music*, trans. Roger Lustig (Chicago: University of Chicago Press, 1989).

18. *On Poetry*, trans. W. H. Auden, 11.

19. *Shiʿr* 5:18 (Spring 1961), 171.

20. *Lan*, 4-15.

21. *Al-Adab* 9:7 (July 1961), 2; *Al-Adab* 9:4 (April 1961), 18; *Al-Adab* 9:3 (March 1961), 67. See Kheir Beik, *Le mouvement moderniste*, 135-37, for a more detailed discussion of the modernists' "vulgarization" of the poetic lexicon.

22. The letter was originally published in *al-Nahar*, February 3, 1961. It was reprinted in *Zaman al-shiʿr*, 225-31.

23. Al-Hajj, *Lan*, 15. As Badini notes, *al-saratan* is in part an autobiographical trope: al-Hajj's mother died of cancer when he was seven years old, a trauma whose impact he has acknowledged and emphasized. See *Une figure*, 23-25.

24. *Lan*, 85. In his letter from Paris, Adonis lauded al-Hajj for this break with previous notions of eloquence: "The scream [*al-surakh*] has rarely been a mode of poetry, but at this moment in our history, it becomes a psychological necessity. For he who would rouse the drugged sleepers, screaming alone might not be enough."

25. *Lan*, 44.

26. Ounsi El Hage, *Éternité volante: Anthologie poétique*, trans. Abdul Kader El Janabi et al. (Paris: Actes Sud, 1997), 11.

27. *Antonin Artaud: Selected Writings*, ed. Susan Sontag (Berkeley: University of California Press, 1988), xix. Sontag's essay, published in the *New Yorker* in 1973, introduced Artaud to nonspecialist American readers. In what follows, I will use the English translations from Sontag's anthology, by Helen Weaver.

28. Al-Hajj's translation of thirteen poems by Breton, along with a short commentary, was published in *Shiʿr* 6:24 (Fall 1962), 72-107. For his version of the Song of Songs, see *Nashid al-Anashid* (Beirut: Dar al-Nahar lil-Nashr, 1967). This is in fact a mixture of two nineteenth-century translations, the Van Dyck Bible and the Jesuit Bible of al-Yaziji and Augustin Rodet. Al-Hajj "arranged" [*wazzaʿa*] his translation into a dramatic text with speaking parts for a male speaker, a female speaker, and a chorus.

29. *Shiʿr* 4:16 (Fall 1960), 69-106. Further citations to this article will appear parenthetically in the main text. The early poems, as well as "L'enclume des forces," texts that date from the mid- to late 1920s, were all published in the first volume of Artaud's *Oeuvres complètes* (Paris: Gallimard, 1956), referenced by al-Hajj in his commentary (94).

30. *Selected Writings*, 139-45 (cf. *Oeuvres complètes*, 1:363-72). It may be that al-Hajj's interest in this episode reflects his own desire to distinguish himself from the earlier Egyptian surrealist movement headed by Georges Henein.

31. *Selected Writings*, 361, 368; *Oeuvres complètes*, 8:192-96.

32. Georges Charbonnier, *Antonin Artaud* (Paris: Éditions Seghers, 1959), 48-49. Al-Hajj's account of Artaud's trip to Mexico is also indebted to Charbonnier. One long passage of "Man Against Destiny" translated by al-Hajj ("Like life, like nature, thought goes from the inside out . . .") is cited by Charbonnier, 128-29. It is from this same study that al-Hajj seems to have taken the text for his translation of Artaud's "Lettre à Pierre Loëb" (Charbonnier, 202-6).

33. *Lan*, 41-42, 21.

34. *84* (1948), 102.

35. *Writing and Difference*, trans. Alan Bass (Chicago: University of Chicago Press, 1978), 234. And see Gilles Deleuze, *The Logic of Sense*, trans. Mark Lester with Charles Stivale (New York: Columbia University Press, 1990), 82-93. Derrida's "La parole soufflée" was first published in *Tel Quel* in 1965; "The Theater of Cruelty and the Closure of Representation" was published in *Critique* in 1966. Both essays were republished in *L'écriture et la différence* in 1967. Deleuze's study was first published in 1969.

36. Derrida's essay recovers the antihumanist premises of Heidegger's critique of existentialism while also indicting its continued commitment to humanist metaphysics: "The thought of Being, the thought of the truth of Being in whose name Heidegger de-limits humanism and metaphysics nevertheless remains a thought *of* man. In the question of Being as it is raised in metaphysics, man and the name of man are not displaced. And they certainly do not disappear. There is, rather, a sort of re-evaluation or revalorization of the essence and dignity of man." "The Ends of Man," *Philosophy and Phenomenological Research* 30:1, 49–50. Althusser is cited in Greif, *The Age of the Crisis of Man*, 304.

It is a measure of humanism's continuous strength in American intellectual life that Roger Shattuck, who along with Sontag did the most to introduce the twentieth-century French avant-garde to an American public, could write in exasperation, "In Artaud one finds none of the attitudes that could keep him firmly within the domain of the human." Artaud's project of "sustained exaltation, the permanent high, is not humanly possible.... His whole approach to the theater as liquidation, as orgy, declares his intolerance of simply being a man." See "Artaud Possessed" in *The Innocent Eye: On Modern Literature and the Arts* (New York: Farrar, Straus and Giroux, 1984), 169–86. The essay originally appeared in the *New York Review of Books* as a review of Sontag's anthology.

37. Frantz Fanon, *The Wretched of the Earth* (New York: Grove Press, 1968), 311.

38. *Writing and Difference*, 169–95. The same trope is more marked in "The Theater of Cruelty," in which Artaud's dramaturgy is said to announce "the limit of representation." At the end of the essay, Derrida writes, "That [Artaud] thereby kept himself at the limit of theatrical possibility, and that he wanted simultaneously to produce and to annihilate the stage, is what he knew in the most extreme way" (*ibid.*, 234, 249).

39. Gilles Deleuze and Félix Guattari, *Anti-Oedipus: Capitalism and Schizophrenia*, trans. Robert Hurley, Mark Seem, and Helen R. Lane (New York: Penguin Books, 2009), 8–9. And see the sequel, *A Thousand Plateaus*, trans. Brian Massumi (Minneapolis: University of Minnesota Press, 1987), 149–66.

40. Antonin Artaud, *The Theater and Its Double*, trans. Mary Caroline Richards (New York: Grove Press, 1958), 119.

41. The five translations are gathered under the title "Cinq adaptations de textes anglais" in *Oeuvres complètes* 9:127–52.

42. *Selected Writings*, 448–51; *Oeuvres complètes* 9:169–72. In the "Post-scriptum" Artaud appended to his translation of chapter 6 of *Through the Looking-Glass*, published in *Arbalète* magazine in 1947, he writes, "I had the feeling, while reading the little poem of Lewis Carroll about the fish [viz., "I sent a message to the fish"] ... that this little poem was thought up and written by me, in some other century, and that I was rediscovering my own work in the hands of Lewis Carroll." "In any case," Artaud finishes the note, "you could compare this little poem with Lewis Carroll's English text and you would realize that it belongs properly to me [*m'appartient en propre*] and is not at all the French version of an English text" (*ibid.*, 147).

43. As if to reinforce this ambiguity, al-Hajj later translated for *Shiʿr* a folio of poems by Breton, including his surrealist blazon, "L'Union libre," in which Artaud's amputations are precisely and lovingly restored: "My love an otter in the tiger's jaws / Her mouth a rosette bouquet of star of the highest magnitude / Her teeth footprints of white mice on white earth / Her tongue smooth as amber and as glass / My love her tongue a sacred host stabbed through." *Shiʿr* 6:24 (Fall 1962), 73–76. See the translation of Mary Ann Caws in *The Yale Anthology of Twentieth-century French Poetry* (New Haven: Yale University Press, 2004), 145. It is perhaps this species of fetishism that attracted al-Hajj to the biblical Song of Songs, his other large-scale translation during this period (cf. "Thy teeth are like a flock of sheep," "Thy lips are like a thread of scarlet"). Similar tropes appear in his own poetry

in a recognizably surrealist register: e.g., "Your navel swallows the world like a whirlpool"; "The nipple of your breasts hangs from a dog's neck." *Lan*, 51, 101.

44. *Writing and Difference*, 233, 243. These remarks on fidelity and infidelity frame the essay's most openly polemical moment, in which Derrida dismisses the situationists' claim on Artaud and implicitly asserts his own: "Assuming, which we do not, that there is some sense in speaking of a fidelity to Artaud, to something like his 'message' (this notion already betrays him), then a rigorous, painstaking, patient and implacable sobriety in the work of destruction, and an economical acuity aiming at the master parts of a still quite solid machine, are surely more imperative, today, than the general mobilization of art and artists, than turbulence or improvised agitation under the mocking and tranquil eyes of the police" (*ibid.*, 244).

45. *A Thousand Plateaus*, 164.

46. Cited in Derrida, *Writing and Difference*, 328 (cf. Artaud, *Oeuvres complètes*, 1:19–20.)

47. *Selected Writings*, 35; *Oeuvres complètes*, 1:36. The phrase "*des tours par lesquels on s'exprime et qui traduisent avec exactitude*" is a motif of Charbonnier's essay (cf. 27, 30, 52) and is also quoted by al-Hajj, who translates "*al-turuq allati yuʿabbir biha wa-allati tutarjim bidiqqa*" (95).

48. "The Activity of the Surrealist Research Bureau," *Selected Writings*, 107; *Oeuvres complètes*, 1:347. The passage is quoted by Charbonnier, *Antonin Artaud*, 34–35. Shattuck, "Artaud Possessed," 184.

49. On Artaud's notion of "*l'impouvoir*" or "unpower," see Derrida, "La parole soufflée," 176–77. The word is taken from *The Nerve Meter* (1925), where Artaud evokes "a powerlessness to crystallize unconsciously the broken point of the mechanism" (*Selected Writings*, 82).

50. *Shiʿr* 5:18 (Spring 1961), 154. The cited line is from *Lan*, 30. The idea that cancer singles out individuals rather than infecting collectives is a commonplace in the literature on the disease. As Sontag notes in her analysis of popular and literary stereotypes, which stem in many cases from earlier stereotypes about TB, "In contrast to the great epidemic diseases of the past (bubonic plague, typhus, cholera), which strike each person as a member of an afflicted community, TB was understood as a disease that isolates one from the community. However steep its incidence in a population, TB—like cancer today—always seemed to be a mysterious disease of individuals, a deadly arrow that could strike anyone, that singled out its victims one by one." *Illness as Metaphor and AIDS and Its Metaphors* (New York: Doubleday, 1990), 37–38.

51. *Lan*, 53–57.

52. *84* (1948), 112. On masturbation in modern Arabic literature, see Joseph Massad, *Desiring Arabs* (Chicago: University of Chicago Press, 2007), 305–10. Massad does not discuss al-Hajj's poem, focusing instead on the scandal of Sonallah Ibrahim's *Tilka al-Raʾiha* [That Smell] (1966)—a novella excerpted in *Shiʿr* after it had been banned in Egypt.

53. In what follows, all citations are to the standard Van Dyck Arabic translation of the Bible.

54. *Lan*, 37.

55. *Ibid.*, 90. This echoes a phrase from Adonis's "Marthiyat al-ayyam al-hadira": "*Kalimatuna la warith laha*" [our words have no inheritors].

56. *Ibid.*, 19. The final phrase was excised from later editions.

57. *84* (1948), 119.

58. Even for al-Hajj, this particular speech seems to have crossed the limit. In any case, it was not one he chose to transmit to future readers. In the third edition of *Lan* (Beirut: Dar al-Jadid, 1994), the final line is rendered harmlessly elegiac: "You can hardly hear—its scream is so loud—my weeping! [*bukaʾi*]."

Chapter 5: The Countercanon: *Adonis's* Anthology of Arabic Poetry

1. *Al-Tariq* 19:5 (1960), 15.

2. Husayn Muruwwa, *Turathuna . . . kayfa naʿrifuhu?* [Our Heritage . . . How Shall We Know It?] (Beirut: Muʾassasat al-Abhath al-ʿArabiyya, 1985), 9 (first published in *Al-Thaqafa Al-wataniyya* in August 1955).

3. György Lukács, *Essays on Thomas Mann* (London: Merlin Press, 1964), 144.

4. "Ibn al-Muqaffaʿ fi adabina al-qawmi," *al-Tariq* 17:5 (May 1958), 13–16; "Abu Nuwas wa-l-shuʿubiyya," *al-Tariq* 21:5 (May 1962), 34–41; "Al- Mutanabbi . . . shaʿir al-jihad al-ʿarabi," *al-Thaqafa al-wataniyya* 6:5 (May 1957), 11–14; "the reactionary pedagogy": Muruwwa, *Turathuna*, 12. The culmination of Muruwwa's revisionary efforts was *al-Nazaʿat al-maddiyya fi-l-falsafa al-ʿarabiyya wa-l-islamiyya* [Materialist Trends in Arabic and Islamic Philosophy], a two-volume study published in 1978 that sought to ground medieval Arab thought in what he called "its true, objective history" (Beirut: Dar al-Farabi, 1978), 6. For a conspectus of Muruwwa's argument, see Steve Tamari, "Reclaiming the Islamic Heritage: Marxism and Islam in the Thought of Husayn Muruwwah," *Arab Studies Journal* 3 (Spring 1995): 121–29.

5. Steiner, *After Babel*, 436.

6. *Adab* 5 (Winter 1963), 87–92. Adonis's French source is *Oeuvres philosophiques et mystiques de Shihabaddin Yahya Sohrawardi*, ed. Henry Corbin, vol. 2 (Tehran: Institut franco-iranien, 1952).

7. Adonis, *al-Thabit*, 1:64.

8. Adonis, *al-Hiwarat*, 15.

9. Adonis, *al-Thabit*, 1:22–23.

10. Muhammad Husayn Tabatabiʿi, quoted in Mahmoud Ayoub, "The Speaking Qurʾān and the Silent Qurʾān: A Study of the Principles and Development of Imāmī Shiʿī tafsīr," in *Approaches to the History of the Interpretation of the Qurʾān*, ed. Andrew Rippin (Oxford: Clarendon Press, 1988), 187.

11. "Esoteric knowledge," Adonis, *al-Thabit*, 1:252; "The best speech," 1:153; "Singular in expression," 2:133; "Metaphor," 1:153 (and cf. 1:149, 2:130); "The etymological derivation," 1:322–33. Adonis is explicit about his aim of identifying a "modernist" tradition within the *turath*, as in his remarks on atheism and humanism: "The sacred, as far as atheism is concerned, is the human itself, human reason, to which there is nothing greater. It puts reason in the place of revelation, and man in the place of God. . . . It is, in other words, the first form of modernism in Arabic-Islamic culture" (1:130). Adonis's understanding of *taʾwil* as a method of historicizing religious texts has found echoes in the work of specialists, who have at times borrowed his categories. The Egyptian hermeneutician Nasr Hamid Abu Zayd writes that all religious texts are "subject to the dialectic of the constant [*al-thabit*] and the transformative [*al-taghyir*]. For while texts are fixed in their utterance, they are subject to dynamism and change in the way they are understood," *Naqd al-khitab al-dini* (Cairo: Sina lil-Nashr, 1994), 111.

12. Casanova, *World Republic*, 238–40.

13. "Theses on the Philosophy of History," in *Illuminations*, trans. Harry Zohn (New York: Schocken Books, 1968), 255.

14. Steiner, *After Babel*, 390.

15. Adonis, *Diwan*, I: 10. Future citations will be kept to the main text, with the volume number in roman numerals followed by the page number.

16. Adonis, *al-Hiwarat*, 1:6.

17. Theodor Adorno, "Valéry Proust Museum," in *Prisms*, trans. Samuel and Sherry Weber (Cambridge: MIT Press, 1981), 175.

18. The trope of resurrection or *"ihya'"* is itself a classical one, alluding to al-Ghazali's *Ihya' 'ulum al-din* [Revival of Religious Sciences]. Here again, Adorno's comments on Proust are apposite: "For him it is only the death of the work of art in the museum which brings it to life. When severed from the living order in which it functioned, according to him, its true spontaneity is released" ("Valéry Proust Museum," 181).

19. Chris Baldick, *The Modern Movement, 1910–1940* (Oxford: Oxford University Press, 2004), cited in John G. Nichols, "Ezra Pound's Poetic Anthologies and the Architecture of Reading," *PMLA* 121:1 (2006), 170.

20. "A living museum of facts": *Active Anthology*, ed. Ezra Pound (London: Faber, 1933), 247. On Diego's anthology, see Octavio Paz, *Los Hijos*, 204–5. On Moore and Beier's anthology, see André Lefevere, "Anthologizing Africa," in *Translation, Rewriting, and the Manipulation of Literary Fame* (New York: Routledge, 1992), 124–37.

21. Jameson, *A Singular Modernity*, 35.

22. Gerardo Diego, *Antología poética en honor de Góngora* (Madrid: Revista de Occidente, 1927), 10–11 [my translations].

23. The stone is also a keyword in Adonis's early poetry. For example, here is his three-line poem, "*Hajar*" [Stone], from *The Songs of Mihyar*: "I worship this gentle stone. / I see my face in its lineaments [*taqati' ihi*]. / I see in it my lost poetry." "*Wadi'a*" [gentle], in the first line, is an unexpected word, bearing melancholic connotations of farewell (*al-wada'*) and archival ones of deposition and storing (*al-wad'*). In the second line, the poet handles the stone as if it were a mirror or a skull, in which he witnesses his own fragmentation: "*taqati' al-wajh*" [lineaments of the face] is an idiom, but the singular form of the first noun signifies interruption, fragmentation, discontinuity. These ambiguities resonate in the final line, in which the poet discovers that the verse he bid farewell to, or perhaps never wrote, has somehow been inventoried in the stone. The stone as an object of "worship" is in this sense a profane fetish or melancholic emblem of a world without divinities, belonging equally to the pre-Islamic world of the *jahili* poets as well as the postreligious world of Mihyar.

24. Massad, *Desiring Arabs*, 95.

25. *The Selected Letters of Ezra Pound, 1907–1941*, ed. D. D. Paige (New York: New Directions, 1971), 101. I owe this reference to Richard Sieburth. Jameson notes the special temporality that attends this kind of revisionary reading, in which the past suddenly becomes invested with futurity: "To affirm the 'modernity' of this or that historical phenomenon is always to generate a kind of electrical charge: to isolate this or that Renaissance painter as the sign of some first or nascent modernity is . . . always to awaken a feeling of intensity or energy that is greatly in excess of the attention we generally bring to interesting events or monuments of the past" (*A Singular Modernity*, 35).

26. Andras Hamori, "Mukhtārāt," in *The Encyclopaedia of Islam*, 2nd ed.

27. "*Diwan*" in Arabic thus also means "department" or "secretariat," a connotation it received from Persian. See A. A Duri's entry in *The Encyclopaedia of Islam*, 2nd ed.

28. Adonis, *al-Thabit*, 1:319.

29. The classic reference work for this body of thought is Hourani's *Arabic Thought*. For a reconsideration that builds on Hourani's insights, see the essays collected in Jens Hanssen and Max Weiss, eds., *Arabic Thought Beyond the Liberal Age: Towards an Intellectual History of the Nahda* (New York: Cambridge University Press, 2016).

30. The most sophisticated exposition of this late modernist logic is Octavio Paz's notion of "the tradition of rupture," in his study of modernist and avant-gardist poetry, *Children of the Mire*, trans. Rachel Phillips (Cambridge: Harvard University Press, 1974). Paz's text, first presented as the Norton Lectures of 1971–72, theorizes modernism as a cultural dialectic of self-scission, "a continual breaking away, a ceaseless splitting apart" (27). Like

Adonis, Paz insists on modernity's multiple pasts as opposed to orthodoxy's monolithic tradition: "Modernity is condemned to pluralism: the old tradition was always the same, the modern is always different. The former postulates unity between past and present; the latter, not content with emphasizing its own differences, affirms that the past is not one but many" (2). All this bears an unmistakable resemblance to Eliot's dynamic concept of tradition and his attempt to reclaim the English Metaphysicals while dismissing the nineteenth century. The same logic permits Paz to claim Latin American *modernismo*'s continuity with British and French Romanticism, recoded in a modernist idiom of irony and revolution, while distinguishing it from the Spanish version, condemned as "superficial and declamatory, patriotic and sentimental" (78). For Paz, who is more concretely historical in this case than Adonis (or Eliot), Spain's sentimental Romanticism was the outgrowth of an enfeebled middle class that never developed a capacity for self-criticism, the engine that drives Paz's narrative of self-scission. But this historical referent is gradually lost in the final chapter of his book, which records the ever more rapid schisms in Latin American modernism, running from *modernismo* to *postmodernismo* to *vanguardia* to *postvanguardia*. A comparison of Adonis and Paz, who share a contemporary interest in indigenous myth, mysticism, translation, and cross-cultural poetics, would reveal a great deal about the identity and plurality of late modernism.

31. Adonis's identification of Egyptian poets of the *Nahda* with a contemporary strain of political poetry is clear in his chapter on Sami al-Barudi in *al-Thabit wa-l-mutahawwil*, 4:39–53. Al-Barudi was the most prominent Egyptian poet of the nineteenth century as well as the editor of a celebrated anthology, the four-volume *Mukhtarat al-Barudi* (1909), and so doubly a rival. Adonis writes, "There is no doubt al-Barudi's poetry had a revivalist function, meaning that it was a technical revision of the past [*iʿada muttaqana*]. This revival may well have carried some political-patriotic significance, in the sense that it encouraged self-confidence and resolution in the face of the enemy, or in the struggle against him. It may be that al-Barudi's poetry played an important role in raising national consciousness, but this role is not, technically speaking, poetic" (4:49). Adonis's polemic against the *Nahda* is pursued in his other anthologies, most of them published in the early 1980s, of the Egyptians Shawqi, ʿAbdu, and Rida.

32. Husayn Muruwwa, *Dirasat naqdiyya* (Beirut: Dar al-Farabi, 1976), 231–36. Adonis's fondness for fragmentation culminates in a later poetic anthology, *Diwan al-bayt al-wahid fi-l-shiʿr al-ʿarabi* [Anthology of the Single Verse in Arabic Poetry] (London: Dar al-Saqi, 2010), which transmits a version of the *turath* in the form of epigrams.

33. Felix Klein-Franke, "The Hamāsa of Abū Tammām, Part II," *Journal of Arabic Literature* 3 (1972): 144–45. My account of Abu Tammam's compilation of the *Hamasa* is especially indebted to Suzanne Stetkevych's study, *Abū Tammām and the Poetics of the ʿAbbasid Age* (Leiden: Brill, 1991).

34. Adonis, *al-Hiwarat*, 9.

35. Adonis also admits to rearranging lines in his *Anthology*. "I have not always maintained the succession of verses in the poem," he writes at the end of his first introduction, "at times moving a verse forward, and at times dropping it back in order to establish the structure of the verses and sequence of thoughts. But I have resorted to this very rarely, when poetic necessity compelled me" (I 32).

36. Cited in Hamori, "*Mukhtārāt*."

37. Adonis, *al-Thabit*, 2:126–33.

38. For a complete English translation of al-Khuraymi's poem, see *The History of al-Ṭabarī*, vol. 31, *The War between Brothers*, ed. and trans. Michael Fishbein (Albany: SUNY Press, 1992), 139–50.

39. Walter Benjamin, *The Arcades Project*, trans. Howard Eiland and Kevin McLaughlin (Cambridge: Harvard University Press, 1999), 460, 473.

40. *Ibid.*, 474.

Chapter 6: "He Sang New Sorrow": Adonis and the Modernist Elegy

1. Jorge Luis Borges, *Collected Fictions*, trans. Andrew Hurley (New York: Penguin, 1998), 235–41.

2. Fredric Jameson, "Magic Narratives: Romance as Genre," *NLH* 7 (1975), 135, emphasis in the original. This essay was revised in *The Political Unconscious*, where Jameson writes, "The emergence, first of modernism, with its Joycean or Mallarméan ideal of a single Book of the world, then of the post-modernist aesthetic of the text or of *écriture*, of 'textual productivity' or schizophrenic writing—all seem rigorously to exclude traditional notions of the literary kinds, or of systems of the fine arts, as much by their practice as by their theory. Nor is it difficult to see why this has been so. Genres are essentially literary *institutions*, or social contracts between a writer and a specific public, whose function is to specify the proper use of a particular cultural artifact" (Ithaca: Cornell University Press, 1981), 106.

3. Rosanna Warren, "Sappho: Translation as Elegy," in *The Art of Translation*, ed. Rosanna Warren (Boston: Northeastern University Press, 1989), 202.

4. *Diwan al-nahda* 9, 13. For a summary study of Shawqi's own elegies, see Antoine Boudot-Lamotte, *Aḥmad Ṣawqī: L'homme et l'oeuvre* (Damascus: Institut Français de Damas, 1977), 160–77. An especially helpful historical approach is provided by Yaseen Noorani, "A Nation Born in Mourning: The Neo-Classical Funeral Elegy in Egypt," *Journal of Arabic Literature* 28 (1997), 38–67. Noorani notes that the number of funeral elegies composed by Shawqi and his contemporary, Hafiz Ibrahim, is remarkably higher than the number composed by the preceding generation of poets, led by al-Barudi.

5. Abdelfattah Kilito, *The Author and His Doubles*, trans. Michael Cooperson (Syracuse: Syracuse University Press, 2001), 32. Similarly, ancient Greek critics often traced the etymology of "elegy" to "*e e logoi*," "to speak well of."

6. The poem is included in Adonis's *Diwan al-nahda*, 162–66; also see Ahmad Shawqi, *al-Shawqiyyat*, vol. 2 (Cairo: Matbaʿat al-Istiqama, n.d.), 73–76. For a close reading and informative contextualization, see Hussein N. Kadhim, *The Poetics of Anti-Colonialism in the Arabic Qaṣīdah* (Leiden: Brill, 2004), chapter 2, "Empire as Occasion: Ahmad Shawqī's Elegy for Damascus," 34–84.

7. Adina Hoffman, *My Happiness Bears No Relation to Happiness* (New Haven: Yale University Press, 2009), 260–61; Mahmoud Darwish, *Diwan* (Beirut: Dar al-ʿAwda, 1994), 1:204–5.

8. For details, see Stephen Widener's "The Divinity of the Profane: The Representation of the Divine in the Poetry of Adūnīs," in *Representations of the Divine in Arabic Poetry*, ed. Gert Borg and Ed de Moor (Amsterdam: Rodopi, 2001), 216–17.

9. Peter M. Sacks, *The English Elegy: Studies in the Genre from Spenser to Yeats* (Baltimore: Johns Hopkins University Press, 1985), 1–37.

10. Jaroslav Stetkevych notes the presence of this trope in the genre of the *nasib* as well as that of the *rithaʾ*: "The stopping at the abandoned encampment and the questioning are thus symbolic stances kindred to those of the visitation of the grave and of its questioning. . . . There is here the promise to those who read the Orphic poets' verses that tombs shall speak to them as they first spoke to the poets themselves." "Toward an Arabic Elegiac Lexicon: The Seven Words of the Nasib," in *Reorientations: Arabic*

and Persian Poetry, ed. Suzanne Pinckney Stetkevych (Bloomington: Indiana University Press, 1994), 116.

11. *Kitab al-tahawwulat wa-l-hijra fi aqalim al-nahar wa-l-layl* (Beirut: al-Maktaba al-ʿAsriyya, 1965).

12. In Borges's Andalusian short story, Averroës recounts the gratitude he once felt, while marooned in Marrakech, for some lines of poetry that ʿAbd al-Rahman supposedly composed in his palace in Córdoba: "Thou too art, O palm!, / On this foreign soil." The philosopher comments, "A remarkable gift, the gift bestowed by poetry—words written by a king homesick for the Orient served to comfort me when I was far away in Africa, homesick for Spain." Borges, *Collected Fictions*, 240.

13. Muruwwa, *Dirasat naqdiyya*, 81–89.

14. *Al-Masrah wa-l-maraya* (Beirut: Dar al-Adab, 1969).

15. In his lukewarm review of *al-Masrah wa-l-maraya*, Jabra Ibrahim Jabra complained that Adonis's poetry, precisely through such devices as the mask and the mirror, was becoming dangerously encyclopedic. Noting the poet's "identification" with Odysseus, Faust, Sisyphus, and Zarathustra, Jabra exclaims, "But what is the link between all these figures? By becoming all of them, you become none of them. Hamlet is Hamlet, not a confused mixture of Abi al-ʿAlaʾ, Montaigne, and d'Artagnan. And Adonis is not Faust." *Shiʿr* 10:39 (Fall 1969), 123.

16. *Anthology*, II 27. This is a periphrasis of a poem cited in the *Anthology*, where al-Maʿarri writes, "My clothes are my winding sheets, my home is my tomb, and my life is my death" (II 497).

17. *Ibid.*, II 28

18. Sacks, *The English Elegy*, 37. Other Arab poets sought to re-politicize the genre, while maintaining Adonis's use of the elegy as a poem of revision and inheritance. See, for example, ʿAbdalwahab al-Bayati's "Elegies for Lorca," in his collection *al-Mawt fi-l-hayat* [Death in Life] (Beirut: Dar al-Adab, 1968). Al-Bayati's poems elegize his Spanish confrere through the mediations of Gilgamesh's lament for Enkidu and Lorca's own elegy for the bullfighter, "Llanto por Ignacio Sánchez Mejías" (a poem translated into Arabic by Subhi Muhyadin in *Shiʿr* 5:18 (Spring 1961), 108–22).

19. Twenty years after the publication of "A Mirror for Abi al-ʿAlaʾ," Adonis collaborated on a translation of al-Maʿarri into French, *Rets d'éternité*, trans. Adonis and Anne Wade Minkowski (Paris: Fayard, 1988).

20. *Le regard d'Orphée*, 51.

21. *Ibid.*, 51.

22. Fuad Ajami, *The Arab Predicament: Arab Political Thought and Practice Since 1967* (New York: Cambridge University Press, 1981), 32.

23. *Shiʿr* 2:7/8 (Summer/Autumn 1958), 4.

24. *Mawaqif* 1 (1968), 2.

25. *Mawaqif* 2 (Winter 1969), 168–72. Adonis presents this last phrase as a variant of Lenin's complaint to Maxim Gorky about the populist poet Demyan Bedny (a favorite of Stalin's), whom Lenin accused of "being led by his readers, whereas he needs to be in advance of them." Adonis quotes Lenin's judgment on Bedny again in his essay "On Poetry and Revolution," an expansion of the lecture printed in *Mawaqif*, which is notable for its explicitly Leninist slant on cultural politics, especially his notion of the intellectual vanguard. See *Zaman al-shiʿr*, 87–117.

26. *Mawaqif* 2 (Winter 1969), 3. It is telling that when, in an interview given in 1964, Adonis was asked to define his politics, he answered, "I'm a leftist insofar as leftism is typified by a faith in man [*al-insan*]—in his freedom, dignity, and self-determination" (*Al-Hiwarat*, 18).

27. Two of the English versions are partial translations: "A Grave for New York," trans. Lena Jayyusi and Alan Brownjohn, in *Modern Arabic Poetry: An Anthology*, ed. Salma Jayyusi (New York: Columbia University Press, 1987), 137–40; and "The Funeral of New York," trans. Mirène Ghossein, Kamal Boullata, and Samuel Hazo, in *Transformations of the Lover* (Pittsburgh: International Poetry Forum, 1982), 59–76. This translation was revised by Hazo for his anthology, *The Pages of Day and Night* (Marlboro: The Marlboro Press, 1994), 57–74. The other versions are "A Grave for New York," trans. Kamal Abu Deeb, www.jehat.com/ar/adonees/adonis-bio-3b.htm; and "A Grave for New York," trans. Shawkat Toowara, in Adonis, *A Time Between Ashes and Roses* (Syracuse: Syracuse University Press, 2004), 124–77. The French version is "*Tombeau pour New York*," trans. Anne Wade Minkowski (Paris: Sindbad, 1986). The Spanish translation switches the genre yet again: see "*Epitafio para Nueva York*," trans. Federico Arbós (Madrid: Hiperión, 1987).

28. *Mawaqif* 2:11 (September–October 1970), 3–4. The prepositional phrase *min ajli* [for the sake of] is a slightly elaborate construction—the Arabic *li-* would be more conventional—and so Adonis's reuse has the air of a quotation. It is worth noting that Adonis also contributed a long poem, "*Muqaddima li-tarikh al-muluk al-tawāʾif*" [Introduction to the History of Petty Kings], a poem he initially dedicated to Gamal Abdel Nasser, to an anthology entitled *Kitabat ʿala qabr ʿAbd al-Nasir* [Writings on the Grave of Abdel Nasser], ed. ʿAbd al-Muʿti al-Hijazi (Beirut: Dar al-ʿAwda, 1971). This collection is an anthology based on the Renaissance model of the *tombeau*.

29. Dominique Moncond'huy, "Qu'est-ce qu'un tombeau poétique?" in *Le Tombeau poétique en France*, ed. Dominique Moncond'huy (Poitiers: La Licorne, 1994), 8 [my translation].

30. Leo Bersani, *The Death of Stéphane Mallarmé* (Cambridge: Cambridge University Press, 1982), 33.

31. Toorawa's translation provides a helpful key to Adonis's citations from the French, to which my own reading is indebted. Al-Khal published two folios of translations of Whitman in *Shiʿr* 2:7/8 (Summer/Autumn 1958), 44–56; and 7:28 (Autumn 1963), 64–80.

32. *Waqt bayna al-ramad wa-l-* (Beirut: Dar al-ʿAwda, 1972). Future quotations will be cited parenthetically in the main text.

33. Early in Ameen Rihani's *Book of Khalid* (1911), the two protagonists sail into the storied harbor: "Is this the gate of Paradise," one wonders, "or the port of some subterrestrial city guarded by the Jinn? What a marvel of enchantment is everything around us!" Ameen Rihani, *The Book of Khalid* (Beirut: Librairie du Liban, 2000), 34–35. Adonis's awareness of the *mahjar* writers' prior claim on New York City (and on Whitman) is evident throughout his *tombeau*. The poem ends with an evocation of Gibran and Adonis rising on opposite banks of a Lebanese river (96).

34. Meddeb, *Tombeau*, vii–xi.

35. Jean-Luc Nancy, afterword to Abdelwahab Meddeb, *Tombeau of Ibn Arabi; and, White Traverses*, trans. Charlotte Mandell (New York: Fordham University Press, 2010), 110.

36. Ibid., vii.

37. The Arabic translation of Meddeb's text by the Moroccan poet Muhammad Bennis is *Qabr Ibn ʿArabi* (Cairo: Supreme Council of Culture, 1999). Bennis's own early interest in the *rithaʾ*, as well as his Adonisian-ʿAbbasid inheritance, is evident from the series of elegies he published as "Bab al-Marathi" [Chapter of Elegies], in *Mawaqif* 2:9 (May–June 1970), 12–13.

38. Meddeb, *Tombeau*, 3.

39. See Yasser Elhariry's erudite analysis of how Meddeb's *Tombeau* reimagines the francophone lyric by insinuating itself among "the tongues and company of *jāhilī*, Sufi,

and modern French poets." *Pacifist Invasions: Arabic, Translation, and the Postfrancophone Lyric* (Liverpool: Liverpool University Press, 2017), 134–51. It seems only fair to note that this particular constellation of poetries was first mapped by Adonis, who also provides Meddeb with his generic model.

Epilogue: Tehran 1979—Damascus 2011

1. "Tahiya li-thawrat Iran," *al-Safir*, February 1, 1979, 1.
2. The first of Adonis's articles on the Iranian revolution, "Between Stability and Transformation: On the Civilizational Significance of Iran's Islamic Movement," was published in *al-Nahar*, February 12, 1979; the second, "After the Bliss of Victory, Some Fear and Anxiousness," was published two weeks later on February 26, 1979. Both articles were reprinted in *Mawaqif* 34 (Winter 1979), 149–60, under the title "Bayn al-thabat wa-l-tahawwul: khawatir hawla al-thawra al-islamiyya fi Iran" [Between the Fixed and the Dynamic: Thoughts on the Islamic Revolution in Iran].
3. "The Spark of Bouazizi," in *Printemps Arabes: Religion et révolution*, trans. Ali Ibrahim (Paris: Editions de la Différence, 2014), 29. This is a collection of Adonis's essays and interviews following the Arab Spring, translated into French. "I Will Never Agree," *al-Hayat*, May 26, 2011.
4. *Akhbar al-adab*, May 27, 2012.
5. *Al-Hayat*, June 22, 2013. Al-ʿAzm was writing in response to Khalida Said's defense of her husband's positions in an op-ed published in *al-Hayat* on May 17, 2013.
6. "Adunis wa-l-naqd al-munfalit min ʿiqalihi" [Adonis and Criticism That Has Lost Its Grip], *Dirasat ʿarabiyya* 18:4 (February 1982), 58.
7. "Here is the thing," "Bayna al-thabat wa-l-tahawwul," 152; "Let us clearly acknowledge," *ibid.*; "total revolution," *ibid.*, 156; "the prime mover," *ibid.*, 155.
8. *Ibid.*, 153.
9. Adonis, *al-Thabit*, 1:161–72. Khomeini often referred to this history as well, as in his famous ʿAshura sermon of June 3, 1963, in which he compared the shah to Yazid (the first Umayyad caliph, who ordered the murder of the Prophet's grandson Hussein).
10. *Ibid.*, 1:322. The "General Conclusion" of the encyclopedia's first and most important volume is focused on the topic of *taʾwil* and the political lexicon of Shiism.
11. Janet Afary and Kevin B. Anderson, *Foucault and the Iranian Revolution* (Chicago: University of Chicago Press, 2005), 222. Afary and Anderson's book includes an appendix of English translations of all Foucault's writings on Iran, which I will refer to in what follows.
12. "Do you know," in *Foucault and the Iranian Revolution*, 201; "What, for us," *ibid.*, 251; "Uprisings belong," *ibid.*, 263 [translation modified]. Foucault repeated his claims about the inability of Marxist categories to capture the Iranian revolution many times, e.g., "What is happening in Iran is enough to worry today's observers. In it they recognize not China, not Cuba, and not Vietnam, but rather a tidal wave without a military leadership, without a vanguard, without a party" (*ibid.*, 211).
13. "Inflexibility," *ibid.*, 218; "unwavering intransigence," "Khomeini *says nothing*," "Khomeini *is not a politician*," 222; "By 'Islamic government,'" 206. All emphases in the original.
14. "Something that is the basis," *ibid.*, 196; "Recent events," *ibid.*, 195; "At the dawn of history," *ibid.*, 203. This paragraph was reproduced in an article in French that Foucault published the following week in *Le nouvel observateur*, cf. *ibid.*, 208. The idea that it was the shah who represented backwardness was a trope of Khomeini's own discourse. "It is the

shah himself who is opposed to civilization and lives in the past," he told French journalists. "The shah carries out the imperialists' policies and attempts to keep Iran in a state of backwardness and degeneracy" (*Le Monde*, April 24, 1978).

15. In his lecture "Governmentality," delivered at the Collège de France in the spring before he visited Iran, Foucault situated the emergence of this theme in the sixteenth century, in response to the collapse of feudalism and the outbreak of the Reformation, in a way that strongly foreshadows his remarks on Khomeini's revolution: "There is a double movement, then, of state centralization, on the one hand, and of dispersion and religious dissidence on the other. It is, I believe, at the intersection of these two tendencies that the problem comes to pose itself with this particular intensity, of how to be ruled, how strictly, by whom, to what end, by what methods, and so on. There is a problematic of government in general." *Power: Essential Works of Michel Foucault, 1954-1984*, ed. James D. Faubion, trans. Robert Hurley et al. (London: Penguin, 2002), 3:202. In the same vein, during an interview in Iran in the fall of 1978, Foucault drew an explicit parallel between Shiism and German Anabaptism, noting that he was "astonished by the connections and even the similarities that exist between Shi'ism and some of the revolutionary movements in Europe at the end of the Middle Ages, up to the seventeenth or eighteenth centuries. These were great popular movements against feudal lords, against the first cruel formations of bourgeois society, great protests against the all-powerful control of the state" (*Foucault and the Iranian Revolution*, 186).

16. Foucault probably received this idea from the Iranian dissidents themselves, who often downplayed the long history of the clerisy's cooperation with the Safavid state. At times, Foucault seemed to recognize there was nothing inherently antistatist about Shiite doctrine. In one of his articles from Iran, he acknowledged that "[the Shi'ite clergy] has administered the official religion." And yet, he continued, "[the mullahs] have been most often on the side of the rebels" (*Foucault and the Iranian Revolution*, 202).

17. "Who sought in Iran," *ibid.*, 264; "a continual refusal," "Bayna al-thabat wa-l-tahawwul," 153. I would dissent from Afary and Anderson's argument that Foucault "privileged premodern social relations over modern ones" (*Foucault and the Iranian Revolution*, 26) and that his enthusiasm for the revolution stemmed from a nostalgic desire to find "alternate forms of non-Western modernity" (*ibid.*, 10). They are more correct when they call Foucault an "antimodernist" (*ibid.*, 123)—but the logic of his opposition is one of rupture, not regression or exoticism.

18. "Bayna al-thabat wa-l-tahawwul," 156.

19. *Ibid.*, 160

20. Adonis, *al-Hiwarat*, 211.

21. *Mawaqif* 36 (Winter 1980), 135–58.

22. "Adunis wa-l-naqd al-munfalit," 59.

23. "Min al-muthaqqaf al-ʿaskari ila-l-faqih al-ʿaskari" [From the Armed Man-of-Letters to the Armed Jurist], *al-Nahar*, July 17, 1980. This article, along with the previous two, is reprinted in "Thalathat nusus hawla al-thawra al-iraniyya" [Three Texts on the Iranian Revolution], in *al-Thabit wa-l-mutahawwil*, 166–75. Fuad Ajami's account of the episode, one of the few in English, is therefore misleading. Ajami argues that "It fell to the poet Adonis to divine early on the destination of [the Iranian] revolution in essays he wrote in 1979 and 1980." He then implies that Adonis's warning about "the armed jurist" came early on, whereas in fact it came a year and a half after Khomeini took power and so can hardly be counted as an early divination (*The Dream Palace*, 142–46).

24. "Putting an end," "Abʿad min al-nizam wa awsaʿ min al-siyasa," *al-Safir*, July 13, 2011; "The Discourse of 'the Arab Spring,'" *Printemps Arabes*, 49. In an interview published in January 2012, Adonis struck the same note: "Because the concern of leftist currents has

been to participate in power one way or another, they haven't effected any real social or political change.... One might glean a definition of the Arab 'left' from its insatiable thirst for power" (*ibid.*, 147).

25. "Such a change," *al-Hayat*, May 26, 2011; "Society doesn't necessarily change," *Printemps Arabes*, 49. Cf. Adonis's address to a conference on the Syrian conflict in early 2013: "The fundamental issue in Syria is not merely the dictatorial politics of the regime. The dictatorship is less of a political structure than a sociocultural one—a structure grounded in the way people think, not in the exercise of power. What, then, is the point of a revolution that only seeks to overthrow the regime without changing this way of thinking?" (*Printemps Arabes*, 173).

26. "Al-ʿaql al-muʿtaqal" [The Captive Mind], *Mawaqif* 43 (Fall 1981), 3–10. The title is an allusion to Czesław Miłosz's analysis of intellectual life in Stalinist Poland. I have translated Adonis's Arabic version of Nietzsche's aphorism, which has "*bashar*"—"humans" or "men"—in place of the German "*Geist.*" The original text is: "*Die Schlange, welche sich nicht häuten kann, geht zu Grunde. Ebenso die Geister, welche man verhindert, ihre Meinungen zu wechseln; sie hören auf, Geist zu sein.*"

SELECTED BIBLIOGRAPHY

ʿAbbas, Ihsan. *Badr Shakir al-Sayyab: Dirasa fi hayatihi wa shiʿrihi* (Beirut: Dar al-Thaqafa, 1969).
———. *Ittijahat al-shiʿr al-muʿasir* (Kuwait: al-Majlis al-Watani lil-Thaqafa wa-l-Funun wa-l-Adab, 1978).
Abdel-Malek, Anouar. *Égypte, Société Militaire* (Paris: Éditions du Seuil, 1962).
Abdul-Hai, Muhammad. *Tradition and English and American Influence in Arabic Romantic Poetry* (London: Ithaca Press, 1982).
Adonis. *Awraq fi-l-rih* (Beirut: Dar Majallat Shiʿr, 1958; 2nd ed., Dar al-Adab, 1988).
———. *Aghani Mihyar al-Dimashqi* (Beirut: Dar Majallat Shiʿr, 1961).
———. *Chants de Mihyar le Damascène*, trans. Anne Wade Minkowski and Jacques Berque (Paris: Gallimard, 2002 [1961]).
———. *Mihyar of Damascus, His Songs*, trans. Adnan Haydar and Michael Beard (Rochester: BOA Editions, 2008 [1961]).
———. *Diwan al-shiʿr al-ʿarabi*, 3 vols. (Beirut: al-Maktaba al-ʿAsriyya, 1964).
———. *Kitab al-tahawwulat wa-l-hijra fi aqalim al-nahar wa-l-layl* (Beirut: al-Maktaba al-ʿAsriyya, 1965).
———. *Al-Masrah wa-l-maraya* (Beirut: Dar al-Adab, 1969).
———. *Waqt bayna al-ramad wa-l-ward* (Beirut: Dar al-ʿAwda, 1972).
———. *A Time between Ashes and Roses*, trans. Shawkat Toowara (Syracuse: Syracuse University Press, 2004 [1972]).
———. "Tahiya li-thawrat Iran," *al-Safir*, February 12, 1979.
———. *Diwan al-nahda* (Beirut: Dar ʿIlm al-Malayyin, 1982).
———. *Zaman al-shiʿr* (Beirut: Dar al-ʿAwda, 1987).
———. *Ha anta ayyuha al-waqt* (Beirut: Dar al-Adab, 1993).
———. "Conférence d'Adonis donnée à la Fondation Saint-John Perse le 9 octobre 1993," *Souffle de Perse* 4 (1994), trans. Anne Wade-Minkowski, 4–9.
———. *Al-Thabit wa-l-mutahawwil*, 4 vols. (Beirut: Dar al-Saqi, 2002).
———. *Le regard d'Orphée: conversations avec Houria Abdelouahed* (Paris: Fayard, 2009).
———. *Diwan al-bayt al-wahid fi-l-shiʿr al-ʿarabi* (London: Dar al-Saqi, 2010).
———. *Al-Hiwarat al-kamila, v.1 (1960–1980)* (Damascus: Bidayat lil-Nashr wa-l-Tawziʿ, 2010).
———. *Al-Aʿmal al-shiʿriyya al-kamila*, 3 vols. (Beirut: Dar al-Saqi, 2012).
———. *Printemps Arabes: Religion et révolution*, trans. Ali Ibrahim (Paris: Editions de la Différence, 2014).
———. *Violence et Islam: entretiens avec Houria Abdelouahed* (Paris: Éditions du Seuil, 2015).
Adorno, Theodor. *Prisms*, trans. Samuel and Sherry Weber (Cambridge: MIT Press, 1981).
———. *Aesthetic Theory*, trans. Robert Hullot-Kentor (Minneapolis: University of Minnesota Press, 1998).
Afary, Janet, and Kevin B. Anderson. *Foucault and the Iranian Revolution* (Chicago: University of Chicago Press, 2005).
ʿAhd al-nadwa al-lubnaniyya (Beirut: Dar al-Nahar, 1997).
Ajami, Fuad. *The Arab Predicament: Arab Political Thought and Practice Since 1967* (New York: Cambridge University Press, 1981).

———. *Beirut: City of Regrets* (New York: W.W. Norton, 1988).
———. *The Dream Palace of the Arabs* (New York: Random House, 1999).
Al-Adab al-ʿarabi al-muʿasir: Aʿmal muʾtamar Ruma al-munʿaqad fi tishrin al-awwal sanat 1961 (Paris: Manshurat Adwaʾ, n.d. [1962]).
al-ʿAlim, Mahmud Amin, and ʿAbd al-ʿAzim Anis. *Fi-l-thaqafa al-misriyya* (Beirut: Dar al-Fikr al-Jadid, 1955).
Amateis, Jacques. *Yusuf al-Khal wa majallatuhu 'Shiʿr'* (Beirut: Dar al-Nahar, 2004).
Amin, Samir. *Delinking* (London: Zed Books, 1990).
Anderson, Amanda. *Bleak Liberalism* (Chicago: University of Chicago Press, 2016).
Artaud, Antonin. *Oeuvres complètes*, 26 vols. (Paris: Gallimard, 1956).
———. *The Theater and Its Double*, trans. Mary Caroline Richards (New York: Grove Press, 1958).
———. *Selected Writings*, ed. Susan Sontag (Berkeley: University of California Press, 1988).
ʿAsfur, Jabir. "Aqniʿat al-shiʿr al-muʿasir," *Fusul* 1:4 (July 1981), 123–48.
Auerbach, Erich. *Time, History, and Literature: Selected Essays*, ed. James I. Porter (Princeton: Princeton University Press, 2014).
Awad, Rita. *Usturat al-mawt wa-l-inbiʿath fi-l-shiʿr al-ʿarabi al-hadith* (Beirut: al-Muʾassasa al-ʿArabiyya lil-Dirasat wa-l-Nashr, 1974).
Badawi, M. M. *A Critical Introduction to Modern Arabic Poetry* (Cambridge: Cambridge University Press, 1976).
———, ed. *Modern Arabic Literature* (Cambridge: Cambridge University Press, 1992).
Badini, Dounia. *Une figure de la modernité poétique libanaise: Ounsi el-Hage* (Beirut: Université Saint-Joseph, 2007).
———. *La Revue* Shiʿr / *Poésie et la modernité poétique arabe: Beyrouth (1957–70)* (Paris: Sindbad, 2009).
Barakat, Halim. *Al-Madina al-mulawwana* (Beirut: Dar al-Saqi, 2006).
Barnhisel, Gregory. *James Laughlin, New Directions, and the Remaking of Ezra Pound* (Amherst and Boston: University of Massachusetts Press, 2005).
———. *Cold War Modernists: Art, Literature, and American Cultural Diplomacy* (New York: Columbia University Press, 2015).
Barut, Muhammad Jamal. *Al-Hadatha al-ula* (Sharjah: Manshurat Ittihad Kuttab wa-Udabaʾ al-Imarat, 1991).
Batatu, Hanna. *The Egyptian, Syrian, and Iraqi Revolutions: Some Observations on Their Underlying Causes and Social Character* (Washington: The Center for Contemporary Arab Studies, 1984).
Bazzun, Ahmad. *Qasidat al-nathr al-ʿarabiyya: Al-itar al-nazari* (Beirut: Dar al-Fikr al-Jadid, 1996).
Beard, Michael, and Adnan Haydar. "Making Mihyar: The Familiarization of Adunis's Knight of Strange Words," *Literature East and West* 25 (1989), 79–103.
Benjamin, Walter. *Illuminations*, trans. Harry Zohn (New York: Schocken Books, 1968).
———. *The Arcades Project*, trans. Howard Eiland and Kevin McLaughlin (Cambridge: Harvard University Press, 1999).
Bennis, Muhammad. *Qabr Ibn ʿArabi* (Cairo: Supreme Council of Culture, 1999).
Bérard, Victor. *Les Phéniciens et l'Odyssée*, 2 vols. (Paris: Librairie Armand Colin, 1927).
Berman, Marshall. *All That Is Solid Melts into Air* (Penguin: New York, 1988).
Bernard, Suzanne. *Le Poème en prose de Baudelaire jusqu'à nos jours* (Paris: Librairie Nizet, 1959).
Bersani, Leo. *The Death of Stéphane Mallarmé* (Cambridge: Cambridge University Press, 1982).
Beshara, Adel. *Lebanon: The Politics of Frustration—the Failed Coup of 1961* (New York: RoutledgeCurzon, 2005).

Bonnefoy, Yves. *Al-Aʿmal al-shiʿriyya al-kamila*, trans. Adonis (Damascus: Manshurat Wizarat al-Thaqafa, 1986 [1982]).
Boudot-Lamotte, Antoine. *Aḥmad Ṣawqī: L'homme et l'oeuvre* (Damascus: Institut Français de Damas, 1977).
Bourdieu, Pierre. *The Rules of Art: Genesis and Structure of the Literary Field*, trans. Susan Emanuel (Stanford: Stanford University Press, 1996).
Bradbury, Malcolm, and James McFarlane, eds. *Modernism, 1890–1930* (New Jersey: Humanities Press, 1978).
Bürger, Peter. *Theory of the Avant-Garde* (Minneapolis: University of Minnesota Press, 1984).
Casanova, Pascal. *The World Republic of Letters* (Cambridge: Harvard University Press, 2004).
Charbonnier, Georges. *Antonin Artaud* (Paris: Éditions Seghers, 1959).
Coleman, Peter. *The Liberal Conspiracy: The Congress for Cultural Freedom and the Struggle for the Mind of Postwar Europe* (New York: Free Press, 1989).
Colla, Elliott. "Badr Shākir al-Sayyāb, Cold War Poet," *Middle Eastern Literatures* 18:3 (2015), 247–23.
Crossman, Richard, ed. *The God That Failed* (New York: Columbia University Press, 2001).
Culler, Jonathan. "Apostrophe," *diacritics* 7 (1977), 59–69.
Daghir, Sharbil. "Tawashujat al-idiyulujiya wa-l-hadatha: Antun Saʿada wa Adunis," *Fusul* (1997), 145–72.
Danielson, Virginia. *The Voice of Egypt: Umm Kulthūm, Arabic Song, and Egyptian Society in the Twentieth Century* (Chicago: University of Chicago Press, 1997).
Darwish, Mahmoud. *Dhakira lil-nisyan* (Beirut: Riad el-Rayyes, 2007 [1986]).
———. *Memory for Forgetfulness*, trans. Ibrahim Muhawi (Berkeley: University of California Press, 1995 [1986]).
———. *Diwan*, 2 vols. (Beirut: Dar al-ʿAwda, 1994).
Dahlhaus, Carl. *The Idea of Absolute Music*, trans. Roger Lustig (Chicago: University of Chicago Press, 1989).
Deleuze, Gilles. *The Logic of Sense*, trans. Mark Lester with Charles Stivale (New York: Columbia University Press, 1990).
Deleuze, Gilles, and Félix Guattari. *A Thousand Plateaus* (Minneapolis: Minnesota University Press, 1987).
———. *Anti-Oedipus: Capitalism and Schizophrenia* (New York: Penguin Books, 2009).
Derrida, Jacques. "The Ends of Man," *Philosophy and Phenomenological Research* 30:1 (1969), 31–57.
———. *Writing and Difference*, trans. Alan Bass (Chicago: University of Chicago, 1978).
DeYoung, Terri Lynn. "And Thereby Hangs a Tale: A Study of Myth in Modern Arabic Poetry" (PhD diss., University of California, Berkeley, 1988).
———. "T. S. Eliot and Modern Arabic Literature," *Yearbook of Comparative and General Literature* 48 (2000), 3–21.
Di-Capua, Yoav. "Homeward Bound: Ḥusayn Muruwwah's Integrative Quest for Authenticity," *Journal of Arabic Literature* 44 (2013), 21–52.
———. *No Exit: Arab Existentialism, Jean-Paul Sartre, and Decolonization* (Chicago: University of Chicago Press, 2018).
Elhariry, Yasser. *Pacifist Invasions: Arabic, Translation, and the Postfrancophone Lyric* (Liverpool: Liverpool University Press, 2017).
Eysteinsson, Astradur, and Vivian Liska, eds. *Modernism*, 2 vols. (Amsterdam: John Benjamins, 2007).
Fanon, Frantz. *The Wretched of the Earth* (New York: Grove Press, 1968).
Franco, Jean. *The Decline and Fall of the Lettered City: Latin America in the Cold War* (Cambridge: Harvard University Press, 2002).

Freud, Sigmund. "Mourning and Melancholia" (1917), in *The Standard Edition of the Complete Psychological Works of Sigmund Freud*, ed. and trans. James Strachey, 24 vols. (London: Hogarth Press, 1953–74).
Friedman, Susan Stanford. *Planetary Modernisms: Provocations on Modernity across Time* (New York: Columbia University Press, 2015).
Gates, Carolyn L. *The Merchant Republic of Lebanon: Rise of an Open Economy* (London: I. B. Taurus, 1998).
Gerardo, Diego, ed. *Antología poética en honor de Góngora* (Madrid: Revista de Occidente, 1927).
Geroulanos, Stefanos. *An Atheism That Is Not Humanist Emerges in French Thought* (Stanford: Stanford University Press, 2010).
Goode, James F. *Negotiating for the Past: Archaeology, Nationalism, and Diplomacy in the Middle East, 1919–1941* (Austin: University of Texas Press, 2017).
Greenberg, Clement. "Modernist Painting," in *The Collected Essays and Criticism*, 4 vols., ed. John O'Brian (Chicago: University of Chicago Press, 1960).
Greif, Mark. *The Age of the Crisis of Man* (Princeton: Princeton University Press, 2014).
Guilbaut, Serge. *How New York Stole the Idea of Modern Art: Abstract Expressionism, Freedom, and the Cold War*, trans. Arthur Goldhammer (Chicago: University of Chicago Press, 1983).
al-Hajj, Unsi. *Lan* (Beirut: Dar Majallat Shiʿr, 1960) [3rd rev. edition, Beirut: Dar al-Jadid, 1994].
———. *Nashid al-anashid* (Beirut: Dar al-Nahar lil-Nashr, 1967).
———. *Éternité volante: Anthologie poétique*, trans. Abdul Kader El Janabi et al. (Paris: Actes Sud, 1997).
Hartman, Michelle, and Alessandro Olsaretti. "'The First Boat and the First Oar': Inventions of Lebanon in the Writings of Michel Chiha," *Radical History Review* 86 (Spring 2003).
Hasan, ʿAbd al-Karim. *Qasidat al-nathr wa intaj al-dalala* (Beirut: Dar al-Saqi, 2008).
Hawi, Khalil. *Kahlil Gibran, His Background, Character and Works* (Beirut: The Arab Institute for Research and Publishing, 1963).
Hawwari, Salah al-Din. *Shuʿaraʾ al-mahjar al-janubi* (Beirut: Dar wa Maktabat al-Hilal, 2009).
Hoffman, Adina. *My Happiness Bears No Relation to Happiness: A Poet's Life in the Palestinian Century* (New Haven: Yale University Press, 2009).
Holt, Elizabeth M. "'Bread or Freedom': The Congress for Cultural Freedom, the CIA, and the Arabic Literary Journal *Ḥiwār*," *Journal of Arabic Literature* 44 (2013), 83–102.
Hourani, Albert. *Arabic Thought in the Liberal Age, 1978–1939* (Cambridge: Cambridge University Press, 1983).
———. "Visions of Lebanon," in *Toward a Viable Lebanon*, ed. Halim Barakat (Washington, DC: Center for Contemporary Arab Studies, 1988).
Hunt, John. *Generations of Men* (Boston: Little, Brown, 1956).
Hyland, Steven. "'Arisen from Deep Slumber': Transnational Politics and Competing Nationalisms among Syrian Immigrants in Argentina, 1900–1922," *Journal of Latin American Studies* 43 (2011), 547–74.
Fakhreddine, Huda J. *Metapoesis in the Arabic Tradition: From Modernists to Muḥdathūn* (Leiden and Boston: Brill, 2015).
Furani, Khaled. *Silencing the Sea: Secular Rhythms in Palestinian Poetry* (Stanford: Stanford University Press, 2012).
Iber, Patrick. *Neither Peace nor Freedom: The Cultural Cold War in Latin America* (Cambridge: Harvard University Press, 2015).

Inboden, William. *Religion and American Foreign Policy, 1945–1960: The Soul of Containment* (Cambridge: Cambridge University Press, 2008).
Jabra, Jabra Ibrahim. *Adunis: dirasa fi-l-asatir wa-l-adyan al-sharqiyya al-qadima* (Beirut: Dar al-Sira' al-Fikri, 1957).
———. *Tammuz fi-l-madina* (Beirut: Dar Majallat Shi'r, 1959).
Jacobs, Matthew F. *Imagining the Middle East: The Building of an American Foreign Policy, 1918–1967* (Chapel Hill: University of North Carolina Press, 2011).
Jacquemond, Richard. *Conscience of the Nation: Writers, State, and Society in Modern Egypt* (Cairo: American University in Cairo Press, 2008).
Jameson, Fredric. *The Political Unconscious* (Ithaca: Cornell University Press, 1981).
———. *A Singular Modernity* (London and New York: Verso, 2002).
Jayyusi, Salma Khadra. *Trends and Movements in Modern Arabic Poetry*, 2 vols. (Leiden: Brill, 1977).
Jeffers, Robinson. *The Double Axe* (New York: Liveright, 1948).
Jihad, Kadhim. *Adunis muntahilan* (Cairo: Maktabat Madbuli, 1993).
———. *La part de l'étranger: la traduction de la poésie dans la culture arabe* (Paris: Sindbad, 2007).
Johnson-Davies, Denys. *Memories in Translation: A Life Between the Lines of Arabic Literature* (Cairo: American University in Cairo Press, 2006).
Kadhim, Hussein N. *The Poetics of Anti-Colonialism in the Arabic Qaṣīdah* (Leiden: Brill, 2004).
Kalliney, Peter. "Modernism, African Literature, and the Cold War," *Modern Language Quarterly* 76:3 (September 2015), 333–68.
Kassir, Samir. *Beirut*, trans. M. B. DeBevoise (Berkeley: University of California Press, 2010).
Kaufman, Asher. *Reviving Phoenicia: The Search for Identity in Lebanon* (New York: I. B. Tauris).
Kermode, Frank. *Not Entitled* (New York: Farrar, Straus and Giroux, 1999).
al-Khal, Yusuf. "Lubnan al-wasit," *al-Huda* 57:2 (February 24, 1954).
———. "Fi mahiyyat al-shi'r," *al-Adib* 11:15 (November 1956), 3–4.
———. *Al-A'mal al-shi'riyya al-kamila, 1938–1968* (Beirut: al-Ta'awuniyya al-Lubnaniyya lil-Ta'lif wa-l-Nashr, 1973; 2nd ed., 1979).
———, trans. and ed. *Diwan al-shi'r al-amriki* (Beirut: Dar Majallat Shi'r, 1958).
———. *Qasa'id mukhtara* (Beirut: Dar Majallat Shi'r, 1962).
al-Khal, Yusuf, Adonis, Buland Haydari, Desmond Stewart, Munir Bashshur, and Ibrahim Shukrallah, trans. *T. S. Eliot, Tarjamat min al-shi'r al-hadith* (Beirut: Dar Majallat Shi'r, 1959).
Khalaf, Samir. *Lebanon's Predicament* (New York: Columbia University Press, 1987).
———. *Civil and Uncivil Violence* (New York: Columbia University Press, 2002)
Kheir Beik, Kamal. *Mouvement moderniste de la poésie arabe contemporaine* (Paris: Publications orientalistes de France, 1978).
Khuri-Makdisi, Ilham. *The Eastern Mediterranean and the Making of Global Radicalism, 1860–1914* (Berkeley: University of California Press, 2010).
Kilito, Abdelfattah. *The Author and His Doubles*, trans. Michael Cooperson (Syracuse: Syracuse University Press, 2001).
———. *La langue d'Adam* (Casablanca: Toubkal, 1995).
Kindley, Evan. *Poet-Critics and the Administration of Culture* (Cambridge: Harvard University Press, 2017).
Klemm, Verena. "Different Notions of Commitment (*Iltizām*) and Committed Literature (*al-adab al-multazim*) in the Literary Circles of the Mashriq," *Arabic and Middle Eastern Literatures* 3:1 (2000), 51–62.

Kristeva, Julia. *Black Sun: Depression and Melancholia*, trans. Leon S. Roudiez (New York: Columbia University Press, 1989).
Lane, Edward. *An Arabic-English Lexicon*, 8 vols. (Beirut: Librairie du Liban, 1997).
Laugesen, Amanda. "Books for the World: American Book Programs in the Developing World, 1948-1968," in *Pressing the Fight: Print, Propaganda and the Cold War*, ed. Greg Barnhisel and Catherine Turner (Amherst: University of Massachusetts Press, 2010).
al-Lawati, ʿAli. *Jinayat Adunis ʿala San Jun Birs* (Paris: Manshurat al-Nuqta, 1990).
Lefevere, André. *Translation, Rewriting, and the Manipulation of Literary Fame* (New York: Routledge, 1992).
Lindkvist, Linde. "The Politics of Article 18: Religious Liberty in the Universal Declaration of Human Rights," *Humanity* 4:3 (Winter 2013), 429–47.
Little, Roger. *Word Index of the Complete Poetry and Prose of Saint-John Perse* (Durham: Durham University, 1965).
———. "The Image of the Threshold in the Poetry of Saint-John Perse," *Modern Language Review* 64:4 (October 1969), 777–92.
Liu, Lydia. "Shadows of Universalism: The Untold Story of Human Rights around 1948," *Critical Inquiry* 40:4 (Summer 2014), 385–417.
Lukács, György. *Essays on Thomas Mann* (London: Merlin Press, 1964).
Mahdi, Sami. *Ufuq al-hadatha wa hadathat al-namat* (Baghdad: Dar al-Shu'un al-Thaqafiyya al-ʿAma, 1988).
al-Malaʾika, Nazik. *Qadaya al-shiʿr al-muʿasir* (Baghdad: Manshurat Maktabat al-Nahda, 1964).
Malik, Charles. "The Metaphysics of Time" (PhD diss., Harvard University, 1937).
———. "Readings in Philosophy, Volume I" (Beirut: n.p., 1939).
———. "The Communist Doctrine of War and Revolution," *World Affairs* 113:3 (Fall 1950), 76–79.
———. "Human Rights in the United Nations," *International Journal* 6:4 (Autumn 1951), 275–80.
———. "The Near East: The Search for Truth," *Foreign Affairs* 30:2 (January 1952), 231–64.
———. "The Relations of East and West," *Proceedings of the American Philosophical Society* 97:1 (February 1953), 1–7.
———. "Call to Action in the Near East," *Foreign Affairs* 34:4 (July 1956), 637–54.
———. "Some Urgent Tasks," *World Affairs* 124:4 (Winter 1961), 103–5.
———. *The Individual in Modern Society* (Corning: Corning Glass Foundation, 1961).
———. *Man in the Struggle for Peace* (New York: Harper & Row, 1963).
———, ed. *God and Man in Contemporary Islamic Thought* (Beirut: American University of Beirut, 1972).
Malik, Habib C. "The Reception of Kierkegaard in the Arab World," in *Kierkegaard's International Reception*, vol. 8, tome 3, *The Near East, Asia, Australia and the Americas*, ed. Jon Stewart (Burlington: Ashgate, 2009), 41–49.
Mao, Douglas, and Rebecca L. Walkowitz. "The New Modernist Studies," *PMLA* 123:3 (2008), 738–42.
Maritain, Jacques. *Khawatir ʿan amrika*, trans. Yusuf al-Khal (Beirut: Dar Majallat Shiʿr, 1958).
———. *Art and Scholasticism and The Frontiers of Poetry*, trans. Joseph W. Evans (New York: Charles Scribner's Sons, 1962).
———. *The Person and the Common Good*, trans. John J. Fitzgerald (Notre Dame: University of Notre Dame Press, 1966).
Meddeb, Abdelwahab. *Tombeau of Ibn Arabi; and, White Traverses*, trans. Charlotte Mandell (New York: Fordham University Press, 2010).

Mermier, Franck. *Le livre et la ville: Beyrouth et l'édition arabe* (Paris: Sindbad, 2005).
Minkowski, Anne Wade. "Biographie d'Adonis," in *Adonis: Un poète dans le monde d'aujourd'hui, 1950–2000* (Paris: Institut du monde arabe, 2000), 202–86.
Mitoma, Glenn. "Charles H. Malik and Human Rights: Notes on a Biography," *Biography* 33:1 (Winter 2010), 232–33.
Moncond'huy, Dominique. "Qu'est-ce qu'un tombeau poétique?" in *Le Tombeau poétique en France*, ed. Dominique Moncond'huy (Poitiers: La Licorne, 1994).
Moody, A. David. *The Tragic Years, 1939–1972*, vol. 3 of *Ezra Pound: Poet* (Oxford: Oxford University Press, 2015).
Moreh, Shmuel. *Studies in Modern Arabic Prose and Poetry* (Leiden: Brill, 1988).
Moretti, Franco. *Modern Epic* (London: Verso, 1996).
——. *Distant Reading* (London: Verso, 2013).
Moyn, Samuel. "Jacques Maritain, Christian New Order, and the Birth of Human Rights," SSRN Working Paper (May 1, 2008), http://ssrn.com/abstract=1134345.
——. *The Last Utopia: Human Rights in History* (Cambridge: Harvard University Press, 2010).
——. "Personalism, Community, and the Origins of Human Rights," in *Human Rights in the Twentieth Century*, ed. Stefan-Ludwig Hoffmann (Cambridge: Cambridge University Press, 2011).
Mufti, Aamir R. *Forget English! Orientalisms and World Literature* (Cambridge: Harvard University Press, 2016).
Muruwwa, Husayn. "Al-Mutanabbi . . . sha'ir al-jihad al-'arabi," *al-Thaqafa al-wataniyya* 6:5 (May 1957), 11–14.
——. "Ibn al-Muqaffa' fi adabina al-qawmi," *al-Tariq* 17:5 (May 1958), 13–16.
——. "Abu Nuwas wa-l-shu'ubiyya," *al-Tariq* 21:5 (May 1962), 34–41.
——. "Min jama'at *Shi'r* ila majalat *Hiwar*," *al-Tariq* 11:21 (November 1962), 8–10.
——. *Dirasat naqdiyya* (Beirut: Dar al-Farabi, 1976).
——. *Al-Naza'at al-maddiyya fi-l-falsafa al-'arabiyya wa-l-islamiyya*, 2 vols. (Beirut: Dar al-Farabi, 1978).
——. *Turathuna . . . kayfa na'rifuhu?* (Beirut: Mu'assasat al-Abhath al-'Arabiyya, 1985).
Al-Musawi, Muhsin J. *Arabic Poetry: Trajectories of Modernity and Tradition* (London and New York: Routledge, 2006).
Nijland, C. "A 'New Andalusian' Poem," *Journal of Arabic Literature* 17 (1987), 102–20.
——. "The Fatherland in Arab Emigrant Poetry," *Journal of Arabic Literature* 20:1 (March 1989), 57–68.
Paz, Octavio. *Children of the Mire*, trans. Rachel Phillips (Cambridge: Harvard University Press 1974).
——. *Los Hijos del limo: del romanticismo a la vanguardia* (Barcelona: Editorial Seix-Barral, 1974).
Perse, Saint-John. *Anabasis*, trans. T. S. Eliot (New York: Harcourt, Brace, 1949).
——. *On Poetry*, trans. W. H. Auden (New York: Bollingen Foundation, 1961).
——. *Œuvres complètes* (Paris: Gallimard, 1972).
——. *Al-A'mal al-shi'riyya al-kamila*, trans. Adonis, 2 vols. (Damascus: Wizarat al-Thaqafa wa-l-Irshad al-Qawmi, 1976, 1978).
Poirier, Richard. *The Renewal of Literature* (New Haven: Yale University Press, 1987).
Pound, Ezra, ed. *Active Anthology* (London: Faber, 1933).
Racy, Ali Jihad. *Making Music in the Arab World: The Culture and Artistry of Ṭarab* (Cambridge: Cambridge University Press, 2003).
El-Rayyes, Riad, ed. *Thalathat shu'ara' wa sahafi: rasa'il min Jabra Ibrahim Jabra, Yusuf al-Khal, wa Tawfiq Sayigh ila Riad El-Rayyes* (Beirut: Riad El-Rayyes, 1996).

Razzuq, Asʿad. *Al-Ustura fi-l-shiʿr al-muʿasir: al-shuʿaraʾ al-tammuziyyun* (Beirut: Manshurat Majallat Afaq, 1959).
Rihani, Ameen. *The Book of Khalid* (Beirut: Librairie du Liban, 2000).
Ross, Kristin. *Fast Cars, Clean Bodies* (Cambridge: MIT Press, 1996).
Rubin, Andrew N. *Archives of Authority: Empire, Culture, and the Cold War* (Princeton: Princeton University Press, 2012).
Ruocco, Monica. *L'intellettuale arabo tra impegno e dissenso: analisi della rivista libanese al-Ādāb* (Rome: Jouvence, 1999).
Saʿada, Antun. "Min al-zaʿim ila al-Duktur Charles Malik," *al-Nizam al-jadid* 1:1 (March 1948), 61–65.
———. *Al-Siraʿ al-fikri fi-l-adab al-suri* (Beirut: al-Matbaʿa al-Tijariyya, 1955).
———. *Al-Athar al-kamila*, vol. 5: *Nushuʾ al-umam* (Beirut: ʿUmdat al-Thaqafa fi al-Hizb al-Suri al-Qawmi al-Ijtimaʿi, 1975).
Sacks, Peter M. *The English Elegy: Studies in the Genre from Spenser to Yeats* (Baltimore: Johns Hopkins University Press, 1985).
Said, Edward. *The World, the Text, and the Critic* (Cambridge: Harvard University Press, 1983).
———. *Out of Place* (New York: Knopf, 1999).
Saʿid, Khalida. *Yutubiya al-madina al-muthaqqafa* (Beirut: Dar al-Saqi, 2012).
Salibi, Kamal. *A House of Many Mansions: The History of Lebanon Reconsidered* (Berkeley: University of California Press, 1988).
Sartre, Jean-Paul. *"What Is Literature?" and Other Essays* (Cambridge: Harvard University Press, 1988).
Saunders, Frances Stonor. *The Cultural Cold War: The CIA and the World of Arts and Letters* (New York: New Press, 2000).
Sayigh, Tawfiq. *Mudhakkirat Tawfiq Sayigh bi-khatt yadihi wa-huwa yastaʿidd li-isdar majallat* Hiwar (Beirut: Dar Nelson, 2011).
al-Sayyab, Badr Shakir. *Qasaʾid Badr Shakir al-Sayyab*, ed. Adonis (Beirut: Dar al-Adab, 1967).
Scholes, Robert, and Clifford Wulfman, eds. *Modernism in the Magazines: An Introduction* (New Haven: Yale University Press, 2010).
Scott-Smith, Giles. *The Politics of Apolitical Culture: The Congress for Cultural Freedom, the CIA and Post-War American Hegemony* (London and New York: Routledge, 2002).
Scott-Smith, Giles, and Charlotte A. Lerg, eds. *Campaigning Culture and the Global Cold War: The Journals of the Congress for Cultural Freedom* (London: Palgrave Macmillan, 2017).
Seale, Patrick. *The Struggle for Syria: A Study of Post-war Arab Politics, 1945–1958.* (New York: Oxford University Press, 1965).
Sharabi, Hisham. *Embers and Ashes: Memoirs of an Arab Intellectual*, trans. Issa J. Boullata (Massachusetts: Olive Branch Press, 2008).
Shattuck, Roger. *The Banquet Years: The Origins of the Avant-Garde in France, 1885 to World War I* (New York: Vintage, 1968).
Shawqi, Ahmad. *Al-Shawqiyyat*, 2 vols. (Cairo: Matbaʿat al-Istiqama, n.d.).
Shehadeh, Nadim. *The Idea of Lebanon: Economy and State in the Cénacle Libanais, 1946–54* (Oxford: Centre for Lebanese Studies, 1987).
Siskind, Mariano. *Cosmopolitan Desires: Global Modernity and World Literature in Latin America* (Evanston: Northwestern University Press, 2014).
Sontag, Susan. *Illness as Metaphor and AIDS and Its Metaphors* (New York: Doubleday, 1990).
Spender, Stephen. *The Struggle of the Modern* (Berkeley: University of California Press, 1963).
Steiner, George. *After Babel* (Oxford: Oxford University Press, 1975).

Stetkevych, Suzanne. *Abū Tammām and the Poetics of the 'Abbasid Age* (Brill: Leiden, 1991).
Suhr-Sytsma, Nathan. "Ibadan Modernism: Poetry and the Literary Present in Mid-century Nigeria," *Journal of Commonwealth Literature* 48:1 (March 2013), 41–59.
Traboulsi, Fawwaz. *A History of Modern Lebanon* (London: Pluto Press, 2007).
Van Gelder, Geert Jan, "The Abstracted Self in Arabic Poetry," *Journal of Arabic Literature* 14 (1983), 22–30.
Von Eschen, Penny M. *Satchmo Blows Up the World: Jazz Ambassadors Play the Cold War* (Cambridge: Harvard University Press, 2006).
Warren, Rosanna. "Sappho: Translation as Elegy," in *The Art of Translation*, ed. Rosanna Warren (Boston: Northeastern University Press, 1989).
Weber, Samuel. *Institution and Interpretation* (Minneapolis: University of Minnesota Press, 1987), 26–27.
Wittkower, Margot and Rudolf. *Born under Saturn* (New York: New York Review Books, 2007).
Yamak, Labib Zuwiyya. *The Syrian Social Nationalist Party: An Ideological Analysis* (Cambridge: Harvard University Press, 1966).
Yaqub, Salim. *Containing Arab Nationalism* (Chapel Hill: University of North Carolina Press, 2003).
Zeidan, Joseph. "Myth and Symbol in the Poetry of Adūnis and Yūsuf al-Khāl," *Journal of Arabic Literature* 10 (1979), 70–94.

INDEX

'Abbas, Ihsan, 222n26
'Abd al-Malik (Umayyad caliph), 158
'Abd al-Rahman I ("Saqr al-Quraysh"), 100, 175–76, 220n6, 235n12
'Abdel Wahab, Mohammed, 124
Abdel-Malek, Anouar, 25, 192
abstraction: Adonis and, 103, 116, 161, 162, 166, 175; as late modernist technique, 9, 10, 43, 92, 94–95, 99, 170; world literature and, 29–30
Abu al-'Atahiya, 164
Abu Nuwas, 63, 118, 119, 149, 151, 165; Adonis's elegy for, 117, 173–74, 177, 179; as modernist precursor, 56, 157, 158
Abu Shadi, Ahmed Zaki, 226n2
Abu Shaqra, Shawqi, 223n33
Abu Tammam, 56, 113, 157, 158, 165, 167–68; *Hamasa* anthologies of, 161–62, 163, 165; "Ode to Amorium," 165–66, 171
Abu Zayd, Nasr Hamid, 231n11
acculturation, 153
Adab, al- (magazine), 30, 38–39, 41, 84, 124, 128; attacks on *Shi'r* by, 52–57, 149; founding of, 35, 46–50
Adib, Albert, 108–9
Adib, al- (magazine), 108, 125
Adnan, Etel, 183
Adonis: *al-Adab* and, 55–56; al-Hajj and, 127, 128, 138, 228n24; al-Khal and, 90, 108, 112; al-Sayyab and, 40, 41; background of, 21–24, 35, 60, 99–100; on Beirut and Lebanon, 4, 21–23, 27, 28; CCF and, 49; criticisms of, 55, 56, 161, 201, 222n26, 223n32; elegy (*marthiya*) in, 170–71, 172–79, 183, 184, 187, 188; influences on, 60, 108, 223n35, 224n42; on Islam, 192–94, 196, 199–200; *Mawaqif* editorship, 181–82; metagrams in, 118, 224n46; melancholy in, 96, 97, 101, 103, 105, 118–19; myth in, 24, 66; on obscurity (*al-ghumud*), 113; Perse and, 29–30, 106–12, 119, 122, 222n26, 224n42; photos of, 39, 45; on poetry, 9, 18, 44, 110, 124, 126, 153–54; politics and, 23–24, 100, 180–81, 189–94, 195, 196–201, 235n26, 238n24; prose poems and, 15, 102, 105–7, 109, 122, 126, 140, 223n35; rivalry with Shawqi, 56, 171; *Shi'r* and 5, 149, 150, 182; SSNP and, 50–51, 56, 57, 99, 100, 102, 174; on Syrian revolution, 200–201; *turath* and, 57, 149–53, 161–62, 187, 231n11; turning away trope in, 55, 99, 101, 104–5, 109, 113–17, 119, 143, 172–73, 224n42
BOOKS: *Aghani Mihyar al-Dimashqi* [The Songs of Mihyar the Damascene], 5, 17, 94–120, 164, 172–74, 220n6, 224n46, 227n14; *al-Masrah wa-l-maraya* [Theater and Mirrors], 177–78; *al-Thabit wa-l-mutahawwil* [The Fixed and the Dynamic], 150–52, 165, 193–94; *Awarq fi-l-rih* [Leaves in the Wind], 102; *Diwan al-shi'r al-'arabi* [Anthology of Arabic Poetry], 153–68, 170, 171, 174, 175, 178, 198, 199; *Ha anta ayyuha al-waqt* [There You Are, O Time], 21–24, 100; *Kitab al-tahawwulat wa-l-hijra fi aqalim al-nahar wa-l-layl* [The Book of Transformations and Emigrations in the Regions of Night and Day], 175–77
ESSAYS AND LECTURES: "Arabic Poetry and the Problem of Renewal," 31–32, 37, 43, 44–46, 162; "Between the Fixed and the Dynamic: Thoughts on the Islamic Revolution in Iran," 189–90, 192–94, 197–98; "Conférence d'Adonis donnée à la Fondation Saint-John Perse le 9 octobre 1993," 108–10,

Adonis, ESSAYS AND LECTURES (*continued*) 223n32; "From the Armed Man-of-Letters to the Armed Jurist," 199–200, 238n23; "Manifesto for Modernity," 198–99, 200, 201; "On the Prose Poem," 15, 122–23, 124, 126, 127; Paris letter to al-Khal, 55–56, 149; "Poetry and Revolution," 181–82, 235n25

POEMS: "Arwad, Princess of Illusion," 223n35; "The Barbarian Priest," 119; "The Crow's Feather," 17; "Delilah," 99; "Dialogue," 101, 112, 114; "The Earth Spoke," 66, 99–100; "Elegy," 112, 117–18, 177, 221n19; "Elegy for Bashshar," 173, 174–75, 179; "Elegy for the Present Days," 101–5, 111, 112–14, 222n26; "Elegy for ʿUmar ibn al-Khattab," 117, 173; "Face Astray," 112; "The Face of Mihyar," 119; "The Hawk," 100, 175–77; "Homeland," 101; "Introduction to the History of Petty Kings," 236n28; "It Is Enough for You to See," 114; "Land of Enchantment," 224n46; "A Mirror for Abi al-ʿAlaʾ," 177–79; "A Mirror for the Mosque of Hussein," 178; "The New Covenant," 96–97, 114, 176; "The New Noah," 11–14, 16–17, 18, 19, 107, 115, 205n24, 207n47; "Odysseus," 223n38; "Only Despair," 102, 105–6; "Psalms," 96, 98, 101, 110, 112, 117, 184; "Resurrection and Ashes, 3, 66; "Salutation to the Iranian Revolution," 189–91, 197–98; "She Might Become My Country," 120; "Singular in Plural Form," 223n38; "Stone," 232n23; "Tombeau for New York," 179–80, 183–87; "Who Are You?," 112, 223n38; "You Have No Choice," 117

Adorno, Theodor W., 8, 154, 225n54, 232n18
ʿAflaq, Michel, 59
Ajami, Fuad, 4, 180, 207n4, 238n23
Ali, Muhammad (Wali of Egypt), 27
ʿAli bin Jahm, 164
ʿAlim, Mahmud Amin al-, and ʿAbd al-ʿAzim Anis, 39

Althusser, Louis, 132–33
Amateis, Jacques, 85, 219n99
American University of Beirut (AUB), 5, 36, 68; Malik and, 69–71, 84
Amin, Samir, 28
Amis, Kingsley, 36
Anderson, Amanda, 10
anthologization, 14–15, 154–56; medieval origins of, 158–59, 161–62
apostrophe. See *iltifat*
ʿAql, Saʿid, 63–64, 79, 80, 99, 218n80
Arab nationalism, 39–41, 47–48, 199. See also pan-Arabism
Arab Spring, 190, 200
Aristotle, 84, 92, 169, 184
Artaud, Antonin, 122, 124, 138, 141–42, 144, 178, 182, 229n36; al-Hajj and, 129–33, 136–37, 228n32; Deleuze on, 134–36; Derrida on, 133–34, 229n38, 230n44
Asmar, Michel, 78–79
Assad, Bashar al-, 190
Asselineau, Roger, 184
Auerbach, Erich, 16, 152
autonomy, 54, 68–69, 76, 108, 192; Adonis and, 98, 108, 159, 163; Beirut modernists and, 39–41, 50, 54, 69, 77, 120, 197; late modernism and, 8–9, 10, 16, 43–44, 167; Lebanon's tradition of, 73–74
Averroes. See Ibn Rushd
ʿAzm, Sadiq Jalal al-, 191, 197, 199

Badawi, M. M., 203n4
Badini, Dounia, 98
Bandung Conference, 35, 47
Barakat, Halim, 97, 98, 113, 221n7
Barnhisel, Gregory, 7, 204n19
Barudi, Sami al-, 233n31
Barut, Muhammad Jamal, 4, 226n2
Bashshar ibn Burd, 117, 173, 174–75, 179
Bashir Shihab II, 79
Bataille, Georges, 174
Batatu, Hanna, 25
Baudelaire, Charles, 16–17, 76, 107, 122, 124, 130, 158, 183
Bayati, ʿAbdelwahab al-, 235n18
Bazargan, Mehdi, 192
Beethoven, Ludwig van, 125–26
Beirut, 1, 4–7, 21–23, 26–27, 201, 207n4; CCF in, 34–35, 44; as "city of

beginnings," 21, 201; Hamra neighborhood, 1, 22, 28, 68
Beirut modernists (1955–1975), 4, 7–10, 15–20, 28–29, 50, 94–95, 186; Arabic literary tradition and, 147–49; criticisms against, 52–55, 127, 152; internationalism and worldliness of, 29–32, 37, 43, 50, 62, 126, 170; language and forms of, 55–56; local color aversion of, 16, 53; maritime tropes of, 17, 55–56, 80, 206n40; music and, 123–26; politics and, 8, 15–16, 23–24, 67, 77, 120, 143–43; state culture aversion of, 26; urban and technological aversion of, 17–18, 80, 206n41. *See also* autonomy; *Shi'r*
Benjamin, Walter, 108, 122, 152; on tradition and catastrophe, 166–67
Bennis, Muhammad, 236n37
Bérard, Victor, 220n100
Berdyaev, Nikolai, 71, 217n70
Berger, Morroe, 42
Berman, Marshall, 6, 18, 50
Bernard, Suzanne, 122–23, 224n46, 226n6
Bersani, Leo, 184
Bible. *See* Jewish Bible; New Testament
Bonnefoy, Yves, 4, 15, 147, 174, 224n42, 225n50
Borges, Jorge Luis, 135, 155, 169–70, 235n12
Bourdieu, Pierre, 8, 54, 204n17
Bradbury, Malcolm, and James McFarlane, 6
Brecht, Berthold, 30, 136
Breton, André, 129, 131, 136, 154, 229n43
Buchman, Frank D., 216n49

Caillois, Roger, 224n46
Camus, Albert, 19
cancer, 128–29, 131–32, 137–38, 140, 228, 230n50
Carroll, Lewis, 134–35, 229n42
Carruth, Hayden, 219n97
Casanova, Pascal, 15, 152
Cénacle libanais, 5, 27, 29, 58, 89, 95, 169, 207n2, 208n20; al-Khal's lecture at, 78–84; CCF and, 78–79, 218n76
Césaire, Aimé, 222n30
Chamoun, Camille, 25, 52, 71, 74

Charbonnier, Georges, 131
Chiaromonte, Nicola, 33
Chiha, Michel, 80, 81
Choucair, Saloua Raouda, x
Chopin, Frédéric, 125
CIA, 9, 10, 33, 49. *See also* Congress for Cultural Freedom
Cixous, Hélène, 221n17
Claudel, Paul, 106
Cocteau, Jean, 113
Cominform, 32–33, 34
Congress for Cultural Freedom (CCF), 10, 32–35, 41–50, 53, 78–79, 209nn34–35; Freedom manifesto of, 34, 210n52; journals sponsored by, 33, 35–36, 46–47, 48–49, 209n35, 211n65, 212n71
Connolly, Cyril, 33
Corbin, Henri, 149
Corm, Charles, 80–81
Crane, Hart, 17
Culler, Jonathan, 114, 117, 119

Daher, Adel, 94, 97–98, 113, 116, 220n2, 221n8
Dahlhaus, Carl, 126
Damascus, 21–22, 100–101, 112, 119, 120, 176–77, 201; Shawqi's elegy for, 172
Danielson, Virginia, 124
Darío, Rubén, 155–56
Dar Majallat Shi'r, 4, 15, 41, 49
Darwish, Mahmoud, 172, 206n40, 223n34
Deleuze, Gilles, 132–33, 134–37
Derrida, Jacques, 132–34, 136–37, 229n36, 229n38, 230n44
DeYoung, Terri Lynn, 220n2
Diego, Gerardo, 155
Dulles, John Foster, 47
Dumont, Jeanne-Léonie, 35

Eisenhower, Dwight D., 25, 47
elegy genre, 14, 29, 96, 117, 174, 179, 235n18; in Adonis's *Diwan*, 164, 165–66, 167–68; Arabic tradition of, 171–72, 175; city elegy (*ritha' al-mudun*), 166, 171, 176–77; modernist, 117–19, 170–88. *See also* Adonis: elegy in; *tombeau* genre
Eliot, T. S., 15, 26, 33, 36, 40, 44, 76, 77, 86, 90, 147, 178, 182, 198, 219n94, 233n30; Perse and, 106, 107–8,

Eliot, T. S. (*continued*)
    122; *The Waste Land*, 15, 40, 66,
    166, 219n96, 219n96
Éluard, Paul, 147
Encounter, 33, 35–36, 46, 210n48, 212n71
engagement (*iltizam*), 38–41, 161, 180,
    182, 198, 210n53
experimentalism, 10, 44, 122

Fakhreddine, Huda J., 14, 203n5, 221n10
Fanon, Frantz, 19, 133
Feuerbach, Ludwig, 182
Flaubert, Gustave, 80
Foucault, Michel, 132, 194–97,
    238–39nn11–17
Franco, Jean, 211n65
Franklin Books Foundation, 41, 47
Frayha, Anis, 68
Frazer, James, 66
free verse (*al-shiʻr al-hurr*), 121
Freud, Sigmund: on melancholia, 119; on
    repression, 120
Frost, Robert, 15, 90
Furani, Khaled, 227n5

Gallimard, Gaston, 35
García Lorca, Federico, 15, 30, 172, 186
genre appropriation, 14
German Romanticism, 63
Ghazali, al-, 56, 213n10, 232n18
Ghorayeb, Beshara, 35
Gibran, Khalil, 27, 62, 156, 226n2, 236n33
Giscard d'Estaing, Valéry, 196
God That Failed, The (anthology), 35–36,
    37–38, 40, 42–43
Goethe, Johann Wolfgang von, 37, 45–46,
    50, 62, 116, 224n44
Góngora, Luis de, 155
Goode, James, 65
Gray, Thomas, 227n7
Greater Syrian Nationalism, 16, 57
Greenberg, Clement, 8
Guattari, Félix, 134, 136
Guilbaut, Serge, 44

Habachi, René, 95, 217n56
hadatha, al-. *See* modernism/modernity
Hajj, Unsi al-, 3, 106, 117, 127–33, 136–46,
    177, 182, 228nn23–24, 229n43;
    al-Adab and, 128; *al-Adib* and,
    125; *al-Nahar* and, 26; Artaud

translations by, 129–33, 136–37;
    Hiwar and, 49; on music, 125–26;
    prose poems and, 124, 127–29,
    138–46. *See also* cancer
    BOOKS: *Lan* [Won't], 5, 55, 120,
        124, 126, 127–29, 131–32, 137–40,
        130n58; *Raʾs maqtuʻ* [A Cut-off
        Head], 132
    POEMS: "The Bubble of Origin,"
        138–42, 144–45; "Country Song,"
        143–44, 146
Hajjaj, al-, 177
Hakim, Tawfik al-, 68
Hallaj, Mansour al-, 56, 117, 118, 173, 177
Hámori, András, 158
Hartman, Michelle, 81
Harun al-Rashid, 166
Hawi, Khalil, 55, 60, 62, 66, 206n41, 213n11
Hazo, Samuel, 183
Hegel, Georg Wilhelm Friedrich, 116, 126
Heidegger, Martin, 132, 229n36; Malik
    and, 18, 70, 75, 82, 215n37, 216n55
hijaʾ (invective poem), 160, 163–64, 169,
    170, 173, 176
Hikmet, Nazim, 30, 40, 147
Hiwar (magazine), 49–50
Ho Chi Minh, 180, 182
Hoffman, Adina, 172
Hofmannsthal, Hugo von, 108
Hölderlin, Friedrich, 95–96
Homer, 65, 86, 88, 89, 106, 113, 115, 119,
    218n85, 223n38
Hourani, Albert, 53, 213n3, 214n15
Hugo, Victor, 172
humanism, 19, 30, 40, 43, 74, 136, 229n36;
    posthumanist discourse, 132–36,
    229n36
Hunt, John, 35, 42, 46–47, 48–49, 53, 79,
    91, 212n78, 213n68, 218n76; *Generations of Men*, 35, 209n39
Husayn, Taha, 68
Husserl, Edmund, 97

ibdaʻ (creativity), 199
Ibn al-Muqaffaʻ, 148–49, 152
Ibn al-Rawandi, 56
Ibn ʻArabi, 187
Ibn Muqbil, Tamim, 156
Ibn Rashiq, 227n8
Ibn Rushd, 70; Borges on, 169–70, 184,
    235n12

Ibrahim, Hafiz 172
Ibrahim, Sonallah, 230n52
Idris, Suhayl, 30, 38–39, 84–85, 91, 181
Iglesias de la Casa, José, 155
iltifat (apostrophe), 55, 113, 119. *See also* Adonis: turning away trope
Imruʾ al-Qays, 56
insan, al- (the human being). *See* man, figure of
internationalism. *See under* Beirut modernists
Iranian Revolution, 189–201
Issawi, Charles, 68
istisqaʾ (prayer for rain), 111
Italian futurism, 8, 17, 36

Jabir bin Hayyan (Geber), 152, 165
Jabra, Jabra Ibrahim, 39, 49, 66, 126, 206n40, 235n15
Jacquemond, Richard, 25–26, 27
jahili (pre-Islamic) poetry, 40, 117, 149, 156–57, 164
Jahiz, al-, 151, 227n8
Jameson, Fredric: on the inward turn, 98–9, 101; on late modernism, 44; on modernism and genre, 170, 234n2; on the temporality of modernism, 155, 232n25
Jargy, Simon, 44–46, 47, 49–50
Jarrell, Randall, 219n8
Jayyusi, Salma Khadra, 203n4
Jeffers, Robinson, 80, 126, 219n87; al-Khal's translation of "Night," 80, 82–84, 86, 89, 92
jeudis de Shiʿr, 4, 36, 41, 62, 147
Jewish Bible, 62, 64, 65, 82, 99, 129, 139–42, 143, 166, 176
Jihad, Kadhim, 222n26
Jiménez, Juan Ramón, 15
Joyce, James, 36, 116

Kaʿab bin Zuhayr, 163
Kafr Qasim massacre, 172
Kalila wa Dimna, 148, 152
Kalliney, Peter, 211n65
Kamil, Mustafa, 171
Karami, Butrus, 79
Kassir, Samir, 7
katabasis, 13, 18, 84, 87, 103, 112
Kermode, Frank, 33, 210n48
Khal, Helen al-, 4

Khal, Yusuf al-, 1, 4, 16, 27, 50, 63, 99, 220n100; Adonis and, 90, 108, 112, 218n75; *al-Adab* and, 35, 46–49, 53, 213n3; *al-Huda* and, 78; *al-Nahar* and, 26, 77, 86, 218n83, 219n99; al-Sayyab and, 40, 41; crucified figure in, 87, 112, 117, 129; institutional efforts of, 90–91; Lebanon trope in, 73–74; Luqyan pseudonymn of, 218n83; Malik and, 18, 69–71, 73, 78, 84, 85; on music, 67, 125; myth in, 66; photos of, 39, 45; on poetry, 8, 15, 76–77, 140, 159; political writings of, 74, 75; SSNP and, 55, 57, 59, 60, 63, 67–68, 70, 74, 77; translation and, 14, 18, 62, 79, 82–83, 86, 92, 109, 111, 184, 227n7; in the US, 78
BOOKS: *al-Biʾr al-mahjura* [The Abandoned Well], 87, 219n99; *al-Hurriyya* [Freedom], 73–74, 218n85; *Diwan al-shiʿr al-amriki* [Anthology of American Poetry], 15, 17, 78, 90–91; *Qasaʾid fi-l-arbaʿin* [Poems at Forty], 55
LECTURES AND ESSAYS: "The Arab Man of Letters in the Modern World," 31–32, 37, 44, 46, 80; "The Future of Poetry in Lebanon," 78–80, 82, 84, 85, 169, 218n75; "On the Philosophy of Poetry," 76; review of al-Malaʾika's *Problems in Contemporary Poetry*, 122; "Thalatta, Thalatta!," 219n99
POEMS: "The Call," 87–88, 104; "The Call of the Sea" (trilogy), 87–89, 103, 219n99; "Freedom," 74; "Lebanon," 73; "My Country," 73–74; "The Poet," 76; "The Return," 87–88; "This Earth Belongs to Me," 73; "The Voyage," 3, 17, 18, 87; "To Ezra Pound," 87
Khalaf, Samir, 22
Khalil ibn Ahmad al-Farahidi al-, 121, 124, 126, 187
Khatib, Mustafa al-, 227n7
Khomeini, Ruhollah, 189–92, 194, 195, 197–201, 237n9
Khuraymi, Abu Yaʿqub al-, 166
Kierkegaard, Søren, 71
Kilito, Abdelfattah, 171, 227n8

Kindley, Evan, 90
Koestler, Arthur, 34, 35, 37, 43
Kristeva, Julia, 119
Kristol, Irving, 33

Lamartine, Alphonse de, 16, 206n38
"Lament for Ur," 166
Lammens, Henri, 59
Laqueur, Walter, 209n35
Larbaud, Valéry, 108
Larkin, Philip, 36
late modernism, 7–9, 20, 44, 50, 89–90, 163; differentiation (autonomization) and, 160; institutions of, 9, 10; internationalism of, 8–9, 15–16, 50; preservation and, 7, 8, 13–15. *See also* autonomy
Lautréamont, Comte de, 110, 122, 223n33
Lawati, ʿAli al-, 222n26, 223n32
Lawrence, D. H., 36
Leavis, F. R., 45
Lebanon: Civil War in, 22–23, 201; modern history of, 24–28, 52, 59, 72–74, 89; poetry tradition in, 79. *See also* Phoenicianism
Leibniz, Gottfried Wilhelm, 97, 113
Lenin, Vladimir, 182, 235n25
Lewis, Wyndham, 17, 154
liberalism, 57, 70, 182, 200; Cold War version of, 9, 29, 32, 43–4, 74, 77; literature and, 10, 95, 98,
Little, Roger, 111, 223n37
Lukács, György, 148
Lu Xun, 30

Maʿarri, Abu al-ʿAlaʾ al-, 56, 63, 157, 177–78
MacLeish, Archibald, 86, 89–92, 94, 106, 108, 111; text of *Shiʿr* manifesto, 92–93, 220n101
madh (praise poem), 160, 163–64, 165–66, 169, 170
Maghout, Muhammad al-, 49, 60, 205n27, 206n41
Mahfouz, Naguib, 27
mahjar movement, 27, 58, 61–62, 97
Malaʾika, Nazik al-, 5, 121–24, 137–39, 227n7
Malik, Charles, 18, 19, 35, 69–78, 82, 85, 90–92, 106, 137, 182, 215n37, 216n49, 216n52, 216n55, 217n62, 217n70; Lebanese Front and, 218n71; photo of, 69; political career of, 25, 29, 71, 74, 78, 317n59
Malki, ʿAdnan, 100
Mallarmé, Stéphane, 107, 113, 158, 161, 163; *tombeaux* of, 183–84
Maʿluf, Shafiq, 61–62, 63–64, 125
Maʿluf, Yusuf Nuʿman, 61–62, 67
Malraux, André, 30, 123
man, figure of, 18–19, 41–43, 58, 94–95, 126–27; Adonis and, 94–98, 161; al-Khal on, 84; Artaud and, 130–31; MacLeish on, 91, 92–93. *See also* personalism; humanism
Mann, Thomas, 33
Mao Zedong, 182, 184
Marinetti, Filippo Tommaso, 17, 36, 154–55
Maritain, Jacques, 71, 74–77
Marxism, 8, 11, 38–39, 40, 53, 132–33, 175, 181; Iranian Revolution and, 192, 194; Malik on, 72, 75
Marzuqi, Ahmad ibn Muhammad al-, 162
Massad, Joseph, 158
Massignon, Louis, 78, 150
Matthiessen, F. O., 78, 80
Mawaqif (magazine), 181–83, 191
Mayakovsky, Vladimir, 17
McNamara, Robert, 180, 184
Meddeb, Abdelwahab, 187–88, 236n39
melancholy, 105, 119, 225n51; in Adonis's *Diwan*, 164–66. *See also* Adonis: melancholy in
Ménassa, Gabriel, 27–28, 29, 81
Mermier, Franck, 4
metagrams, 118, 224n46
Michaux, Henri, 15, 98, 124
Middle East News Service, 78, 218n73
Mihyar al-Daylami, 96–97
Milan conference ("The Future of Freedom"), 209n34
Miłosz, Czesław, 37, 239n26
mirror (*mirʾa*) genre, 177
modernism/modernity: Arabic concept of (*al-hadatha*), 4–5, 28, 157, 192, 198–99, 226n5; authority and, 116, 122; cultural elitism and, 182; definitions of, 203nn4–5, 204n18; differentiation in, 160; Foucault on, 194–97; genre theory and, 170; translation and, 85–86; Jameson

on, 44, 98, 155, 170, 232n25, 234n2; Paz on, 232n30. *See also* late modernism
Moncond'huy, Domninque, 183–84
Monroe, Harriet, 1, 86
Moore, Gerald, and Ulli Beier, 155
Moravia, Alberto, 30
Moreh, Shmuel, 203n4, 226n2
Moretti, Franco, 8–9, 69, 116, 224n44
Moyn, Samuel, 19, 74
Muʿawiya, 158, 177
Mufaddal al-Dabbi, al-, 158, 162
Mufti, Aamir, 16
Muhalhil ibn Rabiʿa, 175
Muhammad, 73, 156, 157, 178
muhdathun, al- (innovators), 157–58
Mukhtar, ʿUmar al-, 171
Muruwwa, Husayn, 39; on Adonis, 161, 175, 181; critique of *Shiʿr* poets, 30–31, 53, 152, 212n72; on the *turath*, 147–49, 150, 231n4
museum trope, 154, 158, 159, 167, 185, 232n18
music, 123–26
Mutanabbi, al-, 56, 149, 157, 163
Muʿtasim, al-, 165–66

Nahar, al- (newspaper), 26, 77, 189–90, 192, 199, 210n49, 218n83
Nahda era, 14, 160–61, 233n31
Nakba, 4, 99
Naksa, 180, 182, 201
naql. See translation
Nancy, Jean-Luc, 187
nasib topos, 164, 234n10
Nasser, Gamal Abdel, 4, 25–26, 27, 52, 70, 102, 104, 212n78, 236n28
Nasserism, 25–26, 47–48, 70, 73, 124, 150, 161, 181, 191, 199, 200
Neruda, Pablo, 40, 147
New Testament, 139–41
Niebuhr, Reinhold, 72
Nietzsche, Friedrich, 13, 19, 71, 105, 113, 126, 154, 182, 201
Nixon, Richard M., 180
Nwiya Boulus, 150

O'Hara, Frank, 18
Okigbo, Christopher, 155, 211n65
Olsaretti, Alessandro, 81
Omahitsu (Wang Wei), 158

Orientalism, 16, 148, 152; Orientalist tropes, 17, 88
Ortega y Gasset, José, 97
Orwell, George, 210n53

pan-Arabism, 9, 25, 30, 47–48, 53, 55, 60, 102, 124, 128, 172, 180, 212n78; Adonis on, 55–56; journals of, 30
Parisot, Henri, 135
Paz, Octavio, 14, 15, 108, 147, 211n65, 232n30
Perse, Saint-John, 15, 16, 17, 122, 126–27, 129, 147, 150, 226n6; Adonis and, 29–30, 106–12, 119, 127, 182, 222n26, 224n42; metagrams in, 224n46
personalism, 18–19, 67, 70, 74–77, 95, 163. *See also* man, figure of; humanism
Pessoa, Fernando, 186
Phoenicia Intercontinental Hotel, 6, 7
Phoenicianism, 80–82, 89, 220n100
Poe, Edgar Allan, 183, 198
Poirier, Richard, 116–17
Pound, Ezra, 15, 17, 18, 36, 40, 85–90, 109, 154–55, 158, 162, 175, 219n97; al-Khal's translation of Canto I, 18, 86, 87; *The Cantos*, 86–87, 155, 166, 219n96; persona technique of, 220n5
professionalism, 9, 68–69
prose poem genre (*qasidat al-nathr*), 15, 29, 36, 106, 107, 121–29, 138–44, 187, 226n2. *See also under* Adonis; Hajj, Unsi al-
Proust, Marcel, 232n18

Qarmatians, 151
Qasim, Samih al-, 172
Quasimodo, Salvatore, 15
Qurʾan, 12–14, 16, 110–11, 151, 169

Radi, al-Sharif al-, 96
Raʾs Shamra excavations, 64–65, 89, 109
Ravel, Maurice, 183
Razi, al- (Rhazes), 56, 152
Razzuq, Asʿad, 26
Renan, Ernest, 80
revolution trope, 35, 67, 130, 159, 192–93, 197; Adonis and, 181–82, 199, 200–201; al-Hajj and, 130, 182; Artaud and, 130, 182; Malik and, 72, 75, 182

Reza Khan, 195
Reza Shah, Mohammad, 189, 195–96
Rihani, Ameen, 27, 61, 62–63, 226n2, 236n33
Rilke, Rainer Maria, 15, 36, 98
Rimbaud, Arthur, 16, 98, 107, 109–10, 128–29, 198, 206n38
Rome Conference, 31–32, 35, 37–46, 49, 50, 53; press reporting on, 210n49
Rougemont, Denis de, 78
Rubin, Andrew, 33

Saʿada, Antun, 54, 57, 58–68, 77, 79, 89, 109, 178, 214n15, 217n70; Adonis and, 99–100; Malik and, 70–71; on music, 63, 125–26; on Phoenicians, 81–82, 83; on world literature, 62–66
  BOOKS: *al-Siraʿ al-fikri fi-l-adab al-suri* [The Intellectual Struggle in Syrian Literature], 60–67, 99, 109, 125; *Fajiʿat hubb* [A Love Tragedy], 125
Saʿada, Khalil, 58
Sacks, Peter, 174, 179
Safir, al- (newspaper), 189–90, 197–98
Said, Edward, 13, 48, 69–70, 218n71
Saʿid, Khalida, 3, 22, 124, 137–38, 225n50
Salah ad-Din, 171
Salih, Tayeb, 212n71
Samné, Georges, 59
Sartre, Jean-Paul, 30, 33, 38–40, 55, 210n53, 215n37
Satie, Erik, 76
Saunders, Frances Stonor, 32–33
Sawt al-Ajyal, 91
Sayegh, Fayez, 217n70
Sayigh, Tawfiq, 39, 47, 49, 213n86
Sayyab, Badr Shakir al-, 39–41, 48, 49, 111; photo of, 42
Schaeffer, Claude, 64–65
Schiller, Friedrich, 63
Schlesinger, Arthur, 32
Scholes, Robert, 24
Scott-Smith, Giles, 10, 34, 209n34
sea-poem genre, 17, 18, 80, 87–89, 106–7, 109–10, 112
Seferis, Giorgos, 108
Senghor, Léopold, 78
Shakespeare, William, 62–63

shakhs, al- (the person). See man, figure of; personalism
Sharabi, Hisham, 71
Shariati, Ali, 196
Shattuck, Roger, 1, 137, 229n36
Shawqi, Ahmed, 56, 63, 171–72, 176, 177, 213n10
Shehadeh, Nadim, 27, 208n20
Shihab, Fuad, 26, 52
Shiʿism, 113, 151, 174, 178, 182, 191, 192, 193–94, 196, 238nn15–16
Shiʿr, 1–5, 7, 29, 35, 46, 62, 91; al-Malaʾika on, 121–22; banning of, 48; classical Arabic poetry in, 149–50; editorial policy of, 29, 84, 89–90, 181, 206n35; international scope of, 15–16, 29–30; layout of, 162; nonpartisan position of, 57–58, 60, 91; politics and, 10, 53–54, 119–20, 213n6; reviews of Adonis in, 97–98; Spring 1962 editorial, 56–57, 122, 221n11; Summer 1958 cover and contents page, 2–3; title significance of, 1, 8, 86; translations in, 14–15, 29–30, 53, 85–89, 109; yearly prize by, 41. *See also* Beirut modernists
Silone, Ignazio, 31, 33, 35, 37–38, 41–43, 44, 48, 49, 50, 63, 78; photos of, 38, 45
Siskind, Mariano, 50
Sontag, Susan, 129, 228n27, 229n36, 230n50
Soyinka, Wole, 155, 211n65, 212n71
Spender, Stephen, 4, 33, 35–36, 40, 44–46, 49, 53, 91, 95, 147, 210n46; on poetry, 36, 44–45, 89, 170
Steiner, George, 7, 149
Stetkevych, Jaroslav, 234n10
Stone, Edward Durrell, 7
Suez Crisis, 26, 47
Suhrawardi, 149–50
Suli, Abu Bakr bin Yahya al-, 157
Suli, Ibrahim bin al-ʿAbbas al-, 164
Surrealists, 128, 130–31, 136, 182, 228n30, 228n43
Syrian War, 190, 191–92, 200–201, 239n25
Syrian Social Nationalist Party (SSNP), 5, 48, 51, 52–57, 70, 91, 102, 119, 164; Adonis and, 21, 50, 56–57, 99–100,

102; al-Khal and, 57, 67–8, 77; Greek Orthodoxy and, 213n7

Tagore, Rabindranath, 40
Tahtawi, Rifaʿa al-, 27
Tammuzi poetry, 66, 94
tarab (musical ecstasy), 123–25, 227n8
Tariq, al- (magazine), 30, 53, 147
Tavernier, René, 218n76
taʾwil (allegoresis), 14, 151–52, 158, 162, 165, 193–94, 231n11
Thaqafa al-Wataniyya, al- (magazine), 30, 53, 147–48
Tilib, Hasan, 191
tombeau genre, 172, 183–88
Toynbee, Alfred, 78
translation (*naql, tarjama*), 13–15, 84–86, 110, 136, 147, 222n26; *al-tasarruf* (translation liberties), 85, 86, 111; Artaud on, 134–35; connotations of word, 14, 85, 205n31; "internal," 15, 152, 167; prose poem and, 122. *See also* Adonis: Perse and; Hajj, Unsi al-: Artaud translations by
Tueni, Ghassan, 217n70
turath (cultural heritage), 14–15, 18, 22, 31–32, 54–57, 121, 147–49, 163, 167. *See also* Adonis: *turath* and
Turk, Niqula al-, 79

Ugaritic literature, 64–65, 88
ʿUmar ibn al-Khattab, 117, 173
ʿUmar ibn Abi Rabiʿa, 79
Umm Kulthum, 124, 125
Ungaretti, Giuseppe, 108, 122
United States: Department of State, 9; Middle East concerns of, 41, 47–49
Universal Declaration of Human Rights, 19, 74, 78, 80, 217n59

ʿUrwa ibn al-Ward, 184
ʿUsba al-Andalusiyya, al-, 61

Valéry, Paul, 15, 84, 227n7
Vietnam War, 180
Virgil, 18, 106

Waddah al-Yaman, 177
Wagner, Richard, 63, 64, 65, 125, 126
Wahhayibi, Al-Munsif al-, 222n26
Walcott, Derek, 222n30
Warren, Rosanna, 171
Wazen, Abdo, 206n38
Weber, Samuel, 68–69
Whitehead, Alfred North, 70, 71
Whitman, Walt, 15, 184–87, 226n2
Wilhelm II, 171
Winters, Yvor, 84
Wittgenstein, Ludwig, 169
Wordsworth, William, 84, 92
world literature, 9, 16, 30, 37, 44–46, 65–66, 210n49; Auerbach on, 16, 45–46; Goethe on, 37, 45–46, 50; Saʿada on, 62–66
Wright, Richard, 35, 211n63

Xenophon, 112, 219n99

Yamak, Labib Zuwiyya, 60
Yaziji, Nasif al-, 79
Yeats, William Butler, 90, 206n38
Yevtushenko, Yevgeny, 30

Zaghlul, Saʿd, 171
Zamakhshari, al-, 224n42
Ziryab, 177
Zukofsky, Louis, 155
Zurayk, Constantine, 68

Translation / Transnation
SERIES EDITOR EMILY APTER

Writing Outside the Nation by Azade Seyhan

The Literary Channel: The Inter-National Invention of the Novel edited by Margaret Cohen and Carolyn Dever

Ambassadors of Culture: The Transamerican Origins of Latino Writing by Kirsten Silva Gruesz

Experimental Nations: Or, the Invention of the Maghreb by Réda Bensmaïa

What Is World Literature? by David Damrosch

The Portable Bunyan: A Transnational History of "The Pilgrim's Progress" by Isabel Hofmeyr

We, the People of Europe?: Reflections on Transnational Citizenship by Étienne Balibar

Nation, Language, and the Ethics of Translation edited by Sandra Bermann and Michael Wood

Utopian Generations: The Political Horizon of Twentieth-Century Literature by Nicholas Brown

Guru English: South Asian Religion in a Cosmopolitan Language by Srinivas Aravamudan

Poetry of the Revolution: Marx, Manifestos, and the Avant-Gardes by Martin Puchner

The Translation Zone: A New Comparative Literature by Emily Apter

In Spite of Partition: Jews, Arabs, and the Limits of Separatist Imagination by Gil Z. Hochberg

The Princeton Sourcebook in Comparative Literature: From the European Enlightenment to the Global Present edited by David Damrosch, Natalie Melas, and Mbongiseni Buthelezi

The Spread of Novels: Translation and Prose Fiction in the Eighteenth Century by Mary Helen McMurran

The Event of Postcolonial Shame by Timothy Bewes

The Novel and the Sea by Margaret Cohen

Hamlet's Arab Journey: Shakespeare's Prince and Nasser's Ghost by Margaret Litvin

Archives of Authority: Empire, Culture, and the Cold War by Andrew N. Rubin

Security: Politics, Humanity, and the Philology of Care by John T. Hamilton

Dictionary of Untranslatables: A Philosophical Lexicon edited by Barbara Cassin

Learning Zulu: A Secret History of Language in South Africa
  by Mark Sanders

In the Shadow of World Literature: Sites of Reading in Colonial Egypt
  by Michael Allan

City of Beginnings: Poetic Modernism in Beirut by Robyn Creswell

Leaks, Hacks, and Scandals: Arab Culture in the Digital Age
  by Tarek El-Ariss

GPSR Authorized Representative: Easy Access System Europe - Mustamäe tee 50, 10621 Tallinn, Estonia, gpsr.requests@easproject.com

www.ingramcontent.com/pod-product-compliance
Lightning Source LLC
Chambersburg PA
CBHW032107220426
43664CB00008B/1159